Let My Nation Go

Let My

A compilation of Talmudic
and Midrashic sources

FELDHEIM

Nation Go

The Story of the Exodus of the Jewish Nation
from Egyptian Bondage

YOSEF DEUTSCH

In this series:
Let My Nation Go (Jerusalem: Feldheim Publishers, 1998)
Let My Nation Live (Brooklyn: Mesorah Publications, Ltd., 2002)
Let My Nation Serve Me (Brooklyn: Mesorah Publications, Ltd., 2004)
Let My Nation Descend (Jerusalem: Feldheim Publishers, 2008)
Let My Nation Wander (Jerusalem: Feldheim Publishers, 2012)
Let My Nation Ascend (Jerusalem: Feldheim Publishers, 2012)
Let Me Join Your Nation (Jerusalem: Feldheim Publishers, 2013)
Let My Nation Be Warned (Jerusalem: Feldheim Publishers, 2014)
Let My World Survive (Jerusalem: Feldheim Publishers, 2016)

FELDHEIM PUBLISHERS
POB 43163/ Jerusalem, Israel

208 Airport Executive Park
Nanuet, NY 10954

www.feldheim.com

Distributed in Europe by:
LEHMANNS
+44-0-191-430-0333
info@lehmanns.co.uk
www.lehmanns.co.uk

Distributed in Australia by:
GOLDS WORLD OF JUDAICA
+613 95278775
info@golds.com.au
www.golds.com.au

Edited by: Yaakov Yosef Reinman
Series design: Deenee Cohen, DC Design
Cover illustration: Deb Hoeffner
Inside illustrations: Shepsil Scheinberg
Typography: Mendelsohn Press

Printed in Israel

In memory of
my grandfather

ישראל בן זאב
Reichman

who epitomized

אוהב שלום ורודף שלום

In memory of
my great uncle

יונה דוב בן אהרן
Schwartz

who died

על קידוש השם

In memory of
my grandparents

מאיר בן מרדכי
Deutsch

חיילא לאה בת אליעזר
Deutsch

whose tiresless efforts
built the community
of Chug Chasam Sofer in Bnei Brak,
as well as its fundamental institutions

In memory of

אהרן צבי אביגדור
בן משה יצחק
Fish

רבקה רחל
בת יקותיאל זלמן זאב
Fish

who dedicated their lives to

צדקה והרבצת תורה

is

In memory of

אליעזר בן שמואל
LUTZ

רבקה בת יצחק
LUTZ

who were מוסר נפש to keep Shabbos
שומרי תורה ומצות and to be
in America during the Depression

ספר זה מוקדש
לעילוי נשמת ידיד נפשי
מוה"ר יהושע ב"ר קהת בורק

This book is dedicated
to the memory of

Reb Yehoshua Borek zt"l

Two years before his untimely passing
I asked him to do me the honor of reviewing my manuscript.
This book, cover to cover, benefited immeasurably
from his brilliance and vast knowlege,
but I myself benefited even more
from his warm friendship and wise counsel.
His passing has left an aching void in my life,
a void that can never be filled.
May he be a *meilitz yosher* for all of us.

ת.נ.צ.ב.ה.

בע"ה

RABBI ARYEH MALKIEL KOTLER
BETH MEDRASH GOVOHA
LAKEWOOD, N.J. 08701

אריה מלכיאל קוטלר
בית מדרש גבוה
לייקוואוד, נ. דז.

בס״ד

TALMUDICAL YESHIVA OF PHILADELPHIA

6063 Drexel Road
Philadelphia, Pennsylvania 19131
215 - 477 - 1000

Rabbi Elya Svei
Rabbi Shmuel Kamenetsky
Roshei Yeshiva

בס״ד ראש חודש ‏ מרחשון תשנ״ז

Dear Rav Deutsch שליט״א

     While perusing your manuscript, I realize how much toil you invested in your book. You present to your readers an extensive collection of well known and not well known מאמרים.

     It is my hope that many people will benefit from your work. Learning about the נפלאות ונסים which are the direct intervention of הקב״ה for the sake of כלל ישראל is a means of strengthening our faith in Him. However, many דברי חז״ל are לא כפשוטן and need much interpretation. It is impossible to understand them at face value. To get the full value of your ספר, one would have to study with a רב or תלמיד חכם who is well versed in דברי חז״ל.

     May you be counted amongst the מזכי הרבים that are blessed with the זכות of מעמידי תלמידים הרבה.

Sincerely yours,

Shmuel Kamenetzky

Rabbi Shmuel Kamenetsky
Dean

RSK:sm

Table of Contents

Introduction

The idea of writing this book came to me while I was standing in front of my fifth grade class in Shalom Torah Academy of Twin Rivers, New Jersey. I had been teaching Chumash in the fifth grade for several years, and was always inundated with all sorts of questions regarding the experiences of the Jewish people in Egypt. Some of these were easily answered. Some were not.

The difficult ones sent me to my *sefarim* to seek the answers. However, for every answer I found, two more questions were thrown at me. It suddenly struck me that I needed to do a comprehensive study of the entire subject, a fascinating and rather daunting idea. From there, it was just a short step to the decision to compile these findings into a book which could be used by teachers and students alike.

The subject of the Exodus from Egypt certainly deserves a comprehensive treatment. The Exodus is one of the foundations of Judaism, and indeed, many of the *mitzvos* and observances of the Torah memorialize the Exodus. The significance of the Exodus is discussed exhaustively by the major commentators, and there are innumerable *midrashim* that provide details to augment the story as it appears in the Chumash. The purpose of this book is to weave a dramatic narrative by drawing on these sources, a narrative that would hold the interest of the average reader.

Putting together this book was not an easy task. There are literally thousands of *midrashim* and commentaries regarding all the aspects of the Exile and the Exodus, and very often, they even conflict with each other.

By necessity, I had to pick and choose among them to create the tapestry presented here, but I tried to mention some of the differing opinions in the footnotes. I make no claims by any means that the picture presented here is the definitive account of what happened in Egypt. It is merely one version that can be extrapolated from the available information, an attempt to convey the spirit of the time through a colorful panorama of events. Someone taking an alternate through this information could very well formulate a different version. There are many sides to the Torah, and all have validity and value.

It must also be pointed out that *midrashim* are sometimes meant to be taken literally, sometimes metaphorically. Often we have the guidance of the commentaries on this question, but sometimes we unfortunately do not. In this book, the *midrashim* are presented as they appear, and it is left to the individual reader to seek out in-depth interpretations of the more obscure passages.

This book would not have been possible without the invaluable participation of all the talented people who assisted me. I owe a debt of gratitude to Rabbi Yaakov Yosef Reinman, who edited the entire manuscript and gave me the benefit of his counsel at every step of the way.

I would also like to thank Rabbi Eliyahu Levine who helped me gain an understanding of some of the more difficult *midrashim*, and Rabbi Henach Ginzberg, who reviewed the source material for accuracy, added additional references and translated all the footnotes into Hebrew.

I would like to express my appreciation to Rabbi Osher Chaim Lieberman, and to his *rebbetzin*, who offered many valuable suggestions for the book.

Special thanks to my *rebbe*, Rabbi Yirmiyah Gugenheimer, who gave me much support and *chizuk* when I needed them most.

I would also like to express my appreciation to Mrs. Deenee Cohen for her excellent graphic design and Shepsil Scheinberg for his outstanding illustrations.

Along the way, many friends contributed in different ways to the success of this book, and I would like to give honorable mention to Leiby Purec, Shimon Saltz, Hershel Ganz and Nochum Barkin.

A special note of thanks to my close friend, Yisroel Kalman, who gave me invaluable assistance.

I would also like to take this opportunity to express my deepest gratitude to my dear parents, Mr. and Mrs. Mordechai Deutsch, whose professional advice and insight helped this book come to fruition; and to my dear parents-in-law, Mr. and Mrs. Michael Lutz, who helped me and guided me from the earliest stages of the book until its very completion; and to my dear brother Eli and his wife Rivky, who assisted me with their advice, guidance and expertise.

It would be impossible for me to express the extent of my gratitude and appreciation to my wife Chaya, who stood by me at every step of the way and gave me the strength to persevere and complete this work, to make this dream into a reality.

Last but foremost, I offer a prayer of humble gratitude to the Ribono Shel Olam for granting me the *zchus* of contributing to His holy Torah and bringing honor and glory to His holy Name.

Yossi Deutsch
Rosh Chodesh Adar, 5758

PROLOGUE
The Prophecy

The story of the exodus of the Jewish people from Egyptian bondage is one of the most spectacular in the history of the world, and also one of the most important. In many ways, it fulfilled the very purpose of Creation.[1]

In the beginning, Hashem created the world as a setting in which His holy Torah could be studied and fulfilled. The first two thousand years of the history of the world were all a prelude to the climactic Giving of the Torah to the Jewish people at Mount Sinai. If the Jewish people had not accepted the Torah, the world would have been returned to a state of emptiness and void, since there would have been no justification for its continued existence.[2]

For the first two thousand years of its existence, the world went through a cycle of ups and downs. Society went through virtuous periods, but more often, it went through periods of corruption

---

1) מדרש לקח טוב יח-א, עבודת הקודש פרק ל״ח 2) שבת פח., ע״ז ג.

and decline when idol worship infected virtually all of mankind. During all this time, the holy Torah was held in reserve for that elusive opportunity when it could be entrusted to mankind, when people would be worthy and capable of being the guardians of such a precious and holy gift.

Generation after generation appeared and passed away. Society degenerated and was destroyed in the Great Flood (Mabul). It was reborn with the righteous Noach and his family, but as time went on, the seeds of corruption sprouted once again. Idol worship and wickedness spread across the face of the earth, and the Torah was left waiting in its Heavenly abode, waiting for that time when at long last it would be brought down into the world.

And then, like a ray of sunshine in the dark night, Avraham appeared. Born to a wealthy family in Ur Kasdim, he recognized the existence of Hashem at a very young age, and disregarding the great risks, he proclaimed it to the world. Hashem loved Avraham for his courage, integrity and devotion to his Creator, and He promised Avraham that he would become the father of a great nation.

The formation of the noble and holy Jewish nation was thus begun, a nation bound by a special covenant to the Creator, a nation that would be worthy to receive the holy Torah and bring it into the world. It would take many years for this process to be completed. Ultimately, it would lead to the Giving of the Torah at Mount Sinai, but first, the fledgling Jewish nation would have to go through some very painful experiences. They would be strangers in a land that was not theirs and they would be reduced to slavery and bondage in Egypt. Yet painful as these experiences were, they were all part of Hashem's Master Plan designed to prepare the Jewish people spiritually for the Giving of the Torah, the fundamental purpose of Creation.

Why was it necessary for the Jewish people to be enslaved in Egypt as a prelude to the Giving of the Torah? Why is the Exodus from Egypt such an important part of the identity of the Jewish people? Why does remembering the story of the Exodus, play such a pivotal role in so many of the Jewish festivals and observances? These questions go to the heart of the Torah, the Jewish people and their relationship with the Creator. The many answers that emerge from a detailed study of the story of the Exodus reflect the wide range of views among the numerous commentators who have addressed these issues. Together, they form a rich tapestry that touches on most of the fundamental principles and concepts of Judaism, a tapestry that reveals how deeply the Jewish soul is rooted in the story of the Exodus.

The first intimation of the bondage in Egypt came when Avraham was seventy years old, at the Bris bein Habesarim, "the Covenant between the Parts." At that time, Avraham still had no children, and he was concerned that he would have no successors to carry on in his place. According to the celestial signs, he had seen that he was incapable of having children with Sarah and that Yishmael, his son from Hagar, would be his only offspring. Nevertheless, Hashem reassured Avraham that he would still have children, that his descendants would be as numerous as the stars in the heavens and that they would inherit the prized dominion of Eretz Yisrael, which at the time was called Canaan.

Avraham accepted Hashem's assurance that he would still have children without any question or reservation. He did, however, ask Hashem by what merit his children would earn the land of Eretz Yisrael. Hashem replied that by offering sacrifices to Him they would create a bond of closeness between themselves and their Creator, and this would earn them the right to inherit the holy Eretz Yisrael.[3] Moreover, if they fulfilled the commandments of the Torah and continued to bring sacrifices faithfully, they would be spared the punishments of exile and Gehinnom.[4]

At first glance, it would seem that Avraham's asking for an explanation of the grant of Eretz Yisrael to his descendants was perfectly innocent and reasonable. Nevertheless, our Sages tell us that this question had very serious repercussions for his descendants in future generations. Because of this question the Jewish people would have to suffer through hundreds of years of exile in Egypt before they could be brought to Mount Sinai to receive the Torah.

How did the asking of this seemingly innocent question lead to the exile in Egypt? What was the intended purpose of the exile, and how was it accomplished?

Avraham's question was indeed innocent and reasonable. However, it was an indication that his faith in Hashem, although of

---

3) רש"י בראשית טו-ו ומקורו תענית כז:, מגילה לא, בראשית רבה מד 4) בראשית רבה שם, תנחומא פקודי, מדרש החפץ טו-ו (וכו'), לקח טוב האזינו נט וע"ע גבורות ד' למהר"ל פ"ח

a very high order, was somewhat less than absolute. Had his faith in
Hashem been truly absolute, there could not have been any need for
reassurance or understanding. He would have accepted the promise
of the Land at face value, even if it was simply an unearned gift. But
Avraham felt ever so slightly unsure about the granting of the Land
to his descendants, and this was the reason for his question.

This presented a very serious problem for the future of the Jewish people. A tiny "flaw" in the root of the nation would be magni-
fied as generations and centuries went on, and when the time would
come, the Jewish people might not be worthy enough to receive the
Torah, Heaven forbid. Therefore, the Jewish people had to be put
through the crucible of exile and bondage to elevate the level of their
faith in Hashem and their reliance on His salvation. In this way, they
could be conditioned to approach the levels of faith of their forefather Avraham, and they would become worthy of being redeemed
and brought to Mount Sinai to receive the Torah.[5]

Other commentators suggest that the Egyptian exile was in no
way an atonement for any shortcoming on the part of Avraham himself or on the part of his descendants. Rather, it was meant to condition the Jewish people to accept the Torah with the appropriate zeal
and enthusiasm. Had they been living in comfort and ease when the
time came to receive the Torah, they might not have been willing to
accept the Torah's restrictions of their material desires. But living as
slaves in Egyptian bondage, their spirits were humbled. When
Moshe offered to redeem them on the condition that they would
accept the Torah, they were fully eager to become servants to
Hashem and his commandments. This was only possible after they
had endured 210 years of exile in Egypt.[6]

Still others suggest that Hashem sent the Jewish people into exile

5) בנדרים לב. מפני מה נענש אברהם אבינו ונשתעבדו בניו למצרים וכו' ברא"ש (שם) א' דאין שאלת הגמ' אלא
מה גרם לו לחטוא אבל בכתוב מפורש שסבת הגלות הי' במה אדע אולם במהרש"א שם הובאו דבריהם ז"ל שבציון
3) וששאל זכות ולא כקורא תגר. רש"י (שם) מעתיק ב' הביאורים (וע' בילקוט הגרשוני פ' לך דבר נחמד בזה).
רמב"ן (בראשית יב-י) כ' דשרש הגלות נבע מחוסר אמונתו שהביא שרה למצרים ואמר אחותי היא. 6) זבח פסח
בשם ר"ן. של"ה פסחים, שפתי כהן שמות, צפנת פענח, אברבנל טו-יב, מכתב מאליהו ח"ב דף 173. בזבח פסח
ותולדות יצחק אי' בפנים אחרת וזאת למודעי שהגלות לא הי' על גופם בלבד אלא גם על נשמותיהם. ע' רמב"ם הל'
עכו"ם סוף פ"א, בשל"ה פסחים (תורה אור) אי' בשם הפרדס שער השערים שהיו ישראל משוקעים במ"ט שערי
טומאה ולכן אילו לא הוציא הקב"ה את אבותינו באותו יום הרי אנו ובנינו משועבדים כי היינו נופלים ח"ו לשער
הנ"ן ולא הי' הי' יתכן הוצאה (ולכן הוצרכה החפזון) בזוה"ק (ח"א קיז.) כתוב שהתגרות הטומאה הי' שם גדול כל כך
שאפי' מלאך לא ירד תמן פן יתעב ולהבין מדוע מבחרא מצרים למלוי הגזרה ע' זו"ח ח"ג פד: דרשות הר"ן דרוש
ג' דף לח (דפוס מכון שלם), גבורות ד' פ"ד, שפתי כהן שמות, דרשת חתי"ס ח"ב דף רנז.

in Egypt so that He could bring them out with a display of the most spectacular miracles the world had ever seen. This would demonstrate His awesome power to Pharaoh, Egypt and all the rest of humanity. It would be a fitting prelude to the Giving of the Torah at Mount Sinai.[7]

The Decree of Exile

Hashem told Avraham that his descendants would be in exile for 400 years. [8] However, the exile did not enter its harshest phase from the very beginning. Rather, it developed gradually in three stages, corresponding to the three divine decrees of exile. In the first stage, the descendants of Avraham were to live in a land that was not theirs. In the second stage, they would be enslaved, and in the third stage, they would be subjected to torment and suffering.[9]

The first stage began with the birth of Yitzchak, when Avraham was 100 years old. From this time until the Exodus was fully 400 years.[10] Although Yitzchak and his children lived in Canaan, the land did not yet belong to them; they lived in "a land that was not theirs." When Yitzchak was 60 years old, his son Yaakov was born. Yaakov's son Yosef was sold into slavery in Egypt, and eventually, Yaakov and his entire family also went down to Egypt and settled there. Yaakov was 130 years old when he and his family arrived in Egypt; 190 years had passed since the birth of Yitzchak. From this time until the Exodus was 210 years, and the duration of their actual enslavement was even less.[11] It was a great chessed from Hashem that the four hundred years should be calculated in a way that would not require the Jewish people to be subjected to actual enslavement for the entire four-hundred-year period.[12]

Down to Egypt

In order to fulfill the decree of exile, Hashem created a path that would bring Avraham's children into Egypt.[13] When Yosef's brothers sold him to Arabs, he was taken to Egypt and sold there into slavery. As time passed, Yosef was given his freedom, and he rose to the high position of viceroy,

---

7) לקח טוב האזינו לב–ג, דרשות הר"ן דרוש א' באורך 8) בראשית טו-יג 9) הגדה מהר"ל, ויאמר לאברהם (ועי' ציון 15) 10) רש"י שם 11) בראשית טו–יג 12) (ע' שפת אמת פסח תרס"ג ביאור נפלא בזה) 13) תנחומא וישב - ג.

second-in-command to the Pharaoh of Egypt. (Pharaoh was not a name but the official title of all the Egyptian kings.[14]) Under his guidance, Egypt prepared great stockpiles of grain, and when famine struck, all the surrounding countries had to rely on the Egyptian grain reserves to keep from starving to death. Like most other people in Canaan, Yosef's brothers went down to Egypt to purchase food. There, after much intrigue, they were reunited with their brother Yosef, who had become the effective ruler of Egypt. When Yosef invited his father Yaakov and the entire family to come join him in Egypt, they all complied. The Jewish people were now in Egypt. The second stage of the prophecy of exile was about to be fulfilled.[15]

At that time, Yaakov's family numbered seventy people in all.[16]* These included: Reuven and his four sons; Shimon and his six sons; Levi and his three sons; Yehudah, his three sons and two grandchildren; Yissachar and his four sons; Zevulun and his three sons; Dan and his son; Naphtali and his four sons; Gad and his seven sons; Asher, his five sons and two grandchildren; Yosef and his two sons; Binyamin and his ten sons; Dinah; and Yocheved.[17] This was the nucleus from which the great Jewish nation would spring forth during the Egyptian exile.

When Yaakov went down to Egypt to join his son Yosef, he knew of the prophecy of exile Hashem had revealed to Avraham, and he understood that his descent to Egypt signaled the fulfillment of the next stage of that decree. "Do not be afraid to go down to Egypt,"[18] Hashem had told him. "It is all part of the decree I have revealed to Avraham."[19] Yaakov's children and grandchildren also understood the significance of their journey to Egypt, yet they all went willingly, fully prepared to endure the travails of exile that Hashem had decreed.[20] They accepted upon themselves the yoke of exile and undertook not to rebel against the oppressive kingdom.[21]

---

* Hashem placed Yosef in Egypt so that Yaakov would be forced to come there as well. (Raavan, *Bereishis*)

---

14) תורה שלמה שם מילואים -ה וע' בספר הישר דכ' במה הוקבע כך 15) גבורות ד' סוף פרק ט ובאר דג' גזירות הללו, גירות עבודה וענוי אתו מכח ג' החטאים שפרט הגמ' נדרים לב. על אאע"ה. (ע"ע ערבי נחל פ' עקב) 16) בראשית מו-כו 17) בראשית מו (ח-כח) ע' ב"ב קכג. דהקשה כשתמנה אי אתה מוצא אלא ס"ט ומשני יוכבד היא ונולדה בין החומות (וכן בסוטה יב.) בפדר"א לט כ' שהשכינה הושלמה המנין לשבעים בבראשית רבה צד-ט (וכן באב"ע) נמנה יעקב. וי"מ חושים בן דן וי"מ סרח בת אשר ועי' במהרש"א (בב"ב שם) ובגבורות ד' י"ג דקשו"ט בהתירוצים. 18) בראשית מו-ב (וכו') 19) הגדת רש"י 20) הגדת ריטב"א, אוה"ח שמות א-א 21) שפתי כהן שמות א-א)

Although he knew he was leading his family into exile, Yaakov did not hesitate to go. He took his whole family and all his possessions and brought them to Egypt.[22] They would not be returning, he knew, for many, many years. He did not bring them to Egypt because life would be more comfortable there; if so, he would have returned right after the famine was over.[23] He brought his family to Egypt, because Hashem had decreed that he take them into exile.[24]

22) בראשית מו-ו (וכו') 23) אוה"ח שם 24) הגדה ע"פ יעב"ץ

The Exile
Begins

1

Yaakov was already entering his twilight years when he arrived in Egypt with his family, but he was suddenly faced with one of the most critical tasks of his life. He knew that difficult trials and tests lay ahead for his offspring and that they would have to remain strong in spirit to withstand the corrupting influences of Egyptian society. The manner in which Yaakov established their presence in Egypt from the beginning would have a great effect on their future.

From the first, Yaakov insisted that he and his family be treated as foreign guests.[1] He wanted his children to feel as strangers in a strange land rather than members of Egyptian society, because this would keep them from assimilating with the Egyptians.[2] He wanted his descendants always to feel out of place in Egypt, always to feel a desire

---

1) הגדת מהר״ל וע״ד שכתב רמב״ן בראשית יב-טו כשירד אברהם אבינו למצרים

2) הגדת הנצי״ב

to leave the land of Egypt, because that would make them worthy of being redeemed at the appointed time.[3] Had he allowed them to assimilate with the Egyptians, the Jewish people would never have been worthy of leaving Egypt.[4]

For the same reasons, Yaakov wanted a place of residence for his family far from the major population centers of Egypt. He chose the Land of Goshen, an outlying district well to the north of the large Egyptian cities.[5] Many years earlier, Avraham and Sarah had come down to Egypt during a time of famine, and the reigning Pharaoh had taken a liking to Sarah. He wanted to marry her and offered her a dowry which included the Land of Goshen.[6] Now, when Yaakov selected Goshen as his preferred place of residence, the Pharaoh who reigned in his time was willing to accommodate him.

Having selected a fairly isolated place of residence, Yaakov now turned his attention to fortifying his family against the corruption and immorality of the Egyptians.[7] Most of all, he wanted to prevent his family from assimilating into Egyptian society. Therefore, he sent his son Yehudah to prepare the way for the rest of the family by establishing a *yeshivah* in Goshen.[8] For the remainder of his life, Yaakov taught his children Torah in the *yeshivah* of Goshen, as his father Yitzchak had taught it to him, and he conditioned them to do good deeds and always obey the will of Hashem.[9]

For the first years of their stay in Goshen, while Yosef and his brothers were still alive, life was peaceful and prosperous for Yaakov and his family.[10] All their needs were provided by Yosef, and they lacked for nothing. Yosef inscribed each of them in the royal ledger as a privileged recipient of a regular stipend of bread.[11] Moreover, the Egyptians admired and respected them because of their noble character and because of their familial relationship to Yosef, the illustrious viceroy of Egypt. They were the family of Yosef.[12] But for all their physical comfort and prosperity, the children of Yaakov found life in Egypt singularly unpleasant and distressing. Brought up in holiness and purity, they could not come to terms with living in a place as *tamei* (spiritually contaminated) as Egypt.[13]

3) מלבים שמות א-א 4) הגדת מהר"ל, מלבים שמות א-י 5) בראשית מז-ד, הגדת הנצי"ב, וע' תרגום יונתן יב-לא
ורלב"ג בראשית טז-ג 6) פרדר"א כו 7) ילקו"ש וארא קפ"ב 8) רש"י בראשית מו-כח 9) תנחומא שמות א,
שמו"ר יא-ד 10) תוספתא סוטה י-ג 11) לקח טוב כי תבא כו-ה 12) ספר הישר, מלבים ריש שמות 13) הגדה
ע"פ שמחת הרגל

The Passing of the Old Generation

Seventeen years after arriving in Egypt, Yaakov blessed his sons and then passed away. Each of his sons had established his own tribe during the intervening years, and Yaakov's blessings highlighted the particular strengths and missions of each tribe and set the tone for their special roles in the future of the Jewish people. The leadership now passed into the hands of his sons, who are known to us as the Shevatim or tribal patriarchs. For the next fifty-eight years, the Shevatim ruled the growing Jewish nation with great skill and wisdom. Then, one by one, they too began to pass away. The first of the Shevatim to die was Yosef, and twenty-two years later, Levi was the last to pass away.[14]

As soon as Yosef passed away, the first cracks in the spiritual defenses of the Jewish people began to appear. Their great leaders had grown old and would soon all be gone, and some elements of the younger generations began to seek acceptance and approval from their Egyptian neighbors. "Let us be like the Egyptians," they told each other. "Why should we try to be different?" And so, they began to change. Many abandoned the *mitzvah* of *bris milah*,[15] the covenant that set them apart from all other peoples. They dabbled in the popular Egyptian practice of sorcery and magic.[16] They intermingled with the Egyptians and frequented their theaters and circuses.[17] They did anything that would make them appear intelligent, knowledgeable and "with it" in the eyes of the Egyptians.[18]

Hashem saw all this and decided to have a new king ascend to the throne of Egypt,[19] a king who "had no knowledge of Yosef."[20] By the time Levi died,[21] the Egyptians began to change their behavior towards the Jews.[22] The great and respected patriarchs were gone, and the alien nation they had left behind filled the Egyptians with unease. Little by little, the Egyptians confiscated their property—their houses, their fields, all their real estate.[23] They also suspended the bread stipends Yosef had allotted to his family members.[24] Relations between the fledgling Jewish nation and the new Pharaoh of Egypt steadily deteriorated[25]—until the Jews were eventually reduced to slave labor.[26]

---

14) ספר הישר 15) שמו"ר א-ח (וע' שפ"א שמות תרל"ה) 16) הגדת ריטב"א 17) ילקו"ש שמות קס"ב 18) הגדה ע"פ מנחת אהרן וע' ספורנו דברים ד-ז 19) ילקו"ש שם 20) שמות א-ח 21) סדר העולם ג 22) אוה"ח שמות א-ו ועי' גבורות ד' ט 23) ספר הישר 24) לקח טוב כי תבא כו-ה 25) תוספתא סוטה י-ג 26) אוה"ח שמות א-ו ויעויין שם במלבים דכתב דשנאתם הי' ניכר גם בחיי יוסף וכשנפטר יעקב לא יכלו לצאת ממצרים עם הארון בלי רשות

The New King

Who was this new king who "had no knowledge of Yosef"? Some suggest that he was literally a new king who had taken over the reins of government. Others suggest that he was a new king only in the figurative sense, but in reality, he was the same king who now decided to follow new policies and enact new laws.[27]

According to some commentators, this new Pharaoh replaced the five-hundred-year-old nineteenth Egyptian dynasty.[28] He was a descendant of Cham,[29] a commoner with no royal background.[30] Some suggest that his real Egyptian name was Mallul,[31] while others suggest that his name was Amunifus.[32] Other commentators are of the opinion that he was of royal lineage, descended from the Egyptian dynasty of Ramses, and that he himself may have been known as Ramses II.[33]

There is also a view among the commentators that this particular king was the son born to Pharaoh when Yosef was still imprisoned. As part of the national celebration that took place on the occasion of his birth, the wine steward was released from prison, and this ultimately led to Yosef's release.[34]

This new king, whoever he may have been, took note of the hostility of the Egyptian people towards the young Jewish nation growing in their midst, and he decided to act upon it.

The Jewish People, a Nation Apart

The hostility of the Egyptians towards the Jews in their midst was understandable. Although some elements among the Jews had begun to assimilate into Egyptian society, the great majority of the Jews kept their distance.

After many years of living in Egypt, the Jews were still easily distinguished from the Egyptians.[35] They lived near each other, kept their distinctive Hebrew names and spoke to each other only Lashon Hakodesh (Biblical Hebrew, "the holy language").[36] They made a pact among themselves to preserve their language and to be kind to each other.[37] They always greeted each other warmly and

שם (29 'מלואים ה - תורה שלמה נג (28 למשכון בגשן ומקניהם טפם לעזוב הוכרחו וגם פרעה
שם שלמה תורה (33 ירחמיאל ספר (32 היׁשר ספר (31 יד 'ד גבורות ,שם בלולה ובמנחה ח-א שמות ע"אב (30
ג"כ א"תנדב (37 הלקט שבלי הגדת (36 האברבנל הגדת (35 ח-א שמות בחיי רבנו (34

courteously.[38] Their table manners were more refined than those of the Egyptians.[39] They did not follow the Egyptian styles in the way they cut their hair[40] or in the clothes they wore; the men also wore *tzitzis*.[41] Their modesty was impeccable, and no two families shared living quarters.[42] They never slandered one another, and they kept the laws of family purity.[43]

The Jews were proud of their heritage, their customs and their deeply ingrained morality, and they carried themselves with a dignity and noble assurance that was recognizable even from afar. "There goes a Jew," an Egyptian could state with assurance when one of them passed by.[44] This self-assured separation and unwillingness to assimilate aroused the resentment of the Egyptians.

The hostility of the Egyptians towards the Jews only brought them closer together. And as the exile grew more and more oppressive, this strong feeling of solidarity helped ease the pain and the bitterness, because all the Jews knew they could rely on each other in times of need and distress.[45]

Because of this steadfast adherence to the preservation of Jewish identity, the observance of Jewish laws and customs and the devotion of the Jewish people to each other, they were eventually redeemed from their exile in Egypt.[46]

Phenomenal Fruitfulness

Although Yosef and the rest of the holy Shevatim passed away, Hashem's love for their descendants did not diminish.[47] He had promised Avraham, Yitzchak and Yaakov that he would make their descendants into a great nation, and now, as the numbers of their beloved grandchildren grew and multiplied, Hashem showered them with His blessings.[48] The Jewish people suddenly began to reproduce in phenomenal numbers.[49]

According to some views, all Jewish women gave birth to twins.[50] According to others, they gave birth to six children at a time, three males and three females.[51] Some commentators even suggest

38) שפתי כהן שמות **39)** לקח טוב ו-ו **40)** שם, פסיקתא זוטרתא כי תבא עה"כ ויהי שם לגוי וגו' וע"ע בהגדת רשב"ץ **41)** הגדת ריטב"א, ויש לצרף לזה מש"כ בפרשת דרכים דרוש א בשו"ת חשק שלמה דמשום ספק ישראל ספק בן נח הוצרכו האבות להתעטף בציצית בשבת ואי לבן נח חשיבי הוצאה היא ואינם בגדר עכו"ם ששבת ואי לא מה טוב. וא"ש שמצינו שאכן עשו תחבולה זו **42)** שפתי כהן שמות **43)** ויקרא רבה לב-ה. ואע"פ שנפלו הרבה, בזה הזהירו וע' בהגדה ע"פ יעב"ץ **44)** הגדת יציאת מצרים **45)** הגדת ריטב"א **46)** ויקרא רבה שם **47)** מדרש הגדול א-ז **48)** שמו"ר א-ח ומתני"כ שם **49)** מדרש הגדול שם **50)** תנחומא פקודי ט **51)** גור אריה שמות א-ז,

that it was not unheard of for a woman to have sixty children at a time, as do scorpions.[52]

The sudden phenomenal fruitfulness of Jewish women manifested itself not only in multiple births, but in other ways as well. Every Jewish woman was blessed with children; not a single one remained barren.[53] Girls who were married at a very young age also began having children.[54] No Jewish woman miscarried.[55] The babies were all sturdy and robust, and they all grew to be tall and strong.[56]

As time went on, the Jewish population in Egypt exploded. Women gave birth every nine months, so that Jewish families had six ten-month-old babies and six one-month-old babies in the house all at once,[57] according to the views that women bore six children at a time. In fact, the growth was so rapid that 600,000 children were born on one particular night.[58]

The land of Goshen was no longer large enough to contain the burgeoning Jewish population, and numerous Jews began to settle in the central areas of Egypt. Their numbers began to rival those of the Egyptians,[59] and eventually, there were virtually twice as many Jews in Egypt as there were Egyptians.[60*]

The Jewish people became like thorns in the eyes of the Egyptians.[61] Wherever they went, the Egyptians saw multitudes of Jews before their eyes, and the sight disgusted them.[62] These alien people, who stubbornly insisted on maintaining their separate identity and not assimilating into Egyptian society, were taking over the entire country through the phenomenal growth in their population. Something had to be done.[63]

---

* Yaakov would have had more children had he not been injured in the thigh during his struggle with Eisav's ministering angel. (*Sefer Tzror Hamor*)

גליון הש"ס ברכות סג: (52 שמו"ר א-ח ורש"ש שם. בגבורות ד' י"ב איתא דכל השיטות אזלי במספר שש משום שענו את ישראל בששת ימי המעשה בלי הפסק (ע' לקמן פ"ה ציון 147) וכתיב כאשר יענו כן ירבה לכן נתרבו תמיד במספר זה (53 הגדת נצי"ב (54 נצי"ב שם (55 ילקוט מעין גנים א-ז (56 רבנו בחיי שמות א-ו (57 אברבנל שמות א-ז, הגדת האלשיך, שם מבאר תבת וישרצו שהרבוי הי' עצום כל כך שנרצים כשרצים קטנים הרצים אנה אנה בבית (58 מדרש הגדול שמות א-ז, ספר הישר, וע' בבראשית רבה עט דלפני פטירתו של יעקב כבר נולדו ששים רבוא (59 העמק דבר שמות א-ז, גם אז נשארו רובם בגושן, ע' רמב"ן שמות יב-לא וטור שם ח-ח (60 מדרש משלי יט (61 סוטה יא. (62 דברים רבה כת"י מובא בתורה שלמה כט (63 שמו"ר א-ח, בהגדת חכמי ירושלים מובא שהעירוב עם מצרים הי' נגד רצון ד' ולכן כשיצאו מגושן הוצרך כביכול לשלוח מלך קשה שעל ידי גזירותיו יובדלו מהם

The Labor Decrees

2

Egyptian society was thrown into crisis by the incredible explosion of the Jewish population. The situation grew worse with every passing day. Fear and uncertainty filled the hearts of the Egyptians. Tensions flared, and the Egyptian people grew restless and angry.

The unrest did not go unnoticed in Pharaoh's palace. A delegation of ministers, advisors and prominent citizens requested an audience with Pharaoh to discuss the emergency situation.

"Your majesty!" one minister declared. "Something must be done about the Jews.[1] We must do something to reduce their numbers."[2]

"Fools!" Pharaoh replied. "Where is your gratitude? If it hadn't been for Yosef, we would all have starved to death. You know that. He filled our storehouses with grain, so that during the years of famine we had more than enough food to eat and

---

שם (2 שמו״ר א-ח (1

also to sell to our neighbors. Because of Yosef, Egypt became very rich. Are we to repay the great service he did to our country by harming his family?"[3]

"But your majesty," the minister persisted, "that is precisely the problem. We sold enormous amounts of food to our neighboring countries and took enormous amounts of their treasures in return. We became rich, and they became poor. What if these people decide they want their money back? We could be in for big problems. According to our intelligence reports, there is a real possibility that the Canaanites will start a war with us to recover some of the treasure they were forced to give us during the famine—if they didn't want to starve to death. What if the Jews ally themselves with the Canaanites and attack us? They could destroy us and drive us out of our own land!"[4]

"That's right, your majesty," a second minister spoke up. "These Jews are dangerous. When they were still a tiny group, no more than a handful of people, they were already winning wars against much larger numbers of people. And now that there are so many of them, they are far more dangerous than ever. Imagine what would happen to us if they joined forces with our enemies."[5]

"I couldn't agree more, your majesty," a third member of the delegation added. "You know, it's not as if these Jews who are multiplying all around us are willing to become Egyptians. They are not interested in assimilating with us or intermarrying with our people. They keep apart from us and are very close-knit among themselves. They are aliens. Strong, united and highly dangerous aliens. Your majesty, they are trouble!"[6]

"Your majesty, if I may add one thought," said yet another member of the delegation. "There is something very uncanny about the way these Jews are multiplying. It's not just that there are so many of them being born all the time. It's that they are all so disgustingly healthy and strong. There are no weak or sickly children among them. Just large and robust ones. It certainly doesn't seem as if nature will correct this impossible situation any time soon. We have no time to waste. We must do something to stop their growth— right now!"[7]

---

3) שם ורע׳ בהגדת האלשיך דכתב שלא נבע מלבו הטוב רק שירא מאלקי ישראל 4) בעה״ט שמות א-יב 5) ספר הישר 6) אוה״ח שמות א-ט 7) שם

Pharaoh had listened carefully to everything that was said, but he was still not convinced. "I agree that we have to monitor this situation very carefully," he said. "But I am not prepared to take any drastic action against the Jews just yet. Let us not forget so easily that we owe a great debt of gratitude to Yosef."

The members of the delegation felt greatly disappointed as they left Pharaoh's presence. They were enraged at Pharaoh's refusal to take action—and determined that the matter should not end there. They mustered all their support and staged a palace revolt, deposing Pharaoh from his throne and throwing the entire government into crisis.

After three months of intrigue and chaos, the deposed Pharaoh asked for a new meeting with the delegation.

"Gentlemen," he began, "I am sure you will be glad to hear that I have had a change of heart. I have given it much thought and decided that you were right after all. The Jews really are a grave threat to our national security. Let us come up with a plan of action. I can assure you that I will support whatever plan is chosen."

The Egyptians were relieved to hear the former Pharaoh speak these words. They all agreed that it would be in the best interests of the country for him to return to his throne and lead Egypt through this time of crisis. Stability and continuity were absolutely necessary if Egypt was to avert disaster at the hands of the Jews.[8]

"Your majesty," one of the leading ministers declared excitedly, "we are overjoyed that you have agreed to face the danger posed by the Jews. We must kill them immediately."

"Not so fast, not so fast," Pharaoh replied, shaking his head. "We cannot do such a thing. Whatever we do, we must be clever and cunning.[9] How will it look to the rest of the world if we killed the Jews? Are we barbarians? My father invited the Jews into the land, and I cannot very well start killing them just like that. What will our people say to mass murder in their own land? This is a civilized country. The people won't stand for it![10] Besides, if we mount a frontal attack on the Jews, it may turn out to be a very difficult thing to accomplish. The royal descendants of Yosef are very influential and well-connected. Many factions in the land might go over to the side of the Jews, and then we would have a full-fledged civil war on

שם (10 רמב״ן שמות א-י (9 שמו״ר שם (8

our hands. No one wants that![11] No, my good man, that is not the way to approach this matter. We need a clever plan, a plan based on guile and subterfuge. We must consult our wisest people and devise a way to outsmart the Jews and, even more important, to outsmart their Lord."[12]

The Egyptians accepted Pharaoh's points. They agreed to wait until a clever plan could be devised and not to go off and do something hasty and foolish. Still, they remained in a state of high distress. They lay in their beds at night, unable to sleep. What was to be done about the Jews? How would it all end?[13]

Bilam's Advice

Once he made up his mind to move against the Jews, Pharaoh did not waste any time. He called a meeting of his council of wise men for the purpose of devising a plan of action.

The most respected among Pharaoh's advisors was a man named Bilam. Bilam was not a native Egyptian. He was the son of Angias, king of a North African nation. Many years before, a grandson of Eisav, a man named Tzfo, conspired with Angias to attack the Jewish settlements in Egypt. Angias provided Tzfo with an army and the services of his son Bilam, who was a sorcerer and a wizard. At first, Bilam was reluctant to attack the Jews in Egypt. Instead, he helped Tzfo make many other conquests for his father's kingdom. Eventually, however, the wars spilled over into Egypt. Jews and Egyptians fought together against the invaders and repelled them. Many years later, after Tzfo's death, Bilam returned to Egypt as a palace wizard in Pharaoh's employ. As expected, Bilam rose to speak as soon as the meeting of the council was convened.[14]

"Your majesty, if I may be so bold," Bilam began. "In your great wisdom, you have determined that it would not be feasible to order the execution of the Jews and that only cleverness will extricate Egypt from this mess. I think all of us here are fully in agreement. So! How do we get rid of the Jews? I think the first step must be to drive a wedge between them and their Lord. We and all our gods are powerless against Him—if He chooses to protect the Jewish people. But He is very strict and demanding. If the Jews disobey Him, He will

---

11) פענח רזא שמות א-י

12) שמו"ר א-ט, ילקו"ש קסב, הגדת זבח פסח 13) מנחה בלולה שמות א-יא 14) ספר הישר

become angry and abandon them. This, then, is what I suggest. Let us do what we can to get them to transgress their laws. Best of all would be if we could convince them to worship our gods. That would really get their Lord furious!"[15]

The meeting was adjourned, and Pharaoh issued his first decree against the Jews. At this time, the Jews had already been given the *mitzvah* of *bris milah*, circumcision. This great *mitzvah* symbolized the covenant between Hashem and Avraham and set the Jewish people apart from all other peoples. Therefore, Pharaoh banned the practice of circumcision in all Egypt. The attack on the Jews had begun.

Although some Jews had abandoned *bris milah* on their own after the death of Yosef in order to assimilate with the Egyptians, the majority had held steadfast to this precious *mitzvah*. And now it was banned by royal decree! Only the tribe of Levi, the priestly caste, disobeyed Pharaoh's decree and continued to practice the *mitzvah* of *milah*.[16] The rest of the Jews felt they had no choice but to comply with the evil decree, and the practice of *milah* effectively came to an end. The forced transgression of the *mitzvah* of *milah* caused great pain to the Jews, but they did nothing about it. This was what Pharaoh had wanted. Now, he hoped, their Lord would grow angry and abandon them.[17]

At the next meeting of Pharaoh's council of advisors, Bilam again rose to speak.

"Your majesty, let me congratulate you on your first decree against the Jews. It is undoubtedly a step in the right direction. Now, we must build on that foundation."

"What would you suggest?" Pharaoh asked.

"If I may be so bold, your majesty," Bilam replied, "I suggest that we give them a taste of their own medicine."

"Their own medicine? How so?"

"Let me explain," Bilam continued. "If we examine the history of the Jews, we find one deception after another. We all know about Yaakov, Yosef's father, the respected patriarch of the Jews who brought his family to Egypt and settled in Goshen. Well, do you also know that he deceived his older brother Eisav into selling him his birthright? And wait! If that's not enough, he also disguised himself as his older brother and deceived his father Yitzchak into giving him

15) הגדה ע״פ יעב״ץ (16 שמו״ר יט-ה (17 שמו״ר א-ח ומהרד״ו, פרדר״א כט, אלשיך א-יב

Eisav's blessings. Then he went off to Charan, married Lavan's two daughters, swindled his father-in-law of his sheep and then ran off like a thief in the night. I heard these stories directly from one of Eisav's grandsons, a man named Tzfo who served in my father's armies. And where do you think Yaakov learned to deceive?"

Everyone leaned forward, eager to hear the answer to this question.

"So where?" asked Pharaoh. "Where did he learn it?"

"From his own father, of course," Bilam declared triumphantly. "Yitzchak went down to Philistia during a famine and told everyone that his wife was really his sister. Can you imagine? So, it's not surprising that Yaakov was a deceiver. And what's more, his own children were deceivers. Shimon and Levi told the people of Shechem to circumcise themselves if they wanted to marry Jewish women. Three days later, when the people of Shechem were at their weakest, Shimon and Levi killed them all! I tell you, your majesty, these are deceitful people, and the only way we can triumph over them is by being deceitful ourselves!"

"All right, Bilam," said Pharaoh. "I give you permission to be deceitful. What do you propose?"

"Well, we obviously can't just go out and kill them," Bilam replied. "Our people won't stand for it, and besides, you can't expect the Jews to sit still and let us do whatever we want to them. They are sure to offer resistance, and then we'll have a royal battle on our hands. No, I say we do something else. Life in Egypt is too soft and comfortable right now for the Jews. We have to make it hot for them. We have to bring suffering and pain and sorrow to the Jews. Then we can expect nature to take its course, and they will slowly fade away."[18]

"Excellent, Bilam, excellent!" Pharaoh declared with relish. "I love it. But tell me, how do we do this thing?"

"Very simple, your majesty," Bilam replied. "We start with taxes. After all, who can object to taxes? Every government levies taxes, and everyone pays taxes.[19] Yes, your majesty, we shall begin with taxes."

Taxes! Pharaoh was delighted with the idea. He issued a decree imposing very heavy taxes on the Jewish residents of Egypt.[20] There

---

18) דברי הימים למשה ור' בזוה"ק ח"ב לג. שעצת איוב הי' ויעץ כן שירא לנפשו וע"ע בספר הישר 19) רמב"ן ורבנו בחיי א-יא (וכו') 20) שמות א-יא

was no escape. Slowly but surely, all the wealth of the Jews was drained away, until finally they were all left destitute. Starvation stared them in the face, and still the Egyptian tax collectors demanded their heavy payments.

"Just because you have no money doesn't exempt you from paying your fair share of the taxes," the Egyptians told them. "But we have a solution for you. We have employment available on many of our construction projects. You can work for us, and we will pay you for your work. Then you'll have money with which to pay your taxes. And who knows? Maybe you'll even have something left for food for your children."

The Jewish people had no choice but to agree to this arrangement.[21]

The Egyptian master plan to inflict unbelievable suffering on the Jews was beginning to take form. The crushing tax burden was leading to the exploitation of the Jews as laborers,[22] and all in a cunning fashion that avoided a public outcry by the Jews.[23]

Pharaoh felt sure he could outsmart the Jews and prevent them from becoming a powerful nation.[24]* Gratified by the success of his early decrees, he began to plan his many future decrees, each designed to weaken the Jewish people or destroy them.[25]

The Hebrew name for Egypt—Mitzraim—took on special significance, because its root is related to the Hebrew word for pain. For the Jewish people, Egypt had become synonymous with pain.[26]

---

* Some suggest that the Egyptians would have been content to have the Jews leave Egypt or to sell them to other nations. (Sforno, Akeidah, *Shemos* 1:10-11)

---

21) הגדת הגר"א 22) שם 23) רמב"ן שמות א-י 24) שמות א-י 25) ע' שמו"ר א-יב וכן ו-ד ומהרד"ו שם 26) לקח טוב שמות א-יג

The Jews Are Enslaved

3

Pharaoh issued four major decrees which reduced the Jewish people to slavery. The first was intended to draw all Jews into the employ of the king.[1] However, for his plan to be successful, Pharaoh had to conceal his true intentions from the Jewish people.[2] He had to present himself to them as a benevolent ruler interested in their welfare.[3] In this way, he would lull them into a false sense of security and draw them into his trap. But Pharaoh—whose Hebrew name פרעה can be reconfigured as פה רע, meaning "evil mouth"[4]—was an expert at this sort of trickery.

Once the decision was made, royal criers circulated in all the Jewish neighborhoods of Egypt.

"Hear ye! Hear ye!" the criers announced. "His Royal Highness, Pharaoh, King of Egypt, is seeking volunteers for his new construction projects.[5] The population of Egypt has grown rapidly,

1) שמו"ר א-יב ומהרז"ו שם 2) רמב"ן שמות י-א 3) שמו"ר א-יא 4) הגדת זבח פסח
5) רמב"ן שמות א-יא

and new cities have to be constructed to house all the new people.

"Any Jewish resident of Egypt who volunteers to work on these projects will be greatly rewarded. Any Jewish resident who works on the construction of the residential sections of a new city will have first choice on new residential quarters for his family.[6] Any Jewish resident who works on the construction of other official buildings will receive gifts from the royal treasury.[7] Lay one brick, and you will receive one gold coin.[8] Lay two bricks, and you will receive two gold coins.[9]

"This is a great opportunity for all Jewish residents of Egypt! You can show your gratitude to Pharaoh for his kindness and hospitality, and you can earn rewards for yourselves and your families. Hurry! Hurry! Register now!"

Numerous Jewish people responded to Pharaoh's call for volunteer labor. They flocked to the construction sites to register for the royal labor battalions and receive their assignments.

When they arrived, they found many Egyptians already at work,[10] their enthusiastic shouts blending with the pounding and grinding of their tools. If the Jews had harbored any suspicions that they were being drawn into a spider's web, the sight of all these Egyptian laborers set their minds at ease. This was clearly a genuine program, a national undertaking to be shared equally by Egyptian and Jew.

As the day wore on, the spirits of the laborers began to flag from the heat of the merciless sun and the difficulty of the work. Suddenly, there was a loud commotion. A contingent of heavily armed soldiers marched onto the construction site, followed by a company of heraldic trumpeters. With great fanfare and pomp, the richly embroidered royal litter appeared, and Pharaoh himself stepped out into the afternoon glare.[11]

A gasp greeted the unexpected appearance of the Egyptian monarch, but the article suspended from a leather band around his neck caused even greater shock. It was a bricklayer's mold. The symbolism was not lost on the assembled laborers. The great king of Egypt had a deep personal involvement in this project. His heart and spirit were with the laborers. He had come to the construction site to

---

6) בעה"ט שמות א-יג וע' לקמן שלא קיים הבטחתו 7) לקח טוב שמות א-יג 8) מדרש אגדה א-יג 9) מדרש החפץ
שמות א-יג, דעת זקנים א-יא 10) ספר הישר 11) הגדה ע"פ אבודרהם

show the laborers how much the project meant to him and to boost their morale.

But the shocks did not end there. An even greater shock was in store for the laborers at the construction site. To everyone's dismay, Pharaoh actually grabbed a shovel and a basket and began to collect finished bricks from the brickmakers' benches.[12] Pharaoh doing manual labor? Unheard of! Clearly, this project was closer to Pharaoh's heart than any other he had ever undertaken.

The effect on the laborers was electric. No longer could anyone slack off in his work or even dare express reservations about doing manual labor. After all, Pharaoh himself did not consider the work beneath him![13]

Whether it was because of the promised rewards or because of Pharaoh's personal visit, the Jewish laborers responded to the entire scenario with a great outburst of productivity.[14] They extended themselves to the limits of their capacity—and far beyond. Huge mounds of bricks arose beside the Jewish brickmakers' benches, and instant walls sprang up wherever Jewish bricklayers labored. At day's end, the Egyptian overseers calculated the number of bricks each Jewish brickmaker had manufactured and the construction work each Jewish bricklayer had done—and this became the daily quota expected of them![15] And all without additional pay![16]

Time passed. Pharaoh continued making weekly visits to the construction sites, but the Egyptian laborers began to take on new roles. Slowly but surely, all the Egyptians laborers were promoted to the rank of taskmaster.[17] No longer did they stand side by side with the Jewish workers doing manual labor. Now they had whips in their hands instead of shovels and trowels. They marched back and forth checking on the Jewish laborers. Should a Jew dare stop working[18] or fail to meet his assigned daily quota, the taskmaster's whip would crack through the air and land on the poor Jew's back with a resounding thud.[19] And if a Jew should be diligent enough to fulfill his required quota before the day was through, he was given even more work to complete.[20]

Pharaoh's diabolical scheme finally became clear to the unfortunate Jewish laborers trapped on the Egyptian construction sites.

---

12) ילקו״ש קסג 13) סוטה יא. 14) מדרש הגדול שמות א-יג מובא במדרש אגדה בדעת זקנים ובצרור המור 15) שם 16) ספר הישר 17) שם 18) שם 19) ילקו״ש שם 20) אוה״ח שמות א-יד

With deep chagrin, they compared Egypt to a horseradish, called *marror* in Hebrew. A horseradish is soft in its early stages of growth, but as it ripens it becomes hard and very rough. Egypt, too, had at first been so kind to its Jewish guests, but now it was treating them harshly.[21] Others made the wry observation that Pharaoh's given name Mallul was almost identical to Marror, which means bitter in Hebrew. Pharaoh had indeed embittered Jewish lives with his harsh decrees.[22]

The Jewish Police

Now the Egyptians devised a plan to gain the maximum efficiency out of each Egyptian overseer. They established a Jewish police force to supervise the work of the Jewish laborers. Each Jewish policeman was put in charge of ten laborers, and one Egyptian overseer was assigned to each ten Jewish policemen. In this way, a single Egyptian could control one hundred Jewish laborers.[23]

It was the responsibility of each Jewish policeman to see that his group completed its work,[24] producing no less than six hundred bricks each day.[25] If any laborer slacked off, the Jewish policeman was instructed to flog him until he resumed his work. If by the end of the day the quota was not filled, the Jewish policeman was to point out those responsible for the shortfall. These unfortunate men would then be punished by the Egyptian overseer.

The Jewish policemen, however, did not cooperate. They treated the laborers of their groups kindly, and they never informed to the Egyptian overseers on any laborer that did not fulfill his quota. The Egyptian overseers were infuriated.

"If you don't tell us who is responsible for the shortfall," they would say, "you yourselves will have to bear the whipping in their stead."

Still, the Jewish policemen refused to comply. "We will gladly take the punishment," they replied, "but we will not inform on our Jewish brothers."

True to their word, the Egyptian overseers beat the policemen severely, but they maintained their silence. In the end, Hashem rewarded them. When Moshe had to appoint judges to the Sanhedrin after the Jewish people received the Torah, Hashem told him to

---

21) פסחים לט.   22) ספר הישר   23) יפה תואר וע' במעם לועז   24) ילקו"ש קס"ז   25) מדרש ויושע בפסוק
מרכבות

choose these righteous Jewish former policemen. They had shown themselves ready to carry the burden of their people, and this qualified them to serve on the Sanhedrin.[26]

Shevet Levi Avoids Labor

Among all the Jewish people, only Shevet Levi (the Tribe of Levi) managed to avoid the harsh labor decrees. The elders of Shevet Levi had suspected that the appeal for volunteer labor was part of a plot to entrap the Jews. They were faced with a serious question: Should they set themselves apart from the rest of the Jewish people and evade the labor decrees? After much deliberation, they decided that since they were destined to do the *avodah* in the Mishkan and the Beis Hamikdash it would be inappropriate to allow themselves to be demeaned by slave labor. They decided not to comply.

Upon the advice of their elders, the people of Shevet Levi did not register for the royal labor battalions. Instead, they sent a message to the royal recruiters that an epidemic had swept through Shevet Levi and practically all the people were sick and incapacitated. Moreover, they claimed, all the people of Shevet Levi were scholars and priests and were worse than useless as manual laborers. Therefore, they would have to decline the opportunity to participate in the king's project.[27]

The Egyptians were not very concerned with the absence of the Leviim. Hordes of other Jews had already reported for work, and the labor projects proceeded without the participation of the Leviim. At day's end, the amount of work each Jew had done was calculated, registered in the royal records—and then established as his quota for the future! The Leviim, however, had done no work, and therefore, no quota could be established for them. Nor could they even be inscribed on the labor rolls, for the Egyptian taskmasters would not deviate in the slightest degree from the specific directive of Pharaoh. Pharaoh had decreed that all future daily labor requirements would equal the amount of labor done on the first day. The Leviim had done no labor on the first day and were therefore exempt from all future labor.[28*]

26) ילקו״ש קס״ג 27) דעת זקנים שמות ה-ד 28) ילקוט כת״י מובא בתורה שלמה

Presently, the absence of the Leviim came to Pharaoh's attention. Fortunately for the Leviim, a royal protocol instituted by Yosef many years earlier came to their rescue. During the Great Famine, Yosef had decreed that everyone who could not afford food from the royal granaries must transfer his land to Pharaoh in exchange for food. Members of the priestly class, however, were not required to give up their lands for food. Out of respect for the priesthood, all priests were exempt from the common law of the land. Because Yaakov had instructed that Levi and his descendants were to concentrate on learning Torah, Shevet Levi was now considered a priestly class, and according to the normal protocols of the Egyptian government, they were entitled to priestly privileges. Pharaoh, therefore, decided to grant Shevet Levi an exemption from the labor decrees.[29]

Pharaoh's decision was also influenced by his great reverence for the saintly Yaakov. When Yaakov felt he was about to die, he left instructions that the Leviim should not carry his casket during his funeral procession. He felt that people destined to carry the Holy Ark of the Torah should not be carrying the casket of a deceased person. Pharaoh, therefore, drew an analogy to himself. If the holy Yaakov had considered it disrespectful to have Levi carry his casket, certainly he, Pharaoh, should not subject them to slave labor.[30]

Pharaoh's Grand Scheme

The pieces of Pharaoh's grand scheme were falling into place. Except for Shevet Levi, the Jews had been successfully maneuvered into submitting to the royal labor battalions.[31] They were trapped and at the mercy of Pharaoh's labor decrees. Pharaoh felt confident that the next stages of his scheme could now be implemented and the systematic destruction of the Jews could at last begin.

Pharaoh's plan for the destruction of the Jews was designed to be executed in three stages. The first stage would sap their physical strength and make them easier to control. The second stage

---

* Shevet Levi's clever and bold plan to avoid slave labor did result in negative consequences for them. Since they did not suffer equally with the rest of the Jewish people, they did not receive a portion of Eretz Yisrael.

29) ע' רמב"ם הל' עכו"ם א-ג, אמת ליעקב ויגש 30) הדר זקנים שמות א-יג, במדרש הגדול שם איתא שרק לעמרם לא הי' חלק בעבודה 31) שמו"ר א-יב

would diminish their reproductive capacity and bring about a drastic reduction in the Jewish population of Egypt. The third stage would destroy the morale and spirit of the Jewish people and bring about their complete and perpetual subjugation to their Egyptian masters.[32]

The harshness of the labor itself was also gradually increased. At first, the Jewish laborers were responsible for gathering the lime and forming it into bricks; the straw needed for the brickmaking process was provided by their Egyptian taskmasters. As time went on, the daily production quotas imposed on the hard-pressed Jewish laborers were gradually increased, and the work load became heavier and heavier. Years later, the Jews would even be required to gather their own straw for brickmaking—a very time-consuming task—but they were not allowed the slightest reduction in their required production quotas. This put tremendous pressure on the laborers, making their burden crushing to the point of unbearability.[33]

The First Stage

The first stage of Pharaoh's plan was launched with the announcement of plans to rebuild the ruined cities of Pisom and Ramses.[34] This was a huge construction project which involved building gigantic storage facilities[35] and massive fortifications,[36]* in addition to the normal requirements for residential, commercial and administrative districts.

The public was told that these cities were needed to store the vast treasures Egypt had acquired from the Canaanites in exchange for food during the Great Famine many years earlier. The Egyptians feared that the Canaanites would attack them and try to recover their treasures, and they made plans to defend themselves.[37]

Storage was also needed for the enormous amounts of grain that accumulated in the royal granaries. During the Great Famine, Yosef had issued a decree that one fifth of all grain produced in Egypt each year was to be given to the king. The Egyptian people

---

* Others suggest that these were cities of idol worship. Pharaoh thought that leading the Jewish people into idol worship would ensure that Hashem would never redeem them. (Yavetz, Haggadah)

---

32) ע' גבורות ד' טו ובהגדתו 33) רבנו בחיי שמות א-י וגם ה-ח 34) שמות א-י-א וע' ובמהרש"א סוטה יא 35) שמות רבה א-י במהרז"ו וע' מדרש הגדול א-יא 36) ספר הישר 37) ילקוט ראובני וע' בבעה"ט שמות א-יב

accepted this imposition, because otherwise they would have gotten no food and starved to death. And thus, every year, rivers of grain poured into the royal granaries, more grain than the government could handle. The storage cities of Pisom and Ramses would now serve to contain the overflow.[38]

The Jewish laborers in Pharaoh's labor battalions were now directed to build these cities. They were told that they had a particular responsibility for this project, because they were indirectly responsible for the destruction of the original cities of Pisom and Ramses. Years before, a grandson of Eisav named Tzfo had mustered an African army and invaded Egypt with the intent of destroying the Jewish settlements.[39] Although the invasion was repelled by Egyptians and Jews fighting side by side, the war caused great damage to Egypt, including the destruction of Pisom and Ramses. The Jewish laborers were now told that since they had been the cause of the destruction of these cities they should take the leading role in the rebuilding project.[40*]

All this is what Pharaoh told the public, but the true purpose of the Pisom and Ramses project was to destroy the physical strength of the Jews.[41] It was to be the first stage in the systematic destruction of the Jewish people. Pharaoh had secret information about Pisom and Ramses that made these cities ideally suited for his cunning and diabolical plans. He had discovered that these cities stood on unstable ground.[42] Any buildings now erected on such land were sure to collapse, no matter how well or how often they were rebuilt. If a deep foundation was laid, it would disintegrate and sink into the ground. Whatever was built during the day collapsed at night.[43]

The Jewish laborers assigned to this construction project were thus in jeopardy of their lives, never knowing when the building they were constructing would collapse over their heads.[44] But even if they survived, they were doomed to work on this project endlessly, building and rebuilding and rebuilding without any hope of ever completing their work. This was totally useless labor, a tremendous waste of human energy. Yet this was exactly what Pharaoh wanted.

---

* This was known as the ancient Egyptian city of Tanis. (Targum Yonasan)

---

38) מלכים שמות א-י״א 39) ע׳ לעיל פרק ב׳ ציון יד 40) ספר הישר 41) סוטה יא. 42) שמו״ר א-י, במהרז״ו, מלכים שמות א-י, ע׳ רש״י ותוס׳ עה״ת 43) בעה״ט 44) מדרש אגדה א-י״א, רש״י סוטה יא., בעה״ט ה-טז

He wanted to drain off the physical strength and energy of the Jewish people, leaving them weak and helpless against their Egyptian masters.[45]

The Second Stage

The second stage of Pharaoh's plan could now be implemented. Special labor programs designed to control the Jewish population were now put into effect.[46] After much research and brainstorming, the Egyptian labor officials had discovered that plowing was the labor most effective as a tool for population control.[47] And so, Jewish labor battalions were sent off to work in the fields, digging and plowing under the harsh glare of their Egyptian taskmasters.

When evening mercifully came and the day's excruciating work was finally done, the laborers prepared to return to their homes.

"Where are you going?" the taskmaster would say. "You can't go home. Field work requires many hours of uninterrupted work. By the time you go home and come back, too many hours will be wasted. No, you must stay here until the work is completed. Stay where you are."

Left without a choice, the fortunate ones among the Jewish laborers were allowed to go off to sleep on the cold ground in the fields or in the taskmaster's hut. The less fortunate ones were forced to continue working into the night,[48] digging for their Egyptian taskmasters.[49]

All this was just a ruse. The Egyptians were not concerned about the work the laborers might miss if they returned home for the night. All they wanted was to break up the Jewish homes and families so that no children would be born.[50] Similarly, the Egyptians sent the Jews into the forest to trap animals. They had no need for these animals, and their intention was solely to keep the Jews away from their homes and minimize the growth of the Jewish population.[51]

Yet to the astonishment of the Egyptians, the Jewish people continued to grow and flourish despite all the efforts of the Egyptians to control them. On the contrary, the more the Egyptians persecuted the Jews, the more they multiplied.[52] They were like grass in the

---

45) שמו"ר א-יא ובמהרז"ו, מלבים א-יא, הגדה ע"פ אמרי שפר (46 שכל טוב שמות א-יא, שמו"ר א-יב (47
מדרש כת"י מובא בתורה שלמה לד (48 שמו"ר א-יב, ח-ט, פדר"א לט (49 רמב"ן שמות א-יא (50 שמו"ר א-
יב (51 אלי' רבא ז (52 שמות א-יב

field. The more it is cut, the more luxuriantly it grows.[53]

By nature, a person subjected to stress and anxiety is unlikely to have children, and if he does, there is an increased possibility of birth defects and deformities. But the Jews continued to have more and more robust children, regardless of how much they were persecuted.[54] Clearly, this was a great miracle. Hashem proclaimed, "I promised Avraham that his children would become as numerous as the stars in the sky. Does Pharaoh think he can outsmart Me? We shall see whose word comes true!"[55]

The Jewish people understood the purpose of Pharaoh's decree, and they found ways to defeat it. The labor decrees included all young men, ages twenty and up, the normal age when young men father children. The Jewish people now arranged to have their children marry at the age of thirteen, thus gaining seven uninterrupted years of potential fatherhood.[56]

The Jewish women, for their part, heroically did all they could to foil Pharaoh's evil plan. They went out into the fields to be together with their husbands and keep their families intact. They spoke words of encouragement to their exhausted husbands, telling them, "Take heart. Do not allow yourself to be broken. Hashem will soon redeem us. We won't be slaves forever. One day soon, we will be free again. Be strong, and have faith."

They then went to draw water for their husbands. Hashem caused little fish to collect inside the jars of water these valiant women drew. The women cooked the fish and fed them to their husbands, and they gave their husbands the hot water for washing. In this way, the Jewish men were sustained by the encouragement, nourishment and company of their wives, and the continuity of the nation was assured. Children continued to be born, and the Jewish people flourished and grew.[57]*

Frustrated by the lack of success of the first two stages of their plan, the Egyptians set their hopes on the third stage of their plan.[58] The Egyptian experts had devised a program of abusive labor that

---

* Shevet Levi, who did not work, was not included in this blessing. Only those who suffered from the harsh labor decrees were blessed with extraordinary growth. (*Megaleh Amukos*, Haggadah; Ramban, *Bamidbar* 3:14)

53) הגדת ריטב"א 54) הגדת יד יוסף 55) שמו"ר א-יב 56) רבנו יהודה החסיד שמות א-יב, זקוקין תדב"א כג 57) שמו"ר א-יב 58) רמב"ן שמות א-יא

would break the morale and spirit of the Jewish people. Now they set it in motion.[59]

The Third Stage

The third stage of the Egyptian plan thoroughly embittered the lives of the Jewish people[60] by making them do work which was exceedingly harsh. The Egyptian labor researchers had ascertained that doing heavy work to which one is not accustomed puts one under tremendous strain. Therefore, the taskmasters assigned men to the work of women, while women were told to do the work of men.[61] Men were put to work washing, baking, cooking and sewing, while women were sent outside to plow, plant and build.[62] This reversal of labor roles was a cause of great suffering for the Jewish people. It brought no benefit to the Egyptian government other than to break down the Jewish morale.[63]

The taskmasters drove the Jewish laborers mercilessly, forcing them to work day and night with practically no interruption.[64] The tasks were so difficult that all two hundred and forty-eight human limbs were strained by the work.[65]

The Jews were assigned thirty-nine different kinds of work.[66]* They were required to plant grains, beans and vineyards in their proper season.[67] They were also required to tend to the animals of the Egyptians, to feed and watch them, even though their other responsibilities did not allow them enough time for this.[68] They were required to sweep the streets and cart away the city waste.[69] They were also required to catch fish for the Egyptians.[70] Just when a Jew became accustomed to the work he was doing, the Egyptians would change his assignment in order to subject him to as great a strain as possible.[71]

Finally, the bitter labor began to have a noticeable effect on the Jews. The people were exhausted and dispirited, and the birth rate

---

* When the Jewish people were redeemed, they were required to refrain from these thirty-nine kinds of labor on Shabbos.

---

59) שמו"ר א-י (וכו') 60) שמות א-יד 61) שמו"ר א-יא 62) שמו"ר שם, יפ"ת, תנחומא ויצא ט וידוע דלשון כרפס הוא נוטריקון ס' פרך וקאי אששים רבוא שנשתעבדו. ויתכן שהרמז בסדר הפוך להורות שעצם עבודתם הי' מהופך וכבפנים 63) נצי"ב, הגדת הגר"א, וע' (בחומש צל העדה) בפי' עיר בנימין שרצה בזה פרעה שיתלמדו זה מזה אופן עבודתם ועי"ז יתערבו ויכשלו בחטא ועי"ז יכעס עליהם ד' ויהי' ביכלתו לשעבדם ללא פחד 64) שמו"ר יח-ט 65) בעה"ט שמות א-יד 66) תוס' פסחים קיז, ולשון התורה עבודת פרך רומז ע"ז כי פר"ך בא"ת ב"ש בגימטריא ל"ט 67) ילקו"ש וארא קפ"ב 68) זבח פסח 69) ילקוט שם 70) מדרש ויושע בפסוק וברוב גאונך 71) הכתב והקבלה שמות א-יג

began to fall. The children, who had always been so robust, were now becoming sickly, and some of them did not survive. Despair and disease were becoming rampant in the Jewish settlements.[72]

Pharaoh was not satisfied, however, with what he had accomplished thus far. Having enslaved the Jews, he now decreed that they should be subjected not only to the domination of the king and the government but also of ordinary Egyptian citizens.[73] Any Egyptian could order a Jew to do menial tasks for him, such as carting away the animal wastes from his property, and he often did this to the accompaniment of a barrage of curses, taunts and physical blows.[74] Sometimes, the Egyptians would send a Jewish laborer to the forests to capture wild animals for sporting events. Afraid to refuse the orders, the Jew would attempt to snare these dangerous wild beasts, only to be devoured and ripped apart.[75]

After a hard day's work, when the Jewish laborer felt he would finally be able to find a moment of rest, the Egyptian would often tell him, "I have more work for you. Go gather straw for my home. Then you can chop some wood and fill my jugs with water."[76] And usually, the Jewish laborer's only reward for all his efforts was a piece of *matzah*[77] or a crust of bread.[78] Hunger was his constant companion, in addition to the lice infesting his clothes, which he was not allowed to wash.[79]

Women, too, were not exempt from the demands of common Egyptian citizens, many of them being assigned work as housemaids.[80] Driven beyond the limits of their endurance, many of them became ill and debilitated.[81] Occasionally, an Egyptian would offer to reduce the workload of a Jew if he paid homage to the Egyptian gods. Those Jews still strong in their faith rejected these offers, saying, "Just as our forefather Avraham did not abandon his faith in Hashem, neither will we!"[82]

Even when the Jews could find a brief respite in their homes, they were still subjected to misery and privation. By royal decree, the large Jewish population was confined to Goshen, and this resulted in conditions of terrible overcrowding. Large families were crammed together in tiny living quarters in unsanitary conditions.

72) מדרש הגדול שמות א-יד, בהגדת ריטב"א כתוב דחוסר האומץ גרם רפיון ביכלתם לפרות ולרבות 73) רבנו בחיי שמות א-י 74) רמב"ן שמות א-יא 75) ילקו"ש וארא קפ"ב 76) תנחומא ויצא ט 77) הגדת הגר"א 78) רמב"ן שמות א-יא ובמדבר יא-ה 79) בעה"ט וארא ח-יד 80) הגדת האברבנל וע' בהגדת הפנים יפות 81) פרדר"א מח 82) תנדב"א כג

There was no joy, no laughter, no song, only sadness and misery. Pharaoh had achieved the degradation of the Jewish people.[83]

The Bitterness of Exile

The Jewish people had been singled out from among all the seventy different nationalities that lived in Egypt.[84] The Egyptians feared the Jews, and their oppressive decrees were all directed against the Jews. The Egyptians had succeeded in enslaving the Jewish people and making their lives one great mass of misery and bitterness.

As much as the Jews suffered in public, they suffered even more in private. This private suffering, known only to Hashem,[85] was so intensely painful and bitter that death would have been considered a sweet and welcome alternative to a life of slavery in Egypt.[86]

The Jews were in the midst of an exile that could not have been more bitter. They were trapped in a wicked land that was ruled by a wicked king, who issued wicked decrees.[87] And there was no escape. The Egyptians had twenty-four different safeguards against unauthorized flight. The Jewish people were so deeply ensnared that they lost all hope of ever extricating themselves by their own power. Their only hope clearly lay in the help of Hashem.[88]

During this dark time in the story of the Jewish people, a small glimmer of light appeared. A daughter was born to Amram and Yocheved, both from Shevet Levi. She was their first child, and they named her Miriam, because the suffering of the Jews was so *mar*, so terribly bitter.[89*]

---

* This took place eighty-six years before the Jewish people would be redeemed from Egypt and marked the beginning of the period of harsh oppression. (*Seder Olam*, ch. 3; *Tanchuma Yashan*, Bo 86)

---

83) רבנו בחיי שמות ג-ט 84) תנחומא ויצא ט במדרש הגדול (שמות א-יד) אי׳ שגלות זה היה הגלות הכי קשה מכולם וע׳ בגבורות ד׳ ח׳ (וכ״א מארי׳ ז״ל) דבגלות מצרים הי׳ כלול כל הד׳ מלכיות 85) הגדת האברבנל 86) הגדת כלי חמדה 87) הגדת הגר״א 88) זבח פסח 89) ילקו״ש קס״ה.

A Decree
of Death

4

Although the Jewish people suffered greatly in their Egyptian bondage, Pharaoh was feeling very impatient. His intention had been to arrest the growth of the Jewish people and destroy them through his cruel labor policies, but it was not happening. The time had come to take more drastic steps and make another decree. Pharaoh called a meeting of his council of advisors to discuss the various courses of action that might be successful against the Jewish people.[1]

"Gentlemen, we have a serious problem to discuss here," Pharaoh began when his advisors had come together. "We all know the terrible danger our beloved motherland faces from the presence of the Jews. You are all aware of the labor programs which have been instituted to destroy these dangerous foreigners, but we have been frustrated

---

1) שמו״ר א-יג במהרז״ו, יפ״ת

at every turn. Clearly, the Jewish God is very powerful, and He has been protecting the Jews from harm, no matter what we have done to destroy them.

"I think we have been very clever in dealing with the Jews themselves. We've outsmarted them with our policies and trapped them into slavery, but we have not succeeded. Why? Why haven't we been able to break them and destroy them? There can only be one answer. They have enjoyed divine protection from their God. Gentlemen, I tell you, it is useless for us to try to outsmart the Jews. No! That is not enough! We must outsmart the Jewish God. Only then will we be successful!"

"But how can we do this thing, your majesty?" the advisors called out in puzzlement and frustration. "We are no match for the Jewish God."

"Do not be so fainthearted, gentlemen," Pharaoh said. "I have called this meeting so that we can put our heads together and come up with a plan. I believe we can do it.

"Now, listen carefully. Before we can outsmart the Jewish God, we must understand His particular ways. Then we must turn them to our advantage. I have given much thought to the matter, and this is what I think. The Jewish God avenges Himself in a manner called *midah keneged midah*, measure for measure. He always repays His enemies in the same measure by which they sin against Him.[2] That is how He works. Now, all we have to do is kill the Jews in such a way that their God won't be able to bring retribution upon us. Does anyone have any suggestions?"

There was a murmur of hushed conversation among the advisors, and then Bilam rose to his feet.

"Your majesty," he began. "First, I must compliment you on your extraordinary insight. As usual, you have penetrated to the heart of the problem and come up with a brilliant solution. We can indeed outsmart the Jewish God, and the key, as you have said, is His policy of *midah keneged midah*.

"It seems to me that there are basically four methods by which we can kill the Jews. We can put them to the sword. We can toss them into the flames and burn them. We can stone them to death. Or we can toss them into the water and drown them. I suggest that we

---

choose this fourth method, and I will tell you why. Drowning has an important thing in its favor, while the other three methods not only lack the advantage of drowning, they also have additional disadvantages of their own. Let me explain.

"We have to worry about two things. Number one, will we be successful in our plan or will the Jewish God cause us to fail? Number two, even if we are successful, will the Jewish God destroy us in revenge? Agreed?"

The question was greeted by nods and murmurs of approval.

Satisfied, Bilam continued. "Let us first consider death by fire. Can we be successful? I think not. Avraham, the forefather of the Jews, was thrown into the flames of a furnace by King Nimrod of Babylon because of his refusal to serve idols and betray his God. The Jewish God rescued Avraham from the flames, and He would probably rescue Avraham's grandchildren as well, in the merit of their grandfather. No, I don't think fire is the answer.

"Then how about death by the sword? Again, we must look back into history. Yitzchak, the second forefather of the Jewish people, bared his neck for the blade of his father Avraham's knife when the Jewish God tested him at the Akeidah. Yitzchak was willing to be brought as a sacrifice, and in this great merit, the Jewish God will never allow the Jewish people to be put to the sword.

"So, you ask, how about stoning them to death? Also not such a good idea. Before he died, the saintly Yaakov, the third forefather of the Jewish people, compared his descendants to a stone when he blessed them. He did this in order to protect them, so I don't think we would succeed in stoning them to death.[3]

"This leaves us with the choice of drowning them. I don't see any special protection for the Jewish people with regard to water. And not only that, we will actually be able to avoid the vengeance of the Jewish God if we drown the Jews, because after the Great Flood, He promised never to bring another flood upon the world. So measure for measure, in this case, will be impossible! Your majesty, I think this plan just might work!"[4]

Pharaoh was delighted with Bilam's words, but he still had one more thought to present to his advisors.

"Gentlemen, I am very gratified that such a brilliant plan is

---

materializing here at this meeting. However, there is one more aspect to this business that I would like to discuss. We are not quite ready for these plans. We have to remember that we are a great and honorable kingdom, and we cannot do something publicly that will bring us shame and disgrace. Drowning, I am afraid, will call too much attention to what we are doing. As for now, we will have to use other methods, methods that can be more easily concealed. I have some ideas as far as this is concerned which I will reveal at a later time.[5] In the meantime, I am more concerned with making sure we destroy all the Jews. How do we do this?

"As always, the key is to be found in the historical record. There have been many occasions on which one man or group tried to destroy another but failed. Kayin tried to make sure that he would be the ancestor of all mankind by killing his only brother Hevel. Kayin was a fool. He should have waited to kill Hevel until after their father Adam had died. But he didn't. Adam was still alive when Hevel died, and he had another child, a son named Shess. And as it turned out, Shess became the ancestor of mankind, not Kayin.

"Many years later, we find Eisav plotting to kill his brother Yaakov. Eisav thought himself a clever fellow. He would learn from the mistakes of Kayin. He would wait until their father Yitzchak died, and then he would kill Yaakov! Clever? Ha! Eisav was just as much a fool as Kayin was. By waiting so long, he gave Yaakov the opportunity to have children. And so many children! Don't we know about it here in Egypt unfortunately? No? So, even if Eisav had been successful in killing Yaakov, what good would it have done? Nah, Eisav was no clever fellow if you ask me.

"But I, Pharaoh, am truly the clever one. I will attack the newborn children. I will snuff out their miserable little lives right from the very beginning.[6] Those who have already been born will grow old childless and die. Then we will be rid of the Jews once and for all. Actually, it is only necessary to kill the male children. We can allow the female children to live. Let them be used to satisfy the appetites of our people.[7] Besides, females are not a threat to us in case of war, since women do not bear arms.[8] Let them be sold as maidservants to the people of Cham; nothing is more humiliating

5) רמב"ן שמות א-י"א 6) ויקרא רבה כז-י"א 7) לקח טוב שמות א-ט"ז בתכלית גזירתו יער"ש ביפ"ת א-י"ג ובמהרש"א סוטה שם דהי' למעט מספר בנ"י ובתרגום יונתן א-ט"ו ובמזרחי א-ט"ז דהי' להפטר ממושיעןן של ישראל 8) הדר זקנים א-ט"ז

than that.[9] Let their children also be sold as slaves,[10] except for the male children, of course. Those we will put to death. Over time, they will become assimilated and forgotten, and they will never be redeemed.[11]

"Yes, indeed. I will nip the problem in the bud. But we must be careful. We must still be concerned about the vengeance of the Jewish God, who is quite powerful, as we all know.[12] We don't want Him to punish us for the sin of murder, which is forbidden to all people.[13] But I have an idea. I will accomplish the full destruction of the Jewish people without dirtying my own hands or the hands of any Egyptian people!"[14]

"How so, your majesty?" his advisors wanted to know.

"Simple, gentlemen. It all goes together with my plan to kill the newborn Jewish children. You see, I will force the Jewish midwives to kill the babies as soon as they are born.* I shall accomplish my goals, and yet, I shall be totally blameless.[15] Are there any other comments before we adjourn this meeting? How about my stargazers? Have you anything to say?"

One of the royal stargazers rose to his feet. "Yes, your majesty, we have taken many readings of the configurations of the stars, and we have consulted with each other to determine the true interpretation. We have some interesting information for you and perhaps a suggestion." He paused for effect.

"Well, go ahead, speak up," said Pharaoh impatiently. "What have you seen in the stars?"

"Your majesty," said the stargazer. "We agree with your statement that it is of the utmost importance to kill the male children rather than the female children. You see, according to our readings, it appears that there is a very great danger to Egypt from the male babies of the Jews. We have seen that a boy will soon be born to the Jews who will redeem them from bondage.[16] Therefore, all the stargazers in the royal astrology department agree that the male children must all be killed."

---

* Aharon was born to Amram and Yocheved at this time. He was born three years after Miriam. (*Shemos Rabbah* 1: 13) He was named Aharon because of the terrible decree that was issued while he was in his mother's womb. (*Yalkut Shimoni* 165, *Sefer Hayashar*)

---

9) הגדה ע"פ יעב"ץ (10 עקידה שמות א-טז (11 אוה"ח א-טז (12 שמו"ר א-יד (13 רש"ש ומהרד"ו שם
14) שמו"ר א-יד (15 שמות א-טו, שמו"ר א-יד (16 לקח טוב שמות א-טז

Pharaoh and the Midwives

Shortly after the meeting was adjourned, Pharaoh discreetly summoned to the palace the two chief Jewish midwives[17]— a woman named Yocheved and her daughter Miriam.[18] These midwives supervised over five hundred midwives who served the entire Jewish community of Egypt. They were paid well for their work, and even after they paid the royal taxes, a substantial sum remained for themselves.[19]

Yocheved and Miriam also had professional names which they used in their roles as midwives. Yocheved was called Shifrah, because she would smooth the skin of the newborn children and then wash and bathe them. Miriam was called Puah, because she would sing and coo to the children to make them stop crying. The Torah uses these names when telling the story of the midwives to acknowledge the great merit of their kind deeds.[20]*

When these two righteous midwives were ushered into Pharaoh's presence, he came straight to the point.

"Welcome, my good midwives," he said. "I have special instructions for you which I command you to carry out without fail. I have decreed that from now on all Jewish male babies will be put to death at birth, while all female babies will be allowed to live. I am now giving you the honor of fulfilling my commands. When you are called to the home of a Jewish woman giving birth, I want you to put the male babies to death. That is an order!"[21]

Miriam, who was five years old, was horrified by Pharaoh's cruel command. She whispered to her mother, "Woe to this man! Hashem will punish him for his evil deeds."

Pharaoh heard her words and exploded in a fit of burning anger. "Do you think I didn't hear what you said?" he bellowed. "What insolence! What gall! Guards, guards! Arrest this insolent little Jew and put her to death."

"Your majesty, your majesty, have mercy on me, I beg of you,"

---

* Others believe that the midwives were two gentile women who would later convert to Judaism. (*Midrash Tadshei* 21; Malbim)

Yocheved pleaded. "Please spare my little daughter's life. She is only a little child, what does she know? She doesn't understand about affairs of state. Your majesty, please let her live. Please be merciful."

Pharaoh glowered at the Jewish midwives, but Yocheved's conciliatory words had taken the edge off his fury.

"Very well, I will let her live," he said. "You are obviously a wise and level-headed woman. I will let her live for your sake."[22]

"Thank you, your majesty. Thank you for sparing my daughter's life."

Pharaoh thought for a moment. Even though he had decided to kill the Jewish male babies, there were important problems to be considered. The honor of the kingdom was at stake. If word got out that Pharaoh had ordered the slaughter of babies, it would bring shame and disgrace to the kingdom. In order to deal with this problem, he would have to enlist the help of the midwives.

"Listen carefully," he said. "When people ask you why the babies are dying, I want you to say they were stillborn.[23] Under no circumstances are you to say you put them to death by my orders. Do you understand?"

"Yes, your majesty."

"Now listen carefully," Pharaoh continued. "I understand that this is not easy for you, and therefore, I am prepared to reward you handsomely.[24] Just carry out my orders and be discreet about it, and you will see how generous I can be. But woe is to you if you disobey me. I will cast you both into the flames, along with every member of your household and all your possessions.[25] Do you understand?"

"Yes, your majesty, we understand," Yocheved replied.

"Good, good. This then is what you will do. When you assist the Jewish mothers in childbirth, look at the birthing stone for indications as to whether it will be a male or a female child. If it is a male, put it to death.[26] I want it to look like a stillborn.[27] All you need to do is place your finger on the infant's nose so that it will suffocate.[28] And most important, make sure you get there in time—before the mother can hide the child and claim she miscarried."[29]

---

22) שמו"ר א-יג וברש"ש שם 23) רמב"ן שמות א-י 24) אמרי נועם שמות א-טז 25) ספר הישר 26) סוטה יא:;

שמו"ר א-יד 27) רמב"ן שמות שם, אוה"ח שמות א-טז 28) לקח טוב שמות א-טז 29) רש"י סוטה יא:

The Midwives Fear Hashem

As soon as they left Pharaoh's presence, the midwives looked at each other in disbelief. The midwives were shocked by Pharaoh's words. "Our father Avraham opened an inn for all passersby," Yocheved declared. "He provided food and shelter even for the worst pagans. Does Pharaoh really expect us, Avraham's grandchildren, to stoop so low? He is not telling us to stop feeding the babies. He actually wants us to kill them! Outrageous!"[30]

The midwives never even considered obeying Pharaoh's command. They feared Hashem, not Pharaoh, and they did all in their power to keep the children alive.[31] Not only didn't they kill the babies, they brought nourishing food and water for the babies.[32] If the mother of the newborn child was too poor to provide for her child, the midwives would collect food for the baby from the wealthier families.[33] If the donated food did not cover the need and more food had to be bought in the market, they would pay for it with their own money.[34]

Sometimes, children were born with life-threatening illnesses or deformities. Under normal circumstances, it would have been beyond the scope of the midwives to make heroic efforts to cure these children. They would have offered words of encouragement and left the newborn child in the parents' care, while they themselves went on to help the next mother waiting to give birth. After Pharaoh's decree, however, the midwives took personal responsibility for the recovery of these unfortunate children. "If these children die," they told each other, "people may think it is our fault. They may think we followed Pharaoh's orders and killed the children. Heaven forbid!" And thus, whenever such a child was to be born, these righteous midwives prayed to Hashem with all their might for the recovery of the child. And Hashem listened to their prayers and cured the children in their merit.[35]

All in all, the extraordinary kindness and devotion of the midwives was so precious to Hashem that he let the Torah bear eternal witness that "the midwives feared Him."[36]

---

30) שמו"ר א-טו 31) שמות א-יז 32) שמו"ר א-יז 33) סוטה יא: 33) שמו"ר א-טו 34) רע"ב שמות א-טו 35) שמו"ר א-טו

36) לקח טוב שמות א-יז

In the meantime, the activities of the midwives did not go unnoticed in the royal palace. Pharaoh angrily summoned the midwives
to appear before him.

"You have disobeyed me!" he thundered at them. "You have
ignored my commands and kept the Jewish boys alive. Why have
you committed this terrible crime?"[37]

"Your majesty, we are not at fault," the midwives cleverly
replied. "Jewish women are not like Egyptian women. Each Jewish
woman is like her own midwife. They give birth like animals, without any assistance in their delivery.[38] They are healthy and strong
and have no problem delivering without our help.[39] They pray to
their God for a quick and healthy delivery, and He answers their
prayers.[40] In fact, it's been days since anyone has called us to come.[41]
When we hear that they are about to give birth, we go to them, but
by the time we get there, the child is already born. There is nothing
left for us to do."[42]

"Why not?" asked Pharaoh. "Why don't you just put the babies
to death as soon as you get there?"

"It wouldn't work, your majesty," they replied. "The Jewish
women are all expert in the entire birthing process. They would
immediately notice if we were doing something out of the ordinary.
And if a baby died while we were there, they would suspect us of
being responsible. Our reputation would be destroyed, and the Jewish people would never again allow us into their homes to deliver a
child."[43]

Pharaoh looked at them skeptically. "Bah!" he snorted. "What
nonsense! I don't believe a word of what you're saying. You are just
a pair of Jewish liars."

"Oh no, your majesty," the midwives responded. "We can prove
it to you. Call in your public officials and ask them how many children are being born in Egypt."

Still skeptical, Pharaoh summoned the appropriate official and
asked him how many children were being born. The man gave an
astronomical figure that stunned Pharaoh.

"Ahem," he said as he turned back to the midwives. "Perhaps
you are not such big liars after all. There aren't enough midwives in

---

37) שמות א-יח   38) סוטה יא: וברש"י, ורש"י, רלב"ג שמות א-טז 39) שכל טוב שמות א-יט 40) תרגום יונתן א-יט

41) ספר הישר 42) סוטה יא: ברש"י שם, שמר"ר א-טז 43) ספורנו שמות א-יט

all of Egypt to assist in so many births. It seems you are right. The Jewish women are giving birth without any professional assistance.[44] Very well, you can go."[45]

The great number of Jewish births that had so shocked Pharaoh was not coincidental but the result of a special act of divine providence. "What good is Pharaoh's decree," Hashem declared, "if I have not given My consent? I will show Pharaoh that his will can not supersede My will in determining the destiny of the Jewish people."[46]

Although his plan had been foiled, Pharaoh did not give up. Determined to discover the Jewish babies at the instant of birth, he had houses built near the houses of the Jews.[47] In these houses, he installed Egyptians who were instructed to spy on the Jews. When a Jewish child was born it would begin to cry, and when the Egyptian babies heard the cries, they too would begin to cry and wake their parents. In this way, the Egyptian could discover the birth of the child at the first moment and summon the midwives—who were required to kill the child.[48] To make discovery even easier, Pharaoh built maternity clinics in the Jewish areas and ordered all women to go to these clinics when they felt they were about to give birth.[49]

Pharaoh's new plan, however, did not work. The Jewish women never came to the clinics, nor did the midwives kill the babies in their homes. The midwives defended themselves by saying that the Jewish women gave birth so quickly that it was impossible for the midwives to appear early enough to snuff out the lives of their babies.[50] Once again, Pharaoh's plans did not work against Hashem's will.[51]

The Midwives Are Rewarded

Hashem rewarded the midwives greatly for their kind and righteous acts. They were blessed with eternal life in the world to come and a happy and secure life in this world.[52] In fact, as we have seen, Hashem actually caused the extraordinary rise in the Jewish birth rate to protect the midwives from Pharaoh's accusations of disobedience.[53] This protection also extended to Yocheved's son Moshe, who was saved from the

44) דעת זקנים שמות א-כ 45) שמו"ר א-טז, יפ"ת 47) שמות א-כא 48) לקח טוב שמות א-כא
49) טור שמות א-כא 50) שם 51) שמו"ר א-טז 52) לקח טוב שמות א-כ 53) שמו"ר א-טז, דעת זקנים א-כ, רבנו
מיוחס שם

drowning waters of the Nile through the merit of his mother.[54]

The midwives were also blessed with outstanding children and descendants. Yocheved gave birth to Moshe, who received the Torah from Hashem on behalf of the Jewish people; indeed, the Torah would always be associated with him by being called "Toras Moshe." Among her descendants, Yocheved would count all the Kohanim and Leviim, her son Aharon being the first Kohein and her son Moshe being the first Levi. Among her descendants, Miriam would count Betzalel, whose skill and wisdom were instrumental in the construction of the Mishkan, and the royal house of David Hamelech who ruled over all the Jewish people.[55]

Through their righteous deeds, the midwives also earned the great honor and privilege of bringing sustenance and comfort to the Jewish people.[56] In the merit of Moshe, the Jewish people were sustained in the desert for forty years by the *mann* that fell from the heavens each day. In the merit of Aharon, the Jewish people were enveloped and shielded by the holy cloud pillars that guided them through the desert for forty years. In the merit of Miriam, the Jewish people were provided with water in the desert by a miraculous spring that traveled with them for forty years, until she passed away.[57]

Pharaoh's Dream

One hundred and thirty years had now passed since the Jewish people first came to Egypt. The sojourn of the Jewish people in Egypt had begun with prosperity and peace but had degenerated into a nightmare of slavery, oppression and attempted genocide. At this time, Pharaoh had a dream.[58]

In his dream, Pharaoh saw himself sitting on his throne when an old man appeared. The old man was holding a scale, which he showed to Pharaoh. All the people of Egypt—men, women and children—were placed on one side of the scale, while a lamb was placed on the other side of the scale. To Pharaoh's amazement, the little lamb outweighed the other side of the scale.[59] The old man then put all the gold and silver of Egypt next to the Egyptian people on the scale, and the lamb, alone on the other side, still outweighed

54) שמו"ר א-כה, יפ"ת 55) שמו"ת 55) שמו"ר א-סז (וכו') 56) רע"ב שמות א-טז 57) שפתי כהן חקת כ-י 58) ילק"ש קסד
59) ספר הישר, מדרש דברי הימים למשה

everything. Then all the armaments of the Egyptians were placed alongside the Egyptian people and their treasures—and still, the lamb outweighed everything![60]

Pharaoh awoke from his sleep, shaken and terrified. He knew it had great significance, but he could not fathom its meaning. Without wasting any time, Pharaoh called together his soothsayers, magicians, stargazers and wise men. He described his dream to them in full detail and asked for their interpretations.

Bilam was the first to respond. "Your majesty, if I may be so bold," he began. "I think it is fairly obvious that the reference is to the Jewish nation, which is compared to a lamb. This lamb in your dream indicates that an important Jewish child will soon be born. The significance of his outweighing all the Egyptian people, treasure and armaments is that he will lead the Jews in a revolt against Egypt and destroy it. If you recall, this is also what the stargazers predicted at the last meeting. Now we have confirmation from your dream. I say we waste no time and destroy the Jews once and for all—right now! That is my opinion, your majesty. Perhaps some of your other advisors would like to offer their comments on the matter."

"Thank you, Bilam," said Pharaoh. "As usual, you have taken a forceful position, and I value your opinion. However, I am willing to hear from some of my other advisors. I think I should like to hear the opinions of Yisro and Iyov. First, let us hear from Yisro."

"I am honored, your majesty," said Yisro. "But I am afraid I do not agree with Bilam. Whoever tries to harm the Jews ultimately fails and suffers. The Pharaoh in the time of Avraham took Sarah from her husband and was stricken. Avimelech, the king of Plishtim, took Rivkah from her husband and was also stricken. What's more, I think we owe a great debt of gratitude to the Jews. Yosef saved Egypt during the days of the Great Famine. I think it is ungrateful on our part to harm the Jews."

Yisro's words angered Pharaoh immensely, but before he responded to Yisro, he called on Iyov to speak.

Iyov responded with great reluctance. "Your majesty, I must beg your pardon," he said. "This is a very difficult question, and I am afraid I have nothing to say on the matter. This land is yours, your majesty. Do with it as you wish."

---

60) מעשיות התמני מובא בתורה שלמה דף נ

Iyov's response disturbed Pharaoh, although not as much as Yisro's response had disturbed him. Once again, he called on Bilam to speak.

"Thank you, your majesty," Bilam said. "As I said, we must destroy the Jews, but that will not prove so easy. Avraham was saved from fire in Ur Kasdim when King Nimrod threw him into the furnace. Yitzchak was spared death by the knife at the Akeidah. Yaakov was enslaved by Lavan and still emerged free and wealthy. The only way to destroy the Jews is by drowning them in water. We must send out soldiers to find all the Jewish children and drown them. Only by doing this can we hope to destroy this male child who will revolt against Egypt, this lamb who outweighs all of Egypt.[61] I have spoken of this before, and I am voicing my opinion again. We must destroy the Jews now!"

Pharaoh was gratified by Bilam's speech, but his anger against Yisro continued to smolder. Yisro decided not to risk the fruits of Pharaoh's wrath. He fled to Midian, where he started a new life.[62]

Hashem repaid each of the participants in this meeting according to the role he played. Bilam who had urged the slaughter of the Jews would perish by the sword. Iyov who remained silent was condemned to a life full of pain. Yisro who spoke in defense of the Jews merited that his descendants should serve on the Sanhedrin.[63]

Pharaoh's New Decree

Following Bilam's advice, Pharaoh now issued a new decree. All male Jewish newborns are to be thrown into the river, while all females are to be left alive![64]

Pharaoh summoned his generals and issued his commands. "You are to send your soldiers to Goshen, seek out every newborn Jewish male and toss him into the river. I want to make sure that we kill the Jewish savior.[65] I want you to follow the midwives, and as soon as they enter a home where a woman is giving birth, I want you to ambush them and get the child."[66]

So it was. The decree was issued, the soldiers dispatched to carry it out. But Pharaoh was still concerned about his reputation

61) ספר הישר 62) שם 63) סוטה יא., תרגום יונתן במדבר כב-ה מביא שבלעם הי' לבן בן בתואל וי"מ שלא הי'
כ"א גלגולו וכן שאיוב הי' גלגולו של תרח אבי אברהם 64) ספר הישר 65) שם 66) מלבים שמות א-כב

and honor. He did not want to be known as a killer. Therefore, he instructed his soldiers not to toss the Jewish babies directly into the river. Instead, they were to place the babies on the ground alongside the river, so that when the river would rise, the babies would be swept away and drowned. Pharaoh's hands would thus be clean and he would not be guilty of murder.[67]

The soldiers now went off to Goshen to search for Jewish baby boys. A reign of terror descended on the Jewish settlements. The soldiers grabbed the children wherever they could find them. Sometimes, they even tore the babies from the arms of their crying mothers.[68]

As the baby hunt gained momentum, Pharaoh was caught up in the blood frenzy taking place in Goshen. He forgot about his desire to keep his decrees secret. He forgot about his earlier concern for his honor and reputation. He forgot about his fear of being branded a murderer. No longer was he concerned about anything else but the killing of Jewish babies. More than anything, he wanted the Jewish people dead. "Throw the babies directly into the river!" he commanded his soldiers. "Enough is enough!"[69*]

Word of the cruel decree spread among the Jewish people like wildfire. Panic and despair gripped their terrified hearts. In desperation, the Jewish fathers would run to the magistrates of their districts.

"Help us!" they would plead.

"What is the matter?" the magistrate would ask.

"They are killing our children!" the Jewish fathers would cry out in anguish. "You must stop them. They are murderers. Arrest them!"

"That's a terrible accusation to make," the magistrate would say. "Do you have any proof? Do you have any witnesses?"[70**]

"No, we don't," the fathers would reply.

"Then I cannot help you," the magistrate would say.

---

* Some suggest that Pharaoh wanted the Jewish children drowned rather than slaughtered because the Egyptians could not stand the sight of blood. They also did not slaughter animals for this reason. (*Chemas Hachemdah* in *Torah Sheleimah* 47)

** All this was part of the Egyptian scheme to maintain a respectable public image. The charade in the courts was meant to delude the Jews into thinking they were protected by the law.

---

67) לקט שמואל, בפנים יפות מבואר ששמו התינוקות בתוך עריסתן ובכה"ג שמו אותן על שפת הנילוס ולפי"ז
מה שעשתה יוכבד עם משה לא הי' נראה לדבר זר (68 ספר הישר (69 הגדת האור החיים (70 רמב"ן שמות א-י

Slowly, all the Egyptians came to the realization that the Jewish people were totally helpless. The soldiers were searching out their children and killing them, and no one stood in their way, not the government, not the courts. The Jews had become fair game, and all Egyptians joined the baby hunt.[71] Egyptian schoolchildren were excused from classes and sent to the bathhouses to see which women were pregnant, and how far along they were in their pregnancies. Careful records were kept of the expected dates of delivery, and when the time came, the Egyptians were waiting to pounce. As soon as a male child was born, he was snatched from his mother and thrown into the river.[72]

Hide the Children!

As the danger grew, the Jewish people began to hide their children in secret cellars and underground tunnels. For a while, the Egyptians could not find these children, and they managed to survive. But the Egyptians did not accept defeat so easily. They would bring their own sleeping babies to the homes of the Jews. Then they would shake them awake until they started to cry. When the hidden Jewish babies heard the sound of babies crying, they also began to cry, and their hiding places were revealed.[73*] The Egyptians often starved their babies in order to make them cry more easily.[74]

The Egyptian women, who were just as ruthless as their husbands, specialized in tracking down the little Jewish toddlers who had eluded the baby hunt. They would come to the Jewish homes carrying their young toddlers on their shoulders. The young Egyptian children, who did not yet know how to speak, would begin to make mumbling sounds, and the hidden Jewish child would imitate those sounds. The Egyptian women would then run quickly to report the location of the hidden children to the authorities.[75]

Even the Egyptian children got involved in the frenzy. Instead of playing normal children's games, they would scatter throughout the Jewish neighborhoods, looking for signs of hidden Jewish children. As soon as they would hear the sounds of newborn Jewish children,

---

* Many Jews would bribe the Egyptians with jewelry to prevent them from divulging the whereabouts of the children. (*Sefer Chemdas Yamim*)

---

71) הגדת הבעה"ט 72) שיר השירים רבה ב-טו 73) שמו"ר א-נ 74) מדרש אגדה ג-ו 75) ספר הישר

they would run to tell their fathers. The Egyptian fathers would come quickly, grab the children and throw them into the river.[76] In addition, the parents of the hidden Jewish child were also executed—for the terrible crime of having tried to save their child from drowning.[77]

Miracles Protect the Children

It was becoming increasingly clear that the Egyptian surveillance systems would discover every Jewish newborn boy and result in his being put to death. The Jewish women had no choice but to leave their homes and go into hiding.[78] They fled into the fields and the apple orchards. There, under an apple tree, Hashem caused them to fall asleep so that they could give birth to their children without pain. There, under an apple tree, they left their children and tearfully returned to their homes.

These infants were now all alone under the apple trees, but Hashem did not abandon them. He sent down an angel to care for the children, to wash and feed them and care for all their needs. The angel placed two rocks near each child, one to give milk, the other to give honey. The children were also provided with butter and with rubbing oil. Their hair grew long, reaching till their knees, so that they were clothed properly. In this way, they grew and matured in the fields, away from their homes, their parents, their families.

Eventually, the Egyptians heard about the Jewish children growing in the fields, and they sent police to seek them out and kill them, but as soon as the Egyptians arrived in the fields, the children sunk into the ground and disappeared from sight. The Egyptians brought plows and dug deep furrows in the fields, but they could find no trace of the children. Finally, the Egyptians left, satisfied that the children had perished deep in the bowels of the earth. But as soon as they were gone, the children sprouted from the ground like grass in the springtime.[79]

These children remained in the fields until they were self-sufficient. Because of the special blessings which protected them, they grew up healthy, mature and as well-adjusted as any child brought

---

76) ילקו"ש וארא קפ"ב 77) מלבים שמות ב-א 78) ספר הישר 79) ספר הישר, מדרש ויושע, דברי הימים למשה, שמו"ר א-יב, הגדה ע"פ כל בו, ע' בפרד"א מח וברד"ל דגזירה זו נמשכה לג' ירחים ושאהרן הכהן נולד תמן

up in the normal way.[80] When they were fully grown, they went back to their home, and miraculously, each one was able to locate and recognize his own parents. The parents, in turn, recognized their sons by their strong resemblance to their fathers.[81] These were the children who would someday stand at the Yam Suf, reflect on the miracles that were performed for them in the fields and say of Hashem, "This is my God, and I will glorify Him."[82]

And what of the children who were thrown into the water? There were as many as 600,000 children in this group,[83] and Hashem watched over them, too, by sending angels to protect them. The angels caught the children as they were tossed into the river and carried them away to a rock in the desert. These children were also fed by rocks that gave honey and milk, and rocks that provided them with rubbing oils. They remained in the desert until they grew up.[84]

Once again, Hashem declared, "Look and see whose decree stands, Mine or Pharaoh's."[85] It is with this in mind that we say in the Haggadah, "*Vehi She'amdah*, and this is what stood by us . . ." Hashem saved the Jewish people from all of Pharaoh's decrees, so that Hashem could keep His promise to the Patriarchs that their children would be saved.[86]

The Net Is Spread Wider

Back at the royal palace, Pharaoh's frustration at the failure of his policies was leading to fear and panic. One day, the stargazers came to him with a very disturbing report.

"Your majesty," they said. "We have been taking many readings in the constellations about this savior who is soon to be born to the Jews. There seems to be an element of uncertainty in this matter."

"Uncertainty?" Pharaoh mused. "You mean the whole thing may be a mistake?"

"Oh, no, your majesty. There can be no doubt about the basic story. We see in the stars that there will be a Jewish savior. We cannot determine, however, if he will be Jewish . . . or an . . . Egyptian."[87]

"An Egyptian?" Pharaoh asked incredulously. "But that's impossible. What kind of Egyptian would want to lead the Jews in a revolt against his own people? Nonsense!"

---

80) הגדת ריטב"א 81) מדרש ויושע ויושע בפסוק אז ישיר 82) שמו"ר א-יב, דברי הימים למשה, ספר הישר, מדרש ויושע 83) בראשית רבה צג-ג 84) שיר השירים רבה ב-כג, דברי הימים למשה, ילקו"ש קפ"ב 85) שמו"ר א-טז 86) הגדה ע"פ כל בו 87) שמו"ר א-יח וברש"ש. ברש"י ושפתי חכמים, א-כב

"We understand your disbelief, your majesty," the stargazers replied. "We are all totally in agreement with your sentiments. Nevertheless, there are clear indications that an Egyptian will lead them in revolt. We also see that the downfall of the savior of the Jews will be water. Therefore, we strongly urge you to drown all the babies born at this time, so that you can be sure that this savior has been destroyed."

Pharaoh saw that he had no choice. "Throw all the baby boys into the river," he told his soldiers. "Not only the Jewish ones but the Egyptian ones as well. We cannot take a chance on having this savior of the Jews survive."[88]*

Now that it affected their own children, the Egyptian people began to protest Pharaoh's cruel decree. It is impossible, they claimed. The savior of the Jews could only be a Jew. An Egyptian would never do such a thing.[89] But it was to no avail. Pharaoh refused to rescind his decree.

In actuality, although Pharaoh and the Egyptians found it hard to believe that an Egyptian would lead a Jewish revolt against his own motherland, the stargazers were not entirely mistaken in their readings. Only their interpretation was mistaken. The savior of the Jews was, of course, Moshe, the young Jewish child rescued from the river by Pharaoh's daughter Basya and brought up in the royal palace. Although Moshe was Jewish, he appeared to the stargazers as an Egyptian because of his upbringing.[90]

Furthermore, the "downfall by water" which they sensed was not referring to drowning in the river. It referred to the incident at Mei Merivah when Hashem told Moshe to bring forth water from the rock by talking to it, and he struck the rock instead.[91]

And thus, during this dark and dreadful time, while the Egyptians hunted down Jewish babies and flung them into the river, the savior of the Jewish people was born.

---

* Some suggest that Pharaoh tried to convince the Egyptians to serve their god the Nile by throwing in their children. (*Yedei Moshe*)

---

88) שמות א-כב ובידי משה על המדרש שם 89) שמו"ר שם 90) שם ובענף יוסף 91) שם ובענף יוסף 91) סוטה יב., שמו"ר א-יח.

The Birth of a Leader

5

The Egyptian campaign to kill all the Jewish male babies brought deep despair to the hearts of the Jewish people, even to the greatest among them, a man named Amram ben Kehas.[1] Amram was the acknowledged leader of the generation.[2] He was blessed with the gift of prophecy,[3] and served as the head of the Sanhedrin[4] and as a teacher of the *mitzvos* to the Jewish people.[5] Amram was as righteous as an angel,[6] one of the people in history who never committed a sin.[7]

When the Egyptian decree to murder the Jewish baby boys went into effect, Amram did not see the point of bringing any more children into the world only to have them thrown into the river. Therefore, he decided to divorce his wife and stop having children. Following his example, the rest of the Jewish people also separated from their wives and divorced them.[8]

---

1) ילקו"ש קסה 2) שם 3) מלבים שמות ב-א 4) שמו"ר א-יג 5) רמב"ם מלכים ט-א
6) מנחה בלולה וארא ו-יח 7) ילקוט ראובני 8) סוטה יב.

Miriam, who was five years old at the time, protested to her father. "I think your decree will have even harsher results for our people than Pharaoh's decrees. Pharaoh's decree only threatens our male children, but your decree threatens both male and female children. Those who die by Pharaoh's decree will have at least come down to this world and will have a share in the World to Come. But those who are prevented from being born by your decree will never have appeared in this world and will not have gained a share in the World to Come. Also, Pharaoh's decree is only a very serious threat, not certain death, but your decree guarantees that no children will be born.[9] What's more, I saw in a prophecy that my parents will give birth to a child who will redeem the Jewish people from Egyptian bondage."[10]

Miriam's words made a deep impression on Amram. He announced in the Sanhedrin that all Jews should keep their wives and continue to have children, even in these times of dreadful peril.[11] Then he went off to the city in which his former wife Yocheved was living, with the intention of bringing her back to his house.[12]

Amram and Yocheved were immediately remarried.[13] At the wedding, little Miriam danced ecstatically and also taught her two-year-old brother Aharon to dance along with her. The two young children understood that this remarriage signaled the beginning of the process of Jewish redemption.[14] The wedding was performed with great fanfare, because Amram wanted the rest of the Jewish people to take note of what he was doing and follow suit.[15] And this is indeed what happened. When everyone saw their great leader return to his wife, they too returned to their wives.[16]

At the time of her remarriage, Yocheved was one hundred and thirty years old, but she miraculously regained her youth. Her skin became soft, her wrinkles disappeared, and the glow of youth returned to her face.[17]

---

9) שם, ואף שלא ידעה, כדברה כך הי' שהצילם ד' וכדלעיל (10 ספר הישר, במדרש אגדה שמות טו-כ מובא שאחר לידת משה פקעה נבואתה (11 מדרש הגדול שמות ב-א (12 מלבים שמות ב-א, בזוה"ק איתא שמלאך גבריאל רקד בשמחת נשואיהם עיין תרגם יונתן במדבר יא-כו שבזמן שהיתה יוכבד גרשה מעמרם נשא את אלצפן בן פרנך ונולד ממנה אלדד ומדד (13 ילקו"ש קסה, זית רענן (14 רמב"ן שמות ב-א (15 מושב זקנים שמות ב-א (16 סוטה יב. (17 שם, רמב"ן ס"ל שהיתה בת נ' ולרלבג בת נ"ח

Moshe Is Born

On the seventh day of Adar, in the year 2368,[18] six months and a day after Amram and Yocheved were remarried,[19] a child was born to them.[20] He would be named Moshe, and he was destined to take the Jewish people out of Egypt.

Although the child was born three months prematurely, the Torah tells us that he looked "good" at his birth, because the entire house was illuminated by his presence. He shone with a sublime spiritual light that was brighter than the sun and the moon, the light that permeated the world during the days of creation.[21] The child glowed like an angel.[22] He was exceedingly beautiful,[23] and he did not cry.[24] Although premature, he was fully developed. He had a full head of hair, and his nails were fully grown.[25] Furthermore, he was born circumcised, an indication that he was pure and holy, with an outstanding good nature and personal characteristics.[26]

With the birth of his son Moshe, Amram came to Miriam and kissed her on the head. "My daughter," he said. "Your prophecy has been fulfilled. The savior of the Jewish people has been born."[27]

The Child Is Endangered

Amram and Yocheved knew that Pharaoh's stargazers had discovered that the savior of the Jewish people was about to be born. They also knew that the stargazers' calculations of when this event would happen was based on the child being carried to the full term of a nine-month pregnancy. Moshe, however, was born after six months of pregnancy, three months before the stargazers expected him to be born. Therefore, Moshe's concerned parents had three months of relative peace before the hunt for the Jewish savior would burst forth in all its ferocity.[28] They concealed their luminous son in an underground cavern beneath their house, and they waited.[29]

---

18) סדר עולם י', בשיטות שונות בתאריך לידתו והמסתעף ע' במכילתא כאן, אסתר רבה ז-יא, שלשלת הקבלה ובכמה כת"י המובאים בתורה שלמה דף נו 19) רש"י שמות שם 20) סוטה שם ויער"ש במכילתא, ספר הישר שמו"ר א-יג ובדעת זקנים 21) שם, זוה"ק שמות כא, דברי הימים למשה 22) ילקוט ראובני, פרדר"א מח, ומבואר דמיום הלקחו לבית פרעה נסתלקה ממנו אור הגנוז עד שעת מתן תורתנו 23) מדרש החפץ שמות ב-ב 24) מנחה בלולה שם 25) רשב"ם ודעת זקנים שם 26) שמו"ר א-כ ובריפ"ת, ע' סוטה יב: ד"טוב" אנבואתו קאי 27) מגילה יד., סוטה יד. 28) סוטה יב., שמו"ר א-כ 29) פרדר"א מח, בעה"ט שמות ב-ג

As the three months drew to a close, the Egyptian hunt intensified as expected. Pharaoh sent Egyptian women with their children into the Jewish neighborhoods, hoping that their cries and mumbles would cause the hidden Jewish children to respond and reveal their hiding places. When they returned empty-handed, Pharaoh called in his stargazers and asked them if they had any information about the child. They told him that the child was still alive. Enraged, Pharaoh ordered that no stone be left unturned in all of Egypt until the baby was found.

The investigation finally began to bear fruit. Word of Moshe's whereabouts reached the royal palace, and Pharaoh immediately sent his soldiers to seize the child.[30] Yocheved realized she could no longer hide her precious son. The situation was desperate. Something had to be done.[31]

Adrift in the River

Yocheved knew that Pharaoh was tracing the progress of the child through his stargazers and that no matter what she did he would be kept informed. Therefore, she needed to do something that would convince Pharaoh and his stargazers that the boy was no longer a threat. She decided to set the child adrift on the river in a specially constructed floating basket. The stargazers would sense what she had done and report to Pharaoh that the child had finally been thrown into the river. Thinking that his decree had been successful, Pharaoh would relax his vigilance and call off the baby hunt.[32]

Yocheved took her son Moshe down to the river, placed him in a basket and set him adrift in the water. She had made the basket out of swamp reeds so that it would escape notice in the reedy marshes of the river.[33] She had made it of a sturdy yet pliable construction so that it would remain afloat in both calm and rough waters.[34] She had covered it with tar and pitch to make it watertight[35] and drilled small airholes into the sides.[36]

Not knowing what the future would bring, Yocheved went home with a great sadness in her heart. Hashem had contrived that

---

30) ספר הישר, פרדר״א שם 31) רמב״ן שמות ב-ב 32) שמו״ר א-כא, וכו׳, בספר ירחמיאל (המובא בתורה שלמה
נא) אי׳ שעשתה כן עפ״י חלום שראתה מרים לפני ט׳ ירחים, בהבא לה זקן והגיד לה שיולד להם בן ויניחו אותו
על המים, ועל ידו יתיבשו המים ויגאלו 33) שמות ב-ג ובדעת זקנים, ילקוט ראובני 34) סוטה יב. 35) רש״י
ורשב״ם שמות ב-ג 36) אברבנל שמות ב

this should occur on the sixth day of Sivan, the date on which the Jewish people would receive the Torah many years later,[37] because He wanted this somber day to become an occasion of happiness in the future.[38] In the meantime, however, sadness and concern over the plight of their child reigned in the home of Amram and Yocheved.

"What has become of your prophecy?" they asked young Miriam. "How will he become the savior of the Jewish people now that he has been thrown into the river?"

Miriam was deeply distressed by the turn of events and the sadness of her parents. She slipped out of the house and ran to the riverside to see what would become of her brother Moshe and the future she had prophesied for him.[39]

She took up a position a short distance from the river and waited to see what would develop.[40] Along with her, the Shechinah, the Divine Presence, also watched over the chosen savior of the Jewish people.[41]*

Miriam did not have long to wait. Her righteous act, so full of kindness and devotion, was rewarded with results after one quarter of an hour.[42]** And in the merit of this righteous act, the Jewish people would wait for Miriam in the desert for seven days when she was afflicted by *tzoraas* and could not travel.[43]***

In Heaven, too, a vigil was being kept over the floating basket and the luminous child it contained. The angels looked down upon the suffering and anguish of the future savior of the Jewish people, the one who would someday receive the Torah from Hashem on behalf of his people, and they begged Hashem to bring the child's ordeal to a merciful end. Hashem heeded their pleas and sent Moshe's salvation in the person of Basya, the daughter of Pharaoh.[44]

---

* Moshe's basket lay near the underwater site of Yosef's casket, who protected him. According to this view, Moshe was placed in the Nile. (*Minchah Belulah*)

** Others note that because she waited for seven hours she was worthy of having the Jewish people wait for her in the desert for seven days. (*Yalkut* in *Torah Sheleimah* 61)

*** Others say that Moshe was in the water for seven days. Yocheved would come feed him at night, while Miriam would protect him from predatory birds during the day. (*Midrash* in *Torah Sheleimah* 60)

---

37) סוטה יב:, בשמו"ר א-כד מפורש דהנחתו בתיבה על הנילוס הי' בכ"א בניסן 38) מדרש הגדול שמות ב-ג
39) מגילה יד. שמו"ר. שמו"ר א-כב ביפ"ת ומהרד"ו 40) שמות ב-יד 41) שמו"ר א-כב ביפ"ת, רבנו בחיי שמות ב-ד
42) תוס' סוטה יא., ילקוט ראובני 43) סוטה ט: 44) פרדר"א מ"ח וברד"ל

Pharaoh's Daughter

Although it was only the beginning of Sivan, summer barely having begun, the day on which Moshe was placed in the river was unusually hot.[45] The heat was so intense that anyone who ventured outside was instantly sunburned and overcome. Pharaoh's daughter wanted to bathe to refresh herself, but unfortunately, she suffered from *tzoraas* and could not bathe in the palace.[46] Therefore, she went down to the river to bathe in its cool waters.[47] Pharaoh's daughter also had another purpose in mind. She was revolted by the idol worship in the palace and attracted to the purity and holiness of Judaism. By bathing in the river, she felt she would cleanse herself of the corruption of the palace.[48]

As befit the princess of a great kingdom,[49] she was accompanied by thirty ladies-in-waiting,[50] all of them from the finest nobility of the land.[51] But when they reached the riverside, her attendants wandered off to search for precious stones and gems that were sometimes found there.[52] Basya was all alone when she caught sight of the basket floating among the reeds.

The daughter of Pharaoh was drawn to the basket by a great curiosity, but it was too far out of her reach. She stretched out her hand for it, and a miracle occurred. Her arm kept getting longer and longer, drawing ever closer to the basket, which was one hundred and twenty feet (sixty cubits) away.[53] Finally, her arm extended all the way to the basket, and she grabbed hold of it. The moment her hand touched the basket, another miracle occurred, and she was suddenly healed from her *tzoraas*.[54]

Clearly, this was no ordinary basket, and Basya trembled as she opened it to see what was inside. To her amazement, it was a young child[55] with a canopy over his head.[56] It was undoubtedly a holy child, because touching his basket had cured her from leprosy.[57] A brilliant spiritual glow enveloped him[58] because of the Shechinah that hovered over him.[59] He was a beautiful child,[60] fully developed like an adolescent,[61] although he was just a newborn.[62]

---

45) דברי הימים למשה, רד"ל בפרדר"א 46) פרדר"א שם 47) דברי הימים למשה 48) שמו"ר א-כג במדרש הגדול
חיי שרה כג-א איתא שנתגלה לה דעל ברכיה יגדל מושיען של ישראל והלכה כל יום ליאור לחפשו ולהצילו,
וכשראתה אז משה שמחה בידעה שנתקיימה 49) אוה"ח שמות ב-ה 50) שפתי כהן שם 51) מלבים שם 52) מדרש
בתורה שלמה סג, במדרש החפץ איתא שהלכו אולי ימצאו תינוקות שנטמנו 53) שמו"ר א-כג, מגילה טו: לקח
טוב שמות ב-י 54) שמו"ר שם, תק"ז כא, שם מח 55) שמות ב-ו 56) שמו"ר א-כד ובמהרד"ו. חופה קטנה זו הי'
סימן שעשתה אמו לומר שמסתברא שלא תראה חתונתו 57) אוה"ח שמות ב-ו 58) סוטה יב: 59) מלבים שמות
ב-ו 60) ספורנו שמות שם 61) אב"ע ורמב"ן שמות שם 62) מלבים שם

While Basya stared in disbelief at this child she had discovered in the river, the angel Gavriel came down and caused Moshe to begin crying so that Basya should take pity on him.[63] Moshe began to cry, thinking, I may never again see my sister who is waiting for me.[64] Little Aharon, who was waiting nearby and feared for his brother's safety, also began to cry.[65]

The tears had their intended effect. They touched Basya's tender heart, and she took pity on the child. "Why would such a complete and perfect child be thrown into the river?"[66] she wondered. "I must save this precious child."[67] After taking a closer look at the child, she noticed that he had a *bris milah*, and she was convinced she had found a Jewish child.[68] Nevertheless, her resolve to save the child was not shaken.

Meanwhile, Basya's ladies-in-waiting returned from scavenging for gems and other precious stones and realized the significance of their mistress's discovery. She had discovered a hidden Jewish child, and she obviously intended to save him.

"Your highness, you cannot do this thing," they protested. "If a king issues a decree and none of his subjects obey it, at least his own children should obey it. What you are doing here goes against your father's decree. Surely, you of all people should obey his decrees."

At that moment, the angel Gavriel came and struck down these ladies-in-waiting until all but one lay dead on the riverbank.[69] Of the thirty ladies, Gavriel left only one alive, because it was unfitting for the king's daughter to return to the palace unattended.[70]

Although Pharaoh's daughter had pulled the child from the river, he did not stop crying. Perhaps the child is hungry, she thought.[71] She found an Egyptian woman who could suckle the child, but he refused to nurse.[72] She searched along the riverside for other Egyptian women who might be able to feed the child, but no matter whom she brought, he would not nurse.[73] Hashem would not allow the mouth that would someday speak with Him to nurse from a person who is defiled. He would not allow an Egyptian nurse to say, "I nursed the mouth that speaks with the Shechinah."[74]

---

63) שמו"ר א-כד (64 שמו"ר שם (65 ילקו"ש קסו, פענח רזא שמות ב-ו יש שמוסיפים שגם המלאך בכה (66
ספורנו שם (67 אב"ע שם (68 שמו"ר א-כד וביפ"ת, כ' האלשיך כי בהיותו גדול כל כך הוכיחה שמזרע היהודים
הוא (69 שמו"ר א-כג וביפ"ת (70 שמו"ר שם, שפתי כהן ב-ה (71 אוה"ח שם (72 דברי הימים למשה (73 שמו"ר
א-כה ובמהרד"ו (74 שמו"ר שם

finding a Nurse

Perhaps I should get him a Jewish nurse,[75] she thought. In any case, it would be dangerous to entrust this Jewish child to an Egyptian woman who might kill him.[76] And besides, it would probably be better for him to be fed by one of his own people.[77]

As Basya struggled with her dilemma, Miriam appeared at her side and asked, "Would you like me to get you a Jewish nurse for the child?" Hashem had made all this happen in the open, so that Miriam could approach the king's daughter without fear and worry.[78]

"Yes, indeed, little girl," Basya replied. "Go get me a Jewish nurse." She had no idea that this young Jewish girl was in fact the sister of the mysterious child.[79]

As quickly as a full-grown girl, Miriam ran off to do as she was told. She returned with a nurse,[80] none other than Moshe's mother Yocheved.[81] Miriam did not tell Basya she was Moshe's sister or that Yocheved was his mother.[82]

"Take this child home and nurse him for me," Basya said to Yocheved. "I will pay you well. You will receive two gold coins for each day of your service."[83]

"Thank you, your highness," said Yocheved.

"Look closely at this child," Basya continued. "Look how beautiful he is, how healthy-looking. I want you to return him to me this way."[84]

"Yes, your highness," said Yocheved. "You can rest assured. I will take care of the child as if he were my own."

"Excellent," said Basya. "And I want you to promise me one more thing. During all the time the child is entrusted to your care you may not nurse any other child but him.[85] Is that understood?"

"Yes, your highness," said Yocheved. "I promise."

Because of her act of kindness, Pharaoh's daughter, whose Egyptian name was Tarmus,[86] was accorded the great honor of being named Basya, "the daughter of Hashem."[87] She was also rewarded by being allowed to enter Gan Eden while still alive.[88] And although

---

75) שם 76) מלבים שמות ב-ז 77) אברבנל שם 78) מלבים שמות ב-ה 79) שמו"ר א-כה ובמתנ"כ 80) רש"י ומלבים שמות ב-ה 81) ילקו"ש קסו 82) שם, שמו"ר שם ובמתנ"כ 83) ספר הישר, מדרש ויושע בפסוק עזי 84) ילקו"ש שם 85) רבנו בחיי שמות ב-ט כי אהרן הי' בן ג' וכבר כלו ימי יניקתו 86) ע' תורה שלמה סג 87) פרדר"א מח 88) מדרש משלי לא-טו

she was a firstborn child, she was protected from death during the plague of the firstborn.[89*]

How wondrous are the ways of Hashem! The child Moshe, set adrift upon the river and destined to grow up in Pharaoh's palace, was returned to his family so that his early nurturing would be among the Jewish people.[90] Yocheved, his mother, was rewarded for her righteousness by actually being paid to nurse her own son.[91] And not only did Pharaoh fail in his attempt to destroy Moshe, his own daughter saved him.[92]

In Pharaoh's Palace

For two years, Yocheved cared for her son in her own home. At the age of three months, he was already endowed with the gift of prophecy, declaring, "In the days to come, I shall receive the Torah from the flaming torch."[93] And from then until he was returned to Pharaoh's daughter at the age of two, Moshe was taught the whole Torah by an angel, maturing into an exceptional scholar even at that very tender age.[94]

Moshe was two years old when he was returned to Basya in Pharaoh's palace.[95] He had grown far taller than other children his age.[96] Basya now decided to give him a name, which she chose with the help of divine inspiration.[97] She had learned Hebrew from the Jewish women of Egypt,[98] and now she chose to call him Moshe, "drawn from the water,"[99] a name which commemorated the miracle of Moshe's rescue from the water.[100] In this way, Hashem ensured that Moshe would always be called by a Jewish name and always be reminded of his people and his heritage.[101]

Moshe actually had ten other names, but of all his names, Hashem chose to identify him in the Torah by his name Moshe. This name had been chosen by Basya, and Hashem wanted to show regard for her extraordinary act of kindness.[102]

---

* Some say she was not Pharaoh's real daughter at all. Rather, she was one of two abandoned infant sisters who were brought to the palace because of their great beauty. The sister, who would later be given the name Tziporah, was adopted by Yisro. She would later become Moshe's wife. (*Midrash Talpiyos; Sifsei Kohein*)

---

89) פסיקתא דרב כהנא ז 90) מלבים שמות ב-ח וכו׳ 91) שמו״ר א-כה, ילקו״ש שם 92) ברכת פרץ שמות וכענין ונהפוך הוא דמגילת אסתר 93) דברים רבה יא-ט 94) שפתי כהן שמות ב-י 95) שמו״ר א-כו 96) רש״י שמות ב-יא, שמו״ר א-כו ובמהר״זו, י״מ שכבר הי׳ גבוהה עשר אמות 97) רבנו בחיי שמות ב-י 98) דעת זקנים שמות שם 99) ריב״א שמות שם 100) רבנו בחיי שם 101) מלבים שמות ב-י 102) שמו״ר א-כו, ויקרא רבה א-ג

The names were as follows:

- ⟜ MOSHE—given by Basya—because she "drew him" from the water.[103]
- ⟜ TUVIA—given by his parents—because he looked "good" when he was born.
- ⟜ YERED—given by Miriam—because she went "down" to the water on his account.[104]
- ⟜ CHEVER—given by Amram—because through his son, he "connected" to the wife whom he had previously divorced.[105]
- ⟜ YEKUSIEL—given by Yocheved—because she "hoped" Hashem would return her child.[106]
- ⟜ SHEMAIAH—given by the Jewish people—because Hashem "listened" to their cries in his days.[107]
- ⟜ AVI-ZENUACH—given by Aharon—because his parents "left" each other and returned on Moshe's account.[108]
- ⟜ AVI-SOCHO—given by his nurse—because for three months he was hidden from the Egyptians in a "*sukkah*," a concealed place.[109]
- ⟜ AVI-GDUR—given by his grandfather Kehas—because Moshe was like a fence that protected other children from being thrown into the water. Pharaoh's decree ceased when Moshe was thrown in the water.[110]
- ⟜ BEN NESANEL—because the Torah was "given" to him by Hashem.[111]
- ⟜ AVIASAR—because Hashem "overlooked" the sin of the Golden Calf because of Moshe.

His Egyptian name was Monios.[112]

Hashem wanted Moshe to be raised in the palace, where he would be introduced to Egyptian scholarship and become accustomed to dealing with important people.[113] To accomplish this, He imbued Basya with a deep emotional attachment to the child she had rescued from the river and a longing to have him beside her. Moreover, Basya desperately wanted a son who would be heir to the

103) שמות ב־י 104) ילקו״ש קסו, ספר הישר, י״מ דנקרא כן ע״ש שירד המן בזכותו כדאיתא בתענית ט.
105) ילקו״ש שם וי״מ על שם שחבר עם ישראל למלכם ב״ה 106) ילקו״ש שם וי״מ ע״ש שנתן תקוה בד׳ בלבבם
107) ילקו״ש שם וי״מ ע״ש ששמע ד׳ תמיד לבקשותיו 108) ילקו״ש שם, זית רענן כתב דנקרא כן מפני שגרם
שב״י יזניחו מלעבוד ע״ז 109) ספר הישר, זית רענן מביא מביא שאחות זו נשכרה לסייע מגודל הכמות הנצטרכת
לתינוק בריא כזה וי״מ דנקרא כן ע״ש שהי׳ ראש להנביאים שזכו ברוח קדשם 110) ספר הישר וי״מ ע״ש שעשה
גדרים וסיגים למנוע אותם מלעבור פי ד׳ 111) ויקרא רבה שם 112) אב״ע שמות ב־י 113) מלבים שם

throne of Egypt. Moshe would now take the place of the son she never had. Moshe's return to the palace was, therefore, an occasion of great excitement for Basya. She let it be known that she had given birth to a child,[114] and introduced Moshe to everyone as her own son.[115] Basya's claim was accepted by everyone in the palace.[116]

Although it was important for Moshe to be brought up in the halls of power, the Egyptian palace was not a fitting place for a person of Moshe's holiness. It was so full of idol worship, sorcery and all sorts of Egyptian abominations that Moshe lost his divine glow when he entered its gates.[117] Nevertheless, he never ate the palace food or drank the palace beverages. An angel would prepare food for him and bring it to him.[118]

Moshe moved easily into his new role as the young Egyptian prince. Basya fluttered over him like a doting mother, never allowing him to leave the protection of the palace.[119] Pharaoh also grew to love young Moshe, hugging and embracing him and taking him on his lap. Sometimes when seated in Pharaoh's lap, Moshe would playfully snatch Pharaoh's crown from his head and throw it to the ground.[120]

One time, when Moshe was three years old, the royal family was gathered around the dinner table in the palace. Queen Alparonis was sitting to the right of Pharaoh, and Basya was sitting with Moshe to his left. Many ministers and high officials were also in attendance, among them Bilam and his sons Ianus and Iambrus. Suddenly, Moshe stretched out his hand, snatched Pharaoh's crown, and unlike his usual habit of throwing it to the ground, he placed the crown on his own head.

A stunned silence descended on the great chamber as the young child sat there with the royal crown perched on his head. Then pandemonium broke loose.

"Your majesty, your majesty," Bilam's voice rose above the clamor. "May I speak?"

"Speak, Bilam," said Pharaoh. "What do you have to say?"

"Your majesty, if I may be so bold," Bilam began, "this incident fills me with foreboding. I have not forgotten your dream about the little lamb who outweighed all of Egypt, its people, its wealth and its armaments. And I don't think you have either, your majesty."

114) תורה שלמה סט 115) אב"ע שם 116) ספר הישר 117) ילקוט ראובני 118) שפתי כהן שמות ב-י
119) שמו"ר א -כו 120) שם, רבנו בחיי שמות ב-י

"Indeed, I haven't," said Pharaoh. "I think of it often."

"Then surely you have not forgotten its interpretation. A savior will be born to the Jewish people who will lead them to freedom. Well, your majesty, it seems to me that we have found your little Jewish lamb. This little child here must be the one!" He pointed dramatically to Moshe. A shocked gasp escaped his spellbound audience. "Yes, your majesty, I believe we have a Jewish child here who is already scheming to wrest your crown from you and place it on his own head. The spirit of the Jewish God is upon him. And I say kill him! Chop off his head right now!"

A murmur of assent rippled around the room, and Pharaoh also nodded his head gravely. Before he could give his consent, however, one of the other ministers present, who was actually the angel Gavriel in disguise, rose to his feet and asked to be heard.

"Speak," said Pharaoh.

"Your majesty, it seems to me that we are behaving like people who are afraid of their own shadows," he said. "Are we to be reduced to killing innocent children because of our fear? Come, look at this boy. He is only a child. We all know who he is. He is Pharaoh's own grandchild who is accustomed to playing with his grandfather's crown, not some secret Jewish impostor who is scheming to usurp the throne of Egypt. Are we to kill Pharaoh's own heir because of some wild, baseless accusations?"

"Pretty words," cried Bilam, "but we are not fooled. This child is not what he seems. He is scheming to destroy Egypt. He is the lamb of the dream!"

"I don't agree," said the angel Gavriel disguised as the minister. "But to set your mind at ease, let us put him to the test. Let us bring out a tray of gold and precious stones and metals. Among these, we will place some hot coals. Let us see if he is clever enough to tell the difference between the good and the bad."

The minister's plan found favor with Pharaoh and his advisors. The tray was brought and placed in front of Moshe, while all the spectators, including a terrified Basya, held their breaths. Slowly, Moshe reached for the precious stones, but an angel redirected his hands to the hot coals. He grabbed a coal and brought it to his lips and tongue. Everyone breathed a sigh of relief, and the taut bubble of tension burst. The festivities resumed, and the incident was forgotten.[121]

121) שמו"ר שם, ספר הישר, דברי הימים למשה ילקו"ש קסו, מדרש ויושע בפסוק עזי

The only remaining sign of Moshe's close brush with death was his burned mouth, which left him with impaired speech for the rest of his life. This was to atone for the few drops of impure milk the Egyptian women tried to put into Moshe's mouth when he was pulled from the river.[122]

Moshe Meets His People

As Moshe grew older, he enjoyed all the privileges and honors of a prince in the royal household. He was dressed in the royal purple and wore a crown studded with precious stones.[123] All who beheld his beauty could not turn their eyes away.[124] As he matured, Moshe's extraordinary wisdom and talents were recognized by Pharaoh, and he was given a position of great responsibility in the palace.[125] He succeeded in all his endeavors, earning the admiration and respect of the entire palace.[126] He also took advantage of his position by learning all the secrets of the wise men and developing poise and confidence in dealing with adversaries of the highest level. These skills would prove invaluable in the future, when he had to go up against Pharaoh himself without being intimidated.[127]

When Moshe was twenty years old,[128*] a mature, wise and gracious adult,[129] he felt that the time had come for him to see his parents and make personal contact with his Jewish heritage. He decided to go to Goshen where the Jewish people lived.

Moshe traveled to Goshen in a style befitting a prince, escorted by a contingent of armed guards.[130] As he neared his destination, he saw Jewish laborers struggling under the crushing burden of their tasks.

"Why do you work so hard?" he would ask them.

The Jewish laborers responded to his sympathetic interest, and they poured out their hearts to him. They told him about the terrible decrees Pharaoh had issued against the Jewish people, how they were oppressed, persecuted and on the verge of destruction. They

---

* There are many different opinions as to Moshe's age at this time, depending on the age at which he could be considered "grown" and on whether or not he went to Kush. He was either twelve (Ramban), eighteen (*Yalkut*) twenty-nine (*Shalsheles Hakabalah*), forty (*Shemos Rabbah*) or sixty (*Bereishis Rabasi*).

122) שפתי כהן שמות 123) דברי הימים למשה 124) תנחומא שמות ח 125) קהלת רבה ט-יב 126) פרדר"א מח
127) רלב"ג ורבנו אפרים שמות ב-י 128) שמו"ר א-כז 129) שמו"ר א-כט, רמב"ן ושפתי כהן, שמות ב-י
130) ספר הישר, שמו"ר א-כז, מהרד"ו שם

also told him about the crucial role of the archvillain Bilam, who had advised Pharaoh at every step of the way and who had even wanted to have the child Moshe killed for placing Pharaoh's crown on his own head.[131]

Moshe's heart went out to his unfortunate brethren. He saw his brethren stumbling under the unbearable loads placed upon them. He saw heavy loads fit for strong people placed on the shoulders of weak people, loads fit for men on the shoulders of women, loads fit for the young on the shoulders of the elderly.[132] Moreover, he could see that working with cement was the most difficult labor possible,[133] and he came to the fields every day to see if he could ease their harsh burden.[134]

He would leave his royal entourage by the roadside and go into the fields to be with the Jewish laborers.[135] He wanted to share in the pain and suffering of his flesh and blood.[136] His royal upbringing had not made him insensitive to the feelings of his less fortunate brethren.[137] "I wish I could carry your burden," he would cry out. "I wish I could give my life for you."

Not only did Moshe give the Jewish laborers sympathy and comforting words, he actually rolled up his sleeves and helped them physically as well. He ran to put his own shoulder under the burden of each and every Jew he saw.[138] When he saw Jews bleeding from the abrasions of their loads, he ran to bandage their wounds.[139] When he saw cement dust blown into the eyes of the Jewish laborers by the strong winds, he would run to remove the dust from their eyes.[140] And saddest of all, when he saw the unattended bodies of Jews who had perished in the fields and wastelands, he would give them a decent burial.[141]

Hashem took note of Moshe's compassion for the Jewish people and said, "Since you have left your palace and gone out to be a brother to the Jewish people, I will come down to speak with you at the Sneh."[142] Because of these qualities, he was also considered worthy of being prophet and king of the Jewish people.[143]

After he had assessed the situation of the Jews in the fields, Moshe devised a plan whereby he could continue to visit them

---

131) ספר הישר 132) ויקרא רבה לז-ב, מהרד"ו על שמו"ר א-כז 133) שמו"ר א-כז 134) ספר הישר 135) שמו"ר
שם ובמהרד"ו 136) מדרש הגדול שמות ב-י, מלבים ב-י"א 137) מלבים שם 138) שמו"ר א-כז 139) מדרש מובא
בתורה שלמה דף עה 140) כנ"ל בדף קעה 141) שם 142) שמו"ר א-כז 143) ויקרא רבה לז-ב במהרד"ו

without calling suspicion to himself and also help alleviate their suffering. The key was to convince Pharaoh that Moshe's involvement with the Jews was for the benefit of the kingdom.[144] With this new plan in mind, Moshe returned to the palace and asked for an audience with Pharaoh.

"Your majesty," he said. "I have just returned from an inspection tour of Goshen and the surrounding districts. I am convinced that your great construction projects will never reach completion."

"Indeed?" said Pharaoh. "And on what do you base this rather amazing prediction?"

"Quite simple, your majesty," Moshe replied. "The success of your projects depends on efficient use of your slave labor force. According to my observations, the slave labor policies are anything but efficient."

Pharaoh was intrigued. "Go on," he said.

"If someone needs animals to do his fieldwork, he feeds them and takes proper care of them, doesn't he? It would be foolish to do otherwise. The animals would wither away and die, and then what would he do? Well, I'm sorry to report to you, your majesty, that your slaves are not even being treated like draft animals. They are being abused by improper work loads, and they are dying like flies. Soon, you will be left with no slave labor. Who will finish your projects? Our own Egyptians?"

"You make a good point," said Pharaoh. "What do you suggest we do?"

"Well, to begin with, I think each laborer should only be given a work load for which he is suited," Moshe replied. "Afterwards, we will see what other improvements can be made."

"Very well," said Pharaoh. "You have been groomed for this sort of thing, and I have full confidence in your abilities. I am placing you in charge of the project. Do as you see fit."

Moshe wasted no time in instituting the new policies. Every Jewish laborer was now given only as much work as he could reasonably be expected to do.[145]

Some time later, Moshe returned to Pharaoh with another suggestion.

"Your majesty, the condition of your Jewish slaves is much

---

144) שמו"ר שם   145) מדרש מובא בתורה שלמה דף עה

improved," he reported. "But some serious problems still exist."

"Speak," said Pharaoh.

"As things stand now," Moshe continued, "the slaves work seven days a week. They never have the opportunity to rest. This is pure folly. No human being, or any other living creature for that matter, can work for any length of time without rest. Working slaves without rest drains their strength without giving it a chance to be replenished. This is bad labor policy. Tired slaves produce shoddy work, and after a while, they don't even do that. They simply die."

"Your point is well-taken," said Pharaoh. "What do you suggest?"

"I suggest we allow them one day of rest every week. We should make it the same day every week, so that there will be some semblance of order to the policy. There is no doubt in my mind that we will profit from it in the long run."[146]

"Very well," said Pharaoh. "I have full confidence in you. Do what must be done."

Ecstatic, Moshe returned to the Jewish people and informed them that henceforth they would be allowed a day of rest every week. He had calculated the dates from the Shabbos of the week of creation, and based on those calculations, he had chosen the day he considered to be Shabbos.[147] On these precious days of rest, Moshe would strengthen the faith of the Elders by reading to them from the Book of Iyov,[148] and he would gladden the hearts of the common people by helping them study scrolls that discussed the impending redemption.[149]

Moshe's purpose in arranging the observance of a day of rest on Shabbos was to ease the burden of the Jewish laborers.[150] Years later, Hashem would give the Jewish people the *mitzvah* of Shabbos, and to Moshe's great joy, the day chosen by Hashem coincided exactly with the day he had discovered through his calculations. This joy is commemorated in the Shabbos morning prayer entitled "Yismach Moshe."[151]

Now Moshe's thoughts turned to the future. He realized that, before anything more could be done to help the Jewish people, their

146) שמו"ר א-כח, ספר הישר, דעת זקנים שמות ה-ד 147) ילקוט מובא בתורה שלמה, בראשית רבתי א-ו (וכו')
בדף יג, ע"ע שמו"ר א-כח. בתורה שלמה מילואים ה' מובא שהי' כששים שנה לפני יצ"מ וע"ש בדף ע"ו והלאה
בנוגע שמירת השבת לפני'ז. האבודרהם כתב שטען משה לפרעה שלא שייך שיראו סימן ברכה מעבודה ביום
שהמזל שבתאי שבתקופה והיות ולא יצליחו תן להם למנוחה יעו"ש 148) שלשלשת הקבלה דף כו ועד שנצטוו
במרה רק חלק מהם שמרו אותה ע' בתורה שלמה שם 149) שמו"ר ה-יח 150) שמו"ר ה-כח 151) שמו"ר א-כח

principal enemies had to be destroyed. First among their enemies was Bilam, who had championed the labor decrees and had also attempted to have Moshe killed when he was only three years old. Moshe decided to have him executed, but before he could put his plan into action, Bilam discovered that he was in danger. He took his sons Ianus and Iambrus and fled to the protection of King Kukinus of the land of Kush.[152]

Moshe Kills an Egyptian

One day, when Moshe was in the fields, he saw an Egyptian hitting a Jewish man.[153] The Jew, a man named Dassan, was not one of the workers but a supervisor.[154] Dassan ran to the princely Moshe for protection from his Egyptian tormentor.[155]

"Help me, great prince!" Dassan yelled. "He is trying to kill me."

"What is happening?" Moshe asked him. "Why is that Egyptian hitting you?"

"Egyptian taskmasters come wake us at the crack of dawn," Dassan replied. "This morning, when he came to my house, he set eyes on my wife Shlomis bas Divri, and he violated her. And now, he is trying to cover up his crime. That is why he is trying to kill me."[156]

Moshe was shocked and infuriated, for although he had grown up among Egyptians, he was not accustomed to their corruption.[157] With his powers of *ruach hakodesh*, he confirmed that the Egyptian had indeed violated Dassan's wife, and that he was indeed trying to kill Dassan. Moshe decided that the Egyptian deserved to die,[158] but he did not reach his decision through anger.[159] First, he reasoned, the Egyptian deserved to die for simply hitting a Jew.[160] Second, the Egyptian was considered a *rodef*, one who is trying to kill another person, and as such, anyone is permitted to kill him and save his intended victim. Third, the Egyptian had transgressed one of the seven Noachide laws by violating Dassan's wife, and as such, he deserved to die.[161]

ובמדבר"כ 152) ספר הישר, דברי הימים למשה 153) ספר הישר, פרדר"א מח, מלבים 154) פרדר"א שם וברד"ל, שמו"ר א-כח וברש"ש, י"מ שהיה לוי ומנכדי קהת ע' בילקו"ש קסו והלאה 155) ספר הישר, שלשלת הקבלה כב 156) שמו"ר א-כח וע' שכל טוב שמות ב-יא, ספר הישר, ופרדר"א לשיטה אחרת בזה 157) ספר הישר, רמב"ן ספורנו ומלבים שמות ב-יא 158) שמו"ר א-כח וברד"ל 159) מלבים שמות ב-יב 160) סנהדרין נח: 161) שם, שמו"ר א-כח מתנ"כ ויפת שם

Still, Moshe was not satisfied. What if the Egyptian was destined to have worthy children whose future birth would now be prevented by his death? Using his *ruach hakodesh* once again, Moshe looked into the personal future of the Egyptian and discovered that all his descendants were destined to be wicked people and not one of them would convert to Judaism. There was now no reason to be lenient with him.[162]* Having reached his own decision, Moshe now consulted with the angels who were always in his attendance. They, too, agreed that the Egyptian deserved to die.[163]

With all questions about the sentence of death resolved, Moshe looked around to make sure no one was watching, and then he immediately killed the Egyptian.[164] Although Moshe normally carried no weapons,[165] he needed none. He killed the Egyptian by pronouncing the letters of Hashem's Name. The Egyptian was consumed by fire and died instantly.[166] Moshe then cast his eyes on the Egyptian's dead body and reduced it to a mound of dust.[167]** He took the remains of the Egyptian and buried them in the sand amongst the Jewish people. Had he buried the remains in the field they might have been discovered, and the Egyptian's family would search for the killer.[168] The Jewish people, however, are compared to sand. Just as sand moves silently from place to place, so would the Jewish people keep Moshe's secret.[169]

This episode was a turning point in Moshe's life. The act of coming to the rescue of another Jew helped him attain the spiritual growth and level of prophecy he would need to fulfill his destined role as the savior of the Jewish people.[170] More immediately, the repercussions of this incident would cause him to flee Egypt in fear for his life.

---

* She had already conceived from the Egyptian (Riva). This child would one day curse Hashem's Name and be sentenced to death. (Rashi, *Vayikra* 24:10)

** Others suggest that he struck him with his fist or with a spade and crushed his skull. (*Shemos Rabbah*, ibid.) Yet others suggest that Moshe killed the Egyptian with his breath. (*Lekach Tov*)

---

162) שמו"ר א-כט במהרד"ו ויפ"ת, רש"י שמות ב-יב ריב"א כתב שכבר הוקלטה 163) שמו"ר שם, ילקר"ש קס"ז, ע' ברבנו בחיי ב-יב ילקוט ראובני ובתורת חיים דהי' המצרי גלגולו של קין ומשה הי' גלגולו של הבל ועכשיו הגיע הזמן שהבל הרג את קין 164) שמות ב-יב 165) שמו"ר שם ביפ"ת 166) שמו"ר א-כט, ילקוט מובא בתורה שלמה פ, בהשאלה אי הי' שם מ"ב או שם ע"ב ע' בשכל טוב, רבנו אפרים ורבנו בחיי 167) ילקוט ראובני 168) שמו"ר א-כט, לקוטי אנשי שם שמות ב-יד, בילקוט ראובני איתא דכשמת המצרי נתגלגלה נשמתו של קין קרח שנולד באותו זמן 169) שמו"ר א-כט 170) רמב"ם עה"ת שמות ב-יב

Dassan and Aviram

The next day, the entire area was abuzz with the disappearance of the Egyptian overseer, and the very air was heavy with menace. Nevertheless, Moshe went out again to see what he could do to help the Jewish people without regard for his personal safety.[171] To his dismay, he saw two enraged Jewish people yelling at each other.[172] They hurled curses at each other, and seemed to be on the verge of attacking each other with murderous intentions.[173] As he drew closer, Moshe saw that one of these men was none other than Dassan, the man whose life he had saved the previous day. The other was a man named Aviram.[174]

The argument between these two men was directly related to the incident of the previous day. Dassan's wife Shlomis was the sister of Aviram. Because she had been violated by the Egyptian, Dassan felt she was no longer fit for him, and he decided to divorce her. Mortified, she ran to tell her brother Aviram about Dassan's intentions. Aviram confronted Dassan and berated him, and the two brothers-in-law began to fight.[175*]

As Moshe was trying to stop the confrontation, Dassan raised his hand to strike Aviram.

Moshe was horrified by the sight of two Jewish people fighting, a reaction which well suited the future leader of the Jewish people.[176] "*Rasha!* Wicked man!" he cried out. "Why would you strike your fellow Jew?"[177] Clearly, Moshe was of the opinion that a Jew who merely raises his hand against another Jew is already considered a *rasha*, a wicked man.[178]

The two brothers-in-law now formed a common front against Moshe. "Who made you a master and judge over us?"[179] they wanted to know.

Moshe was taken aback by this unexpected attack on him.

"That's right," one of them pressed on. "A man is not suitable to be a judge until the age of forty, and you are merely twenty years old."[180]

---

* The Torah writes that Dassan and Aviram were brothers. (*Parshas Pinchas* 26:9)

---

171) שמו״ר א-כז וביפ״ת, מלבים שמות ב-יג 172) שמות ב-יג 173) ילקו״ש קסז, שמו״ר א-כט, כלי יקר ב-יג
174) שמו״ר א-כט 175) שלשלשת הקבלה דף כב, ילקוט קסו וכר׳, שמו״ר א-כח וברד״ל, ספר הישר, ילקוט ראובני
176) מלבים שמות ב-יג 177) ילקוט קסז, שמות ב-יג 178) סנהדרין נח: 179) שמו״ר א-ל 180) שמו״ר שם וברד״ל,
עי׳ ילקו״ש ורבנו בחיי, י״א שהי׳ לפני היותו בר מצוה, וי״א שדינא הוי דעד עשרים וחמשה אינו יכול לדון

"You are not an accepted authority among our people," the other added. "Why should we listen to you?[181] Have you been appointed a judge over us?"[182]

"Do you know who we are?" the first one continued. "We are not just anybody. We are the aristocrats of our nation. We are not simple people whom you can push around. We are the supervisors of the simple people, and you have no right to judge us, even if you were a judge."[183]

"Do you think we don't know who you are?" said the other. "You're no 'son of Basya' who can come here and tell us what to do. You're no Egyptian prince! You're the son of Yocheved, a Jew like the rest of us. Who do you think you are coming here and telling us what to do?"[184]

At this very moment, while Moshe was being ridiculed, Hashem said, "The very words they have used to belittle Moshe will bring him greatness. I will give him laws to enforce, and he will 'judge' the Jewish people."[185]

Dassan and Aviram were not satisfied with having insulted Moshe. Now they began to threaten him.

"So what do you intend to do?" Dassan asked him. "Do you intend to kill me like you killed the Egyptian? Are you surprised that I know about it? I know you killed him by pronouncing Hashem's Name. Well, you can't do the same to me, since I have committed no crime.[186] I'll tell you what we plan to do. We plan to tell Pharaoh what you did to the Egyptian yesterday."[187]

When Dassan and Aviram made their vicious statements out loud and in public, Moshe came to a painful realization.[188] "I thought that by hiding the remains of the Egyptian the incident would remain a secret," he said to himself. "Now I see that there are Jewish people who are prepared to speak *lashon hara*.[189] I also know something else. For a long time, I have been wondering why the Jewish people must suffer such harsh slavery. I know the decree of exile revealed in Avraham's prophecy was inevitable, but why did it have to be this harsh? Now I know. It is because there are slanderers among the Jewish people,[190] and I fear this may prevent them from ever being redeemed."[191]

181) מלבים שמות ב-יד 182) שם 183) שמו"ר א-ל במהרז"ו, טור שמות ב-יד 184) שמו"ר שם, מתנ"כ ויפ"ת
185) ילקוט ראובני 186) מלביי"ם וכלי"י שמות ב-יד, ע"ע יפ"ת שמו"ר ה-כב 187) שמו"ר א-ל
188) שמו"ר שם במהרז"ו, ספורנו שמות ב-יד 189) שמות ב-יד, וברש"י, שמו"ר שם 190) שמו"ר שם, רש"י
ושפתי חכמים שמות ב-יד, ילקו"ש קסז 191) רש"י שם ויש לדון אי הי' אותם בלבד או שגם אחרים חטאו בזה וע'
כל"י שמות ב-יד

Sentenced to Death

Dassan and Aviram promptly went to deliver their slanderous report to Pharaoh.[192]

"Your majesty," they said. "Moshe is bringing shame and dishonor to the royal house and the crown itself."

Pharaoh was not interested. "Let him be," he said.

"Moshe is easing the burden of labor on the Jews," they reported.

Pharaoh was still not impressed. "Let him be," he said. "That is not your concern."

"You know, of course, that Moshe is not Basya's son," they said. "He is actually a Jew."

Pharaoh refused to be provoked. "I don't care," he said.

"Did you know that he is a murderer?" they persisted. "He killed an Egyptian. We saw him do it."

"A murderer?" Pharaoh said. "Tell me more."

"He didn't even use a weapon, your majesty," they said. "He killed a man by uttering the Name of Hashem. Isn't this man dangerous?"

Pharaoh realized that Moshe was indeed dangerous. Even though he could not walk around the palace bearing arms, he would still be able to kill Pharaoh at any time by uttering the Name. This was too much for Pharaoh to ignore. "A murderer!" he exploded. "This I simply cannot ignore. Arrest him at once!"[193]

Moshe was arrested, brought before Pharaoh for judgment and sentenced to death.[194] Dassan and Aviram were rewarded handsomely for informing on Moshe, and they became very rich.[195]

"Off with his head!" the judges proclaimed.

The soldiers ran to bring Moshe from his prison cell to the place of execution.[196] Because Moshe was such a tall man, a large and specially sharpened sword, unlike any other in the whole world, was prepared for the occasion.[197] Moshe's head was laid upon the block, and the executioner lifted the sword high. The blade swished through the air faster than the eye could see and struck Moshe's outstretched neck, but miraculously, nothing happened. There was not even a small cut on Moshe's neck. The executioner swung again. The blade of the sword broke, but Moshe did not even suffer a slight

---

192) ילקו"ש קסז 193) פני דוד שמות ב-יד, ילקו"ש קסז, ילקוט ראובני 194) ילקו"ש שם 195) שפתי כהן במדבר טז-יג 196) שמו"ר א-לא, ריב"א שמות ב-יא 197) שמו"ר שם במהרז"ו

scratch. His neck had miraculously turned to marble.[198] Ten times
they repeated the attempt, and ten times they failed.

The executioners decided that Moshe was a magician whose
powers would prevent death by the sword. Another method would
have to be tried.[199] Moshe was led onto a great platform, where he
would wait until they decided on another method of execution.[200]

Another miracle occurred. The angel Michael came down in the
guise of the executioner, while the executioner suddenly assumed
the guise of Moshe.[201] The angel Michael, who had assumed the
form of the executioner, then killed the executioner, who had
assumed the form of Moshe. Hashem now planted the thought in
Moshe's mind that it would be a prudent time to make his escape.
Moshe jumped from the platform and ran for the door.[202]

The assembled Egyptians thought that Moshe had finally been
executed. Pharaoh, however, was not fooled for very long. As soon
as he saw Moshe running for the door, he began to yell, "Grab him!
Grab him!"

No one responded to Pharaoh's commands, because a wondrous thing had happened. Miraculously, they had all become deaf.

Desperately, Pharaoh motioned and signaled to the guards to
grab Moshe, but miraculously, they all became blind. Pharaoh now
tried to yell with all his might to bring soldiers from other parts of
the palace, but miraculously again, Pharaoh found himself mute. He
could not speak one word![203]

In the confusion, the angel Michael grabbed Moshe and spirited
him out of Egypt to a place three days' journey away.[204]

In another version, when the executioner tried to kill Moshe, the
sword bounced off Moshe's neck that had turned to marble, and cut
the throat of the executioner himself, killing him instantly.[205]

In Moshe's absence, Hashem appointed his brother Aharon to
serve as the prophet for the Jewish people. He tried to dissuade the
Jewish people from worshipping idols like the Egyptians among
whom they lived, but they did not heed his words. Because they
did not uphold the covenant their forefather had made with
Hashem, Hashem caused Pharaoh to intensify the labor decrees,

198) ילקו"ש שם, דברי הימים למשה, ירושלמי ברכות ט-ה 199) ריב"א שמות ד-יא, דברים רבה ב-כט
200) ריב"א שם 201) ספר הישר, שמו"ר שם, דברי הימים למשה 202) שמו"ר שם וביפ"ת, רש"י שמות ד-יא
203) תנחומא שמות י', רש"י שמות ד-יא 204) דברי הימים למשה וי"מ שהי' כדי הילוך מ' יום וע' בדעת זקנים
205) דברים רבה ב-כט, שמו"ר א-לא, ספר הישר, דברי הימים למשה

and the Jewish people continued to suffer the terrible miseries of exile and bondage.[206]

Moshe in Kush

During this time, there was a war between the great and powerful kingdom of Kush and the people of Kedem and Aram. Kukinus, king of Kush, marched off at the head of his army to do battle with the enemies of the kingdom. Bilam, who had sought asylum in Kush after he fled Egypt, was placed in charge of the capital city in the absence of the king.

The fortunes of war went well for Kukinus. He won victory after victory, took many captives and levied heavy taxes against his defeated enemies. But on the home front, things were not going so well. In the absence of the king, Bilam had persuaded the people of the capital to rebel and seize the city. The people did as he suggested and chose Bilam to be their king. Then they prepared to prevent the return of Kukinus, their rightful king. They built great walls around the city. At one opening, they dug a deep moat and filled it with water so that no one could pass through to enter the city. At the other opening, they placed scorpions and snakes to prevent entry to the city.

When Kukinus returned, he saw the great walls and mistook their significance. "How wonderful!" he declared. "While I was off fighting the war, my people built these walls to defend the city against Canaanite invaders."

When he approached the city, however, the bitter truth dawned on him. Bilam had taken control of the city and usurped his throne. Kukinus decided to attack.

The fighting was heavy on the first day, and one hundred and thirty soldiers of the king's army died. On the second day, an advance chariot force tried to cross the moat into the city, but they all drowned in a great whirlpool that swirled around them. They then attempted to enter the city through the gateway defended by the snakes, and many more soldiers were killed. There was no choice but to call off the attacks and lay siege to the city.

The siege was already nine years long when Moshe appeared on the scene. He was twenty-seven years old at the time, a fugitive from the kingdom of Egypt. Moshe was exceedingly tall, handsome and strong, and Kukinus took an immediate liking to him. He appointed Moshe general of his army and placed him in charge of the siege.

Some time later, the king died, and his followers were faced with a dilemma. They wanted to abandon the siege, but they were afraid that if they withdrew they would be pursued by the forces inside the city and slain. Perhaps it would be better to maintain the siege indefinitely, even if they perished in the process. They decided to appoint Moshe as their king. They also gave him the hand of Kukinus's widow in marriage. In order not to offend them, he accepted the queen as his wife, but the marriage was never consummated, since Moshe would not violate the covenant Hashem made with Avraham never to marry into the family of Canaan.

On the third day of Moshe's reign as king of Kush, the soldiers in his army, who had been separated from their families for nine years, asked Moshe what he planned to do. Moshe told them that he had a plan that would allow them to be reunited with their families very soon. He told them to bring fledgling storks from the forest and train them to forage for food in the manner of hawks. When the storks were fully grown, Moshe instructed that they be deprived of food for three whole days.

At the end of the day, Moshe told his men to arm themselves and mount their horses. Bringing the starving storks with them, they approached the gateway to the city which was guarded by the snakes. When they neared the city, the soldiers released the storks. The storks streaked for the squirming mass of snakes and devoured every single one. The entrance to the city was now clear, and Moshe's army swarmed through with their swords brandished and attacked. Eleven hundred of the city's defenders fell that day, while Moshe's army suffered no casualties. In the heat of the battle, Bilam and his sons slipped away and returned to Egypt.

Meanwhile, reports of the death of Kukinus reached the kings of Aram and Kedem, and they decided to invade Kush. Moshe mustered an army of thirty thousand men and repelled the invaders.

After Moshe had reigned as king of Kush for forty years, one of Kukinus's sons laid claim to the throne. The queen threw her support behind her son. Since he was now old enough to rule, she contended, he should be allowed to do so. He had a right as the son of the former king and a native of Kush. Moshe, on the other hand, was a stranger who did not follow the customs of Kush and did not worship idols. A delegation of the highest officials in the land approached Moshe and told him of the queen's comments. Moshe agreed to abdicate the throne in favor of Kukinus's son. The members of the delegation were relieved at his cooperation, and they sent him off with a great fortune and many gifts.[207*]

Hashem now instructed Moshe to go to Midian, where he should begin to prepare himself to redeem the Jewish people.[208]

Ephraim Tries to Leave Egypt

While Moshe was in Kush, a terrible tragedy occurred in Egypt. Thirty years before the redemption was to take place, the people of Shevet Ephraim attempted to leave Egypt—with disastrous results.

The Elders of Shevet Ephraim, based on mistaken calculations, had decided that the divinely ordained period of exile had come to an end, and the time had come to leave Egypt. As descendants of Yosef, the viceroy of Egypt, they were treated as royalty by the Egyptians. They were not required to submit to slave labor, and in fact, they were free to leave Egypt if they so chose. They used their free time to train as warriors. The one hundred and twenty thousand Egyptian soldiers guarding the borders of Egypt to prevent the escape of the Jews were instructed not to stop the people of Ephraim if they attempted to leave.[209]

With great excitement, the people of Ephraim prepared to go to Eretz Yisrael. They packed their personal belongings and also took substantial amounts of money.[210] They did not bother packing provisions for a long journey, because they assumed they would be able to buy whatever food they needed along the way. Thousands of the men also armed themselves should they encounter any hostilities.[211] The men of Ephraim were very powerful fighters, one of whom could take on a thousand of the enemy.

The people of Ephraim left Egypt and traveled along the northern route, which was the most direct route to Eretz Yisrael. When

---

* Others suggest that Moshe was now seventy-seven years old and had lived a wanderer's life for sixty years. (Ramban, *Shemos* 2:23)

207) דברי הימים למשה, ספר הישר 208) ילקוט מובא בתורה שלמה דף פז, ע' מדרש החפץ שמות ב-טו

209) ילקוט ראובני, שפתי כהן בשלח 210) ספר הישר 211) שם

they reached the outskirts of the Philistine city of Gath, they came across some shepherds tending their flocks in the fields. The people were hungry, and they asked the shepherds to sell them some sheep. The shepherds refused. The powerful soldiers of Ephraim, concerned for their hungry families, were not to be frustrated by the refusal of simple shepherds, and they took their sheep by force.

The shepherds raised a loud hue and cry, which brought the people of Gath running. When they saw all these armed men and what they had done, they girded themselves for war.

On the first day, the fighting was heavy, and there were casualties on both sides. The people of Gath sent an urgent appeal to the other Philistine cities—Gaza, Ekron, Ashdod and Ashkelon—to come to their aid in battle. By the third day of the war, the people of Ephraim, tired and hungry, found themselves facing the massed forces of all the Philistine cities, forty thousand men strong. In the ensuing fighting the people of Ephraim were wiped out, while the Philistines lost twenty thousand men. From Ephraim, only ten people survived. The Philistines carried their dead away from the field of battle, while the fallen people of Ephraim remained scattered in the field for many years, and the valley remained full of bones.

This tragedy befell the people of Ephraim, because although they were free to leave Egypt, they should not have attempted to leave before the entire Jewish nation could go. The survivors now returned to Egypt with their tragic story, and the Jewish people mourned for many days.[212]

---

212) ספר הישר, ע' רש"י סנהדרין צב: מה שטעו בחשבונם, י"מ שיחזקאל החיה את עצמותיהם ע' רד"ק דברי הימים א-ז, י"מ שעשרים אלף מתו וי"מ מאתים אלף ע' שמו"ר כ-יב, פרדר"א מח, תרגום יונתן יג-יז ובספר הישר

Moshe in Midian

6

Moshe was sixty-seven years old when he arrived in Midian. Nearly fifty years had passed since he had fled Egypt, but he never allowed himself to forget that he was still a fugitive, and he never ceased to thank Hashem for saving him from the sword of Pharaoh.[1]

In Midian, Moshe chose to live near a well,[2] because just as his forefathers Yitzchak and Yaakov had found their wives alongside a well, he would, too.[3] He also chose a place which was not very inhabited, because he was a fugitive and didn't want to be recognized.[4] To protect himself against the divinations of Pharaoh's magicians, he placed a metal rod above the well. This would distort their vision, making them think he was on a metal bridge that spanned a waterway but giving them no clue to his actual whereabouts.[5]

---

1) דברים רבה ב-כט וברד"ל, ילקו"ש קסח   2) שמות ב-טו, ילקו"ש שם   3) שמו"ר א-לב   4) תנחומא שמות יא ובעץ יוסף, אב"ע שמות ב-טו   5) ספר המובחר מובא בתורה שלמה צ

At that time, Pharaoh's former advisor Yisro also lived in Midian. He had been forced to flee in disgrace and fear for his life when he had dared suggest that the Egyptians should not persecute the Jewish people.[6] When he had arrived in Midian, his great talents and personal qualities had been recognized by the people, and he had been appointed the priest-king of Midian. In this role, Yisro paid homage to all the idolatrous gods of the world,[7] not because he believed in them particularly but because this allowed him to live an honored and luxurious life.

After some time, Yisro became disillusioned with his lifestyle. He came to the realization that idol worship was foolish nonsense, and that honors and luxuries were not adequate compensation for living a life of total falsehood. He decided to repent and change his life.[8] He called a meeting of his most prominent followers, told them he had decided to retire and relinquished his control of the temples. He did not tell them his real reason for resigning his high office, because he was afraid they would take offense and kill him.[9]

The people of Midian, however, were not fooled by Yisro's words. They did not think he would give up his high office so easily. Clearly, he had rejected the idols, and for this affront, they ostracized him from their society.[10] No one was allowed to have any contact with him, do any work for him or accept favors from him. No one was to help him tend to his flocks. And no one was to marry any of his daughters. Yisro and his family were thus effectively isolated from the people among whom they lived.[11] Nevertheless, because of his courageous act of rejecting idol worship, Hashem gave him the name Reuel, which means "Friend of Hashem."[12]

Struggles at the Well

Since no one would associate with him, Yisro had to rely on his own family to tend to his sheep. And since he had no sons, he had no choice but to swallow his pride and send his seven daughters into the field with his sheep.[13] Each day, his daughters would take the sheep to the public well very early in the morning. They would fill their pails with water and pour it into

ספר הישר, ילקוט ראובני 7) אב״ע וטור שמות ב-טו, דברים רבה א-ה לקח טוב ורש״י שמות ב-טז, תנחומא 6) שמות יא ובעץ יוסף 8) תנחומא ושמו״ר שם, עיין רש״י יח-טז ובשפתי חכמים ב-טז דעדיין לא נתגייר 9) תנחומא שם ובעץ יוסף 10) שמו״ר א-לה ובעץ יוסף 11) שמו״ר שם ובמהרז״ו 12) שם 13) תנחומא שם ובעץ יוסף

a trough from which their sheep would drink.[14] They would try to leave before the other shepherds arrived, because they did not want to be harassed on account of their father. Later in the day, when all the other shepherds were gone, they returned to the well and allowed their sheep to drink their fill.[15]

Early one morning, when Yisro's daughters were drawing water for their sheep, Hashem caused the other shepherds to arrive before their accustomed time. The shepherds were impatient and had no intention of waiting for Yisro's daughters to finish with their sheep.[16] They snatched the water the girls had drawn from the well and cast them into the well.[17]

Moshe, who lived near the well, saw what was happening and came to the rescue of Yisro's daughters. He tossed a bucket down to them and pulled them out of the well.[18] Then he turned to confront the shepherds.

"What kind of men are you?" he scolded them. "In the way of the world, men draw water from the wells and give it to the women. But not only didn't you draw the water for these girls, you actually went and took their water away."

The shepherds slunk away in silent shame, and Moshe went back to the well to assist the daughters of Yisro. As the shepherds watched in astonishment, the water rose up to meet him. He took some of this water and gave it to the sheep in Yisro's flock.[19] Then he took the rest of the water and gave it to the speechless shepherds. With the tensions in the air much reduced, Moshe spoke to Yisro's daughters about the folly of idol worship and the eternal wisdom of Hashem and His Torah. He also drew the shepherds to him in a spirit of reconciliation and spoke words of inspiration to them as well. The shepherds were deeply impressed by this great man who had suddenly come into their lives, and they never harassed Yisro's daughters again.[20]

Yisro's daughters were beside themselves with gratitude, and they couldn't thank Moshe enough for rescuing them from the harassment of the shepherds.

---

14) רש"י שמות ב-טז   15) שמו"ר א-לב במהרז"ו וידי משה, ויעיון ברמב"ן ב-טז   16) רמב"ן ומלבים שמות ב-
טז והלאה, שמו"ר א-לב וברד"ל   17) שמו"ר א-לב ברד"ל ויפ"ת, ריב"ש ומלבים שמות ב-טז   18) שמו"ר שם
ובמהרז"ו   19) אדר"נ כ, שמו"ר שם   20) ויקרא רבה לד-ח, שמו"ר שם ברד"ל מתנ"כ ומהרז"ו

"Please don't thank me," Moshe told them. "The one you must thank is the Egyptian taskmaster I killed many years ago. Had I not seen him beating a Jewish man, I would not have killed him and become a fugitive hiding in Midian."[21] Of course, Moshe did not really mean that they should be grateful to the wicked Egyptian taskmaster. He meant to point out that whatever happens is the result of divine providence (*hashgachah*) and not in human hands.[22]

Moshe's humble response was very much in character. He never felt it was below his dignity to come to the defense of a tormented Jew against his Egyptian tormentor nor to defend the daughters of Yisro nor to help the shepherds improve themselves.[23] Being brought up as the grandson of Pharaoh had not made him arrogant.[24]

When Moshe left the well, the water receded to its original level. Moshe now realized that this incident would result in him finding his destined wife,[25] since his grandfather Yaakov had also met his destined wife Rachel by the waters of the well.[26]

Moshe Meets Yisro

After the incident at the well, the daughters of Yisro returned home. Yisro was quite surprised to see them so soon after they had left.

"What brings you home so early?" he asked. "Doesn't it always take you much longer to draw water from the well and give all the sheep to drink?"

"Today was different," they replied. "The shepherds came early and stole our water. But then an Egyptian man rescued us from the shepherds and gave water to our sheep.[27*] And an amazing thing happened. When he came toward the well, the water rose up to meet him."

---

* Since Moshe allowed Yisro's daughters to assume he was Egyptian and did not reveal his identity as a Jew, he lost the opportunity to be buried in Eretz Yisrael. He should have trusted in Hashem to save him—as He had before. (*Midrash Vayosha, passuk Azi; Devarim Rabbah* 2:8; *R' Ephraim al Hatorah*) Others add that Hashem judged Moshe meticulously for wearing Egyptian garb, unlike the Jewish people in Egypt who did not change their distinctive garb. (Asher Rost)

---

21) שמו"ר שם 22) עץ יוסף שם וע' בשיחות מוסר מהגר"ח שמולווץ ז"ל מאמר לב תשל"ב בפ' שמות דכתב דאכן כוון משה על אותו מצרי ומעיר בזה הערה נוראה בגדרי חיוב הכרת הטוב 23) מכילתא בשלח א 24) מדרש הגדול שמות ב-יז 25) אדר"נ כ, זוה"ק ח"א יג 26) שמו"ר שם, זוה"ק ח"ב יג 27) דברים רבה ב-ח, שמו"ר שם

Yisro was intrigued. "That is truly amazing. Are you sure he was an Egyptian? What makes you think he was an Egyptian?"

"He wore Egyptian clothing,"[28] they said, for Moshe indeed still wore the clothing he had worn in Pharaoh's palace.

"Well, I don't think he is an Egyptian," Yisro said, "From what you are saying, I would venture to say he is a descendant of Avraham, the man of blessings. I would also venture to say he is a descendant of Yaakov who also had well water rise miraculously towards him. He must be a great man.[29] Where is he?"

"Why, we left him in the fields, near the well."

"Ridiculous. You should have invited him to come stay with us. He seems to be an outstanding person.[30] And besides, is that how we repay the kindness he has shown you?[31] Go quickly. Bring him here to our house. Who knows? Perhaps he will even marry one of you."[32]

Yisro's motives for inviting Moshe to his home were righteous, and in the merit of his kind deed, he was deemed worthy of having his descendants serve on the Sanhedrin in the Lishkas Hagazis of the Beis Hamikdash.[33]

Tziporah, one of Yisro's daughters, was the one who responded immediately to her father's instructions. No sooner had her father finished speaking when she was already running back to the field to get Moshe.[34]

Tziporah, who was destined to become Moshe's wife, was a girl of many special qualities, as was indicated by her name, which is a derivative of *tzipor*, the Hebrew word for "bird." She was swift as a bird to do what was right.[35] She purified her home from idol worship, just as a bird is used to purify a *mitzora*.[36] She was an upright and worthy person who would convert to Judaism, just like the bird is worthy (kosher) to be eaten.[37] Like a bird which is considered pure and holy enough to be brought as a sacrifice, she was pure and holy enough to marry Moshe.[38] The name Tziporah is also a derivative of *tzafra*, which means morning, indicating that her beauty shone as brightly as the morning.[39]

28) עץ יוסף שם   29) מדרש ויושע פסוק עזי, שמו"ר שם, תנחומא שם, ילקו"ש קס"ט, אוה"ח ב-כ   30) ספורנו ומלבים שמות ב-כ   31) אוה"ח שמות ב-כא   32) שמו"ר שם ובמהרז"ו   33) סנהדרין קד.   34) שמו"ר שם 35) שם ובמתנ"כ   36) שם ובמהרז"ו   37) רבנו בחיי שמות ב-כא   38) ילקוט ראובני, ע"פ פענח רזא סוף שמות 39) חזקוני שמות ב-כא, במדרש תלפיות איתא דבתיה וצפורה אחותות היו ונמצאו בצעירתן אסופות ברחוב ומגודל יפותן הובאו לבית המלכים, פרעה נטל בתיה ויתרו קבל צפורה

Moshe in Yisro's House

When Tziporah brought Moshe into Yisro's house, a royal welcome awaited him. Yisro understood that Moshe was destined to be the leader of the Jewish people, the powerful savior foretold in Pharaoh's dream. He asked Moshe many questions about his experiences and listened intently to his replies. Moshe told Yisro about his miraculous escape from Egypt and how he eventually became king of Kush.

As Moshe spoke more and more about his experiences in Kush, Yisro became increasingly skeptical. How could such a thing be true? he wondered. How could the future leader of the Jewish people become king of Kush? Highly unlikely!

Yisro began to suspect that Moshe might not be the great person he seemed to be. It seemed much more likely that he was an adventurer or a teller of fanciful tales. Yisro decided to imprison Moshe in a secret dungeon deep in the ground under his house while he investigated his story. Yisro then became distracted by other things and forgot that Moshe was languishing in the dungeon without any food or drink.

Tziporah, Yisro's daughter, was shocked by the unexpected turn of events. She could not let Moshe perish in the dungeon. Her heart was filled with compassion for the man who had come to her aid. She had to help him, but it had to be done in such a way that no one would know, especially her father and her sisters. Tziporah thought of a plan and approached Yisro.

"Father, you know that I am a very good worker," she said. "In fact, I myself can do just about as much work as all my sisters put together. Isn't that true?"

"Indeed it is, Tziporah," Yisro replied. "You are certainly a very industrious girl."

"Exactly," said Tziporah. "And it is also true that I work better by myself. I can get much more work done. Therefore, I have a plan. Why don't you divide your daughters into two groups? One group will consist of my six sisters. The other will consist of . . . me!"

"Go on," said Yisro. "What are you getting at?"

"Well, Father," said Tziporah, "you can send one group out to tend the sheep and keep the other one here to take care of the house. Can you imagine how much more will get done this way?"

Yisro looked at her intently. "It is a very good idea," he said. "I will do it. Which would you like, to tend sheep or care for the house?"

Tziporah, of course, wanted to remain in the house, but she wanted Yisro to make that decision on his own. "Whichever you choose, Father," she said, "will be just fine with me."

Yisro thought about it for a moment. "I suppose the best would be for you to stay home and your sisters to tend the sheep," he said. "I don't think I should send you out into the fields alone."

"Very well, father," said Tziporah. "As you wish."

Tziporah was delighted. From then on, she had total privacy in her home every day while her father took care of his interests and her sisters were away in the fields. She would take advantage of these times to sneak down to the dungeon and bring food to Moshe. Sometimes, she would even be able to bring him some special delicacies from the kitchen.

This state of affairs continued for ten years.[40] Yisro assumed that his prisoner had long since died in his dungeon, but Tziporah kept him alive through her kindness and devotion.

One day, Tziporah approached Yisro with a question. "Father, do you remember the Jew that came to our house a long time ago?"

"Indeed, I do," said Yisro. "I threw him into my dungeon."

"Well, ten years have passed," said Tziporah, "and no one has come to make inquiries about him. Is it possible that you made a mistake, father? Is it possible that this was no criminal but the great person he seemed to be? I fear we may have committed a grave injustice."

"You may be right, my daughter," said Yisro. "But what can we do about it now? It is too late."

"Perhaps we should go down to the dungeon and see what has become of him."

"What has become of him? What do you think has become of him? It's been ten years! Ten years without food and water. Do you think he might still be alive? Preposterous! Who ever heard of such a thing?"

"Father, if he is a righteous man he may still be alive," Tziporah responded. "Haven't you heard of the greatness of the Jewish God? He saved Avraham from the furnace of Ur Kasdim. He saved

---

Yitzchak at the Akeidah. He saved Yaakov from Eisav. And He has also done wonders for your prisoner. He saved him from drowning in the river when he was a baby. He protected him from the sword of Pharaoh's executioner. He watched over him in Kush. Certainly, He could have watched over him in your dungeon for ten years." Tziporah knew, of course, that Hashem had indeed watched over Moshe for ten years in the dungeon by sending her to bring him food.

"You have a point, my daughter," Yisro replied. "Come, let us go down to the dungeon."

When they reached the dungeon, Yisro could not believe the sight that met his eyes. There stood Moshe, alive as ever, offering up praises and thanks to Hashem. His hair had grown long and his clothes were threadbare, but otherwise he seemed fit and well.

"Moshe!" Yisro called out.

"I am here," Moshe answered.

"Blessed is Hashem, who watched over you for ten years," said Yisro. "He is in fact the Lord, who gives life and takes it away. I am now convinced that you are indeed the savior of the Jewish people who will destroy Egypt."

Yisro took Moshe from the dungeon. He cut his hair, gave him fresh clothing and fed him. From then on, Yisro showered Moshe with honors and much wealth.[41]

Moshe Gets Married

Moshe decided to remain with Yisro, and he asked him for Tziporah's hand in marriage.

"Come, let me show you something," Yisro responded.

He took Moshe out to his garden and showed him a luxuriant, deeply-rooted tree resplendent with blossoms and nuts.

"Let me tell you a story, Moshe," said Yisro. "On the sixth day of creation, a certain staff was created and given to Adam for safekeeping. When Adam left Gan Eden, he took this staff with him. It was then passed down from generation to generation until it came into the possession of Yaakov.[42] When Yaakov came to Egypt, he gave the staff to his son Yosef. When Yosef died, Pharaoh took the staff and put it into

---

41) מדרש ויושע פסוק עזי, ילקו"ש קס"ח, ספר הישר, דברי הימים למשה   42) מדרש ויושע שם, ספר הישר,
בדברי הימים למשה נפרטת כל הסדר מאדה"ר עד האבות

his treasurehouse among all his other valuables.[43]*

"You know the story of my flight from Egypt. Well, I also had my eye on that staff, and when I left, ahem, the staff came along with me. I planted the staff in my garden, and lo and behold, it miraculously grew into this wonderful tree.

"Over the years, many young men have come to ask for my daughter Tziporah's hand in marriage. As you well know, she has outstanding personal qualities. I always tell these young men to try and pull the staff from the ground. The one who pulls the staff from the ground can have my daughter's hand in marriage. Needless to say, no one has ever been successful. In fact, when they attempted to remove it, the tree suddenly swallowed them up.

"That is my story, Moshe. I now say the same thing to you. If you can pull the staff from the ground, you can have my daughter's hand in marriage." [44]

The attempts by all the others had failed, because Tziporah was destined to be married to Moshe.[45] Moshe, however, pulled the tree-staff from the ground with the greatest of ease—to Yisro's great amazement.

Moshe lifted the staff in his hands although it weighed 40 *saah* (approx. 800 pounds). He took a close look at it and realized its extraordinary significance. Engraved into the ancient wood were the Name of Hashem and the Hebrew letters, דצ"ך עד"ש באח"ב, an acronym of the ten plagues that Moshe was destined to bring upon the Egyptians. Clearly, no one but he could have drawn it from the ground.[46]

Yisro now realized that his daughter was destined to be married to the future redeemer of the Jewish people.[47] But before he would allow the marriage to take place, there were certain reassurances that he wanted.

"I agree to let my daughter marry you, Moshe," he said. "But I want some promises from you. I want you to promise to treat my daughter with respect and honor all your marital commitments to her. Do you promise?"[48]

"Of course," said Moshe. "That goes without saying."

---

* Some suggest that this was the very same staff Yehudah gave to Tamar as collateral. (*Pirkei d'Rabbi Eliezer* 40; *Yalkut Shimoni, Chukas* 763)

---

43) שם, ילקוט ראובני, וע"ע במדרש השכם המובא באוצר המדרשים קלט   44) מדרש ויושע שם   45) שם, ספר הישר, דברי הימים למשה   46) שמו"ר ה-ו, פרדר"א מ, תרגום יונתן שמות ד-כ, ב-כא   47) כציון 45 ובמדרש השכם   48) שמו"ר שם ובמהרז"ו

"Second, I want you to stay here in Midian and tend to my flocks of sheep.[49] You must not leave Midian unless I give you my permission. [50] I know that your great-grandfather Yaakov ran off from Lavan without his knowledge, and I don't want you to do the same to me. Do you agree?"

"I agree," Moshe replied. In any case, Moshe realized, Yisro's fame and prestige as a great priest would protect him until the time came for his destiny to be fulfilled. He would undoubtedly be much safer in Yisro's house than elsewhere.[51]

"Third, I want your first son not to be circumcised and to be initiated into the cults of idol worship.[52] This may seem like a strange request, but I have a good reason. I myself worshipped every idol in the world, and only by doing so did I realize how foolish it was and that the only correct path to follow is the service of Hashem. I want your firstborn son to have the same appreciation so that, in the end, he will follow the path of Hashem. Do you agree to my conditions?"[53]

"I agree, and I swear to comply with your will in all these matters," Moshe replied,[54] because he saw with his *ruach hakodesh* that Tziporah was the wife Hashem had prepared for him.[55] Moshe also knew through his *ruach hakodesh* that Yisro would convert to Judaism and not allow his grandson to have even the slightest contact with idol worship. Therefore, there was no need to make an issue of this last condition at this point.[56]

Moshe was seventy-seven years old when he married Tziporah and settled down in Midian as he promised Yisro. Tziporah became one of the seven saintly converts that joined the Jewish nation, exhibiting the same attributes as Sarah, Rivkah, Rachel and Leah.[57] Yisro was delighted with his new son-in-law. He loved him like his own son and always treated him with the greatest respect.[58] For taking the great *tzaddik* into his household and caring for him so honorably, many blessings were bestowed on Yisro's home, and for

---

49) שם 50) שמו"ר א-לג ובמהרז"ו 51) רבנו בחיי שמות ב-כא, באלשיך איתא דסבירא לי' יתרו דכמו שקדושתם של יצחק ויעקב היו עד הקצה ויצאתה הזוהמא ידתה ע"י אחיהם ישמעאל ועשו שעע"ז, כמו כן יעשה משה לבניו 52) ילקו"ש קס"ט ובזית רענן, ספר הישר. במדרש ויושע בפסוק עזי איתא שרצה שבני משה יוחלקו, חצים ילכו בדרך הישמעאלים וחצים השני יתנהגו עפ"י התוה"ק. 53) עפ"י ילקוט בני ירושלים 54) ילקו"ש קס"ט, שמו"ר שם 55) אוה"ח שמות ב-כא עפ"י הזוה"ק, פענח רזא סוף שמות מעיר דתבת "למשה" בגימטר' "צפרה" 56) בעה"ט שמות ב-טז, רבנו בחיי שם, בילקוט ראובני דף כט מובא שאע"פ שכוון לטובה אכן הי' אחד מנכדו עוע"ז 57) ילקו"ש קסח, ילקוט ראובני 58) תנחומא שמות טז, שמו"ר ד-ב

the first time, after seven daughters, Yisro had sons of his own.[59]

Time passed, and Tziporah bore Moshe his first child, a son. Moshe named him Gershom, the Hebrew words for "a stranger there." In this way, Moshe expressed his gratitude to Hashem for leading him to safety as "a stranger there" in distant Midian, far from the murderous designs of Pharaoh.[60] How fortunate he was to be living in Midian, where Hashem had granted him a wife, a child, tranquillity and success.[61] In keeping his promise to Yisro, Moshe did not circumcise his son. For the time being, he let his father-in-law raise his son as he saw fit.[62]

Back in Egypt While Moshe was finding peace and tranquillity in Midian, the situation in Egypt was beginning to come to a head. Nearly two hundred and ten years had already passed since the Jewish people had arrived in Egypt, and the ordained period of exile and bondage was approaching its explosive climax. Despite all the Egyptian persecution and oppression, the Jewish people had grown into a great and multitudinous nation who had, amazingly, avoided intermingling with the Egyptian population throughout the long centuries of their Egyptian sojourn.[63]

The Jewish people clung tenaciously to their own identity by preserving their distinctive style of dress and their traditional laws, and by speaking only Lashon Hakodesh, their own holy language, among themselves.[64] They also lived together in their own communities and neighborhoods to avoid becoming assimilated with the Egyptians.[65]

Yet despite their great efforts to insulate themselves from the Egyptian culture, some Jews did succumb to the lure of idol worship. Pharaoh had known all along that he needed to pry the Jews away from their powerful God, and he had tried to do so by inducing them to sin. Unfortunately, his efforts were not always met with failure.[66]

Hashem took the extenuating circumstances into consideration and did not view the idol worship of those who fell into Pharaoh's trap as a total sin.[67] However, in order to put a stop to this terrible breach in the spiritual world of the Jewish people, He sent Aharon

59) תנחומא שם 60) שמו"ר א-לג וע"ש במהרז"ו, רשב"ם וספורנו שמות ב-כב 61) שמו"ר שם במהרז"ו
62) ילקו"ש קס"ט, ספר הישר 63) הגדת האברבנל בד"ה ויהי שם 64) שם 65) שם וכן בהגדות רש"י ריטב"א
ורשב"ם 66) הגדות רש"י ויעב"ץ, בשיר השירים רבה ד-ז איתא שראובן שמעון ולוי לא חטאו בזה 67) הגדה
ע"פ יעב"ץ

to bring the wayward Jewish men back to their traditional path, and Miriam to bring back the wayward Jewish women.[68] But the wayward Jews continued to transgress, and Hashem allowed Pharaoh to increase the hardships of labor on all the Jewish people.[69]

On the other side, Hashem now began to afflict Pharaoh severely for his crimes against the Jewish people in Egypt. Pharaoh was stricken with *tzoraas* which ravaged his body from head to toe.[70] And for his attempts to kill Moshe, Hashem decreed that Pharaoh would ultimately die from his wounds.[71] Pharaoh had assumed a haughty and arrogant attitude towards the Jews. However, Hashem humbles the arrogant,[72] and Pharaoh would now begin to experience the taste of humiliation.[73] But Pharaoh was extremely stubborn, and his pain and suffering did not sway him from continuing to work the Jewish people as cruelly as ever.[74]

In the meantime, Pharaoh sought relief from his terrible illness by consulting with his doctors and wise men. Bilam had by this time returned to Egypt and rejoined the royal advisory council, and as usual, he was the first to respond.

"Your majesty, if I may be so bold," he began, "I believe I have the solution to your problem. I know of a cure that is only available to great kings or other men of unlimited resources."

"Indeed?" said Pharaoh. "Tell me about this cure."

"It is really quite simple, your majesty. Build a large pond, and fill it with blood. Then you must bathe in it each day. Every day the pond must be filled with fresh blood. Human, of course. The warm blood will cure you of your illness."

"But where am I to get a pond full of human blood every day?"

"I have the answer to that as well, your majesty," said Bilam slyly. "The Jews, your majesty! The Jews! They still grow in Egypt like weeds in your garden. Here is an opportunity to arrest their growth and heal yourself at the same time. Kill the Jewish children, and bathe in their blood!"

"That is a very interesting thought, Bilam," said Pharaoh. "You are certainly a tenacious foe of the Jews, and I appreciate your efforts. Let us now hear from our physicians. Physicians, what is your expert medical opinion?"

The chief royal physician stood up. "Your majesty, Bilam's plan is a good one," he said. "It is consistent with our medical research. However, I would like to add a small point. The blood of children is indeed the best for this purpose, but the blood of firstborn children is even better. It seems that the blood of firstborn children is of a higher quality and more likely to cure you of your illness. As Bilam said, this is a cure that is only available to a king. Who else could bathe in a pond full of fresh blood from firstborn children every single day?"[75]

Pharaoh wasted no time in putting this plan into action. He sent off his soldiers to Goshen to find sources for the fresh blood he needed. The decree against the Jewish children had lapsed after the birth of Moshe many years earlier, and the Jewish people were no longer accustomed to hiding their children. The Egyptian soldiers now stormed into the Jewish neighborhoods, mercilessly snatched young children from the arms of their mothers and carried them off to the royal palace in the capital.[76] Pharaoh had three hundred of these young children slaughtered daily, one hundred and fifty every morning and one hundred and fifty every evening.[77] He had their still warm blood poured into his pond, and he went down to bathe in it. In retribution for this outrageous crime, Hashem would later punish Egypt by killing all of their firstborns.[78]

To his great disappointment, however, Pharaoh's bloody pond did not cure him. Hashem would not allow the doctors to find a remedy for his illness. After ten years of suffering in this fashion, ten years that coincided with Moshe's imprisonment in Midian, Pharaoh's condition took a turn for the worse. His skin erupted in blisters and boils, and infection spread all over his body. On top of everything, he began to have terrible stomach cramps and other intestinal ailments. It seemed there was no end to his suffering.[79]

One day, as Pharaoh sat on his throne, contorted in pain, two officials from the ministry of labor entered.

"Your majesty, we are having problems with the Jews!" they exclaimed. "They have become lazy and are neglecting their work!"

"I won't stand for this!" Pharaoh thundered through his pain. "They think they can take advantage of my condition. They probably joke among themselves and make fun of me. Well, we will see if there is still order in this kingdom. We will see if such mockery will

---

75) ילקוט מובא בתורה שלמה ק"ב, שכל טוב שמות ב-כג, תרגום יונתן שם, ספר הישר, הגדת החזקוני 76) ספר הישר 77) שמו"ר א-לד, בספר הישר שנהרגו שע"ה כל יום 78) שכל טוב שם 79) ספר הישר

be allowed to continue. I will go there in person and get control of the situation."[80]

Immediately, Pharaoh's servants prepared the royal chariot, but Pharaoh's body was too diseased to endure a ride in the chariot over the rough roads. Instead, he was hoisted onto a horse, and accompanied by twenty horsemen and ten runners, he set off for Goshen.[81]

Along the way, the royal entourage encountered an extremely narrow stretch of road that was hemmed in on both sides by fences. The road itself was rutted and scarred by practically impassable ditches. The royal entourage entered this hazardous stretch of road slowly and in single file. As Pharaoh's horse picked its way through the ruts and ditches, it suddenly stumbled and fell. The riders behind could not rein in their horses in time, and they crashed into the fallen king and fell upon him. Pharaoh screamed in excruciating pain as his bones were shattered by the weight of the fallen horses. By the time all the chaos was untangled, any thought of continuing on to Goshen was abandoned, and Pharaoh was carried back to the capital, bruised, battered and barely alive.[82]

When Pharaoh returned to the palace, the royal physicians examined him and realized that the end was near. The king's wounds, injuries and infections were so great that recovery was all but impossible. The queen and all the assembled courtiers wept at the news of the imminent death of their king, and in a spirit of sadness, the thoughts of the royal councilors turned to the selection of a successor to the throne of Egypt.[83]

The choices were not very many. Pharaoh had three sons. The oldest, whose name was Asurai, was a fool. The second son, whose name was Adikum, was sly and intelligent but grotesquely ugly. He was a very fat midget only two and a half feet in height (one *amah* and one *zeres*).[84] Nevertheless, the king held him in high regard because of his sharp intelligence. The third son, whose name was Morion, was immature and unfit to be king. The final selection, however, was in the hands of Pharaoh, and although death stared him in the face, he was still not quite ready to decide.

The old Pharaoh, whose name was Mallul, clung to life for three

---

80) שם 81) שם 82) שם 83) שם 84) שם ועיין מועד קטן יח. דה"י גבוהה אמה

A Successor Ascends to the Throne

more years in his wasted and shriveled body. His flesh decomposed on his gaunt frame and gave off the horrible stench of the grave. Still, Hashem allowed Pharaoh to live in pain and suffering in punishment for his crimes against the Jewish people.

Mallul's miserable life finally expired. He had reigned as pharaoh of Egypt for ninety-four years, and now he was buried in the city of Tzoan. Even in death, his humiliation continued. The pharaohs of Egypt were traditionally embalmed before burial, but Mallul's body was too decayed to be embalmed. And thus Pharaoh was buried beside his ancestors, unembalmed and in disgrace.[85]

The funeral for the deceased Pharaoh was a solemn occasion. The passing of a king who had ruled for nearly a century was commemorated by glowing eulogies and the tearful sobs of the many thousands of mourners.[86] The Jewish people also attended the funeral of the Egyptian monarch, showing outward signs of grief and mourning under the watchful eyes of the Egyptians, but in their heart they rejoiced.[87]

After the funeral, the Jews were not required to return to their labors for the rest of the day, and they took advantage of this time to cry out to Hashem in their agony and suffering, pleading with Him to deliver them from their desperate plight. Ordinarily, the Egyptian overseers would not allow them to congregate and make a public outcry, but on this day, the Egyptians did not object. Strange as it may seem, they thought the Jews were crying out in grief over the passing of the old Pharaoh. Hashem, however, knew that the cries were really prayers to Him, and He was soon to answer their prayers.[88] The Jewish people were making a stand against the Egyptians with typically Jewish weapons—the "voice of Yaakov" rather than the "hands of Eisav." Hashem heard the prayers of His tormented people. The process of the redemption was about to begin, although in the short term, the oppression actually became worse.[89]

Not unexpectedly, Pharaoh had chosen his second son, Adikum, the firstborn of his mother, as his successor to the throne of Egypt. Adikum, now twenty years old, married the ten-year-old

---

85) ספר הישר   86) מלבים שמות ב-כג   87) אברבנל, ושל"ה בהגדה   88) הגדה ע"פ אמרי שפר, מלבים שמות
שם   89) הגדה ע"פ צפנת פענח

daughter of an Egyptian nobleman. Since he was of age and married, the councilors acceded to the wishes of his father and appointed Adikum king of Egypt. Like his father Mallul before him, Adikum was given the honorary title of Pharaoh.[90] In secret, however, the councilors mocked the grotesque new king, whose recently grown beard reached down to his ankles. Among themselves, they referred to him as Avus, the Egyptian word for "Shorty."[91]

There were divided opinions among the Jewish people with regard to the new development. Some feared that the new king would be even worse than his father. Others found the change on the throne an occasion for rejoicing.[92] They were convinced that the new king could not be as evil as his father and that he would abolish the harsh labor decrees as soon as he assumed full control. It did not take long for the first group to be proved right.[93]

As difficult as such a thing would have been to imagine, Adikum showed himself to be not only as evil as his father but far worse. In his inaugural act as king, he went down to Goshen to make a firsthand evaluation of the labor situation. He was not satisfied with what he saw.

"There will be no more slacking off under my administration," he announced to the Jews. "Why haven't you fulfilled your quotas? The lax days are over! My father was too lenient with you, but I shall be strict! I expect all of you to finish your quota, in addition to the requirements of the new labor decrees I shall issue. Should you find it impossible to finish the brick quota, your children will fulfill . . . in a way that you might find rather unpleasant."[94]

Sadly, most of the Jewish laborers could not finish the impossible quota set for them. Furious, the Egyptians snatched the children from the arms of their screaming mothers, one child for every brick short of the quota. They placed the crying children in the walls, crushing their tender bodies to make them take the shape of bricks. Then they plastered over the children with lime and cement, while their pathetic screams could still be heard from within the walls. The screams of the parents who had to watch these atrocities were ignored.[95] The Egyptians had never stooped so low. Even during the decree of throwing the children into the river, the parents were not

---

90) ספר הישר   91) שם   92) שם   93) רמב"ן רבנו בחיי ודעת זקנים שמות ב-כג הגדת רשב"ץ   94) ספר הישר   95) שם
שם

forced to witness the deaths of their beloved children, but now, the children were killed in front of their weeping parents.[96]

The Egyptians were now caught up in a frenzy of sadism. It was no longer enough for them to tear the children from the arms of their parents and cement them into the walls. Now the Egyptians began to force the parents themselves to place their own children into the walls of the buildings.

It was now clear to the Jewish people that Adikum was even worse than his father in his hatred towards the Jewish people.[97] As time went on, he constantly outdid himself in his savage treatment of the Jews. Sadistically, he insisted that the parents themselves cement their children into the walls.[98] He commanded that Jewish children be burned alive in the temple ceremonies of the Egyptian idol worship.[99] He continually increased the labor burden on the Jews, ordering the construction of new government buildings, theaters and burial pyramids to beautify the kingdom of Egypt.[100] The hopes of the more optimistic Jews turned to ashes. There seemed to be no end in sight to the suffering of the Jewish people.[101]

The Jewish Prayers Are Heard

The Jewish people had descended to the lowest levels of misery. Adikum's unbearable labor decrees and the ruthless slaughter of the children caused the Jewish people to cry out in bitter agony.[102] They would have welcomed death rather than endure this kind of pain.[103] The cries of anguish rose up to the heavens, some bemoaning the harsh labor, some bemoaning the pain, some bemoaning the economic exploitation, some simply crying out plaintively for the salvation of Hashem.[104] The angels in the heavens listened to the cries, and responded with the blessing שומע תפילה.[105]

Hashem heard the cries of the righteous praying for their salvation. He heard the cries of the children buried in the walls. He heard the cries of the children being burned alive for the Egyptian sacrifices. He heard the weeping of the children, and through their cries, He recalled the covenant with Avraham, Yitzchak and Yaakov. And

---

96) שמו"ר א-לד ובי"פ"ת 97) ספר הישר, ילקו"ש קס"ט 98) ספר הישר 99) ילקו"ש שם 100) מלבים שמות ב-כג 101) דעת זקנים שם 102) ספר הישר 103) רמב"ן שמות ב-כג 104) מדרש הגדול, אב"ע, ספורנו ואוה"ח שמות ב-כג 105) שבלי הלקט תפילה יח

He decided that the time had come to reap the seeds of redemption.[106]

A spirit of repentance spread among the Jewish people. They resolved to turn away from the sinful ways into which they had slipped because of the burdens of oppression. They accepted their heavenly ordained travails with faith and without resentment, and they prayed to Hashem with purity and sincerity, to the Lord of their fathers, the One who responds to grieving hearts and answers the prayers of the afflicted. They prayed for divine mercy in the merit of the covenant Hashem had made with their forefathers.[107]

Hashem took note of their prayers, the cruelty of Pharaoh and the dire need of the Jewish people.[108] He took note of their repentance. He also took note of the good deeds they would do in the future. He saw that they would rise in faith at Mount Sinai and say, "*Naaseh venishma*. We will do, and we will hear." The time had come to begin the redemption of the Jewish people.[109]

Although in earlier years the Jewish people had also cried out in anguish to Hashem, the time of redemption ordained in the covenant with Avraham had not yet arrived. Hashem had, of course, heard all those prayers and treasured them, but He did not respond until the time for redemption was at hand. But now the time had finally come, and redemption was indeed at hand.[110]

---

106) ילקו״ש קסט, ספורנו שמות ב-כד, ספר הישר   107) הגדת האברבנל, אוה״ח שמות ב-כה   108) הגדת מהר״ל
109) שמו״ר א-לו, רש״י רמב״ן ואוה״ח שמות ב-כה   110) שמו״ר א-לו, רמב״ן שם.

A Messenger Is Chosen

7

While the Jewish people suffered in Egypt, Moshe lived a shepherd's life in Midian, tending Yisro's flocks as he had promised he would. The wealthy Yisro would undoubtedly have provided his son-in-law Moshe with flocks of his own, but Moshe was perfectly content to tend his father-in-law's flocks. Although Yisro was still connected to the pagans, Moshe felt it important to show his gratitude to Yisro for his kindness. Had he tended his own flocks along with Yisro's flocks, people would have assumed that his primary concern was for his own flocks, when in fact it was not so. Moshe was more interested in expressing his gratitude to Yisro than in enriching himself.[1]

The life of a shepherd suited Moshe well at this time. For all intents and purposes, he was still a fugitive from Pharaoh, and as a shepherd who is

---

1) זוה"ק ח"ב כא., תולדות יצחק כתב שהי' רועה צאניו של זולתו שלא יחשדו אותו לגזלן

constantly moving from place to place, he found it easier to conceal his identity and whereabouts from unfriendly eyes.[2] The lifestyle of a shepherd also suited his contemplative nature. While the sheep graze, the shepherd usually has much free and undisturbed time to himself. Moshe took advantage of these opportunities and used the time to reflect on the wondrous ways of Hashem and reach high levels of prophecy.[3] The forefathers of the Jewish people had also lived as shepherds because of this reason, and Moshe was now following in their footsteps.[4] Finally, Moshe preferred the solitude of the fields, far from the temptations of the towns. It was an environment more conducive to holiness.[5]

Moshe was a very conscientious shepherd. With the staff he had extracted from Yisro's garden, he would lead the flocks out to the grazing pastures.[6] Fully aware that he was entrusted with Yisro's property, he was more watchful with the flocks than he would have been with his own.[7] He gave special attention to the care and welfare of each and every sheep. He made sure that the young sheep, whose teeth were still tender, grazed in the soft grass.[8] Moshe was so conscientious that in all the time he tended to Yisro's sheep, he never lost a single sheep or allowed his flocks to come under attack. Under his supervision, the flocks prospered and multiplied far beyond the norm.[9]

The pastures to which Moshe chose to lead his flocks were in the wilderness to the west of Midian.[10] Moshe wanted to make sure that they did not graze in private lands and consume other people's grass.[11] He also saw by his gift of prophecy that the Jewish people would find greatness and glory in the wilderness; that they would receive the Torah there, that they would be fed the *mann* from Heaven;[12] that the Mishkan would be built there, and the Shechinah and the clouds of glory would rest upon it;[13] that the Jewish people would receive the *kehunah* there and become a kingdom there; that a miraculous well would travel with the Jewish people through the wilderness and provide them with water.[14] This was the place where Moshe wanted to spend his time.

One day, while Moshe was tending the flocks, a young lamb ran away into the fields. Unwilling to lose even one lamb of Yisro's flock,

2) אב"ע שמות ב-טו 3) רבנו בחיי ג-א וכל"י שמות שם 4) רבנו בחיי שם 5) שם 6) ילקוט ראובני 7) שמו"ר ב-ג ובים"ת 8) שמו"ר ב-ב 9) פרדר"א מ 10) שמות ג-א 11) שמו"ר ב-ב 12) תנחומא שמות יד 13) שם (14 שם

Moshe ran off to find the missing lamb, but he could not find it. Just
when he was about to give up hope, he caught sight of a stream running near a grassy area. The lamb was standing beside the stream
and drinking. Apparently the lamb ran off because he was very
thirsty, Moshe said to himself. The lamb must be tired and weak, and
it will be too difficult for him to return to the flock on his own power.
Gently, Moshe lifted up the lamb and carried it on his shoulders
back to the rest of the flock. Moshe had passed a test Hashem had
prepared to determine the extent of his caring for every member of
his flock.[15]

Hashem Chooses Moshe

Hashem does not bestow greatness on
someone until He tests him with something small. By showing compassion for
the little lamb, Moshe had proved himself
worthy of leading the Jewish people. Just as Moshe showed himself
capable of nurturing a little lamb and helping it reach its full growth,
so would he be capable of nurturing the fledgling Jewish nation and
helping them reach their full potential. Hashem said, "The one who
cares so well for his flock of sheep is the one I want as the leader of
My flock, the Jewish people."[16]

Furthermore, a leader needs to be mindful of even the most
minor detail, or his most insignificant follower. Only then can he be
considered a "leader" in the truest sense of the word. Moshe had
already shown his compassion for his Jewish brothers when he
went out into the fields to help ease the burden of their labor. Moshe
also risked his own life to protect another Jew from his Egyptian
tormentor. But how small a detail would warrant Moshe's attention? When he exerted himself to care for the wayward little lamb,
he showed how sensitive he was to the most minor details. Hashem
decided that this proved Moshe fit to be the leader of the Jewish
people.[17]

Hashem decreed that just as Moshe exerted himself to chase
after one little lamb to prevent monetary loss to his employer, so
would he judge the Jewish people and thereby protect their wealth.

---

15) שמו״ר ב-ב ברד״ל ומהרז״ו 16) שם, זוה״ק ח״ב כא., בתנחומא ישן שמות איתא שבזכות ששם נפשו בכפו
להציל היהודי מאותו מצרי (שהרג בשם המפורש) זכה להיות רבם של ישראל 17) ע׳ דעת חכמה ומוסר חלק א

Just as Moshe went to the wilderness to avoid possible theft, so would he judge the Jewish people and protect them from theft. Just as Moshe did not abandon hope of finding the lost sheep, so would he be the one who "brings back" the sinful by getting them to repent. Just as Moshe showed patience and care to the sheep, so would he lead the Jewish nation with consummate patience and care.[18]

The Bush on the Mountain

On one of his sojourns into the wilderness, Moshe had a very unusual experience. For forty days, he walked through the wilderness, and not once did the sheep stop to graze. This was a sign that in the future the Jewish people would travel through the wilderness for forty years without eating the produce of the land, only the *mann* that fell from Heaven.[19] After forty days, Moshe noticed that his surroundings had undergone a subtle change. No longer did he seem to be in a desolate place but in a cultivated one. The wilderness seemed to recede before his eyes.[20]

On the fifteenth day of the month of Nissan, a day which would become the first day of Pesach, Moshe reached a forlorn area a three-day journey from Egypt (approx. 87 miles). A mountain loomed up in front of him.[21] At the very summit of the mountain was a small tree, actually a thorn bush (*sneh*). The thorn bush had five sharp leaves growing from each branch.[22] The intense heat and lack of rain had parched it to a withered dryness.[23] Birds flew around the summit of the mountain but did not go near it. They flew down to where Moshe stood and landed at his feet.[24]

The mountain Moshe beheld was the famous Mount Sinai, the mountain from which the Jewish people would one day receive the Torah. The name Mount Sinai symbolized the hostility (*sinah*) Hashem felt towards the gentiles after the Jewish people received the Torah.[25]* The mountain also had four other names, each with its

---

* Some say that the name Mount Sinai is derived from the stones on the mountain which bear inscriptions about the Sneh. (Nervuni, end of ch. 66 in *Moreh Nevuchim*)

18) מאמר כ״א וכ״ד שמו״ר ב-ב ביפ״ת ורד״ל גם בדוד המלך מצינו שלא הובחר עד אחר היותו רועה נאמן, ובאמת כנס״י נמשלו לצאן כמ״ש נוהג כצאן יוסף וכמ״ש כצאן אשר אין להם רועה 19) תנחומא שמות יד מדרש אגדה שמות ג-א, עיין ילקוט ראובני יט, עץ יוסף מעתיק דברי הפסיקתא שלא אכל כלל כל באותם ארבעים יום 20) ילקוט ראובני 21) שם 22) שמו״ר ב-ה ובמהרז״ו, רמב״ן שמות ג-ה כל החמשה יוצאין ממקום אחד (ע״ד הדס) 23) עפ״י אב״ע שמות ג-א 24) ילקוט ראובני זוה״ק ח״ב כא. 25) שמו״ר ב-ד י״מ שנקראת סיני על שם הסנה

own significance and symbolism.[26] It was called the Mountain of God, because on this mountain the Jewish people would accept Hashem as their God.[27] It was called Mount Bashan, because whatever the Jewish people would "eat with their teeth" (*b'shein*) in the future would be in the merit of accepting the Torah.[28] It was called Mount Gavnunim, because when the Jewish people received the Torah they were healed from all blemishes and injuries.[29] It was also called Mount Chorev, because the giving of the Torah empowered the Sanhedrin to issue and execute the death sentence, and it also sealed the decree of destruction for the gentile nations who rejected the Torah.[30]

As Moshe approached the mountain, he saw that the angel Michael, whose appearance always indicated the presence of the Shechinah, was standing on its peak.[31] The thorn bush was burning, and the angel was standing in the midst of the flames. Moshe tried to look away from the miraculous visions that confronted him, because he was a conscientious shepherd who refused to neglect his duties.[32]

Suddenly, Moshe was struck by an amazing thought. The bush was burning vigorously, but it was not being consumed! Moshe called out to the other shepherds in his vicinity and asked them what they thought of this strange vision, but none of them had seen anything at all.[33]

Moshe retreated a few steps to get a more peripheral view of the mountaintop.[34] To his further amazement, he saw that there was no fuel of any kind at the bottom of the bush that could account for the fire.[35] Moreover, only the top third of the bush was aflame, while the rest of it seemed perfectly normal. The fire was also of a strange hue, not red like an ordinary fire but a glowing black streaked with many different colors. Long tongues of this black flame licked the air around the bush, but the bush itself remained intact.[36]

Moshe was perplexed. If this thorn bush (*sneh*) drew enough water from an underground source to prevent it from being consumed, the dampness should have extinguished the flames. If it was dry inside then it should have been consumed. Moshe realized he

---

26) שמו"ר שם 27) שם 28) שם 29) שם במהרז"ו והכוונה כגבינה נקויה שאין בה סיג 30) שם 31) שמו"ר

ב-ה, אגדת בראשית לב, זוה"ק ח"ב כא. וע' ביפ"ת דכתב דהיה גבריאל שהוא שר של אש כמ"ש חז"ל 32) שמו"ר

ב-ו וברד"ל 33) שמו"ר ב-ה וברד"ל, לקח טוב שמות ג-ג 34) כל"י שמות ג-ג 35) רשב"ם שמות ג-ב

36) שמו"ר ב-ה וע"ש במתנ"כ ועץ יוסף, תנחומא טו

was not witnessing an ordinary fire but a prophetic and spiritual vision.[37]

Although, he had been reluctant to leave his sheep, he realized that Hashem had prepared this vision expressly for him and wanted him to give it his attention.[38] Moshe now drew closer to see if he could determine the prophetic message of this vision,[39] taking three steps towards the flame.[40] By straining to understand the vision, he again proved himself worthy of leading the Jewish people to freedom.[41]

Hashem showed this vision to Moshe, because He wanted to condition him to the sort of prophetic vision he would experience when the Jewish people would receive the Torah on Mount Sinai.[42] But why did Hashem send an angel down to the thorn bush specifically? What did the bush signify? What did the fire mean? What did the unburned bush mean?

Once again, we are presented with numerous symbols. A thorn bush is a symbol of pain, and in this case, it signified that Hashem is in pain, so to speak, when He sees the suffering of the Jewish people—like a twin who always feels the suffering of his brother.[43] Also, an encounter with a thorn bush almost always results in injury, and the Jewish people, too, were caught in a situation where injury was inescapable.[44] A thorn bush has flowers as well as thorns, as do the Jewish people have righteous as well as sinful people.[45]

The Hebrew word for a thorn bush, *sneh*, indicated that one of the reasons for the suffering of the Jewish people was the hostility (*sinah*) Yosef's brothers had exhibited towards him in selling him into slavery. Moshe's merits would eventually help them be redeemed.[46] Although a thorn bush normally has no more than three leaves on each branch, this particular bush had five on each branch, indicating that the Jewish people would be redeemed in the merit of their five righteous leaders—Avraham, Yitzchak, Yaakov, Moshe and Aharon.[47]

The lowly and humble thorn bush was a particularly appropriate place for the appearance of Hashem, because He wanted to show that He does not only show Himself on tall mountains.[48] In addition,

---

37) פרדר"א מד וברד"ל רבינו בחיי שמות ג-א   38) שמו"ר ב-י ובעץ יוסף, תנחומא שמות טו ושם   39) רש"י וספורנו שמות ג-ב, ילקו"ש קעא   40) ע' שמו"ר ב-ה ברד"ל וביפ"ת, תנחומא שמות טו ובעץ יוסף, ויש שגירסו חמשה פסיעות   41) תנחומא שם   42) שמו"ר ב-ה ומתנ"כ, שם   43) תנחומא שמות יד, שמו"ר שם   44) שמו"ר שם   45) שם   46) תוס' שבת י:, ילקו"ש קסט, מדרש הגדול ג-ב   47) שמו"ר שם   48) שם, מכילתא ב, ע' תוס' עה"ת שמות ג-ד

the thorn bush, because of its prickly nature, is the only existing wood that was never used for idol worship, and thus, it had a purity that made it worthy of receiving the presence of Hashem in transmitting the prophecy of the impending and long-awaited redemption of the Jewish people.[49] And just as the fire did not consume the humble thorn bush, the fires of exile and bondage in Egypt would not consume the humbled Jewish people.[50]

As the meaning of the prophetic vision of the burning bush entered Moshe's consciousness, he was gripped by an overwhelming sorrow. Here in this vision lay the full extent of the suffering of his brethren in Egypt, and Moshe's heart ached with compassion.[51] Hashem took note of Moshe's deep sympathy for his brethren, and looked on him with favor as the future leader of the Jewish people.[52]

Hashem Speaks to Moshe

Once Moshe understood the full import of his vision, Hashem was ready to speak to him directly.[53] But Moshe had to be conditioned to such a high level of prophecy in gradual stages. Just as someone who had been in the dark cannot be brought directly into the blazing sunlight, Moshe had to be initiated gradually into the levels of prophecy.[54] First, he was shown the miraculous fire. Then he was shown the angel in the fire. Only then would Hashem speak to him directly.[55] And even then He did not speak to Moshe in a loud voice, so as not to frighten him. Nor did He speak in a low voice, since this would be inappropriate to the gravity of the prophecy. Hashem spoke to Moshe in the voice of Amram, his father, in normal tones.[56]

"Moshe, Moshe," Hashem called out in Amram's voice.

"Yes, Father, I am here," Moshe replied.[57]

"I am not your father," Hashem replied. "I am the God of your father and your forefathers. I addressed you in your father's voice so as not to frighten you."[58]

Moshe was elated that his father's name was mentioned by

49) מכילתא שם, טור שמות ג-ד ועיין מדרש הגדול ג-ב 50) שמו"ר שם 51) שמו"ר שם 52) שמו"ר ב-ו ובמהרז"ו שם, תנחומא שמות טו 53) שמו"ר שם, ספורנו שמות ג-ד, ברמב"ן רשב"ם ואב"ע כ' דמלאך דבר אליו בשם ד' 54) רבנו בחיי שמות ג-א 55) שם, שמו"ר ג-א ובמתנ"כ, כבר כאן התחילה מעלת נבואתו המיוחדת לו שמשונה היתה משאר נביאי ישראל כמש"כ ברמב"ם הל' יסוה"ת ז-ו 56) שמו"ר ג-א במהרז"ו ויפ"ת, בלקח טוב טוב איתא שגם דמות המלאך נראה לו כאביו 57) שמו"ר ג-א, ע' שמו"ר וביפ"ת שם דגם באברהם יעקב ושמואל מצינו קריאה כפולה ודרך חיבה היא 58) שמו"ר שם

Hashem in conjunction with the names of the patriarchs, actually being mentioned first. But he was also saddened. Moshe knew that Hashem does not connect His own Name with that of a living person, and therefore, when Hashem referred to Himself as "the God of your father," the clear implication was that Amram had passed away.[59]

"Do not come any closer here," Hashem continued. "You have not yet reached the level of prophecy that would allow you to come closer. Take off your shoes, because this is a holy place. You may not wear shoes in the presence of the Shechinah."[60] The place also had holiness because of the *mizbeyach* Moshe would build there in the future.[61]

Moshe was taken aback. "The God of my father is standing here," he exclaimed, "and I must turn my face aside!" He promptly turned his face away so as not to gaze upon the Shechinah.[62]

Because Moshe showed the proper honor and respect to Hashem by not gazing at the Shechinah, he earned the great privilege of speaking directly to Hashem on Mount Sinai for forty days and nights.[63] He also earned the honor of being considered the king of the Jewish people.[64]

"I have seen the affliction the Egyptians have visited upon My nation," Hashem said. "I have seen the pain and agony they have caused. They have treated the Jewish people far worse than was needed to comply with My decree of exile. I have heard the cries of mothers whose children have been torn from their arms and thrown into the river or plastered into the walls. The Egyptians have broken up Jewish families and expelled them from the comfort of their homes. I will avenge Myself upon the evil Pharaoh.[65]

"I will take the Jewish people and redeem them from the hard, backbreaking labor, the oppression, the pain and the bitterness they have endured till now in Egypt.[66]

"I will take them out to Eretz Yisrael, a land of flowing milk and

---

59) שם, רמב"ן וחזקוני שמות ג-ו, בשכל טוב איתא כי עי"ז גלה לו הקב"ה כי אביו כבר הלך לעולמו דאין הקב"ה
קורא שמו אלא בכה"ג ולולא הודעה זו ודאי הי' משה מסרב לקבל שליחות זו מפני כבוד אביו (60 שמו"ר ב-ו,
רמב"ן שמות ג-ה, ע' תקי"ז יב (ובבאר לחי רואי שם) ושם כא דהיות ופיו נגע בת פרעה נטמא בשרו קצת ועדיין
לא נזדככה לגמרי ולכן לא הי' יכול להתקרב יותר, ברש"ש על שמו"ר ג-ז מפרש הצווי של נעליך מדין שמעוה
רחוקה על פטירת אביו (61 ילקו"ש קסט (62 שמו"ר ג-א, לקח טוב שמות ג-ו (63 שמו"ר שם, בתנחומא בשלח
ט איתא דעי"ז זכה להיות מלך, בבעה"ט ג-ו איתא באופן הפוך דאילו הביט הי' זוכה לראות כל העולמות העליונים
64) תנחומא בשלח ט (65 מכילתא שמות, רמב"ן שמות ג-ט, הגדת הגר"א ועיין תוס' שבת י': (66 שמות ג-ז
ובבעה"ט

honey; a good land with temperate climate and broad open spaces; a land of exceedingly fertile ground and good water in which cattle will graze and produce excellent milk; a land of succulent and sweet fruits bursting with juice.[67]

"Just as I dwell in the highest realms of the heavens, I will place the Jewish people in the choicest of all the lands. Unlike their forefathers, they will not live among the Canaanites. Rather, they will live alone in the land they will have inherited from the seven nations after destroying them.[68]

"Moshe, I am sending you to Pharaoh to order him to send My nation, the Jewish people, from Egypt. You are to be their redeemer, Moshe. If you don't redeem them, no one will."[69]

This wonderful prophecy contained a double blessing. The Jewish people would have been happy just to leave Egypt, no matter where their destiny would take them. And now, Hashem was saying that not only would they be released from slavery, they would be given the choicest land in the world—Eretz Yisrael.[70]

Moshe Is a Reluctant Messenger

"Who am I to take out the Jewish people from Egypt?" Moshe responded with customary modesty and humility. "Who am I to speak to a mighty king like Pharaoh? I am just a shepherd, and he is a great king![71]

Besides, You specifically told Yaakov that You Yourself would take the Jewish people out of Egypt, not I. How can a humble shepherd like me expect to accomplish so dangerous a task as taking the Jewish people out of the mighty Egyptian empire? And even if it would be possible, are the Jewish people worthy of being redeemed from Egypt now?"[72]

"Do not worry," Hashem replied. "It will not be you who takes them out of Egypt but I. You will be My messenger to Pharaoh. I will be with you every step of the way, as I was with you when you escaped Pharaoh's sword. Trust in Me. The vision you have seen here at the *sneh* assures your success as My messenger—without any harm befalling you. As for the worthiness of the Jewish people, they are indeed worthy, since they will accept the Torah on this very

---

67) רמב"ן שמות ג-ח 68) רמב"ן ואב"ע שמות ג-ח 69) שמו"ר ג-ג וברד"ל, הגואל צריך להיות משבט לוי ועד"ז
לעתיד שיגאל אותנו אליהו הנביא כמ"ש בפסיקתא רבתי ד 70) רבנו בחיי שמות ג-ח 71) אב"ע שמות ג-יא, עץ
יוסף על שמו"ר ז-ב 72) שמו"ר ג-ד, רש"י שמות ג-יא

mountain after they are redeemed from Egypt."[73]

"But how am I to care for the Jewish people in the heat of summer and the cold of winter?" Moshe continued. "Will I have enough food for everyone? There are pregnant and nursing women to be fed. There are children to be fed. There are even cattle to feed. Will I have all the varieties of food needed to satisfy all of them?"

"The cakes and dough they take with them from Egypt will satisfy them," Hashem answered Moshe. "It will taste like the *mann*, and it will last them for thirty days until they receive the actual *mann*."[74]

"The Jewish people will of course agree to any conditions if it means getting out of Egypt," Moshe persisted. "But once they have left Egypt, how will I convince them to confront the powerful warriors of Canaan?"

"Do not fear," Hashem replied. "The people will trust in you. They will follow your command even after they leave Egypt."[75]

Moshe Asks for Hashem's Name

The time had come for Moshe to leave Midian behind and go down to Egypt as the messenger of God. But first Moshe had a very important question to ask of Hashem. "When I approach the Jewish people and tell them that the God of your fathers sent me to take them out of Egypt," Moshe wanted to know, "they will ask me for His Name. What shall I tell them?"

"Tell them אֶהְיֶה אֲשֶׁר אֶהְיֶה—I Shall Be What I Shall Be—sent you to them,"[76] Hashem told him.

In truth, a name is restrictive, highlighting a specific quality or attribute, and since Hashem is infinite, no one Name can be applied to Him. All the Names of Hashem are not inclusive Names for Him but indications of a particular Attribute. When He judges, He uses the Name Elokim. When He guides a war, He uses the Name Tzevakos. When He shows pity, He uses the Name Hashem. When He withholds judgment for the sinful, He uses the Name Shakai. And so forth.[77]

The Name אֶהְיֶה אֲשֶׁר אֶהְיֶה—I Shall Be What I Shall Be—signified Hashem's role in the exile and redemption of the Jewish people.

---

73) שמו"ר ג-ד, לקח טוב שמות ג-יא, רש"י שם 74) שמו"ר שם ובמהרז"ו 75) שמו"ר שם ברד"ל ויפ"ת, רמב"ן שמות ג-יא 76) שמות ג-יג והלאה, ראשית חכמה ענוה סב 77) שמו"ר ג-ו, מדרש הגדול שמות ג-יד

The Name infers that Hashem was in the past, is in the present and will be in the future, since He is above the restrictions and boundaries of time. By using this Name in this instance, Hashem was saying that He has been and always will be with the Jewish people. And just as He is with them in this exile, so will He be with them in future exiles.

The revelation about future exiles, however, was only for Moshe's benefit. The Jewish people who were deep in the agonies of their present exile were not in a frame of mind to be told about future exiles. It was sufficient to tell them that "the One who is with them in their present suffering" had sent Moshe to redeem them.[78]

Moshe's Instructions

"Tell the Jewish people that the Lord of their forefathers sent you to them," Hashem instructed Moshe. "The Name signifying compassion will take them out of Egypt in the merit of Avraham, Yitzchak and Yaakov."

Moshe wanted to know why Hashem had not included his father Amram's name in connection with His own Name—as He had done at the *sneh*. Hashem explained that He had attached His own Name to Amram's at the time only in order to set Moshe's mind at ease. Otherwise, He only attaches His Name to the names of the forefathers.[79]

Hashem now told Moshe to call together the "elders" of the Jewish people and tell them, "The Lord of your fathers has appeared to me."[80]

By the word "elders," Hashem was not necessarily referring to old people, but rather to the learned people who guided the Jewish people with their wise counsel.[81] It also included people of high intelligence who would be able to fathom the finer points and implications of Moshe's prophecy[82] and people of great humility who were prepared to listen to Moshe unequivocally.[83] Finally, it included people of outstanding personal achievement, since in their merit the Jewish people were worthy of redemption.[84]

Hashem instructed Moshe to tell the elders that He has

---

78) שמו"ר ג-ו, רש"י שמות ג-יד, ברכות ט: ובמהרש"א, רמב"ן כתב דההבטיחו הקב"ה דכשיתפללו לפניו ית"ש יענם 79) שמו"ר ג-ז, בעץ יוסף מבואר דודאי הוא ית"ש אלקי כאו"א רק דאינו מתגלית בתור אלקי אדם פרטי (והאבות הק' כלליים היה כמ"ש אין קורין לאבות אלא שלשה) 80) שמות ג-טז 81) שמו"ר ג-ח וביפ"ת, רש"י שמות ג-טז 82) שמות ג-טז 83) אברבנל שמות ג-טז 84) שכל טוב שמות ג-יח שמו"ר טו-ד

remembered them, using the words פָּקֹד פָּקַדְתִּי, *pakod pakadeti*. They would recognize this phrase, because there was a tradition among the Jews carried down from Yosef himself that the messenger who mentions this phrase of remembrance will be the true redeemer. Therefore, when Moshe would repeat this phrase to them, they would surely believe in him. They would know that Hashem had decided to redeem them from all the pain and suffering of their Egyptian bondage.[85]

There are a number of hidden meanings in the choice of this word. The numerical value of the word פָּקֹד is 190, signifying that Hashem subtracted one hundred and ninety years from the original decree of four hundred years and would redeem the Jews after only two hundred and ten years.[86] The word *pakod*—which translates as remember—also means a deposit, derivative of the word *pikadon*. Thus, by the use of this word, Hashem indicated that the Jewish people were only given to the Egyptians as a deposit, temporarily, and now, Hashem was prepared to take back His *pikadon*.[87]

This then was the message Moshe was to carry from Hashem to the elders of the Jewish people. He was to tell them that Hashem had, so to speak, been in exile with them and suffered with them. He had taken note of the crimes of the Egyptians and would punish them—not only in Egypt but at the Yam Suf as well.[88] Then He would bring the Jewish people out from Egypt and take them to the land of the seven nations, Eretz Yisrael, the land of flowing milk and honey.[89]

Having given his message to the elders, Moshe was to go to Pharaoh, accompanied by the elders, and say to him, "The Lord of the Ivrim[90] (Hebrews) has called upon me. Please allow the Jews to travel for a three-day journey into the desert to sacrifice to our God."[91]

All along, Hashem's intention had been for the Jewish people to leave Egypt and not return. Nevertheless, Moshe was to ask Pharaoh only for a three-day furlough, because any other request would undoubtedly be rejected out of hand. At first, Pharaoh would also refuse the three-day furlough. The world would see how wicked Pharaoh was, refusing his slaves even a three-day furlough. Eventually, Pharaoh would give in and allow the furlough. The Jewish people would leave Egypt, and when they did not return after three days, Pharaoh would pursue them—right into the sea. The Egyptians would be punished for throwing Jewish children into the river, and Hashem's Name would be glorified.[92]

The request was also to be presented in this way for the benefit of the Jewish people. It would be easier for the common people to accept the new life that awaited them as servants of Hashem in smaller doses. Just as Hashem had revealed piecemeal his command to Avraham to sacrifice his son so as not to overwhelm him, so too would the Jewish people be indoctrinated into their new life a little bit at a time.[93]

After Pharaoh would deny the request, Moshe was to report to the Jewish people and tell them that Pharaoh had refused to allow them to leave Egypt. His ability to refuse, however, did not stem from his own power and freedom of choice. Rather, it stemmed from Hashem's preventing him from giving permission. Hashem will harden his heart. Not only will he deny the Jews permission to leave, he will actually increase the workload of the Jewish people. The Jewish people would have to be patient and trust in Hashem.[94] Pharaoh's refusal would result in Hashem afflicting the Egyptians with ten plagues in Egypt and fifty by the sea. Then Hashem's mighty and powerful Hand would be revealed for the entire world to see.[95]

The Jewish people would leave Egypt triumphantly, and not empty-handed but with great wealth. Hashem had promised Avraham that his children would emerge from exile with great wealth. This promise would be fulfilled.[96]

Actually, this was much more than a promise of blessings, it was a pair of commandments. The Jewish people were prohibited to "leave empty-handed," and they were commanded to "leave Egypt with great wealth."[97] They were to drain Egypt of its gold, silver, money, fine garments[98] and all other wealth, leaving it empty like a pond without fish.[99] The jewelry of the Egyptians would be used to adorn the Jews as they celebrated the holidays and sacrificial offerings in the desert.[100]

---

92) שמו"ר ג-ח, אברבנל שמות ג-יט, מלבים שמות ג-יח, במדרש אגדה שסימן הי' דלעתיד יראו פני ה'

בשלש רגלים 93) רבנו בחיי שמות ג-יח 94) ת"א שמות ג-יט, שמו"ר ג-ט 95) בעה"ט ורשב"ם שמות ג-יט

96) שמו"ר ג-יא ובמהרז"ו 97) מדרש הגדול 98) שמות ג-כב 99) שמו"ר ג-יא ובמהרז"ו דמשל למה הדבר דומה

לתחתית הנהר שאין שם דגים כי כולם על פני המים לחפוש אוכל כן יהיו המצריים אחר שיוקחו מהם רכושם

100) רשב"ם שמות ג-כב

The wealth of Egypt was not to be taken by force. Women were to borrow all kinds of jewelry and clothes from their neighbors. It was to be expected, of course, that when they asked to borrow the valuables of the Egyptians, the Egyptians would claim they had nothing to offer. However, during the plague of *choshech*, darkness, when the Egyptians would be immobilized, the Jews were to search their houses and find the hiding places of all their valuables. Afterwards, when the Jews would come to borrow the valuables, they could pinpoint the location of each and every item.[101]

We are presented here with a perplexing question. How could the Jewish people claim to be borrowing something when in fact they never returned it? Wasn't this dishonest?

There are many answers to this question. In fact, a thousand years later, the Egyptians would sue the Jews in the court of Alexander the Great for the return of their "borrowed" valuables. The Jews would argue in defense that the money was owed to them for two hundred and ten years of unpaid labor—and they would win![102*]

Moreover, much of this treasure had come from the Jewish people themselves, who had given it to the Egyptians as futile bribes to save their children from Pharaoh's decree of drowning.[103**] Much of it was treasure accumulated by Yosef during the Great Famine, when he exchanged the grain in Egypt for the treasures of the world; the Jewish people would eventually return these treasures to their rightful owners.[104] Furthermore, even if the Jews intended to return it, they would not be required to do so, since the Egyptians would give it wholeheartedly as a gift.[105]

In truth, however, the whole question is really moot, since all the treasures in the world belong to Hashem. If He wishes to take the

---

* The Egyptians in the time of Alexander the Great sued the Jewish people for the treasures they took from Egypt. A person named Gevia ben Kosem replied, "We were not paid for all the years of slavery. Multiply that by six hundred thousand, and let us see how much the Egyptians owe us!" The Egyptians left in disgrace.

** Shevet Levi would not be allowed to share the booty of Egypt, because they did not labor in Egypt. (*Mishneh Lamelech* in *Migdal Eider Haggadah* on *Baruch Shomer*)

---

101) תנחומא ישן בא ג, חזקוני כותב דדרכן של הנשים לשאול אולם ודאי שגם האנשים עשו כדבר ד' 102) מגילת תענית ג, סנהדרין צא., בראשית רבה סא-ז, יש שדנו בזה דלכאורה כל העבודה היה משום מס וא"כ אינם מחויבים להחזיר שום כסף לבנ"י וכמה ביאורים נאמרו בזה ויתכן לתרץ עפ"י מש"כ רמ"כ בחו"מ שס"ט סעיף ח ע"ש דכל דינא דמלכותא דינא אינו אלא מפני שיכול לצוות להם תן לי או תצאו וכאן רצו לצאת רק הוא עכב ולכן אין מקום לדין זה ואה"נ אותם שלא רצו לצאת מתו ולא קבלו כסף וזהב מהם ודוק 103) חמדת הימים שמות ג-כב 104) פסחים פז:, שם קיט., יעוין גם אדר"נ מא-ט, בראשית מז-כ ע' עץ יוסף פסחים שם דציין המאורע במלכים א-יד 105) רבנו בחיי שמות ג-כב

wealth of a rich man and give it to a poor man, He does so. And if He instructed the Jewish people to appropriate the treasures of the Egyptians, under whatever pretext, the transfer of the wealth is valid and permanent.[106]

Moshe's First Refusal

After Hashem had given Moshe his instructions, Moshe was still reluctant to go to the Jewish people. When he heard Hashem say that Pharaoh would deny the request of the Jews to leave Egypt, he thought he would lose all credibility. After all, the Jews would reason to themselves, is it possible that Pharaoh would reject the messenger of Hashem? Surely, Moshe cannot be the messenger of Hashem. The Jewish people would not accept him.[107]

"The Jewish people will not believe what I have to say," Moshe therefore protested. "They will say that Hashem did not reveal Himself to me."

Moshe had not judged the Jewish people fairly. He should have understood that if Hashem told him the Jewish people would listen to him they would. Moshe had also misunderstood his instructions. He had never been told by Hashem to go to the Jewish people, only to the elders. Therefore, he had unnecessarily suspected the Jewish people of wrongdoing (*chosheid bichsheirim*) and had spoken *lashon hara* about them.[108]

Hashem was displeased with Moshe's refusal to go, for Moshe had already learned the secrets of His Name![109] He now chose to show Moshe signs that his fears about the Jewish people were unfounded.[110]

The Sign of the Staff

"What are you holding in your hand?" Hashem asked Moshe.

"A staff," Moshe replied.

Hashem knows everything, of course, including what was in Moshe's hand. The key word, however, was "holding." By turning the staff into a serpent, Hashem was indicating to Moshe that he was "holding" on to the nature of the slanderous serpent. The serpent (*nachash hakadmoni*) had also spoken *lashon hara* about Hashem.[111]

---

106) אב"ע שמות ג-כב, ע' רש"י ריש התורה דהכל שלו ית' ונותנו אלינו רק דלזמן מסוים הי' הרכוש גדול בידי מצרים 107) שמו"ר ז-ב, רמב"ן וספורנו שמות ד-א 108) רמב"ן שם, ע' שבת צז. ושמו"ר ג-ב, בלקח טוב שמות ד-ו מבואר שהי' מוציא שם רע 109) ילקו"ש קעא 110) שמות ד-ה, שמו"ר ג-יב 111) שמו"ר שם, מדרש אגדה

"The staff that you are holding will deliver My message if you refuse to do so," Hashem told Moshe. "Throw the staff to the ground."

Moshe did so, and the staff turned into a living serpent. The serpent began chasing Moshe, and he fled from it.[112] Moshe did not fear the serpent itself, because he knew full well that sin rather than serpents cause harm and injury. His fear stemmed from the realization that he had sinned. Because of his sin, he was endangered by the serpent.[113]

To add miracle upon miracle, Hashem told Moshe to seize the serpent's tail, the repository of its venom and the most hazardous part of a serpent's body. Moshe seized it, as he had been told to do, and the serpent became a staff in his hand once again.[114]

"This miracle will be a sign for the Jews that the God of their forefathers has indeed appeared to you," Hashem told Moshe. "When the Jews will see an inanimate object brought to life and then returned to its lifeless state, they will recall the six days of creation, when everything was created from nothing, and they will surely trust in you."[115]

The incident with the serpent also lent itself to misinterpretation. The *Midrash* tells about a pagan woman who worshipped serpents who once approached Rabbi Yosi.

"My god is more powerful than yours," she declared.

"Indeed?" said Rabbi Yosi.

"It's really quite simple," the woman replied. "When Hashem first revealed Himself to Moshe, all Moshe did was turn away his face. But when he saw the serpent, he fled!"

"You are such a fool!" Rabbi Yosi replied. "Where could Moshe have gone had he wanted to flee from Hashem. Hashem is everywhere! All Moshe could do was avert his face. Your little serpent, however, is different. All Moshe had to do was run a few steps, and he was out of reach of the serpent."[116]

There were also other reasons, besides the allusion to *lashon hara*, for Hashem's decision to turn the staff into a serpent. Just as a serpent bites and kills its prey, Pharaoh and the Egyptians were "biting" and killing the Jewish people.[117] And like the serpent became a

lifeless staff incapable of causing harm, so would Pharaoh become helpless against the Jewish people.[118*] Just as the original serpent blas-
phemed against Hashem's mastery of the world, Pharaoh would also
blaspheme and claim that he had made the Nile and controlled it.[119] Just
as a serpent coils its tail towards its ears to block out the commands of
its charmer, Pharaoh would also block out the words of Moshe until
after Hashem would display all His miracles and wonders.[120]

The Sign of Tzoraas

Moshe then asked Hashem for a second sign
which he could show to the elders.[121] Hashem
told him to place his left hand inside his bosom,
in his armpit under his coat, and then take it
back out. Moshe did as he was told, and as he took it out, his hand
turned white as snow, fully covered with tzoraas.[122] Hashem then
told Moshe to put his hand back inside his bosom. When he took his
hand out the second time, it had already turned back to its original
state.

The sign of tzoraas manifested the kindness of Hashem in two
ways. First, when the hand was afflicted with tzoraas, it happened as
he was taking it out, at the latest moment possible. When the hand
returned to normal, it happened as soon as he was putting it back, at
the earliest moment possible. Clearly, Hashem is more inclined to
reward than to punish. Second, the hand turned to tzoraas only after
it was withdrawn. This was to avoid any impression that his entire
body had been afflicted by leprosy.[123]

The sign of tzoraas symbolized the relationship between the Jewish people and Pharaoh. Just as contact with a leper contaminates, so
did contact with the impure Pharaoh contaminate the Jewish people.
And just as Moshe was able to return his hand to its pure state, so
too would the Jewish people be returned to their original purity.[124]

The sign was also a reprimand for Moshe. Tzoraas is the symbol
of lashon hara, since the original serpent was stricken with tzoraas
when he spoke lashon hara about his Creator. Moshe was now smitten with tzoraas for speaking lashon hara about the Jewish people.

---

* Some suggest that Hashem specifically told Moshe to grab its tail, which was a
far more dangerous task than grabbing its head. This was meant to show Moshe
that he would have to risk his life in order to redeem the Jews. (Sefer Peh Kadosh)

---

118) שמו"ר ג-יב 119) מדרש הגדול שמות ד-ג, ביחזקאל כט נמשל פרעה לתנין 120) לקח טוב שמות ד-ג 121)
ילקוט מובא בתורה שלמה קסח 122) רבנו אפרים ואב"ע שמות ד-ו 123) שמו"ר ג-יג וברד"ל 124) פרדר"א מ

Furthermore, the concealed manner in which this took place symbolizes the secretive nature of *lashon hara*.[125]

Finally, the sign of *tzoraas* served as an atonement for Moshe. It was a punishment for requesting a second sign, and not being satisfied with the first sign Hashem had given him.[126] The *tzoraas* also served to purify his body, which had been somewhat defiled when Pharaoh's daughter Basya had touched him as an infant.[127]

Having given Moshe both signs, Hashem reassured him that between the two he would convince the Jewish people of the authenticity of his mission.[128]

The Jewish people were already familiar with the connection between *tzoraas* and the harmful practice of *lashon hara* from the example of Pharaoh and Avimelech who were smitten with *tzoraas* because they tried to harm a Jew.[129] Therefore, they would appreciate the symbolism of leprosy. They would also be impressed by the miraculous changing of healthy skin into *tzoraas* and a staff into a serpent.[130] The staff would announce, "I am the staff that once turned into a serpent and became a staff again." The hand would proclaim, "I was the pure hand that became leprous and then pure again."[131]

The Sign of Blood

Hashem then gave Moshe a further sign to show the elders should he find it necessary. He was to go down to the river, take some water and pour it on the dry land. The water would turn to blood. This would be the conclusive sign.[132] The first two signs were connected to Moshe's having spoken *lashon hara*, but the third sign foretold the first plague visited upon the Egyptians.[133] Furthermore, whoever would see this sign, whether Jew or Egyptian, would realize there was no trickery or red dyes involved. They would first see it as water and as it became absorbed into the ground it would turn to blood.[134]

Unlike the other signs in which the miraculous changes were later reversed, the sign of blood was not reversed. It would never turn back into water. One benefit of this was that no one would be able to claim Moshe had employed magic, since the effects of magic are only temporary.[135]

---

125) שמו״ר ג-יג וע״ש בעץ יוסף 126) כציון 124 127) ילקוט ראובני 128) שמות ד-ח ובאב״ע 129) רש״י שמות ד-ח ובשפתי חכמים 130) רבנו בחיי שמות ד-ג 131) לקח טוב שמות ד-ח 132) אב״ע שמות ד-ח (וכו׳) במלכים מבואר שלא הי׳ מים במדבר ולכן לא הי׳ אות זה שם כ״א במצרים 133) לקח טוב שמות ד-ט 134) מדרש הגדול, מלכים שמות ד-ט, אות זה הי׳ בתור מכה ולא רק כדי שיאמינו בו 135) חזקוני שמות ד-ט

There was also a personal significance for Moshe in this differentiation between the other signs and the sign of blood. The first two signs symbolized Moshe's sin of *lashon hara*. The sign of the blood symbolized Moshe's sin at the Mei Merivah, where he struck the rock to bring forth water rather than talk to it as Hashem had commanded; in that episode, blood ran from the rock before it turned to water. The reversal of the changes in the first two signs indicated that Moshe would be forgiven for the *lashon hara* which he had spoken in private. The lack of reversal in the sign of blood indicated that Moshe would not be forgiven for striking the rock in public.[136]

In another sense, the three signs represented the three Avos—Avraham, Yitzchak and Yaakov—and were meant to strengthen the faith of the Jewish people.[137] Moshe's faith was complete, however, and the signs only served to reassure him that he would change the course of history with his staff.[138]

Moshe's Second Refusal

Seven days after Hashem appeared to Moshe at the Sneh, Moshe was still reluctant to serve as Hashem's messenger to the Jewish people.[139]

"Hashem, I beg You," Moshe implored. "Please do not send me as Your messenger. I am not a man of words who is suited for the task of speaking to Pharaoh. I stutter and have difficulty speaking. Punish me if you must, but please don't send me to Pharaoh."[140]

Moshe had suffered from a speech impediment since early childhood, and certainly as an adult, he would be restricted by this handicap.[141] He was unable to pronounce the Hebrew letters ז,ש,ר,ס,ק, with his teeth, and he was unable to pronounce the Hebrew letters ד,ט,ל,נ,ת with his tongue.[142] He therefore felt unqualified for his mission, since it was inappropriate for a prophet to be deficient in speaking ability.[143] He was also no longer fluent in the Egyptian language, having fled Egypt sixty years before, and he felt it would be unfitting for a messenger of Hashem to speak poorly.[144] And perhaps most important of all, Moshe's great humility made it extremely difficult for him to accept a position which would bring him great honor.[145]

---

136) שמו"ר ג-יג ובמהרז"ו (137 שמו"ר ג-יג (138 רמב"ן שמות ד-ג (139 ויקרא רבה יא-ו ובעץ יוסף, ע"ע שמו"ר ג-יד (140 אב"ע שמות ד-י (141 רמב"ן ורבנו בחיי שמות ד-י (142 רבנו בחיי שם (143 שכל טוב, אוה"ח ומלבים שם (144 רשב"ם שם (145 רמב"ן שמות ד-יג

"Do not worry, Moshe," Hashem reassured him. "Who makes the mute? Who gives them speech? Who makes people deaf, blind or gives them sight? It is I, Hashem!" Hashem was the One who gave Moshe the ability to defend himself at his trial before Pharaoh. Hashem was the One who caused Pharaoh to become mute so that he couldn't order Moshe's execution. Hashem was the One who caused Pharaoh's servants and executioner to become deaf to the orders of Moshe's execution. Hashem was the One who caused them to become blind so that they would not see Moshe escape.[146]

Hashem was the One who put the power of speech into the mouth of Adam and enabled him to speak the seventy languages of the world.[147] Hashem could easily have cured Moshe of his speech impediment, but He wanted Moshe to perform miracles and lead the Jewish people in spite of his handicap. Let people see that his success stemmed not from his glib tongue and gilded oratory. Let them see that Hashem chose a humble and handicapped person whose success would clearly stem from the power of Hashem alone.[148]

There was no need for Moshe to worry. Hashem would lead him and guide him at every step of the way. He would be beside him when he went to Pharaoh. He would place words in Moshe's mouth that he could pronounce easily and correctly. And the words would come out like sharp and swift arrows.[149]

Moshe's Third Refusal

Still, Moshe could not reconcile himself to the idea that he would be the leader of the Jewish people. He felt unworthy. "Please Hashem," he begged. "Send whomever You wish. Just do not send me."

Moshe wanted Hashem to choose his older brother Aharon, who had been a prophet for the Jewish people in Egypt. Besides all his other reservations, Moshe did not want to encroach on anything Aharon might think was due to him.[150]

Moshe also felt there were others more worthy of being Hashem's messenger than he was. Furthermore, Moshe saw prophetically that he himself would never enter Eretz Yisrael with the Jewish people, and therefore, he thought that they would be bet-

146) שמו"ר ג-טו, רש"י שמות ד-יא, דברי הימים למשה (147 לקח טוב שמות ד-יא (148 שמו"ר ג-טו, דרשות הר"ן דרוש ה', פענח רזא שמות ד-יא (149 רמב"ן ואב"ע שמות ד-י, ע"ש ברבנו בחיי, שמו"ר ג-טו (150 שמו"ר ג-טז, מדרש אגדה שמות ד-י, ילקו"ש קע"ב

ter off with a leader—such as Yehoshua—who could actually bring them into the land.[151] Another possibility was Pinchas. In the final days of the world, Hashem will send Pinchas, in his identity as Eliyahu Hanavi, to announce the coming of Mashiach to the Jewish people. Why not send Pinchas now? Or perhaps even Mashiach himself![152]

In fact, Moshe argued, Hashem could even send angels to redeem the Jewish people. He had sent angels to save Lot, the nephew of Avraham. Certainly, six hundred thousand Jews were equally deserving of being redeemed by angels from Heaven![153]

Moshe desperately tried to think of other candidates so that Hashem's honor should not be degraded by a messenger with an obvious handicap.[154]

Aharon Is Chosen as Interpreter

For seven full days, Hashem waited for Moshe to accept the mission. He did not want to give anyone an opening to claim that Hashem, being all-powerful, had acted hastily.[155] Three times Hashem had asked Moshe to be His messenger, and three times Moshe had declined. A person is only given three opportunities to reconsider and repent. Moshe had been given his three opportunities, and Hashem chose not to wait any longer.[156]

Hashem was angry with Moshe for his refusal, especially when he had no valid argument other than his own humility.[157] If Moshe had asked that his defect be cured, Hashem would have done so, but now He would not.[158] Hashem considered Moshe's refusal comparable to an idolatrous act, since Moshe could have turned the Jewish people away from idolatry if he had exhibited perfect obedience.[159]

The time for discussions had passed, and Hashem decided to do as Moshe wanted. He would send another messenger to fulfill the role He had offered to Moshe. Yehoshua would lead the Jewish people into Eretz Yisrael.[160] And to take the Jewish people out of Egypt, Hashem chose Aharon, as Moshe had suggested.

---

151) פדר״א מ, מכילתא, רש״י שמות ד-יג 152) תרגום יונתן שמות ד-יג, ילקו״ש פנחס תשע״א, פדר״א מ, לקח טוב 153) שמו״ר ג-טז 154) רמב״ן שמות ד-יג, במדרש הגדול איתא שראה כל דור ודורשיו ור״ע בינתיה ואמר להקב״ה שיתן על ידן התורה ראה גם מנחות כט 155) מכילתא שמות ג-ח 156) שמו״ר ז-ב וע״ש ביפ״ת, עץ יוסף ומהרז״ו, ואע״פ שכבר נענש בצרעת לא היה אלא לשעה 157) ריב״ש שמות ד-יד 158) רבנו בחיי שמות ד-יד 159) אברבנל שמות ד-יד 160) מכילתא ב

Aharon would serve as Moshe's interpreter rather than the primary messenger. Moshe would speak to Aharon in Lashon Hakodesh, like an angel, and Aharon would translate the words into the Egyptian language and repeat it to Pharaoh.[161] Because Moshe had forfeited the role of speaking directly to Pharaoh, Hashem took away the office of Kohein from him and gave it to Aharon's family. Moshe's family would take over the role originally designated for Aharon's family. They would be the Leviim.[162]

Hashem reassured Moshe that Aharon would be more than happy with this arrangement. He would not resent his younger brother being the chosen messenger of God, nor would he be envious of Moshe's honors and prestige. He would welcome his brother to Egypt with open arms and unmitigated joy. He would conscientiously fulfill his role as the spokesman to the Jewish people, and he would accompany Moshe whenever Moshe spoke.[163] He would do all these things joyously, and because of this great joy that would fill his heart, he would be deemed worthy of wearing the *choshen*, the holy breastplate of the Kohein Gadol, over his heart.[164*]

Hashem now instructed Moshe to take his staff—the one with which he performed the signs of Hashem—and go down to Egypt. Should Pharaoh refuse to heed his warnings, he should strike him with the staff, as a master strikes a disobedient slave.

With this staff, Moshe would bring the plagues upon Pharaoh and the Egyptians, overriding the very laws of nature.[165] With this staff, he would split the waters of the sea. With this staff, he would dissipate the strength of Amalek. With this staff, he would bring forth water from the rock. After Moshe's death, this staff would be set aside for King David and then passed down to all the kings of Yehudah until the destruction of the Beis Hamikdash. This staff will reappear in the hands of Mashiach, and he will use it to destroy the wicked nations of the world.[166]

Hashem had chosen Moshe over Aharon because of his greater level of *kedushah* and *nevuah*. Hashem had wanted Moshe to be His

---

* Aharon had every reason to be upset. He had enjoyed the gift of prophecy long before Moshe arrived in Egypt. Yet Aharon was not jealous. (Rashi)

---

161) שמו"ר ג-יז, מכילתא שם, רש"י שמות ד-טז 162) שמו"ר שם, זבחים קב. 163) רמב"ן שמות ד-יד והלאה 164) שבת קלט. 165) שמו"ר ג-יז, תנחומא וארא ט, ספורנו שמות ד-יז 166) ילקו"ש חקת תשס"ג וע' שכל טוב

sole messenger, because the message would have been more direct. Now, with the inclusion of Aharon as a second intermediary, the message would be somewhat diluted. The Jewish people would hear it from Aharon only after he would hear it from Moshe, who would hear it directly from Hashem. Furthermore, it would have been more impressive to have Moshe carry the message directly in spite of his speech impediment.[167]

Nevertheless, Aharon was a more than worthy choice for his role. Like Moshe, Aharon was the son of the holy Amram and a prophet in his own right, a distinguished member of Shevet Levi, the only tribe that was unswervingly loyal to Hashem throughout all the years in Egypt.[168]

ד-י. מלבים שמות ד-יז (168 ד-יד מלבים שמות (167 ד-יז.

The Mission Begins

8

The mission to redeem the Jewish people from Egypt now became the dominant feature of Moshe's life. He would have gone straight to Egypt from the wilderness, but he had promised Yisro not to leave Midian without his permission and not to return to Egypt.[1]

Moshe hurried back to Midian to obtain Yisro's release from his vows. A dense cloud traveled over his head to indicate that Hashem had annulled his vows to Yisro, but Moshe still sought Yisro's permission. Yisro had treated him with kindness, and Moshe felt a debt of gratitude that obligated him to ask Yisro's permission before he left for Egypt.[2]

Upon his return to Midian, Moshe was welcomed by the news of a newborn son who had been born while he was away at the Sneh in the wilderness. Unfortunately, it was not feasible to

1) שמו"ר ד-א, שם א-כג, תנחומא שמות כ, רש"י נדרים סה., ע"ע שו"ת המיוחסות לרמב"ן סימן רנ"ה 2) לקח טוב שמות ד-יח, נדרים שם

perform a *bris milah* for the new child. The mission to redeem the Jewish people from Egypt took priority over everything else. There was no time for personal considerations. Moshe did, however, give his newborn a name. He called him Eliezer, out of gratitude to Hashem for saving him from the sword of Pharaoh.[3] Moshe gathered his family and prepared to leave, but first he had to speak to Yisro.

"I have decided that it is time for me to leave," Moshe told Yisro. "I appreciate everything you have done for me, and I will always be grateful. A long time ago, I promised I would not leave without asking your permission. I ask for that permission now."

Yisro nodded. "You have my permission, Moshe.[4] But tell me, where do you intend to go?"

"To Egypt," Moshe replied. "I want to see if my Jewish brethren have survived the dreadful oppression of the Egyptians."

"I don't understand," said Yisro. "The Jews are trapped in Egypt and would give anything to leave, and you want to bring your wife and children *into* Egypt?"

"I am convinced that the Jewish people will soon leave Egypt," Moshe replied. "They will go to Mount Sinai and receive the Torah from Hashem. If we don't go to Egypt now, we will not share in this great experience. I want my children to stand at Mount Sinai and hear Hashem declare, 'I am God your Lord.' I cannot deprive them of this."

"I understand," said Yisro. "I give you my permission and release you from your vow. You have my blessings. Go in peace. But I would still advise you not to return to Egypt. Do not forget that you are wanted for murder in Egypt. Do not forget that in Egypt you are still a fugitive."[5]

Hashem, however, reassured Moshe that he had nothing to fear in Egypt,[6] since the people that wanted him dead had already died themselves. Included among these were the family of the slain Egyptian as well as Dassan and Aviram, who had informed on Moshe to Pharaoh. Dassan and Aviram had not actually died, but they had been so impoverished that they were as good as dead.[7] They would

---

3) שמות יח-ד, רמב״ן שמות ד-כ 4) לקח טוב שם 5) שמו״ר ד-ד, שו״ת המיוחסות לרמב״ן שם, רמב״ן על אתר אי׳ שהאמינו בו יותר בגלל שהביא בני ביתו אתו ועיין במדרש הגדול שמות ד-יח דטעמא שלא גלה ליתרו הסיבה האמיתית היתה כי באמת לא אמר ד׳ שיגאלם בודאי אלא התנה עמו אם ישובו אליו ית׳ אז יגאלם וירא משה אולי לא יתעוררו לשוב כדבעי 6) שו״ת המיוחסות לרמב״ן שם 7) נדרים סד:, ר״ן שם ז:, תוס׳ ע״ז ה.. עיין אב״ע לקח טוב, בסנהדרין ק: דדתן ואבירם נבלעו באדמה עם עדת קרח

sit at the city gates and beg passersby for a few pitiful coins.[8] Indeed, ever since they had slandered Moshe to Pharaoh, they had lost all their wealth and status and were now totally ineffective.[9] There was, therefore, no longer any danger to Moshe in returning to Egypt, and he could feel confident that he was not violating the spirit of his vow to Yisro to avoid the dangers of Egypt.[10]

At the same moment Hashem was speaking to Moshe in Midian, telling him to return to Egypt, He was also speaking to Aharon in Egypt, telling him to go out towards Moshe in the desert. Thus, Hashem's voice was heard in two distant places saying two different things at the exact same time, and no one in between could hear a thing.[11]

The wheels had now been set in motion.

Departure from Midian

Moshe took his wife Tziporah and their two children, Gershom and Eliezer, and left Midian. They set out on the journey to Egypt riding upon a donkey. This was no ordinary donkey. It dated back to the six days of creation, and in the thousands of years since its creation, it had enjoyed an illustrious career for a donkey. Avraham had ridden upon this donkey to the Akeidah. Yitzchak inherited the donkey and passed it on to Yaakov, from whom it passed on to Levi, and then to Kehas, and then to Amram, Moshe's father. In the end of days, Mashiach will come riding upon this selfsame donkey to redeem the Jewish people from exile.[12] Moshe was in possession of this donkey in Egypt, and when he fled for his life, he took this donkey with him.[13]

As Moshe rode upon the donkey, he carried in his hand the wondrous staff he had drawn from Yisro's garden. The staff weighed over seven hundred pounds, but miraculously, it carried itself. All Moshe had to do was grip it in his hands.[14]

Along the way, Hashem reminded Moshe of the miracles he could perform through the staff in his hand, including the ten plagues whose symbol was etched into the wood of the staff. There was no need to fear Pharaoh, Hashem reassured Moshe.[15] Hashem

8) מדרש חופת אליהו באוצר המדרשים קעא   9) שפתי כהן קרח טז-יג 10) לקח טוב שמות ד-יט, רש"י ר"ן ונמו"י נדרים שם   11) שמו"ר ה-ט וביפ"ת   12) פרדר"א לא וברד"ל שם דהיא החמור שדברה אל בלעם 13) במדרש תלפיות אות ח'   מסופר עוד שאצטגניני פרעה הגידו לו שהגואל ישראל ירכוב על אותה חמור וירא משה אולי יקחוה ממנו ורק עתה ששמע שכבר מתו אויביו נסע עלה   14) שמות ד-כ, שכל טוב שם, בזוה"ק מובא שמטה זו עמדה אצל הלוחות בקודש הקדשים 15) שמו"ר ה-ו, לקח טוב שמות ד-כא

Himself would harden Pharaoh's heart and keep him alive until all ten plagues would be visited upon Egypt.[16] After each plague, Pharaoh would delude himself into thinking the worst was over, and thus, each new plague would strike him with the full force of an unexpected blow.[17]

Hashem instructed Moshe to approach Pharaoh fearlessly and tell him, "Hashem considers the Jewish people a great nation.[18] They are very dear to Him. He considers them His firstborn child, so much does He love them.[19] There may be hundreds of thousands of Jews, but each one is as beloved to Hashem as an only child.[20] They are the children of Yaakov, who took the birthright from Eisav, and endowed his descendants forever with the rights of the firstborn.[21] Therefore, Hashem commands you, Pharaoh, to release His firstborn from bondage so they can serve Him.[22]

"Do not think He has allowed you to cause them so much pain and suffering because He does not care for them. He has only done it to condition their hearts, as a father trains his beloved son.[23] Hashem will avenge Himself upon you, Pharaoh. Because you cast His firstborn into the river, Hashem will kill your firstborn and the firstborns of the Egyptians. This is your last chance to save yourself, Pharaoh. Let the Jewish people out of Egypt right now, and your firstborn children will be spared."[24]

This was the message Moshe was to carry to Pharaoh, and he was to carry it personally. The palace gates were guarded by two ferocious lions, and anyone passing them would be frightened to death—literally. Only Moshe would be able to pass them safely. Indeed, the lions would lap at his heels like tame dogs, much to the astonishment of Pharaoh.[25]

The Bris of Eliezer

The day Moshe left Midian for Egypt with his family was the eighth day after the birth of his second son. Because of the urgency of his mission, Moshe could not delay his journey for even the short time necessary to perform the *bris* of his son.[26]

---

16) חזקוני שמות ד-כא 17) מלבים שמות ד-כב, וע׳ רמב״ן ז-ג דהי׳ עפ״י שורת הדין 18) דברים לג-יז ובפרש״י
19) שבת לא. 20) אגדת בראשית ה-א 21) שמו״ר ה-ז, שם טו-כז, בחזקוני שמות ד-כב כתוב דעד שהתחיל אהרן
לעבוד במשכן הי׳ מוטל עניני העבודה על הבכורים 22) שבת לא. 23) רבנו בחיי שמות ד-כב וע׳ לעיל בהקדמה 24)
שמו״ר ה-ז, צרור המור סוף וארא, בשמו״ר טו-כז, איתא שנגזר עליו ככה על שעבר על איסור עבודה בבכור יען
וכנס״י נקראת בני בכורי ישראל 25) לקח טוב שמות ד-כב 26) רמב״ן שמות ד-כה, רש״י נדרים לב. ויקרא רבה טו-

Later that day, Moshe and his family stopped at an inn on the road to Egypt. The angel Gavriel came down from Heaven and wanted to kill Moshe.

"You have not given your son a bris milah," the angel accused him. "You have violated the covenant of Avraham!"[27]

The true purpose of the coming of the angel was to save Moshe rather than to kill him. Had the day passed without Moshe giving his son a bris, it would have been the first transgression of Moshe's whole life.[28]

The angel took the form of a snake. It swallowed Moshe from the top down and from the bottom up to the place of the milah.

Tziporah immediately understood the meaning of this action. The angel had swallowed all of Moshe's body except his milah to indicate that Moshe had failed to give his newborn son a bris milah.[29] All Moshe's merits could not protect him from the consequences of his failure to fulfill this great mitzvah.[30]

Tziporah took a sharp stone (or knife) and gave her child a bris, since her husband Moshe was incapable of doing it himself.[31] In her haste, she actually cut Eliezer on his foot.

When the bris of her son Eliezer was completed, she threw the foreskin towards Moshe and the angel.

"Here, I have given my son a bris!" she exclaimed. "Because of this bris, my husband was almost killed!"[32]

"Spit him out!" a voice from Heaven suddenly cried out.

The angel released Moshe's top half, but still held on to his bottom half.[33] Seeing this, Tziporah realized she had not completed the mitzvah. She had done the milah, the circumcision, but she had not done the priah, the uncovering. Quickly, she uncovered the milah, bringing the mitzvah to its complete fulfillment. As soon as she was finished, the angel released Moshe completely.[34] The mitzvah of bris milah was fulfilled, and the danger passed.

One has to wonder about this enigmatic episode. Had Moshe done something wrong in postponing the bris of his son until he arrived in Egypt? And if not, why was his life threatened?

Moshe had in fact made the correct decision, because Hashem's

---

כז 27) זוה"ק ח"א צג., רש"י שמות ד-כד, ספר הישר 28) מלבים שמות ד-כד 29) שמו"ר ה-ח, רש"י שמות ד-כד
30) נדרים לא: 31) רד"ק לקח טוב ואב"ע ד-כה, ע' רמב"ם הל' מילה ב-א ובחזקוני על אתר דלכתחלה נכון למול
עם מתחית אולם בשעת הדחק כשר גם ע"י אבן 32) ירושלמי נדרים ג-ט, קרבן עדה ועי' מנחה בלולה דכמעט
שקצצה את רגליו 33) אלשיך שמות ד-כה 34) רבנו בחיי שמות שם, ע' רש"י ע"ז כז.

commandment to go to Egypt and redeem the Jewish people super-
seded all else. A child who has just had a *bris milah* would not be
considered strong enough to go on a long journey for three days,
and therefore, if Moshe had given his child a *bris*, his journey would
have been delayed. However, when Moshe stopped at the inn, he
should have given his child a *bris* right then and there.[35] The inn
was just a short distance from Egypt, and the child could have traveled into Egypt without being endangered.[36]

In general, someone who is doing a *mitzvah* is exempt from
doing other *mitzvos*. In Moshe's case, however, his involvement in
the *mitzvah* of his mission to the Jewish people did not exempt him
from his obligation to give his child a *bris*. Stopping at the inn had
interrupted that *mitzvah*, and he was immediately required to give
his son a *bris*.[37]

A lesser person than Moshe would not have been punished so
quickly for such an omission under these circumstances. But Moshe
was a *tzaddik*, and Hashem judges *tzaddikim* by the strictest stan-
dards and demands perfection from them.[38]

Aharon and Moshe Meet

As Moshe approached Egypt, his brother
Aharon was coming out to the desert to meet
Moshe, as Hashem had commanded him to
do.[39] The two brothers met at Mount Sinai in
the desert that lies between Midian and Egypt.

It was an emotional meeting, and the two brothers hugged and
kissed each other. So many years had passed since they had been separated from each other, but now they were at last reunited, bound
together not only by their brotherly love but by their common mission to redeem the Jewish people from Egypt. Moshe was to be the
prophet of Hashem and the future leader of the Jewish people, and he
would become a Levi. Aharon had been the prophet for the Jewish
people for the past eighty years and now he was to be the spokesman
for his brother. He would become a Kohein. Each brother
was more than content with his own role and had not the slightest
tinge of jealousy for the role his brother would play.[40]

35) נדרים לב. 36) ר״ן שם, שפתי חכמים ד-כד, ע׳ תרגום יונתן וחזקוני שם ובספר הישר ויש דיון אי הי׳ אליעזר
או גרשום י״מ שהי׳ פטור מכח הבטחתו ליתרו וי״מ דכשיצא ממדין יצא מרשות חותנו ושפיר הי׳ מחויב
37) אוה״ח שמות ד-כד 38) מנחה בלולה שמות שם 39) שמו״ר ה-ט, לקח טוב שמות ד-כז 40) רמב״ן שמות ד-כז,
שמו״ר ה-י ובמהרז״ו ויש להעיר על הריחוק דכאן כתיב שהי׳ מהלך יום א׳ ואלו פגישתם הי׳ בסיני מהלך ג׳ ימים
ויש ליישב

Unlike the earlier sets of brothers mentioned in the Torah—Kayin and Hevel, Yishmael and Yitzchak, Eisav and Yaakov, Yosef and his brothers—there was only love and harmony between Moshe and Aharon, the two brothers who shared the responsibility for the destiny of the Jewish people.[41]

"Where have you been for all these years?" Aharon asked Moshe after their first embrace.

"In Midian," Moshe replied.

"And who are the woman and children traveling with you?" Aharon asked.

"They are my wife and children," Moshe said.

"Where are you taking them?" Aharon asked.

"To Egypt," Moshe replied.

"It is bad enough that there is already so much Jewish misery in Egypt," Aharon replied. "Do you want to create even more Jewish misery by bringing your family into Egypt?"

Aharon's opinion convinced Moshe where Yisro's had not. Moshe now decided to send his family back to Midian.[42]

As the two brothers continued alone into Egypt, Moshe told Aharon all the details of his mission. He described the experience of the Sneh and the revelations he had received there. He also told Aharon that he would be the spokesman to the Jewish people.[43]

The Elders Investigate

As soon as they arrived in Egypt, Moshe and Aharon gathered all the elders of the Jewish people.[44]* Aharon told the elders about the mission which Hashem had entrusted to Moshe, and he showed the elders the miraculous signs.

"Hashem remembers you," Aharon said. "He has instructed us to tell you that *pakod pakadeti*, He remembers."

The elders were very impressed with the display of the miraculous signs, and the mention of the words *pakod pakadeti* dispelled almost all

---

* It is logical to assume that this took place on Shabbos when all the Jewish people were free from work. (*Chasam Sofer al Hatorah*, Va'era 6: 9)

---

41) תנחומא שמות כז (42 מכילתא יתרו א, דעת זקנים שמות ד-כד, על אף שהיו לויים, רצה שלא ייראו צרת אחיהם במצרים ומעונין דכשיתרו צוה לו כן לא שמע (43 רמב"ן רבנו בחיי ומלבים שמות ד-כח, וע' שמו"ר ה- יא (44 לקח טוב שמות ד-כט

their doubts.[45] Nevertheless, they were afraid to commit themselves. They still had painful memories of the tragedy that had befallen the tribe of Ephraim thirty years before, when they had tried to leave Egypt prematurely.[46]

The elders decided to seek the advice of the only surviving child of the sons of Yaakov. It was a very old woman named Serach, and she was the daughter of Asher. She was the closest link to the early generations who had known the secrets of the promise of redemption. Perhaps she would be able to make an accurate evaluation of the claims of Moshe and Aharon.

"A man has come to us claiming to be the messenger of Hashem," they told her. "We have been shown miraculous signs to prove the truth of his words."

"That means nothing," Serach replied.

"He mentioned the words *pakod pakadeti*," the elders continued.

The effect of these words on Serach was electric. "Yes, he is indeed the redeemer!" she exclaimed. "I heard it from my father, who heard it from his brother Yosef, who had it in a tradition dating back to Avraham, that the one who mentions the phrase *pakod pakadeti* will redeem the Jewish people from Egypt."[47]

Still, the elders were not completely satisfied, and they continued to discuss the matter among themselves.

"Perhaps Moshe heard it from his father Amram, not from Hashem," they wondered. "Perhaps he is not really the redeemer."

"No, that cannot be," one of them said. "Moshe left his father's house at a very young age, and he returned to Egypt just recently, long after his father had passed away. He could only have heard this secret sign from his father before he left Egypt, and it is unlikely Amram would have revealed it to Moshe at such a young age. Besides, no one would dare use this phrase unless he was telling the truth. Moshe must indeed be the true redeemer."[48]

This final argument convinced the elders. They bowed and prostrated themselves before Hashem and poured out their gratitude for the good tidings they had received.[49] The long-awaited redemption had finally begun.

---

45) לקח טוב שמות ד-לא, אב"ע ומלבים שמות ד-לא ילקוט ראובני כו 46) פרדר"א מח וברד"ל, ילקוט ראובני כו 47) פרדר"א מח, כתב שרק אמר אות פ' פעמים 48) שמו"ר ה-ב ביפ"ת וברד"ל, ע"ע שמו"ר טו-כז ורמב"ן שמות ג-יח, ויש שהקשו שם המפורש ידע ופקד יפקד לא ידע אתמהה וי"ל 49) לקח טוב שמות ד-לא

The First Confrontation

9

Once the elders were convinced that Moshe was the true messenger of Hashem,[1] a delegation comprised of Moshe, Aharon and the elders immediately set off for the royal palace.[2] As the delegation neared the palace, however, dread of the forthcoming confrontation overcame the elders, and one by one, they started to slip away. By the time the delegation reached the entrance of the palace, only a few of the elders still accompanied Moshe and Aharon. Moshe led the way, and the others followed.[3]

As they entered the palace, the remaining members of the delegation were greeted with a terrifying sight. Numerous doors opened in each direction, and each doorway was guarded by a large contingent of heavily armed warriors.[4] In the distance was an enormous gateway leading into the royal throne room. Intense flames illuminated

---

1) אב״ע שמות ה-א 2) מדרש הגדול שמות שם 3) שמו״ר ה-יד 4) ילקו״ש קעה

this gateway with an eerie glow that chilled the blood of all who beheld it. On either side of this sinister gateway hung the broken and mutilated bodies of slain Jews.

Horrified by this gruesome spectacle, the remaining elders shrunk back. "What a dreadful sight!" they cried out. "Oh, our poor fallen brothers! Better that we should remain slaves than to witness such a sight." With that, they fled from the palace, leaving Moshe and Aharon alone.[5] The elders experienced the consequences of their faintheartedness when the Jewish people received the Torah at Mount Sinai. The elders had to remain at the foot of the mountain, while Moshe and Aharon were allowed to ascend. Moshe, having led the way into the palace, was allowed to ascend to the very top.[6]

As Moshe and Aharon continued toward Pharaoh's throne room, they were accosted by the savage roars of two young lions chained to the gates. Other ferocious beasts also strained at their leashes, snarling at all who came near as if to rip them apart limb from limb. Sorcerers stood beside these beasts, and when they spoke the appropriate words, the beasts became pacified and allowed a visitor to pass. The lion keepers would then release the lions to stand menacingly beside the guest as he spoke to Pharaoh.[7]

When the sorcerer Bilam saw Moshe and Aharon enter the palace, he left instructions for the lion keepers to unchain the crazed lions and place them directly in front of Moshe and Aharon. Undaunted, Moshe lifted his staff over the young lions, and they froze in their tracks. The angel Gavriel came down and transformed the lions into harmless creatures who lapped at Moshe's heels happily like playful dogs. The angel Gavriel also immobilized the fierce warriors who blocked their way, allowing Moshe and Aharon to pass unmolested into Pharaoh's throne room.[8]

In Pharaoh's Throne Room

The throne room was in turmoil when Moshe and Aharon entered. Pharaoh was in a mad rage over the failure of his guards to prevent the two brothers from entering. He ordered some of the guards executed, some of them flogged and some of them expelled from the royal service.[9]

---

5) כציון 2 (6 ריב״א ורע״ב שם (7 ילקו״ש קעו, ספר הישר, דברי הימים למשה (8 ילקו״ש קע״ה, דברי הימים למשה (9 ילקו״ש שם

Moshe and Aharon planted themselves in front of Pharaoh and, without any introductions or greetings, came straight to the point.

"Hashem, the Lord of the Jews, sent us to you," Moshe said through his spokesman Aharon. "He commands you to send His nation Yisrael out of Egypt so that they can serve Him."

Pharaoh stared at Moshe in astonishment and disbelief. Clearly, this was a serious matter, something that could not be dismissed out of hand. Pharaoh needed time to reflect on this strange announcement and formulate an appropriate response.

"Come back tomorrow," he finally said. "I will give you my reply tomorrow."

Without another word, Moshe and Aharon turned and walked away.

As soon as the two brothers had left, Pharaoh called together his sorcerers and advisors, including Bilam and his sons Ianus and Iambrus.

"Gentlemen, we have a problem," Pharaoh said. "Those two Jews that were just here seem to be prophets of the Jewish God. They came to inform me that the Jewish God commands me to release the Jews so they can serve Him."

"I don't understand how they got past the lions," Bilam commented. "I never said the words that pacify them. Why weren't they ripped apart?"

"I don't understand it either," Pharaoh answered. "All I know is that the lions came to them like playful puppies wagging their tails for their master."

"Your majesty, if I may be so bold," Bilam said, "I feel there is really no need to be overly concerned. These Jews are probably magicians, just like us. We will test them and see what they are worth."

"Excellent idea!" Pharaoh cried out, somewhat relieved by Bilam's confidence. "Bring those Jews back to me. I want the Jewish prophets back here at once!"[10]

The day on which this took place was one of the most important days of Pharaoh's life, a day designated for an international display of subservience to the mighty ruler of the Egyptian kingdom. Kings and ambassadors gathered from the distant corners of the civilized world to pay homage to Pharaoh and present him with ceremonial

---

10) ספר הישר, דברי הימים למשה, וראה ילקו"ש שם ואילך

crowns and other precious gifts.[11]* They also brought their idols to greet the great Egyptian king and pray for his welfare. The display was so impressive that Pharaoh was universally acknowledged as the premier monarch of his time.[12]

Throughout the day, Pharaoh sat on his throne, receiving honors and gifts with the nonchalance of a person who believes he deserves everything he is getting—and much more. All around him sat noblemen, wise men, wizards, scribes and men of many talents who spoke the seventy languages. Tables groaned under the weight of mountains of scrolls containing the writings and accumulated knowledge of the nations of the world. The room was abuzz with the sophisticated conversations of scholars and princes and aglitter with the trappings of the highest royalty in the world.

Suddenly, the commotion came to a halt, and an awed silence took its place. All mouths were agape, and all eyes were riveted on a remarkable sight. Two elderly men had appeared in their midst. They were straight and tall, like cedars. Their eyes shone like glowing stars, and their faces were as radiant as the noonday sun. They seemed like heavenly angels who had come among mortal men.[13]

A guard who had come in beside them bowed down to Pharaoh. "Your majesty," he said. "I have done as you commanded. Here are the two Jews who were here earlier. I have brought them back to you."

When Moshe and Aharon began to speak, their words scorched the assembled dignitaries like tongues of fire and filled them with profound reverence. Their pens, scrolls and papyrus fell from their nerveless fingers, and they all kneeled in deference to Moshe and Aharon.[14]

At that point, Pharaoh decided to go off and relieve himself. As soon as he closed the door behind him, however, he was attacked by twelve vicious rats, and within moments, his entire body was covered with rat bites. Pharaoh screamed in pain and terror, to the utter consternation of all the assembled dignitaries. After a period of anxious waiting, Pharaoh returned to the throne room, angry and sullen.[15] He resumed his place without explanation, but his heart

---

* Some suggest it was his birthday.

11) שמו"ר ה-יד ובמתנ"כ 12) רד"ל על שמו"ר ה-יד, תנחומא וארא ה ובעץ יוסף 13) אותיות דר"ע אות ק'

14) שם 15) ילקו"ש וארא קפ"א

was no longer in the festivities. The thought of rats pervaded his consciousness, and he resolved never again to use the facilities in the palace. Whenever he needed to relieve himself, he would go in secret to the Nile River, and he would represent himself to the public as a god who had no need to relieve himself.[16]

Pharaoh's mood was not improved by the presence of Moshe and Aharon. They stood before him proud and defiant, without any signs of servility, their hands empty of gifts for the king. They did not bow to the king or even offer him a greeting.[17]

"Tell me who you are," Pharaoh grumbled.

"We are the messengers of Hashem," Moshe replied through his spokesman Aharon.

"What do you want?" asked Pharaoh.

"I have come with a message from Hashem," Moshe said. "He commands you to send His nation, the Jewish people, out of Egypt so that they can serve Him in the desert."

"Why do you pester me?" said Pharaoh impatiently. "Who is Hashem that I should listen to Him? Have you come to me with gifts as tribute like all the others here?[18] No! You come to me with words! Wait here! I will investigate your ridiculous claims."

Pharaoh left the throne room and went to the innermost chamber of the palace where he kept all the known idols of the world and his records of the different idolatrous cults that existed at the time. He searched long and hard among all the idols and records, but he found nothing. Angrier than ever, he stormed back to his throne room.

"Nothing!" he yelled. "No mention! I have checked all my records, and nowhere is Hashem's Name mentioned.[19] What kind of god is this? Is He strong? Young? Old? How many kingdoms are under His control? How big are His armies?"[20]

"Fool!" Moshe thundered back at him. "Where did you look for Him? In your gallery of dead idols? Hashem is alive, and He rules the entire world. He created the world. He was there before it existed, and He will be there after it ceases to exist. He covers the mountains with grass, and He makes the rain. He responds to the silent pleas of the animals. He forms the child in the womb.[21] He created

16) שפתי כהן וארא ח-טז 17) שמו"ר ה-יד וברד"ל 18) מדרש ויושע בפסוק וירא 19) שמו"ר ה-יד וברד"ל
20) אותיות דר"ע שם, שמו"ר שם 21) שמו"ר ה-יד, תנחומא וארא ה

the winds and the souls of people with the utterance of His Lips. He created the entire universe, and sustains it! He makes peace between fire and water. His bow and arrow is flame and fire. His spear is the torch. His sword is the lightning; He needs no metal. That is who Hashem is!"

"This is total nonsense," Pharaoh replied. "These things were all done by none other than myself. Me! The great Pharaoh! Look around you. Do you see all who came to pay homage to me? I am the ruler of the world. I made the Nile. The Nile belongs to me. It is the work of my hands. I don't need all these other powers you speak about. Why do I need lightning? Why do I need rain? I have made the Nile, and it alone serves all my needs. It slakes the thirst of the soil of Egypt. Look at me! I, Pharaoh, am a god! With my own might and wisdom I created this empire. I don't need anyone or anything!

"Why do you come here with your foolish stories? No one here has heard of your Hashem. My wise men know of no such god. Do you understand me? I never heard of this Hashem. Not Him! Not His power! Nothing! Listen closely. I absolutely refuse to release the Jewish people.[22] Who does He think He is trying to take my slaves from me?[23]

"You can't fool me! I know all the stories the Jews tell each other about their God. I've heard the story about how Avimelech took Sarah, and how your God revealed Himself to Avimelech that night. You hear? One person gets into trouble for one night, and already He revealed Himself. Well, I've had the Jews in my power for two hundred years, and not just one person but an entire nation. Don't you think He should have revealed Himself during all this time? And you come and claim to be messengers. Hah! What nonsense! If He wants to say something to me, let Him say it to me directly!"[24]

Hashem took note of Pharaoh's arrogance and how greatly he differed from the Jewish people. When Jews are raised to prominence, they become more humble, while a gentile like Pharaoh has the audacity to declare, *"Mi Hashem?* Who is Hashem?"[25] But his own words would come back to haunt him. The numerical value of the word *Mi* is fifty—the number of plagues that would afflict the Egyptians in the sea.[26] Hashem would show him that the waters of

---

22) שמות ה-ב וע' מפרשי תנ״ך יחזקאל כט 23) רשב״ם שמות ה-ב 24) מושב זקנים שם 25) חולין פט. 26) שמו״ר
ה-יד

the Nile he claimed to have created would turn to blood.[27]

Pharaoh's ingratitude brought him to this disgraceful state. He had acted as if he did not know Yosef so that he could enslave Yosef's people. As a result, he had fallen to the lowest level yet, actually denying the Creator of the Universe.[28]

Moshe and Aharon ignored Pharaoh's tirade. "The God of the Jews has sent us to you," they continued. "He asks you to allow the Jews to go on a three-day journey into the desert, where we can serve Him, so that we will not fall victim to plague or the sword. The Jews are called Ivrim, because they come from the other side of the river. We do not belong in Egypt, and we are not your slaves. We are Hashem's people.[29] Since the days we left Canaan, we have not sacrificed to Hashem, and now that He wants us to serve Him, we must obey.[30] We cannot sacrifice sheep to Him here in Egypt, because the Egyptians worship sheep and will not allow us to do it.[31] Surely, they will stone us.[32] We have no choice but to go out to the desert."

In spite of Pharaoh's villainy, Moshe and Aharon treated him with the respect due to a king. The mention of "plague" and "the sword" was really an oblique reference to the fate that would befall Pharaoh if he refused to let the Jewish people go.[33]

"Listen to me closely, Moshe and Aharon," Pharaoh responded. "Do you want to help your people or hurt them? Why do you want to make trouble for the Jews? They have work to do, and your coming here will only distract them from their responsibilities. Who knows? When they hear what you have to say, they may think they are free from work, and nothing is further from the truth![34] Just be thankful that you yourselves, as members of Shevet Levi, are exempt from work.[35] If you have nothing to do with yourselves, why don't you just go home? I'm sure you can find something to occupy yourselves with there.[36]

"But wait," Pharaoh continued, "I have an excellent idea. Idleness seems to have led you into mischief. I think it would be best to end the exemption of Shevet Levi from work. From now on, all of you Leviim will be required to work—just like the rest of the Jews. Maybe that will cure your delusions of redemption.[37]

---

27) רבנו בחיי שמות ה-ב 28) לקח טוב שמות א-ח 29) שמות ה-ג וברשב״ם 30) שכל טוב שמות ה-ג 31) דעת זקנים שמות ה-ג 32) ריב״א שמות ה-ג, במעם לעז בא יא-א-ב איתא דוודאי הי׳ כוונתו לעולמים ואף פעם לא אמר מפורש שלא יוסיפו על ל ג׳ ימים רק שכך הבין פרעה מסתמא וע׳ בפנים אחרת באמת ליעקב 33) רש״י שמות ה-ג 34) שם ה-ד 35) חזקוני שמות שם 36) רש״י שם, שמו״ר ה-טו 37) מלבים שם

"But then again," Pharaoh continued reflectively, more to him-self than to anyone else, "maybe it is not such a good idea after all. You Leviim are all rabble-rousers and troublemakers. I think it would probably be best to keep you out of the fields where the Jew-ish laborers are. I don't need you poisoning their minds with these ridiculous notions of freedom and redemption. I think it would be better just keeping the Leviim as they are.[38]

"Ahem, now where was I? Oh yes. Now listen to me, Moshe and Aharon. I want you to put a stop to this foolishness. I mean, I might have been more understanding if you had asked for one or two thousand of your people to go into the desert. But six hundred thousand! And for how long? A three-day journey? That means three days out, one day in the desert, and three days back. A full week! You must be joking! I tell you, stop this foolishness, and let the Jews go back to work.[39] Now, get out of my sight!"[40]

38) שם 39) שמו"ר ה-יז, שפתי כהן שמות ה-ה 40) ספר הישר

Pharaoh Retaliates

10

The meeting with Moshe and Aharon made a strong impression on Pharaoh, but it did not have the desired effect. In fact, it had quite the opposite effect. Moshe's unsuccessful demands for freedom had awakened a strong sense of apprehension in Pharaoh. All the inflammatory talk about freedom and redemption could only cause serious labor unrest throughout Egypt. Pharaoh's reaction was typical. The greatest danger of revolt, he felt, was during the spare time of the Jewish laborers. Therefore, the only solution was to make sure they had no spare time. Immediately, he issued a decree increasing the work load of the Jews.[1] "This would teach Moshe and Aharon to demand freedom for the Jews!," he thought angrily. This would teach them not to defy the glorious king of Egypt![2]

The new decree involved the gathering of raw

---

1) שפתי כהן סוף שמות עפ"י שמו"ר ה-יח 2) דברי הימים למשה

materials for the brickmaking process. The established system had been for cut straw to be delivered from the government storehouses to the laborers in the field, where it would be used to manufacture bricks.[3] A new decree was issued to the Egyptian taskmasters, telling them that the Jewish police under them would now be put to work.[4]

"Do not continue to give them straw to make bricks, as you did yesterday and the day before," Pharaoh commanded his officials. "Let them collect the straw themselves[5] but without failing to fulfill their regular quotas. Make them work harder than ever, because they are becoming lazy.[6] Their idleness leads them to think about frivolous matters,[7] and then they cry out, 'Let us go sacrifice to our God.'[8] It is no wonder they want to sacrifice to their God. They want to thank Him for giving them such an easy life. Well, my esteemed officials of the ministry of labor, it is your job to make them feel like slaves once again. Show those lazy Jews what hard work really means, and then we'll see if they have the energy to waste on such idle thoughts as sacrificing to their God.[9] If you work them hard enough they won't be interested in all these fanciful tales about freedom and redemption."[10]

In order to accommodate the increased work load, Pharaoh ordered the cancellation of Shabbos as a day of rest. Ever since Moshe had instituted the policy of resting on Shabbos, the Jewish people had drawn their spiritual nourishment from those precious moments of serenity. Sitting together and reading from scrolls entrusted to them by Amram that foretold their future redemption, they had felt a strong sense of hope and closeness to Hashem. These days would now be spent gathering straw under the watchful eyes and the snapping whips of their Egyptian taskmasters.[11]

The nights, when they would rest their weary bones, would now be given over to intense labor.[12] Even the noontime break for a paltry meal and a few moments of stolen leisure would now be curtailed. The Jewish laborers would only be allowed to eat while they were working. Pharaoh would see to it that the Jews would have no opportunities for idleness and thoughts of rebellion.[13] Although he had no need for this additional labor, he derived much satisfaction from the pain and suffering he was causing the Jewish people.[14]

---

3) מלבים שמות ה-ו 4) רש"י שם 5) שמות ה-ז 6) רש"י שמות ה-ח 7) לקח טוב שמות ה-ח 8) שמות שם 9) אוה"ח שמות ה-ח 10) שמו"ר ה-יח ובמהרז"ו, תנחומא וארא ו ובעץ יוסף, רש"י ואב"ע שמות ה-ט 11) שמו"ר ה-יח ובמהרז"ו 12) בעה"ט שמות ה-ט 13) לקח טוב שמות ה-כא 14) הגדת הגר"א

The Oppression Intensifies

The officials immediately set out to the fields to implement Pharaoh's new decrees. The taskmasters were told to consult their records of each Jew's production quota, as it was established at the beginning of his enslavement, and raise that quota to new and absurd levels. They also required that each Jew gather his own straw, as Pharaoh had commanded.[15] Children as young as nine years of age were also drafted into the slave labor force to help meet the new production targets.[16]

As soon as he left Pharaoh's palace, Moshe returned to Midian for three months to await his next set of instructions from Hashem.[17] It would be three months before Hashem appeared to him again.[18] In the meantime, as the labor decrees intensified, the Jewish people searched for him across the length and breadth of Egypt,[19] but they could not find him.

The Jewish laborers staggered under the load of the new decrees. They ran through the fields,[20] gathering straw for the clay[21] so as not to fall short of their new daily quotas.[22] They would then return to their brickmaking ovens and mix the straw in with the cement.[23] The mixture would be put into a brick-shaped mold which bore the name of their individual Shevet.[24] The newly-formed brick would be left in the sun to dry, and then it would be baked in an oven.[25]

In the month of Iyar,[26] amid the soft breezes of the spring, the Jewish people were running desperately through the fields, seeking straw for their quotas. As they ran, the Egyptians beat them mercilessly, and the Jews would flee even further into the fields to avoid the vicious beatings.[27]

Sometimes, they would find straw in a field, and overjoyed at their good fortune, they would run toward it. But just as they would be about to take it, an Egyptian would appear, shouting, "Thieves, you may not touch that straw. It is private property."[28] The Egyptian would then attack them so mercilessly that they would run bleeding into the fields, often with fractured hands and legs.

---

15) שמו"ר ה-יח 16) שמו"ר ה-ד 17) טור שמות ה-ד 17) שמו"ר ה-יט, ע' בבעה"ט ד-כא שהלך משה למדין וחזר למצרים ז' פעמים 18) רמב"ן שמות ו-א וברד"ל, מהרש"ל ומהרז"ו בשמו"ר שם, וראה גם במדבר רבה יא-ב 19) שמו"ר ה-יט ובמהרז"ו 20) רש"י שמות ה-יא 21) שם ה-יב 22) שמות ה-יא 23) רש"י ה-ז 24) ילקוט ראובני 25) רש"י שמות ה-ז 26) סדר עולם ג 27) שמו"ר ה-יט, בעה"ט שמות ה-יד 28) מלבים ה-ו, תנחומא וארא ו

It became increasingly obvious that straw could only be obtained on public lands,[29] which were few and far between. The only straw available otherwise was for sale in the marketplace, but the Jews had no money.[30] More and more, Jewish laborers would venture as far as the desert to get the straw. They would return with the scraggly straw of the desert, their feet torn by the desert thorns and bleeding profusely onto the cement.[31] Their wives and children would then thresh the straw so that it would be ready for the next day's brickmaking.[32]

Hashem took note of the terrible hardships Pharaoh's new decrees were imposing on the Jewish people, and He had mercy on His people. He caused a powerful wind to blow into Egypt from the north, bringing with it large bales of straw from what was then the Land of Canaan.[33]

But even as the burden of gathering straw eased somewhat, the burden of the brickmaking quota was crushing. Each Jew was required to make six hundred bricks a day, and for every brick he fell short of his quota, the Egyptians revived the old monstrous practice of cementing a child into the wall in place of the brick.[34] Hashem did not allow this to be forgotten, and when the Jewish people stood at the Yam Suf, he retaliated against the Egyptians by destroying their six hundred chariots.[35]

The Jewish Officers

By the third day, the decree was in full force.[36] The taskmasters inspected the production of each group of laborers and demanded a reckoning from the Jewish police officers who were required to supervise them. The officers worked side by side with the laborers in a futile attempt to reach the unreachable quota.[37] The officers took pity on their fellow Jews and allowed them to fall short in their quotas.[38]

When the taskmasters came and demanded to know which of the workers had failed to reach his quota, the officers remained silent. The taskmasters beat and tortured them, but they refused to speak. "Better that we should be beaten," they would cry out in the midst of their pain, "than to inform on our brothers." Hashem

29) לקח טוב שמות ה-טז, תנחומא שם 30) לקוטי אנשי שם שמות ה-יב 31) פרדר"א מח 32) שם 33) חמדת הימים שמות ה-יב 34) מדרש ויושע בפסוק מרכבות פרעה 35) שם 36) לקח טוב שמות ה-יד וע' רש"ש שמו"ר ה-כ 37) החז"ס עה"ת וארא י-ט 38) שמו"ר ה-כ

rewarded these righteous men by allowing them to serve on the Sanhedrin and giving them the gift of *ruach hakodesh*.[39]

In one particular instance, a pregnant woman named Rachel, the granddaughter of Shuselach, was working late in the cement pits. Unable to leave her work, she delivered right there in the pit, and to her horror, the newborn child was thrown into the cement mix and became part of a brick. The woman cried out in such excruciating pain that the angel Gavriel came down, took the brick into which the child had been cemented and brought it up to the Heavenly Throne. Hashem did not allow this terrible tragedy to go unpunished. One year later, on the night of Pesach, He would kill all the firstborn of the Egyptians in retaliation for what they did to that Jewish child.[40]

Unable to stand by and witness the plight of their brethren, the Jewish police went each day to the royal palace to petition Pharaoh on behalf of the Jewish people, but the guards barred their entrance. They pleaded and cried and even suffered the impatient blows of the guards, but it was all to no avail. One day, however, Pharaoh happened to be passing by when the Jewish police were pleading with the guards. Pharaoh decided to grant them an audience.[41]

"Your majesty," they cried out, "why do you treat us this way? Are we slaves you bought in the marketplace or won as the spoils of war? We came down to Egypt on our own as your guests. We are your servants, and you are killing us. Why, your majesty? Why do you want to kill your loyal servants? How can you expect us to make bricks without giving us straw?[42] We ask our Egyptian taskmasters for straw, but they refuse to give us any.[43] Instead, they beat us and break our bones. How can they expect us to finish our work if they give us no straw? And how can they expect us to finish our work if they beat us constantly?"[44]

"Utter nonsense," Pharaoh replied. "You Jews are just lazy people. Instead of concentrating on your work, you fill your time with idle talk of sacrificing to your God.[45] What you need is a little less free time on your hands. This business about not having enough straw is just an excuse to cover your laziness.[46] Well, I for one am not fooled by this charade! You will absolutely not be given straw, and

---

39) במדבר רבה טו-כ, שמו"ר ה-כ, שמו"ר ה-כב 40) פרדר"א מח 41) רמב"ן שמות ה-כב 42) לקח טוב שמות ה-טו
43) מלבים שמות שם 44) לקח טוב שמות ה-טז 45) רש"י שמות ה-ח 46) מלבים שמות ה-יז

you will absolutely have to fill your quotas anyway![47] As for you miserable Jewish excuses for police officers, I will see to it that you too enjoy the taste of discipline!"[48]

The Jewish police officers found themselves out in the street, worse off than they had been before they managed to gain an audience with Pharaoh.

Three months had passed since the new decrees were issued. It seemed as if the Jewish condition in Egypt had hit rock bottom.

Moshe Returns to Egypt

Unknown to the Jewish police officers, Hashem had already appeared to Moshe in Midian and told him to return to Egypt. As before, Aharon went out into the desert to greet his brother and escort him into Egypt.[49] Along the way, they met the Jewish police returning from their disastrous audience with Pharaoh.[50] "What shall we do?" the Jewish police officers lamented to Moshe and Aharon. "What are we going to report to the Jewish people about this audience? We have no good news to tell them. All we can tell them is that from now on we will be working beside them in the fields."[51]

As Moshe and Aharon continued along their way, they were approached by many more Jewish people, among them Dassan and Aviram.[52] Moshe and Aharon wanted to calm the agitated people and speak words of encouragement to them.[53] But Dassan and Aviram spoke against them, blaspheming against and cursing Moshe and Aharon.[54]

"May Hashem judge you for what you have done to us," they shouted. "And if He really sent you to Pharaoh, then let Him judge what He has accomplished by sending you. But if you went to Pharaoh on your own, then may Hashem judge you both for all the trouble you have caused us.[55] May He judge the harsh labor and suffering that the Egyptians have inflicted upon us because of you.[56] Look what you have done to us by your meddling. Not only have you failed in your efforts to redeem us, you have actually caused the labor decrees to be intensified.[57] Look! Do you smell the odor of death? The wounds in our flesh are beginning to fester! And

47) שמות ה-יח 48) אב״ע שם 49) אב״ע שם רבה יא-ב, מתנ״כ בשמו״ר ה-כ 50) אב״ע שמות ה-יט 51) מלבים שם 52) שמו״ר ה-כ 53) מדרש הגדול שמות ה-כ 54) שמו״ר ה-כ וברש״ש 55) שמו״ר ה-כא 56) מדרש אגדה שמות ה-כא 57) מדרש הגדול שמות ה-כא

the children! Oh, the poor children plastered into the wall! Their pitiful little bodies are decomposing and causing this unbearable stench.[58] You have placed a sword into the hands of the Egyptians, and they are using it to kill us!"[59]

It dawned on Moshe that Pharaoh had rejected every part of the message he had brought from Hashem, and he felt that a good part of the blame belonged to him. If I had been righteous enough, Moshe thought, Pharaoh would surely have heeded my words. I must repent! Although Moshe knew full well that the Jewish people were being enslaved because of Pharaoh's villainy, his humility led him to believe that part of the blame was his as well.[60]

When Moshe realized what the Egyptians had done in his absence, Moshe immediately retraced his steps and went back into the desert. He needed desperately to speak to Hashem, but he could not do so in Egypt itself, a land whose every corner was filled with *avodah zarah*.[61] Instead, he went to a place designated for this purpose outside Egypt.[62]

"Why did these children deserve this kind of death?" Moshe asked Hashem. "Why did they have to be cemented into the walls of buildings?"

"These children are not destined for good things,"[63] Hashem replied. "They will grow to be wicked people,[64] and it is better they die now while they are still righteous than grow up to be wicked people.[65] If you want to see for yourself, take out one of these children, and we will see how he turns out."[66]

(Later, when Moshe returned to Egypt, he went to inspect the buildings and saw a Jewish child in the wall still clinging to life. Moshe took him out of the wall and revived him.[67] The child was named Michah, because he was "crushed" inside the walls.[68] This child would later be one of the contributors of the Golden Calf.[69] In retrospect, Moshe had to admit that it would have been better had this child not been saved. Hashem controls the entire world and always does what is best, even if we do not understand it at the time.)

Moshe continued to pour out his heart to Hashem. "I have read the *Sefer Bereishis*," he said, "about the Dor Hamabul, the Dor

---

58) שמו״ר ה-כא 59) שמות ה-כא 60) ילקוט בני ירושלים בשם לקוטי אנשי שם 61) שמו״ר יב-ה 62) לקח טוב שמות ה-כב 63) שפתי חכמים כי תשא לב-ד 64) רש״י סנהדרין קא: 65) כציון 63 66) כציון 64 67) כציון 64 68) שם סנהדרין קא: 69) שפתי חכמים שם, רש״י סנהדרין קא:, ע״ע רש״י שמות לב-ד, ע׳ באדרת אליהו נצבים דמטפל במה שמשמע שהי״ מיכה תינוק ואי״כ מובן לכאורה האיך הי״ לו חלק גדול בעגל

Hahaflagah and the inhabitants of Sedom. You condemned and destroyed all these people, because they were truly wicked. But what have the Jewish people done to deserve such a terrible fate? If You had to fulfill Your decree to Avraham that his descendants would be enslaved, why could You not have chosen the children of Eisav and Yishmael to bear the slavery You decreed?[70] Is it because the Jewish people are still guilty of *lashon hara*? Surely, they are not the only nation guilty of this sin! Why then do they deserve to be enslaved?[71]

"Is the reason they continue to suffer because the four hundred years of the decree have not yet been completed, and the preordained time of redemption has not yet arrived? If so, why then did You send me to Pharaoh?[72]

"You ask me who I am to come before You and complain about the exile of the Jewish people. But I have a personal involvement here. You sent me as a messenger to Pharaoh, and by coming, I have given the people hope. Unfortunately, only evil has come of my mission. I have been rejected, ridiculed and insulted. I did not feel qualified for this mission, and I have failed. Why did You ever send me?[73] Look what I have wrought! Not only has Pharaoh kept the Jewish people enslaved, he has actually increased their work load.[74] Pharaoh is heartless, a brutal man who lacks compassion and sensitivity to the suffering of the Jewish people.[75]

"What can I do? Oh, what will I say to the Jewish police officers? I had told them that You would redeem them, but now the worst has happened. They were expelled from Pharaoh's presence and ordered to work in the field alongside the other laborers."[76]

"Do not worry, Moshe," Hashem replied. "You yourself will see My mighty Hand persuade Pharaoh to send the Jewish people out. Moreover, he will actually force them to leave Egypt in such haste that they will not have enough time to prepare food for the journey.[77] They are being tormented now, but their future reward for their suffering will be manifold.[78] The redemption will come promptly, and you will witness it."[79]

Hashem had reassured Moshe, but He had also taken him to task for complaining and questioning the ways of Hashem. "Many

---

70) שמו"ר ה-כב 71) יפ"ת בשמו"ר ה-כב 72) רמב"ן ורבנו בחיי שמות שם 73) לקח טוב שמות שם וכו' 74) מדרש הגדול שם 75) שם 76) אב"ע שם 77) רש"י שמות ו-א 78) חמדת הימים, רבנו בחיי שמות ו-א 79) רמב"ן שם

times I appeared to Avraham, Yitzchak and Yaakov, and they did not question Me," Hashem told him. "I told Avraham that a great nation would descend from him through his son Yitzchak, and then I told him to bring Yitzchak as a sacrifice. Avraham did not question Me. But you have questioned Me. Therefore, you will witness My mighty Hand destroy Pharaoh, but you will not witness the destruction of the seven nations and the thirty-one kings during the conquest of Eretz Yisrael."[80]

Moshe had mistakenly thought that when he delivered Hashem's message and Pharaoh rejected it Hashem would instantly bring all the wonders, miracles and plagues upon Pharaoh and the Egyptians.[81] He did not understand that Hashem was waiting for Pharaoh to commit one more sin and reach the pinnacle of his wickedness, and for the Jewish people to earn one more merit to make them deserving of their exodus. Pharaoh's decree of increased labor and his denial of the existence of Hashem brought Pharaoh to the pinnacle of evil, and the additional suffering of the Jews earned that one last missing merit. The time of redemption had arrived.[82]

80) סנהדרין קיא., שמו"ר שם, רש"י שמות ו-א, ריב"א שם וע"ש שם דכתב דזה יחד עם החטא במי מריבה גרם שלא יכנס 81) רמב"ן שם 82) מלבי"ם שם.

Revelations of Redemption

11

Moshe had questioned Hashem's allowing the Jewish people to suffer in Egypt and regretted his own selection as the leader of the Jews, and because of this, Hashem rebuked him.[1] Moshe had no right to question Hashem's judgment. The Avos had never questioned Hashem, even when they had good reason to do so.[2] When Hashem told Avraham to leave the land of his fathers and go to a strange land, he obeyed without question. When Avraham had to pay an exorbitant sum for a burial plot for Sarah, he still did not question Hashem. When Yitzchak moved to a new place on Hashem's instructions and encountered difficulties with his new neighbors, he did not question Hashem. When Yaakov had to spend a large amount of money to settle near Shechem, he did not question Hashem.[3] And because of this unquestioned faith, Hashem made an everlasting

---

1) רש״י וארא ו-ב   2) שמו״ר ו-ד   3) שם, ע׳ סנהדרין קיא. ובמהרש״א

covenant with the Avos to give them the land of Canaan and redeem their descendants from Egypt.[4]

Furthermore, the Avos enjoyed a lower level of prophecy than Moshe did.[5] The Avos only encountered Hashem in dreams and visions, while Moshe encountered Hashem in full consciousness, speaking to Him as a person speaks to his friend. Moshe even asked Hashem to reveal His Name to him, and He did. Someone with such a high level of prophecy should certainly not have questioned Hashem.[6] Nevertheless, Hashem viewed Moshe's error with mercy, since Moshe had only acted out of his deep concern for the Jewish people.[7]

In truth, the Jewish people were not righteous enough to be redeemed on their own merits, only in the merits of the faithful Avos.[8] In the meantime, Hashem had hardened Pharaoh's heart so that he would not escape the full retribution for the crimes he had committed against the Jewish people.[9]

When Hashem saved Avraham from Pharaoh, He did not avenge Himself on Pharaoh. When Hashem saved Yitzchak from Avimelech, He did not avenge Himself on Avimelech. When Hashem saved Yaakov from Lavan, He did not avenge Himself on Lavan. But this time would be different. This time Hashem would avenge the Jewish people and punish Pharaoh for what he did to them.[10]

The Four Terms of Redemption

Hashem now sent Moshe with a message to the Jewish people that He would redeem them in the merit of their future acceptance of the Torah and in the merit of the Avos.[11] As preconditions of the redemption, the Jewish people would have to agree to accept the Torah, to acknowledge the sovereignty of Hashem and to sanctify His Name. Otherwise, they would not be redeemed.[12] The acceptance of Hashem as the God of the Jewish people would be the first

---

4) לקח טוב וארא ו-ה (5 שמו"ר שם, רבנו בחיי וארא ו-ג (6 לקח טוב וארא ו-ג (7 שמו"ר ו-א (8 רש"י וארא ו-ג, שמו"ר ב-ה, שם טו-ד, ועי' בעה"ט וארא ו-ג דהיה בזכותו של יצחק (וכן יהי' לעתיד לבא ע' שבת פט: ובבעה"ט שלהי חיי שרה) ועי"ע דעת זקנים סוף בא ובפענח רזא (9 שמו"ר ו-א (10 מדרש אגדה וארא ו-ג, שמו"ר ו-ב וביפ"ת, רמב"ן וארא ו-ג שהגיד הקב"ה למשה שידעיו אותם שיתגלה במדות שונות, ידון את מצרים בשם אלקים, ולישראל יתגלה בשם הוי' ויראם עליהם ויושיעם, ועי' בזוה"ק בא לו, דכתב שהי' כאחת וגנוז בכל מכה הי' ישועה והארה לבני ישראל וכש"נ נגוף ורפוא, ואותו דבר שהי' להם דינים הי' לנו רחמים וחסדים (וכהדם שלנו אותו דבר הי' מים, ועד"ז הי' לעתיד כמ"ש נדרים ח: (11 בעה"ט וארא ו-ח (12 מדרש הגדול ו-ו ואילך, אוה"ח וארא ו-ח, ועי' בזוה"ק וארא דע"י קבלת אדנותו והאמונה בו ית' יזכו לראות בנפלאותיו

commandment given at Mount Sinai, but even before, the Jewish people had to acknowledge and accept it in order to appreciate the miracles He would perform for them in Egypt.[13] If they agreed to these preconditions, they would be redeemed and given Eretz Yisrael. The holy land would be taken from the Canaanites who were only being allowed temporary residence and given to the Jewish people as a permanent inheritance.[14*]

"Therefore, tell the Jewish people, I am God," said Hashem. "I will *bring* you out from under the Egyptian burden. I will *rescue* you from their forced labor. I will *redeem* you with an outstretched Arm and great judgments. I will *take* you as My nation, and I will be your Lord."[15**]

The Jewish people earned these four different terms of redemption—*bring, rescue, redeem* and *take*—because of four meritorious practices. They did not change their language. They did not change their clothing styles and names. They did not divulge each other's secrets. They began to observe the *mitzvah* of *bris milah*.[16] The four terms of redemption also correspond to the four decrees Pharaoh issued against the Jewish people—the harsh labor, the slaughter of the male babies, the casting of the children into the river and the withholding of straw from the Jewish laborers.[17]

Moshe's task now was to convince the Jewish people that redemption was indeed imminent. This would not be so easy to accomplish, since the Jews were convinced that Egyptian magic prevented escape from Egypt.[18] The Egyptian magicians had placed

---

* They themselves would not enter Eretz Yisrael because of the future sins of the Eigel (the Golden Calf) and the Meraglim (the Spies). They would receive the Torah, but their children would actually inherit Eretz Yisrael.

** We drink four cups of wine during the *seder* on Pesach night to commemorate these four expressions of redemption. We drink the last cup when we say the section of שפוך חמתך in the Haggadah. In that context, we say that Hashem will one day give four cups of retribution to the wicked to punish them for their treatment of the Jewish people. (*Shemos Rabbah* 6:4, Rabbeinu Bachia, *Va'era* 6: 8)

---

13) זוה"ק וארא כה 14) מדרש הגדול וארא ו-ח, בבא בתרא קיז:, שם קיט:, ילקו"ש תשמ"ה, שם תתט"ו 15) וארא ו-ו וכו', שמו"ר ו-ד, עיין מילואים בתורה שלמה וארא א 16) לקח טוב וארא ו-ו, ומבואר דלא ידע מצרים שבדעתם לשאול מהם כסף זהב ושמלות, וזה שאף אחד לא גלה הסוד לשום מצרי הי' חלק מזכותם להגאל ועיין בתכלת מרדכי (פ' בא) דדייק מלשון הכתוב דבר נא באזני העם שהסוד יהי' שמור כל כך שגם הערב רב רב לא ידעו דרק על אותם שהיו בכלל וענו אותם כתיב ואחרי כן יצאו ברכוש גדול (כמ"ש סנהדרין צא. מובא לעיל פרק ז ציון 105) 17) שמו"ר ו-ד ובמהרד"ו, ועיין מתנ"כ ומהרד"ו שם א-יב 18) זוה"ק וארא כה

images of animals, such as dogs, lions, camels and foxes, all around the borders of Egypt. Through their sorcery, they contrived that anyone passing one of these images caused it to begin wailing. The live animals in Egypt would hear these haunted cries and begin to wail themselves. The Egyptian border guards would be alerted that someone was trying to escape, and they would pursue and capture him. It was therefore virtually impossible for anyone to escape Egypt. This then was Moshe's first task. He had to convince the Jews that Hashem would get them out of Egypt.[19]

The Jews Raise Objections

Moshe immediately went back to Egypt[20] and relayed Hashem's message to the Jewish people, particularly to the people of Shevet Levi. He also told the Jewish people to rid themselves of *avodah zarah*, make sure they all had a *bris milah* and to purify themselves in preparation for receiving the Torah.[21] The Jewish people, however, were not especially receptive to Moshe's words.[22*]

"These are only words," some of them said. "We do not have a moment of ease in our lives.[23] At any time, Pharaoh can come and kill us, and you bring us words!"[24]

"Besides, why should we believe you?" others asked. "Last time you came with these announcements of redemption, what happened? Did we get released? No, we did not! We got even harsher working conditions."[25]

"There's also something else," said others. "Last time you never told us that we would have to stop worshipping our idols. We thought that Hashem was prepared to take us out even if we did a little idol worship here and there, you know, like we're all used to. But now you come along with a new story. You're telling us we have to stop completely. That's not so easy, you know."[26]

---

* It was not actually Moshe who spoke to them. Aharon conveyed his words over to the Jewish people. After Aharon's death, his son Eleazar conveyed Moshe's words to the Jewish people. (Ibn Ezra, *Shemos* 4:30; Sforno 7:6, *Va'era*)

---

19) שפתי כהן שמות (20 לקח טוב וארא ו-ט (21 מדרש הגדול וארא שם, רבנו בחיי ו-יג ואותם שעדיין היו ערלים נמלו לפני אכילת הפסח (22 וארא ו-ט ברש"י ושפתי חכמים (23 שם (24 רמב"ן וארא ו-ט (25 ספורנו וארא ו-יב (26 שמו"ר ו-ה וביפ"ת, בשיר השירים רבה מפורש שהשבטים ראובן שמעון ולוי לא עבדו אף פעם

"You can't really expect us to agree to what you ask," said yet others. "After all, we're slaves, you know. Did you ever hear of a slave that could serve two masters? Well, right now we're slaves of Pharaoh, and we're terrified of him.[27] Do you expect us to agree at the same time to become slaves of Hashem? This is too much for us to handle!"[28]

Eventually, of course, the Jewish people would agree to Hashem's preconditions and be redeemed, but because they were not receptive to Moshe's message they themselves would not earn the right to enter Eretz Yisrael. Only their children would.[29]

Moshe Refuses Again

When Moshe returned to his place of meeting with Hashem, Hashem instructed him to go to the royal palace[30] and tell Pharaoh to let the Jewish people leave his land.[31]

Moshe again pleaded with Hashem that he not be the messenger. "If the people of Shevet Levi, who are exempt from labor, don't want to listen to me," he asked Hashem, "how can I expect the rest of the Jewish people to listen to me? And besides, how can a person with a speech impediment like me be a proper spokesman for the Jewish people?[32]

"I have told the Jewish people that they will go free, and still they don't listen to me. Why should Pharaoh listen to me when I tell him to set his slaves free?[33] Isn't Pharaoh much less likely to listen to me than the Jews are? After all, the Jewish people are faithful to You and the message is for their own benefit. But Pharaoh has rejected You and the message is to his detriment.[34]

"And even if there were a possibility that Pharaoh would listen to what I have to say, is it possible that he would listen to someone like me who has a speech impediment? Originally, You only sent me to the elders of the Jewish people to ask them to accompany me to Pharaoh, but You did not tell me to go directly to Pharaoh by myself. In those circumstances, the elders could have spoken to Pharaoh on my behalf, and it would not have been necessary for me to speak. Unfortunately, the elders ran off, leaving just me and Aharon, and I had no choice but to speak. Now, however, You are telling me to go alone with the intention of being the main speaker![35]

---

27) מדרש הגדול וארא ו-ט 28) לקח טוב שם 29) ספורנו שם וראה גם בבא בתרא קי"ז: 30) אב"ע וארא ו-יא
31) וארא ו-יא 32) רבנו אפרים וארא ו-יב 33) מדרש הגדול ודעת זקנים שם 34) אוה"ח וארא שם 35) רמב"ן

"Pharaoh will laugh at me when I tell him I am a messenger from Hashem who rules the entire world. Ambassadors to the royal court are all well-spoken people who are fluent in the seventy principal languages of the world. When Pharaoh realizes that I have a speech impediment and am not fluent in the seventy languages, he will roar with laughter and say, 'If, as you say, Hashem rules the world and created the languages, why has He sent me someone like you? Couldn't He find a better messenger to send to me?'[36]

"And besides, how can I, a prophet the son of a prophet, convince an evil person descended from slaves, such as Pharaoh who is descended from Cham, to heed my words? Pharaoh has no fear of Heaven, not even of his own imaginary gods! Why would he accept my rebuke?[37] He will say to me, 'If the Jews were wrongfully enslaved, why has it taken two hundred and ten years for you to protest? Surely, you can't expect me to release my Jewish slaves just so they will be able to serve another master!'"[38]

Hashem Chooses Aharon

In response to Moshe's concerns, Hashem told him that Aharon would be his intermediary, and therefore, he need not worry about his speech impediment.[39] Aharon now became Moshe's partner in all messages to be conveyed to Pharaoh, as well as to the Jewish people.[40] But the two brothers differed in their level of prophecy. Moshe received his communications directly from Hashem, while Aharon received them in visions.[41]

Hashem now sent the two brothers again to the Jewish people and to Pharaoh. However, He warned them to be patient with the Jewish people, because they were stubborn, excitable and irritable. They should expect the Jews to be troublesome, because they are all descended from kings and royal blood flowed in their veins.[42] In order to make the forthcoming redemption real in the minds of the Jewish people, Moshe and Aharon were to instruct them to begin

---

שם, מלבים שם ו-יא (36 תנחומא דברים ב, לקח טוב וארא ו-ל (37 מדרש הגדול שמות ד-א, שמו"ר ג-יד במהרז"ו
38) מכילתא שמות ג (39 רש"י וארא ו-יג, רבנו בחיי וארא ז-א (40 אוה"ח וארא ו-כח, ע' רמב"ן ו-יב ובמלבים
ו-יג ושם מפסוק כח והלאה דבעצם מבואר במדרשים דעד עתה הי' משה המנהיג לגמרי ואהרן לא היה כי אם עזר
ובכה"ג הי' משה מלכם והיה מולידכם לארצם והיה נבנית בית מקדשנו, ועתה ע"י דיבורו של משה נטלה ממנו חלק
מנשיאותו ולקחו אהרן ולא זכה משה להכנס לארץ ישראל. מלשון המדרש (ויקרא רבה יא-ו) מבואר שלא רק שהי'
עונש אלא שהיה תוצאה מדיבורו, דלפי טענתו היה נמצא שלא ילך לארץ כנען, ולכאר' אינו מובן ועיין באסופת
מערכות על חג הסוכות באושפיזא דמשה ותראה הסבר נפלא בקישור אמירתו שהוא כבד פה לגזירה הנ"ל (41
ר' אברהם בן הרמב"ם וארא ו-יג (42 זוה"ק וארא כו, שמו"ר ז-ג, מזרחי ו-יג

preparing acacia wood from the trees Yaakov had brought from Beersheva for the building of the Mishkan.[43]

Moshe and Aharon were the perfect choices to take the Jewish people out of Egypt.[44] Descended from the prestigious Shevet Levi, the chosen of Hashem,[45] they were both on an equally high status in their deeds[46] and thoroughly righteous,[47] like two precious stones equal in weight.[48] Aharon took precedence when speaking to the Jewish people, while Moshe took precedence when they appeared before Pharaoh.[49]

---

43) שמו"ר יח-י ובמתנ"כ, בראשית רבה צד-ד ובספר המבחר מובא תורה שלמה יח 44) ספורנו וארא ו-כו
45) מלבים וארא ו-יד וכו' 46) משכיל לדוד וארא ו-כו 47) רש"י וארא שם 48) שיר השירים רבה ד-ה 49) מלבים
וארא ו-כו וכו', ברבנו בחיי ו-כג איתא ששבט לוי זכה לששה נביאים, משה אהרן פנחס (זה אליהו) וג' בני קרח.

The First of the Signs

12

Hashem told Moshe, "I have made you a master and a judge, a man of power over Pharaoh." From that day on, Moshe wielded great power over Pharaoh through the plagues and tortures that he would visit upon the Egyptians.[1] There was no longer any need to worry about whether or not Pharaoh would listen to him.

Moreover, from that day on, Pharaoh would look upon Moshe as an angel—with reverence and fear.[2] Moshe would be like a deity to Pharaoh, and Aharon would be his prophet.[3] Moshe would carry the fearsome title of Elohim, the Name used by Hashem when He created the world. He was to use this title only in his dealings with Pharaoh to help bring him into submission.[4] Pharaoh had considered himself a god, but in the face of Moshe's august title, he would realize that he was nothing. Pharaoh had thought the world was governed by

---

1) אונקלוס רש"י ורבנו בחיי וארא ז-א 2) אב"ע שם וראה גם תרגום יונתן שם 3) שכל
טוב שם וע' לעיל פרק ח 4) במדבר רבא יד-ו וברד"ל, מדרש אגדה ז-א

unchangeable natural laws, but Moshe's spectacular miracles and wonders would at last convince him that God above controlled everything.[5]

Nevertheless, despite Pharaoh's evil nature and the disastrous end that awaited him, Hashem instructed Moshe to speak to him with the honor and respect due to a king.[6] Moshe was to speak to Pharaoh only in Hashem's Name,[7] to show Pharaoh that Hashem was master of the world. In this vein, Moshe was to command Pharaoh to let the Jewish people go, and he was to reinforce his words with signs and wonders.[8]

The "signs" to which Hashem was referring were predictions about future events that proved Moshe and Aharon were truly the messengers of Hashem. In the interim, before those events came to pass, Moshe was to perform "wonders," miraculous feats which would convince Pharaoh that Moshe and Aharon were indeed men to be reckoned with and that their signs should be taken seriously even before they actually came to pass.[9]

Hashem then told Moshe not to expect Pharaoh to submit to Hashem's will right away. First, Hashem intended to harden Pharaoh's heart so that he would persist in his refusal to release the Jewish people, thereby causing numerous plagues to be visited upon Egypt.[10]

One could perhaps wonder why Pharaoh should be punished for not letting the Jewish people go if Hashem had in fact hardened his heart. But the truth is that a person is ordinarily given three chances to repent. Only if he persists in his wicked behavior does Hashem close his heart to repentance and thus ensure that he will be punished. Pharaoh was given ample opportunity to repent and set the Jewish people free. Even after the fifth plague, Pharaoh was still able to repent. But when he persistently refused to set the Jewish people free, in spite of the commands of Hashem and in spite of his own afflictions, Hashem hardened his heart and made sure he remained firmly on the road to disaster.[11]

A number of other solutions to this problem have also been suggested. According to one view, Hashem did not actually harden Pharaoh's heart so that he could not repent. He merely sent the

---

5) תנחומא וארא ט ובעץ יוסף, שמו"ר ח-א וביפ"ת 6) שמו"ר ז-ג 7) שכל טוב וארא ו-כט 8) מדרש הגדול שם (9 רמב"ן דברים יג-ג, מנחה בלולה וארא ז-ג, מלבים שם, ראה גם ספורנו ז-ט 10) שפתי כהן וארא ז-ג 11) שמו"ר יג-ג

plagues in such a way that Pharaoh would find it easy to harden his own heart against repentance. For instance, He allowed a sufficient period of time between plagues so that Pharaoh would think the worst was over and he could relax. Thus, even if he had been inclined to give in and allow the Jewish people to leave, he could now change his mind.[12]

In a similar vein, it has been suggested that Hashem did not actually prevent Pharaoh from repenting. He prevented Pharaoh from being forced into repentance by the suffering visited upon him, but He still allowed him to repent of his own free will—that is, in recognition of the supremacy of the command of Hashem and the evil of his own behavior. Hashem therefore hardened his heart so that the suffering would not force him to release the Jewish people even though he really would not have done so of his own free will.[13] Others have suggested that Hashem actually assigned an angel to bolster Pharaoh's resolve to keep the Jewish people enslaved in spite of his suffering, although he still had the ability to repent, if he so chose. This is what was meant by Hashem hardening his heart.[14]

Still others are of the opinion that Hashem did indeed take away Pharaoh's ability to repent. A person can repent and be forgiven only by the grace of Hashem, but Pharaoh was so overwhelmingly wicked that he did not deserve this privilege. Therefore, Hashem hardened his heart and did not allow him to repent.[15] Moreover, Pharaoh's repentance would not have been genuine in any case, since he would still have remained an idol worshipper. He would have been like a *toveil v'sheretz b'yado*, a person who attempts to purify himself by immersion in a *mikveh* while holding an insect in his hand.[16]

In any case, Hashem assured Moshe that Pharaoh would not relent despite all the plagues that would be visited upon Egypt. Finally, after the plague of the death of the firstborn, Pharaoh would pass his limit, and he would never want to see Moshe again. He would beg Moshe to take the Jewish people and leave Egypt, and at that point, Hashem would bring His people forth into freedom.[17] At

---

12) אברבנל וארא ז-ג, סוגיא עמוקה וארוכה היא ולא הצגנו כי אם ראשי פרקים 13) רמב״ן וספורנו שם ויע״ש ברש״י ומזרחי, יפ״ת על שמו״ר יג-ג 14) רוקח ז-ג, ילקוט ראובני מה, מקור האי כללא ביומא לח: בדרך שאדם רוצה לילך מוליכין אותו 15) רמב״ם הלכות תשובה ו-ג ובאור שמח שם, ע״ע שמונה פרקים ח-ח, שפתי כהן בא י-א
16) אברבנל וארא ז-ג 17) אוה״ח וארא ז-ד

that time, Hashem would avenge Himself upon the Egyptians for their crimes against the Jewish people. The death of the firstborn and the subsequent drowning of the Egyptians in the sea would repay them measure for measure for their murderous attacks on the Jewish infants. Until that time, the signs and wonders would continue to resound throughout Egypt as unheeded calls to repentance,[18] but in the end, the full might of Hashem would be revealed. They had scoffed at the master and ruler of the universe, saying, "Who is Hashem?" Now they would be cast into the sea and drowned.[19]

While all this would be going on, the Jewish people would be living safely in the midst of the storm. For fully a year, they would witness the signs and the wonders and the plagues, and in the month of Nissan, they would be redeemed.[20]

Aharon Joins Moshe

At this point, Moshe went to tell Aharon everything he had heard from Hashem. At first, Aharon was under the impression that his mission was exclusively to be Moshe's spokesman to the Jewish people. Now he discovered that he was to accompany Moshe to Pharaoh's palace and, what's more, speak to Pharaoh on Moshe's behalf. Thus, Moshe would receive the message directly from Hashem, he would tell it to Aharon who would convey it to Pharaoh, and Hashem would bring the plagues down on Pharaoh and the Egyptians.[21]

Moshe and Aharon accepted their mission from Hashem with unbounded devotion and enthusiasm, not adding or subtracting anything from the exact letter of their instructions.[22] Moshe would be Hashem's messenger, while Aharon would be Moshe's spokesman, both in carrying the message to Pharaoh and in performing the wondrous signs in front of him in the royal palace.[23]

The two brothers, advanced in years but fearless, now prepared to go to Pharaoh, even at the risk of their lives.[24] Aharon was eighty-three, Moshe was eighty.[25]

18) ספורנו שם 19) לקח טוב רשב"ם ומלבים ואר א ז-ה 20) לקח טוב ור' אברהם בן הרמב"ם שם (21 מדרש הגדול ואר א ז-ב, תנחומא ואר א י' 22) ספורנו שפתי כהן ואוה"ח ואר א ז-ו (23 ספורנו ומלבים שם (24 חזקוני וספורנו שם (25 ואר א ז-ז

Instructions about the Signs

Hashem now addressed both Moshe and Aharon,[26] preparing them to carry out His wondrous signs in the proper fashion.[27] Pharaoh would undoubtedly expect a sign that Moshe and Aharon were indeed Hashem's emissaries, but they were not to show the signs until Pharaoh asked for them specifically.[28] Pharaoh's purpose in demanding a sign would be solely for the purpose of determining if Moshe and Aharon were truly prophets or if they were impostors and adventurers.[29]

The first sign Moshe and Aharon were to show Pharaoh would involve a staff changing into a serpent. Aharon, who would be performing the actual wonders, was to take his staff and throw it to the ground. Once the staff was on the ground, Moshe would call out to the staff in front of Pharaoh, commanding it to become a serpent. Pharaoh would see for himself that only through Moshe's words did the staff change into a serpent.[30]

The staff Aharon was to use was not the holy staff Moshe had taken from Midian when he had fled from Egypt, the staff which dated back to the sixth day of creation and upon which Hashem's Name was engraved. The staff used for the signs would have to devour the staffs of the Egyptian sorcerers, and it would have been unfitting for Moshe's consecrated staff to devour the contaminated staffs of the sorcerers.[31] Aharon's staff, rather than Moshe's, would also be used to administer the plagues, since some of the confrontations with Pharaoh took place on his way to the bathroom at the river in places where Moshe's holy staff could not be taken.[32]

Hashem chose a staff for his first sign to imply that Pharaoh deserved to be struck with a staff like a dog, because Pharaoh always sought to distort the truth through magic and sorcery. He could have given Moshe a more wondrous sign, such as causing the sun to stand still in the sky, but He wanted to show that He rules with a staff and punishes the wicked.[33]

He chose to change the staff into a serpent to show that Pharaoh would be punished for the things he said. Just as the serpent in Gan Eden was punished for speaking disrespectfully about Hashem to Adam and Chavah, so too will Pharaoh be punished for his scornful

---

26) וארא ז-ח 27) מדרש הגדול וארא ז-ט 28) שמו״ר ט-א, שם ט-ה אוה״ח וארא ז-ח 29) רבנו בחיי ומלכים וארא ז-ט, 30) תנחומא וארא יב בעה״ט ומלכים וארא ז-ט 31) זוה״ק ח״ב כח 32) ר׳ אפרים וארא ז-טו, באב״ע ומלכים שם כתוב שהי׳ מטה משה 33) שמו״ר ט-ב במהרז״ו ויפ״ת

statement, "Who is Hashem that I should heed Him?"[34] And just as the serpent in Gan Eden had screamed in pain and horror when his hands and feet were removed as punishment for his sin, so too would the Egyptians scream in pain and horror when the plagues would come upon them.[35]

Moreover, a serpent was an appropriate symbol for Pharaoh. A serpent always coils itself in a crooked way, and Pharaoh also always behaved in a crooked and perverse manner. A serpent is always moving and fidgeting, never truly at rest. Pharaoh, too, would continually change his mind regarding the release of the Jewish people.[36]

The serpent also had a particular significance for Pharaoh, because it was a sea serpent, a creature of the water. The Egyptians worshipped the Nile and the sea serpent who, they believed, was the god that had created it. Pharaoh, in his great conceit, had declared himself a god and the creator of the Nile River, thereby assuming the role of the sea serpent in the eyes of the Egyptians. The sign of the staff would show that Hashem was the true master of the Nile, since the sea serpent itself was completely in Hashem's power. The metamorphosis of the staff into a serpent and its reversal would show that power does not mean greatness. Hashem had given the lifeless staff the power to become a serpent and to devour the staffs of the sorcerers even after it had returned to its original lifeless state. Pharaoh, too, had been given royal powers, but in truth, he was no more than a putrid and powerless piece of protoplasm that would eventually return to nothingness.[37*]

---

* The Torah tells us that Aharon's staff turned into a *tanin*. But what is a *tanin*? Rashi on the *passuk* identifies it as a snake. Rashi on *Iyov* 7:12 and in *Bereishis* and the Mahari Kra in *Yechezkel* 39:3 identify it as a large fish. *Metzudos* in *Yechezkel* and *Yeshayahu* identifies it as a snakelike fish. *Klei Yakar* identifies it as a great and dangerous fish. See also *Midrash Chupas Eliyahu* in *Otzar Hamidrashim* 175, and *Avos d'Rabbi Nassan* ch. 39. Malbim on *Yeshayahu* 27:1 identifies it as a water snake or crocodile. Historians believe that the crocodiles in the Nile were indeed worshipped as gods. They were thought to have created themselves and the Nile and were considered the rulers of all the other Nile wildlife. Perhaps the "great fish" refers to a crocodile, which belongs to the family of reptiles along with snakes. Be all that as it may, Pharaoh was compared to a *tanin* in that he also claimed to have created himself and considered himself master of the Nile. For the purposes of this book, we have followed the widely accepted opinion that the *tanin* was a serpent.

---

34) מדרש הגדול ורבנו בחיי ואראa ז-ט 35) תרגום יונתן ואראa שם 36) שמו"ר ט-ג, רבנו בחיי ואראa ז-י
37) ילקו"ש קפא, בעה"ט ומלבים ז-ט

Having received all their instructions and comprehending all the symbolism and significance of the actions they would perform, the two venerable brothers set off for Pharaoh's palace.

Moshe and Aharon in Pharaoh's Palace

While Moshe and Aharon were on their way to the palace, they were already occupying Pharaoh's thoughts. The possibility of another troublesome confrontation with Moshe was being discussed by Pharaoh's advisors, but Pharaoh dismissed the whole subject with disdain.

"There is no need to worry, gentlemen," he declared in his customary haughty manner. "If Moshe ever steps foot in the palace again, I will kill him. I haven't yet decided if I will have him sliced in half by the sword, hanged from a high tree or burned at the stake. I am going to think about that question for a while, savoring the thought as I play with it in my mind. But of one thing you can all rest assured. He will be put to death!"

Just then, Moshe and Aharon arrived at the palace. Moshe preceded his older brother Aharon into the throne room, because he was held in higher regard by the Egyptians and because Hashem had assigned to him the primary role. Pharaoh took one look at Moshe, and his blustering threats to kill Moshe were completely forgotten. Pharaoh became speechless, transfixed by fear into a lifeless statue.[38] Unknown to the others present, Pharaoh had seen the angel named Eifah who stood at Moshe's side and showed Pharaoh ghastly visions of Gehinnom. Trembling with fear, Pharaoh remained silent and motionless.[39]

As both Moshe and Aharon strode to the center of the throne room, a shiver of terror rippled through the assembled crowd of advisors, sorcerers, magicians, sages, dignitaries and servants.[40]

"What do you want here?" Pharaoh asked them belligerently, just as Hashem had said he would.

"We are emissaries from Hashem," Aharon replied. "Hashem demands that you let the Jewish people out of Egypt."

"How do I know you are really messengers from Hashem?" Pharaoh asked. "Maybe you are just a pair of adventurers and impostors."

---

38) שמו"ר ט-ד וכו', ילקוט ראובני לז, יפ"ת מוסיף דמרוב ענותנותו היה קשה לו להכנס קודם ולא עשה כן כי
אם מרוב תשוקתו למלאות רצון יוצרו במלואה 39) ילקוט ראובני תולדות רלח 40) דברי הימים למשה

This was the signal for Aharon to take his staff and follow the instructions Hashem had given him.[41]

In full view of Pharaoh's entire court, Aharon threw his staff down to the ground.

"Staff, become a serpent," Moshe commanded.

The staff turned into a serpent.[42]

When Pharaoh saw this, he began to chuckle and giggle like a chicken.

"Do you call these wonders?" he sneered, laughing aloud. "Are you bringing magic to Egypt? People usually bring merchandise to a place where it is needed, not where there is an abundance of it! Would you bring brine to Spain or fish to Acco? Of course not! There is plenty there already. Well, my friends, there is plenty of magic in Egypt already. We don't need any more. We are the international capital of sorcerers and magicians. And what you have done is merely a simple act of magic. You are just laughable. This you are showing me? Even my wife can do this simple thing. Guards, summon the queen!" Pharaoh neglected to mention that his wife was a magician and sorceress without peer in all of Egypt.[43]

Indeed, the practice of magic and witchcraft was very widespread in Egypt. For the most part, the practice consisted of sleight of hand and illusions, since the hand is faster than the eye. There were, however, some forms of sorcery which were authentic, drawing their powers from the dark forces and demons. The Egyptians devoted enormous amounts of time to the development of their magical skills, because this allowed them to deny the existence of Hashem.[44]

When the queen arrived, Pharaoh greeted her with a snickering smile.

"My lady, these Jews here are trying to make a mockery of me," he said. "They've thrown this staff onto the ground and commanded it to turn into a serpent. They think they can impress me with such antics. Well, my lady, do you think you can duplicate this great feat?"

"I think so, my lord," she replied. "Guards, hand me a staff!"

41) שם, שמו"ר ט-ה 42) שמו"ר ט-ו, בעה"ט וארא ז-ט, תוס' שם ז-י כתב שלא הי' ראוי למשה לעשות אות זה יען והלשין על בני ישראל כשמטהו הפכה לתנין 43) שמו"ר שם, תנחומא ישן וארא יב, פענח רזא רבנו בחיי וארא ז-יא, ילקוט שמעוני קפא, מדרש הגדול ז-י 44) ע' מורה נבוכים ח"ג לז, רמב"ם הלכות ע"ז יא-טז, רמב"ן וארא ז-יא, שם דברים יח-ט, מהרש"א סנהדרין סז: לקח טוב שכל טוב רבנו בחיי אברבנל ומלבים וארא ז-י ואילך

One of the guards brought her a staff. She snatched it from his hands and flung it to the ground. Instantly, it turned into a serpent.

"That was not very difficult," she said smugly. "It is elementary magic. It can even be done by children who are just beginning to learn the secrets of sorcery."

She ordered the guards to bring several children between the ages of four and five. When they arrived she gave them all staffs and told them what was required of them. Each one was able to turn his staff into a serpent.

A mocking laughter reverberated around the great chamber. "How simple it is!" people cried. "Even a young child can do it!"[45]

The leading magicians of the Egyptian court, Yachani, Mamrai, and Bilam's two sons Ianus and Iambrus, all laughed at Moshe and Aharon.

"Did you intend to bring straw to Ofarfaim, a place overflowing with straw?" they scoffed. "Did you expect us to be impressed by your little magical trick?"[46]

"Do not be so cocky," Moshe answered. "People bring vegetables to places where vegetables are sold, since that is where the customers are. I have come to a market of magic, because you of all people will appreciate this wonder."

Pharaoh roared with laughter. "Sages! Magicians!" he shouted. "Turn your staffs into serpents! Let us show these Jews how foolish this demonstration has been."

All the wise men and magicians turned their rods into serpents and turned to stare mockingly at Moshe and Aharon.[47]

The floor was now covered with slithering serpents. Suddenly, Aharon's serpent lunged forward and devoured all the other serpents.[48*]

The mocking laughter came to a sudden halt, and all the magicians stared in open-mouthed awe at the spectacle unfolding in front of them. The serpents they had produced through their magic were not living creatures, just magical illusions that were incapable of

---

* Others suggest that Aharon's staff turned into a snake, while the staffs of the magicians turned into much larger sea serpents. Then Aharon's small snake devoured the larger creatures, an even greater miracle. (*Midrash Hagadol*)

---

45) כצ'ון 43 46) שמו"ר ט-ז, תרגום יונתן ז-יא, ילקו"ש קפ"ב, מדרש הגדול ז-י, ילקוט ראובני 47) מנחות פה. וברבנו גרשום, שמו"ר שם, מדרש הגדול שם, וע' ילקוט ראובני לז 48) פרדר"א מח, מדרש הגדול וארא ז-יב

devouring other creatures. Aharon, however, had managed to turn his staff into a real serpent, a stunning feat![49]

Bilam was the first to react to this startling development. "Your majesty, if I may be so bold," he began. "These Jews have not proved anything at all. They have simply added a new wrinkle to established magical procedures. A clever little trick, I must say. But I am not impressed. From ancient times, it has been possible to cause one living creature to devour another living creature. But lifeless objects cannot devour anything. Let us conduct a little experiment, if I may suggest it. Aha! Let us all turn our serpents back into staffs, and then let us see their staff swallow ours! Not so simple, eh? Something like that would be a wondrous sign and not just plain ordinary magic."

"Good idea, Bilam," Pharaoh said. He turned to Moshe and Aharon. "So, did you hear what our esteemed sorcerer has suggested? If your staff can swallow our staffs, then you have shown yourselves to be messengers of a divine power. Otherwise, you are nothing but ordinary magicians. We've plenty of those here in Egypt."

Aharon did not hesitate. He grabbed the tail of his own serpent, and it spit out the Egyptian snakes and turned back into a staff. The Egyptian magicians all followed suit, and all their slithering serpents also turned back into staffs. Ten piles of stacked wooden staffs rose up in the center of the floor.

Instantly, Aharon's staff lunged forward and swallowed all ten piles of wooden staffs. And to add wonder to wonder, Aharon's staff did not become bloated from all the staffs it had consumed.[50*] This could no longer be dismissed as magic. It was clearly a higher power at work.[51] In fact, from this time on, anyone who saw Aharon's staff would declare, "There is Aharon's miraculous staff, the symbol of good that will perform miracles for the Jewish people for generations to come."[52]

Pharaoh was duly impressed by Aharon's latest feat. "Any staff that can swallow other staffs without becoming bloated," he grumbled tremulously, "can devour me along with my throne."[53]

---

* Some suggest that the staff did not actually swallow the other staffs. It bit the staffs of the Egyptians and left "teeth" imprints on them. (Maharam)

---

49) ספורנו שמות ד-ג 50) שמו״ר שם, מדרש הגדול, ר׳ אפרים, דברי הימים למשה, ספר הישר 51) זוה״ק ח״ב כח שזה גם אות על תחה״מ אם דומם יוכל להתהפך לחי עצמות שכבר חיו פעם לא כל שכן 52) שמו״ר שם 53) שמו״ר שם, ומדרש הגדול ז-י

Pharaoh quickly called to his wise men to bring the scrolls of the gods from his archives. Perhaps Hashem's Name did indeed appear there but had been earlier overlooked. The scrolls were brought, and Pharaoh and his advisors and sages pored over them. But Hashem's Name was not to be found on the lists of the false gods.[54]

With no explanations to offer, Pharaoh looked at Moshe and Aharon and hardened his heart.[55]*

---

* Some suggest that they did the sign of the *tzoraas* as Moshe did at the Sneh, and the magicians could not rid themselves of it forever. (*Pirkei d'Rabbi Eliezer*)

---

54) דברי הימים למשה 55) שמו״ר שם וביפ״ת, רשב״ם וארא ז-יג.

13

Blood, Frogs and Lice

By denying the existence of Hashem, Pharaoh brought upon himself and his kingdom ten dreadful plagues. Hashem had created the world with ten divine commands solely for the sake of the Jewish people. Pharaoh and the Egyptians had enslaved the Jewish people and were therefore subjected to ten plagues, each corresponding to one of the divine commands through which Hashem created the world. Moreover, Pharaoh had denied the existence of Hashem who had created the world with the ten divine commands. In retribution, he was subjected to ten plagues, each corresponding to one of the divine commands through which Hashem created the world.[1]

The ten plagues also correspond to the ten tests of Avraham. Hashem put Avraham to the test ten times, and each time Avraham passed. In this merit, Hashem sent ten spectacular plagues on the

---

1) לקח טוב וארא ט-יג, הגדה מעשה נסים, בכמה הגדות ובפרט של הר״ר צדוק הכהן מלובלין מבואר בפרטות כל מכה נגד מאמר דיליה

Egyptians, punishing them and delighting the Jewish people who witnessed great miracles being performed on their behalf.[2]

The purpose of the plagues was, of course, not merely to punish the Egyptians. Had Hashem so desired, He could have destroyed all the Egyptians with one devastating plague. Rather, His purpose was to demonstrate methodically to Pharaoh and the Egyptians that He was the Almighty Master of the Universe, to bring them to recognize and acknowledge Hashem's sovereignty, to glorify and sanctify His Name.[3]

Abbreviation of the Ten Plagues

In the Haggadah, Rabbi Yehudah gives a mnemonic for remembering the ten plagues, דצ"ך עד"ש באח"ב,[4] the words engraved on Moshe's staff to remind him of the order of the plagues. This three-word mnemonic, however, is much more than a simple memory tool. It actually categorizes the plagues into three distinct groups, each with its own purpose.[5]

When we categorize the plagues, we must realize that the tenth plague, the death of the firstborn, stands on its own. The first nine plagues were to prove Hashem's existence to the Egyptians, while the tenth was to force them to release the Jewish people. The first nine plagues are comprised of three groups of three plagues each, as in Rabbi Yehudah's division. For the purposes of the mnemonic only, the tenth plague was attached to the third group.[6]

Of the first nine plagues, the first set of three demonstrated the existence of Hashem—in response to Pharaoh's denial of Hashem. The second set demonstrated Hashem's power and authority to control the world—in response to Pharaoh's claim that even if Hashem existed He had no authority over the world. The third set demonstrated that Hashem's power is absolute—in response to Pharaoh's claim that, even if Hashem had powers other gods had equal powers.[7]

The first set of plagues came from below, from the water and the earth, and being a lesser form of plague, they were performed by Aharon. The second set of plagues came from the air, and being a higher form of plague they were performed by Moshe. The last four

---

2) שמו"ר טו-כז, אדר"נ לג 3) ספרי האזינו, מלבים וארא ז-יד 4) הגדה וע"ע כל בו ומחזור ויטרי 5) גר"א
6) מלבים וארא ז-יד 7) שם, ראה גם הגדת ריטבא

plagues came from the sky, and being the highest form of plague, they were performed by Hashem Himself.[8]

Pharaoh received a warning about the first two plagues in each of the three sets of plagues. The third plague in each group came without warning, because once someone is twice warned and does not repent, it is unnecessary to warn him again. When the next set of plagues began, however, a new lesson was being taught, and the warnings would begin again.

The three plagues about which Pharaoh was not warned were lice (*kinim*), blisters (*shechin*) and darkness (*choshech*), three plagues which caused pain and inconvenience to Pharaoh and the Egyptians but did not threaten their lives.[9] Those three plagues also occurred simultaneously with each other. During the plague of lice, the Egyptians were smitten with blisters and darkness, during blisters, they were plagued with lice and darkness, and during darkness, they were plagued with lice and blisters.[10] In addition to this, during each of these plagues, a pestilence or epidemic hovered over the air of Egypt.[11] Each of the first nine plagues also signified Hashem's control of one of the aspects of the world. The tenth plague, death of the firstborn, signifies His direct control over life and death.[12]

PLAGUE	WARNING	ATTRIBUTE	POWER OVER
blood	*warning*	Hashem's existence	water
frogs	*warning*	Hashem's existence	aquatic creatures
lice	*no warning*	Hashem's existence	dust of the earth
wild animals	*warning*	Hashem's authority	land animals
epidemic	*warning*	Hashem's authority	life of land animals
blisters	*no warning*	Hashem's authority	humans
hail	*warning*	Hashem's power	nature
locust	*warning*	Hashem's power	flying creatures
darkness	*no warning*	Hashem's power	day and night

---

8) תוס' על הגדה, רא"ש והדר זקנים, בשמו"ר יב-ד מבואר החלוקה כך:ג' ראשונים מן הארץ וע"י אהרן, ברד ארבה וחושך מן האויר שבין שמים וארץ ע"י משה, ערוב דבר ובכורות ע"י הקב"ה ומכת שחין ע"י כולם יחד, רשב"ם בהגדתו מגדירם כך: ג' הראשונים היו מכות האדמה, כת השנית היו מקרי העולם, כת השלישית מכות האויר, בטור נפרטו בסדר אחר, ישנם בעולם ד' יסודות אש רוח מים עפר. דם צפרדע וברד היו במים, כינים שחין וערב בעפר, דבר ארבה וחושך ע"י הרוח, ובכוריהם מתו ע"י אש, ראה גם באב"ע חזקוני אלשיך ושפתי כהן מש"כ בזה 9) רמב"ן וארא ח-טו, מלבים ז-יד, הגדת מחזור ויטרי, הדר זקנים, רמב"ם הל' סנהדרין יח-ד וכו' ובהגהות מיימני וע"ע סנהדרין פא: 10) הגדה ע"פ יעב"ץ, הגהות מיימני, דעת זקנים, אותיות האחרונות כשח אותיות חשך 11) שמו"ר י-ב, הגדת שבלי הלקט 12) חיי עולם ח"א טו

The Order of the Plagues

The order of the plagues also followed the pattern of a king who subdues a rebellious city. First, he sends his troops to lay siege to the city. As soon as the besieging army is in place it cuts off the water supply of the city. Then they bring in special battalions of troops who let loose wild, bloodcurdling cries to frighten the people inside the city and get them to surrender. If they persist in their rebellion, he brings up archers who send clouds of arrows into the city. Then he brings in barbarian mercenaries who seek out and destroy the livestock of the city. Then he throws a corrosive chemical called naphtha at the surviving livestock, resulting in plague and famine. If the city has still not capitulated, he brings up catapults to hurl boulders at the city. Then he brings battering rams and other artillery pieces to bombard the city and smash its gates and walls. Then his assault troops pour into the city and arrest the rebels. The prisoners are held in dark dungeons while their fate is decided. If there are still pockets of resistance, the leaders of the rebels are executed.

Similarly, Hashem first sent Moshe and Aharon to besiege Pharaoh. The siege began with the plague of blood (*dam*) which cut off the Egyptians' water supply. Then He sent multitudes of noisy frogs (*tzfardeia*) to frighten the Egyptians. When they still resisted, He sent clouds of lice (*kinim*) that penetrated their bodies like arrows. Then He sent wild beasts (*arov*) and pestilence (*dever*) to injure the Egyptians and kill their animals. He then attacked the bodies of the Egyptians themselves with blisters (*shechin*) and hailstones (*barad*). Then He sent locusts (*arbeh*) to overwhelm and subjugate the entire land of Egypt, after which He trapped them in darkness (*choshech*) and killed their firstborn (*makas bechoros*).[13]

There is no doubt, of course, that Hashem could have easily destroyed Egypt with just one of the plagues. But Hashem wanted to draw out the punishment of the Egyptians in retribution for all the pain and suffering they had caused the Jewish people, and He also wanted to demonstrate His power for all the world to see.[14]

---

13) מדרש ויושע פסוק ד', ילקו"ש קפ"ב, פסיקתא דרב כהנא ז (דף י), תנחומא בא ד 14) אלשיך תהלים עח פסוקים מה עד מח

The Duration of the Plagues

Before we begin the account of the actual plagues, it is necessary to point out that there are varying opinions as to the dates and duration of the plagues. According to some opinions, the plagues began in the month of Av,[15] while according to others they began in the month of Iyar.[16] Each plague lasted a month, but there is a difference of opinion if the warning period was seven days and the actual plague about three weeks or vice versa.[17] All are agreed that the total period of retribution for Egypt was twelve months, ending on the fourteenth of Nissan. Significantly, whenever Hashem punishes great numbers of wicked people, the punishment lasts for twelve months, just as the Mabul, the great flood during the generation of Noach, lasted for a full twelve months.[18*]

Hashem Decrees the Plague of Blood

Egypt is a very fertile land, but no rain falls on it. The thirsty soil is watered by the great Nile River which overflows its banks every year and saturates the land with water. Everything in Egyptian society revolved around the Nile River. Pharaoh claimed he was god, and that he had made the river. The river itself was worshipped as a god by the Egyptians. Now, as the plagues began, Hashem decided to strike at the Nile with the first two plagues to show the Egyptians that the Nile was completely in the control of Hashem and had no powers of its own.[19]

The first attack on the Egyptians, therefore, was on their idolatrous beliefs.[20] The great Nile, whom they had assumed to be a god, would turn to foul-smelling blood and lose all credibility in the eyes of the Egyptians.[21] Moreover, had another part of Egypt been

---

* Although the actual plagues began in the month of Av, the judgment of the Egyptians began when Moshe was at the Sneh, exactly one year before the exodus of the Jewish people. (Gra on *Seder Olam 3*)

---

15) רבנו בחיי בא י-ה, שמו"ר ה-יט ברד"ל ורש"ש, סדר עולם ג, גר"א, ע"ע רמב"ן רבנו בחיי ואב"ע בפרשת בא דיי"מ ששלש מכות היו בניסן, באוה"ח ו-ו מפורש דאיכות השעבוד נתמעטה אחר מכת דם אבל עדיין עבדו קצת, באברבנל ח-טז דאחר מכת ערוב לא עבדו כלל 16) מדרש הגדול וארא ז-כה 17) תנחומא וארא יג, שמו"ר ט-טז ברד"ל ויפ"ת, רבנו בחיי וארא ז-כה, רי"מ שהי' לערך כח יום, דעת זקנים מביא שהיה יום של הפסק וכל מכה התחילה בר"ח 18) עדיות ב-י ובראב"ד, תוס' ר"ה יא. 19) לקח טוב וארא ז-כח, שמו"ר ט-ט, רש"י ז-יז 20) שמו"ר שם, רש"י שם 21) מדרש הגדול וארא ז-יז

attacked first, they would have claimed that their own gods were acting out of anger. Clearly, the supposed gods had to be attacked first.[22] It was also appropriate that the water of the Egyptians should be stricken, because the Egyptians had prevented the Jews from purifying themselves in the ritual baths[23*] and because they had enslaved them as water carriers.[24]

Pharaoh apparently had no intention of letting the Jewish people go, Hashem told Moshe.[25] The obvious difference between the wonders performed by Moshe and the simple magic of his own sorcerers had not caused him to change his mind. He had hardened his heart against the obvious truth.[26] The futile anger seethed within him, bringing his blood to a boil and hardening his whole body.[27] Now, he would suffer the consequences of his stubbornness, and Egypt would be devastated by the first of the plagues.[28]

The time had come for the plagues to begin, and Hashem commanded Moshe to strike the source of Pharaoh's drinking water—the Nile.[29] Moshe was to take his staff with him when he confronted Pharaoh, because it would remind him of the staff that swallowed all the other staffs and frighten him.[30] Moshe was to explain to Pharaoh that this time he was not coming to present a sign but to wreak havoc on Egypt. The staff would strike the waters of the Nile, and the river would instantly turn to blood.[31]

Why blood? Because the Egyptians had spilled the blood of the Jewish people.[32] Because they had thrown the Jewish children into the water, staining it with Jewish blood.[33] Because Pharaoh had bathed in the blood of freshly slaughtered Jewish children when he had leprosy.[34]

Hashem now commanded Moshe to go confront Pharaoh at the riverside, where he goes every morning. It would be easier to speak to him there, where he would be alone, than in the palace, where he

---

*The fish in the Nile died as retribution for Pharaoh's having prevented the Jewish people from multiplying like fish. (*Klei Yakar*)

22) שם 23) שמו"ר ט-י 24) תנחומא בא, ילקו"ש קפב, מדרש ויושע 25) אוה"ח וארא ז-יד 26) רש"י וספורנו שם 27) שמו"ר ט-ח וברד"ל 28) מלבים וארא ז-טז 29) שמו"ר כ-א 30) שמו"ר ט-ח וברד"ל והכוונה על האות שעשה משה לפני בנ"י דמשמע דבבית פרעה היה מטה אהרן ועי' לעיל פרק י"ב ציון 32 דבאב"ע מובא שהיה מטה משה גם אז וא"ש שיזכור ויפחד 31) שכל טוב ואב"ע וארא ז-טו וכו' 32) לקח טוב ז-יז 33) משנת ר' אליעזר, זבח פסח, מדרש הגדול שם, מלבים שם ז-כה 34) שפתי כהן וארא ז-יט, משנת ר' אליעזר יט, במדרש תלפיות ערך אותיות אות א' איתא דכמו שדור המבול נענש במים דדומה לחנק יען והשחיתו דרכי הטהרה, כמו כן אירע למצרים על שפגעו בכנסת ישראל דודתו של הקב"ה (וכעניין סוטה)

was always surrounded by dignitaries, servants and guards.[35] There he would not be able to avoid Moshe.[36] The early morning time was also appropriate, since Hashem rewards and punishes early in the morning.[37]

But why was Pharaoh always to be found at the riverside early in the morning?

Pharaoh's palace was built alongside the Nile River, and when the river overflowed its banks and rose onto the land, Pharaoh's palace seemed to float in the water. Pharaoh claimed that his divine powers made the river rise, when the rise was in fact caused by a series of dams which prevented the waters from spilling into the sea. Pharaoh would go out to the river in the morning to make it appear as if he was causing it to rise.[38] Pharaoh would practice his magic and blaspheme against Hashem, saying, "The river is mine. I made the river."[39]

Furthermore, since Pharaoh had told the Egyptian people that he was a god, he could not allow them to see that he had normal human bodily functions. Therefore, he issued a decree forbidding anyone to leave his home before a certain time each morning, and while the streets were empty, he would hurry down to the riverside to take care of his bodily needs. There would thus be an added benefit in Moshe's confronting him while he was in the middle of taking care of his bodily needs. Pharaoh would be embarrassed to have his silly charade exposed,[40] and Moshe would show him that Hashem knew all his secrets.[41]

But Moshe was reluctant to accept this mission against the Nile River. "Does a person who drinks from a well show his gratitude by throwing a rock into it?" Moshe responded to Hashem. "How can I hit the water when these very same waters saved my life when I was an infant? When my mother put me into the river in a basket made of reeds, the waters remained calm and did not sweep me away to my death."[42]

35) טור וארא ז-טו 36) לקח טוב, ריב"ש שם, חזקוני מוסיף דמים הוא מקום נקי מע"ז משא"כ בית פרעה 37) מדרש הגדול וארא ז-טו, מלבים מביא שהזהיר פרעה ע"י הנילוס שיוכחש אמונתו בו ואח"כ הזהירו שנית בפני כל 38) מדרש ד' מלכים, תנחומא בראשית ז, אב"ע אברבנל 39) מועד קטן יח., תוס' שבת עה. 40) תנחומא וארא יד, שמו"ר ט-ח וברש"י, פענח רזא וארא ז-טו, ילקר"ש קפב, תורה שלמה מעתיק קומץ המנחה דאדרבה, ע"י שיראו שיבזה את הנילוס אע"פ שהיא אלוה עוד יתחזקו באמונתם בו שזה אות שהוא יותר אלוה ממנה, בשכל טוב ואב"ע איתא שזה גופא היה אופן עבודתה וכדמצינו בבעל פעור וע"ע ברבנו בחיי שם 41) אוה"ח וארא ז- טז 42) שמו"ר כ-א ובמתנ"כ

Hashem acknowledged the justice of Moshe's words, and as a result, He designated Aharon to strike the river and set off the first of the plagues.[43]

Moshe Meets Pharaoh

Early the next morning, Moshe went down to the riverside near the palace. Sure enough, Pharaoh was taking care of his bodily functions in the river.

Moshe came closer and grabbed Pharaoh's arm.

"Let go of me!" Pharaoh shouted. "Can't you see that I need my privacy now? Don't you see what I am doing?"

"Of course I see what you are doing," Moshe replied. "Some god you are! Since when does a god have to go to the bathroom? How do you explain this to the Egyptians?"

"That's none of your concern," Pharaoh replied. "They are all fools. They'll believe anything I tell them."[44]

"Well, listen to me, your majesty," said Moshe. "Hashem finds your treatment of the Jewish people unacceptable. It is customary in the world for people in a neighborhood to welcome a new neighbor and make things easier for him. But what have you done? You cajoled the Jewish people into settling in Egypt, offering them prime land and sweet words. Once they were settled here, you enslaved them!

"Hashem will punish you for your perfidy![45] Hashem, the Lord of the Jews, has sent me to tell you to release the Jewish people, but you have disobeyed Him.[46] You claimed you did not know Him. Well, Hashem will now send you a symbol that will prove to you once and for all that He exists."

Moshe brandished his staff in the air.

"Do you see this staff? When this staff hits the water, the entire river will turn to blood. Then you will know the truth!"[47]

The Plague of Blood

For three weeks, Moshe repeated his warnings to Pharaoh, but Pharaoh did not respond. Time had run out.

On a Thursday night in the month of Av, Moshe and Aharon went down to the river together.[48]

---

43) שמו״ר ט־י וביפ״ת, משנת ר׳ אליעזר יט 44) מדרש אגדה וארא ח־טז 45) מדרש הגדול בא י־א 46) וארא ז־
טז 47) לקח טוב, תרגום יונתן רמב״ן וספורנו ז־טז וכו׳ 48) פרדר״א ט, רבנו בחיי בא י־ה וע״ע ילקוט ראובני מ

"Stretch out your hand in all directions of Egypt," Moshe told Aharon. "Then hit the river with your staff!"[49]

Aharon did as Moshe told him. He struck the water with the staff, and all the waters of Egypt instantly turned into blood.[50]

All of Egypt was full of blood. There was not a place in Egypt that was spared the plague. The Nile river, the canals, ponds, pools, ditches—every body of water had turned to blood.[51] Only the waters of Goshen, the land where the Jewish people lived, remained pure and did not turn into blood. In the rest of Egypt, however, all the water had turned to real blood, not just the appearance of blood. It looked like blood. It smelled like blood. It tasted like blood. It was blood!

The fish and all other aquatic creatures could not survive in the blood and died.[52]* The Egyptians were overcome by the stench of dead fish blended with the overpowering smell of blood.[53] During the Flood in the times of Noach, the fish survived. In Egypt during the plague of blood, however, Hashem wanted the fish to die, so that no one could claim the god of the fish had caused the plague.[54] Moreover, the fish had fed on the dead bodies of the drowned Jewish children, and now they would suffer the consequences.[55]**

The blood was everywhere. Even the water absorbed in wood and rocks turned to blood. Blood oozed from the Egyptian idols.[56] It sprayed from the beams of every Egyptian home.[57]

Inside their homes, the blood totally disrupted the normal lives of the Egyptians. They could not eat, and they could not drink. Drops of water on ladles and dishes turned into blood. Women making bread saw blood spurt from the dough in their hands. Blood would bubble out of boiling pots and extinguish the flame underneath, ruining all the food. Even foods previously cooked turned bloody.[58] The juice that was squeezed from the fruit turned to blood.

---

* Blood is warmer than river water, and the change in temperature will kill the fish and other small aquatic creatures. (*Ibn Ezra, Baal Haturim, Rabbeinu Bachia*)

** This follows the opinion that the children who were thrown in the water died.

---

49) מדרש הגדול רמב"ן אב"ע ומלבים וארא ז-יט וכו' 50) רשב"ם ואוה"ח וארא ז-כ וכו', רבנו בחיי מביא שרק שורש מימי מצרים זאת אומרת הנילוס הוכה ואידך לא הוזקו כי אם בדרך ממילא 51) מדרש הגדול ורש"י וארא ז-יט 52) רבנו בחיי תוס' ספורנו ומלבים וארא ז-יז וכו' 53) שכל טוב וארא ז-יח 54) לקח טוב ומדרש החפץ וארא ז-יח 55) תולדות יצחק וארא ז-כא 56) מדרש הגדול שם, ריב"ש כתב דההתהפכות לדם היה היה לרגע בלבד ומיד חזר לטבעו ולא יכלו אח"כ לשתות כי נבאשו ע"י הדגים שמתו 57) מדרש הגדול וארא ז-כא 58) מדרש

Even the body fluids of the Egyptians turned to blood.[59]

Those Egyptians that ventured to drink the blood saw their stomachs swell and then burst.[60] Animals died from the lack of water to drink.[61]

Egypt had always prided itself on the exceptional clarity and purity of its water. Whenever a body of water would be in any way contaminated, the Egyptians would use special wood and stone apparatuses to purify the water. But these methods were ineffectual against the mighty power of Hashem. Egypt was flooded with blood, and there was nothing they could do about it.[62]

The Waters of Goshen

All the waters of Egypt had turned to blood, except for the waters of one district—Goshen, the home of the Jewish people. In the rest of Egypt, the people were overcome by a terrible thirst. In desperation, they searched for water in the underground cataracts alongside the Nile, hoping that Aharon's "magic spell" had not affected those waters not visible to the naked eye. But it was a futile effort. Every drop of water within the borders of Egypt, excluding the district of Goshen, had turned to blood.[63]

To make matters worse, all the fish in the Nile choked to death

הגדול ואראז-יט, ספר הישר 59) שמו"ר ט-י ואילך במהרד"ו ויפ"ת, תנחומא ואראיג, ע"ע מדרש הגדול
60) זוה"ק כב ויתכן לצרף מה שהבאנו בציון 34 שהיח כעין סוטה 61) אברבנל ואראָ 62) הגדת ריטבא, הכתוב
והקבלה 63) שמו"ר ט-יא וברד"ל, אב"ע ורי"ש מביאים שיטה דהמים שלמטה מן הארץ לא הוכה, ראה גם
בחת"ס עה"ת שם

on the bloody ooze that had replaced the sparkling waters of the river.[64] The stench of rotting fish hung over Egypt like a malignant cloud, and the lucrative fishing industry, one of the main pillars of the Egyptian economy, was destroyed.[65]

The Egyptian scientists and magicians mounted a determined campaign to reverse the effects of Aharon's "magic spell" and make the waters of Egypt drinkable once again, but these also failed miserably. Slowly, it dawned on the Egyptians that they were totally powerless in the face of this plague, and this drove them to despair.[66]

During this time, word got out that the waters of Goshen had remained fresh and pure, but as soon as an Egyptian drew some water to drink, it turned to blood. The Egyptians realized that the difference was not between Goshen and Egypt but between Jews and Egyptians. Apparently, Aharon had added a wrinkle to his "magic spell" that deactivated it with regard to his own people, the Jews. To counteract this wrinkle, they forced Jews to drink from the same bowl as the Egyptians, but to their astonishment, the water remained fresh and pure in the mouth of the Jew but turned to blood in the mouth of the Egyptian, killing him on the spot.

Presently, the Egyptians discovered that if they bought water from a Jew it would remain water even in Egyptian hands. The assertion of the Jew that he was selling water apparently prevented it from turning to blood. Thousands of parched Egyptians flocked to Goshen. Enormous amounts of money passed into the hands of the Jews in exchange for some priceless drinking water, and the Jewish people became wealthy.[67*]

In the Face of the Evidence

In spite of all their tribulations, the Egyptians refused to be deterred from the path they had chosen for themselves. They refused to admit that the plague of blood was an act of Hashem, the God of the Jewish people. The royal ministries

---

* Some suggest that the Egyptians did not die of thirst. Only sweet drinking water was plagued. Bitter and salty water was available, but was consumed with great reluctance. The Egyptians would much rather purchase sweet water from the Jews than drink the bitter waters. (*Rabbeinu Bachia, Midrash Hagadol, Malbim*)

---

64) וארא ז-כא, וע׳ תוס׳ ריב״ש מושב זקנים פני דוד ור׳ אליעזר מגרמייזא דכל מים שהיה בכלי מתחית לא נפגע 65) רבנו מיוחס וארא ז-יח 66) רש״י וספורנו שם 67) שמו״ר ט-י, מדרש הגדול וארא ז-כ, שפתי כהן וארא ט- א, מעוניין דבפני דוד פ׳ בא וכן בשפתי כהן מובא שלפני כל מכה ומכה טעמו ישראל מעין המכה כדי שיודו לד׳ אח״כ בשעתה

informed the Egyptian people that the plague of blood had been caused by a powerful magical incantation, and to prove it, the Egyptian sorcerers would duplicate the feat.[68]

Some of the sorcerers had been prepared for this in advance. As soon as they heard the warning that the waters of Egypt would turn to blood, they prepared flasks of water, and as the plague struck, they mumbled their silly incantations over the water as it turned to blood. The people who witnessed this demonstration spread the word that they had seen Egyptian sorcerers turn water into blood.[69]

Other sorcerers bought water in Goshen and brought it into Egypt.[70] Then they used their magic to create the illusion that it had turned to blood.[71] "You see," they crowed. "We can also turn water into blood. There is nothing remarkable in what Aharon has done." They failed to mention that the water they had turned into "blood" could not have killed the fish in the river. Therefore, the overpowering stench of rotting fish should have been adequate proof that the plague was not a mere magic trick. But the Egyptians did not want to face the truth, and they ignored the evidence of their own eyes—and noses.[72]

Pharaoh Hardens His Heart

Ironically, the evil Pharaoh, who was the worst villain of all the Egyptians, suffered the least during the plague of blood. Among all the Egyptians, he was the only one unaffected by the plague. Hashem had chosen to give him yet another chance to repent of his own free will. Hashem also wanted to reward Pharaoh for the years Moshe had lived in the royal palace and enjoyed Pharaoh's hospitality. And finally, Hashem wanted the Egyptian people to be filled with awe and admiration at Pharaoh's immunity to the plague, making his eventual downfall that much more humiliating.[73] Having no problems with his own drinking water and fully aware that the people could import water from the Jews in Goshen, Pharaoh did not feel Egypt was on the verge of destruction.[74]

Nevertheless, there was tremendous devastation caused to the

---

68) וארא ז-כב 69) רבנו בחיי שם 70) תרגום יונתן ודעת זקנים ז-כב, ע׳ לעיל בציונים 56 וגם 63, בשכל טוב איתא שחרטומיהם נטלו מי גשם ועשוהו לדם וצ״ב דלא ירדו גשם במצרים 71) לקח טוב וספורנו וארא ז-כב וע׳ סנהדרין סז: 72) אוה״ח וארא ז-כא, ספורנו ז-כג 73) משנת ר׳ אליעזר יט, מדרש הגדול וארא ז-כג, בציון 64 הבאנו דמים שעמד בכלי מתחת לא הוכה וע׳ לעיל דרק מעמודי וגלולי הבית פרצו דם ולא ממאכלם ומבואר היטב במדרש הגדול 74) ר׳ אליעזר מגרמייזא, תוס׳ ואה״ח וארא ז-כב, מסתברא לומר שבדוקא הניח השי״ת מקומות שלא נפגעו כדליעיל כדי שיעשו החרטומים את שלהם ועי״ז יוכבד לב

kingdom by the plague of blood, yet Pharaoh stubbornly refused to budge. The sign of the blood accomplished no more than the sign of the staff becoming a serpent had accomplished.[75]* As soon as Pharaoh saw his own magicians turn water into blood as Moshe and Aharon had done, he hardened his heart and dismissed from his mind all thoughts that the plague was an act of Hashem.[76]

The plague lasted for a full seven days before it finally subsided.[77] It was a long time, however, before the river recovered its purity and the stench of decomposition faded from the land. For the meantime, the Egyptians had to dig new wells for their drinking water. The memory of the plague did not fade so quickly.[78]

The Warning of the Second Plague

Egypt was still reeling from the effects of the plague of blood, when Hashem instructed Moshe to warn Pharaoh about the impending second plague. This time there would be no private early morning meetings at the riverside while the rest of Egypt slept. This time Moshe and Aharon were to confront Pharaoh in his royal palace in the middle of the day when he was surrounded by the royal courtiers. This time all would know that Pharaoh had been warned that a dreadful plague was imminent.[79] If he failed to release the Jewish people, Egypt would be overrun by *tzfardeia*.[80] Unlike a mortal king who conceals his battle plans from his enemies, Hashem sent Moshe to warn Pharaoh about the next plague; He gave him fair warning and a chance to do *teshuvah* before the *tzfardeia* came.[81]

What were the *tzfardeia*? According to most opinions, they were frogs, amphibious creatures who made loud croaking sounds.[82] Their Hebrew name indicates that they knew how to communicate with birds. According to other opinions, they were insects who

---

* Pharaoh explained away the plague of blood by Egypt's close proximity to mountainous Kush. He believed that the red dust of the mountains in Kush had been washed into the Nile, turning it red. (*Haggadah Zecher Yehosef*)

---

75) רש"י ולקח טוב וארא ז-כב וכו' 76) שמו"ר ט-יא 77) וארא ז-כה, שמו"ר י-א וכבר הבאנו אותם שאמרו
שעצם האזהרה היה לשבעה ימים והמכה כ"ג ימים, בלקח טוב איתא שז' ימי ימי הדם היה סימן להנהגת טהרת
המשפחה שלא הניחו אותם לעשות 78) מעם לועז וארא ז-כה 79) לקח טוב ומלבים וארא ז-כו, רוקח מוסיף
שלא יוכל פרעה לטעון אח"כ שלא שמע אזהרתם כי היה עסוק בעסקו ע"י היאור 80) רשי וארא ז-כז
81) שמו"ר ט-ט ובמהרז"ו 82) אב"ע ומלבים וארא ז-כז

croaked all night but stopped when morning came.[83*] Others suggest that they were large amphibious reptiles—crocodiles.[84] Regardless of the identity of the actual *tzfardeia*, all species of amphibious life would overrun Egypt during the plague of *tzfardeia*.[85]

The *tzfardeia* would ascend from the river and invade Pharaoh's house, swarming into his bedroom and bed. Then the *tzfardeia* would swarm into the houses of the servants and the houses of the rest of the nation, attacking their ovens and baking dishes.

After that, the *tzfardeia* would attack Pharaoh himself, then the Egyptians and then Pharaoh's slaves.[86] Pharaoh would be afflicted first, because his immunity to the plague of blood had made him intensely conceited. This time, however, he would have the honor of being the first to suffer.[87] Moreover, Pharaoh was the first to draw the Jewish people into forced labor by pretending to join the laborers, and therefore, he would be the first to suffer.[88]

The plague of frogs was also an escalation over the plague of blood. The plague of blood had shown Hashem's power over water, as did the Great Flood during the time of Noach, but Pharaoh could still have denied the power of Hashem over the land. The frogs swarming over the land, however, would show conclusively that Hashem's power extended over the land as well.[89]

In many ways, the plague of frogs was punishment measure for measure for the suffering the Egyptians had inflicted on the Jewish people.

The Egyptians had prevented the Jewish people from offering the sweet sounds of their prayers and songs to Hashem, and now, the Egyptians would be subjected to the endless croaking of the frogs, a sound which horrified the Egyptians and drove them to the edge of madness.[90] The Egyptians had robbed the Jewish people of their sleep by dragging them off to their labors at the crack of dawn,

---

* Ever since the plague of blood, the birds were reluctant to drink the water. The *tzfardeia* showed the birds that the water in the Nile was drinkable again. (*Rimzei Aish* on *Tana d'bei Eliyahu*)

---

83) ילקו"ש קפב, תנדב"א רבא ז, תוס' עה"ת שם, חצי מנשה, ראה גם בלקח טוב, צפרדע נוטריקון צפור-דַע כלומר דעת הצפוֹר וגם דצפרא לשון בקר דרא וכבפנים 84) ע' אב"ע אברבנל ומלבים וגם ברמב"ן בא י-יד 85) מדרש הגדול וארא ז-כר 86) וארא ז-כח וָהֵלאה, במושב זקנים וכן בבעה"ט איתא שפרעה וביתו הוכו קודם העם יען והם הכבידו על בנ"י ביותר 87) משנת ר' אליעזר שם, מדרש הגדול ז-כו וכו' 88) שמו"ר י-ג, מדרש חסרות ויתרות באוצר המדרשים קצט 89) הגדת ראשית ביכורים 90) זוה"ק, שפתי כהן וארא ז-כח

and now, the Egyptians would be robbed of their sleep by the infernal croaking of the frogs.[91]

The Egyptians had demeaned the Jewish people, not just enslaved them. They had rushed them off to their labors without allowing them time to go to the bathroom, and now, the Egyptians themselves would be demeaned by the frogs that crawled in and out of their intestines.[92] The Egyptians made sport of the Jewish people by sending them out to catch repulsive insects, rodents and reptiles, and now, the Egyptians would suffer the revulsion of the frogs.[93] The Egyptians forced the Jews to eat their bread with filthy hands soiled by dirt and clay, and now, the Egyptians would have to eat bread contaminated by the filthy frogs.[94*] The Egyptians had made the Jewish people carry their merchandise for them, and now, the Egyptians were forced to carry loads of frogs in their bellies.[95] The Egyptians burned Jews on their altars in their pagan ceremonies, and now, the Egyptians would find the food in their ovens swarming with frogs.[96]

The Plague of Frogs

Having received his instructions from Hashem, Moshe set off to warn Pharaoh about the plague of frogs.[97] Once again, Hashem told Moshe that out of gratitude to the river that had once saved his life he should not be the one to initiate the plague. Aharon would be the one to do it.[98] He would extend his staff over the waters of Egypt and bring a flood of frogs onto the land.[99]

---

* The frogs also assaulted the Egyptians with a barrage of deafening noise. The Egyptians had caused the heartwrenching sounds of Jewish mothers screaming and weeping when their children were thrown into the sea and swept away by the current. In retribution, Hashem subjected the Egyptians to the maddening croaking sounds of the frogs—who in a certain way resembled little babies. (*Zevach Pesach, Malbim*) Furthermore, the noise was in retribution for the suppressed cries of the Jewish mothers who stifled any sound while giving birth for fear that the Egyptians would discover their newborn males. (*Zevach Pesach, Sifsei Kohein*) It was also in retribution for the crying of the Egyptians infants that was used to find the Jewish newborn. (*Chida*) According to others, the noise of the frogs was in retribution for the cries and moans of the Jewish laborers. (*Tosefos*)

---

91) לקח טוב ושכל טוב שם 92) תוס' עה"ת ח-ח 93) תנחומא וארא יד, ילקו"ש קפב, שמו"ר י-ד ביפ"ת 94) שפתי כהן וארא 95) ילקו"ש קפב, מדרש כהן וארא 96) שפתי כהן וארא 97) רמב"ן בא י-ב 98) שמו"ר י-ד 99) מדרש הגדול וארא ח-א וכו'

Moshe relayed Hashem's instructions to Aharon, and as soon as Aharon stretched out his hand on the waters of Egypt, a single frog ascended and covered the land of Egypt.[100]

This single frog was enormous, created by Hashem especially to administer the plague. It lumbered out of the water and set off straight for the royal palace. The guards were terrified by its approach, but they did not flee. They hurled stones at it and attacked it with every weapon and instrument in their possession. One Egyptian ran forward and struck the frog a vicious blow. Suddenly, six frogs sprang from the mouth of the monster frog. Again the Egyptian hit the frog, and even more little frogs sprang from his mouth. The Egyptian saw that with each blow he struck the frog brought forth a swarm of new frogs, yet in his blind anger, he kept striking the frog and causing new frogs to appear. The great frog came to a halt and let out a loud, booming croak. Instantly, his croak was answered from every direction by frogs croaking, and all the neighboring frogs answered its call. Frogs from every possible direction swarmed and covered the whole land of Egypt.[101]

The frogs hopped into the royal palace, and headed straight for Pharaoh's bedroom. They leaped into his bed and tunneled into the bedding, croaking and biting as they went.[102] During the plague of blood, Pharaoh had sat comfortably in his room, admiring a sculpture of Sarah commissioned by his grandfather and quite removed from the flood of blood that had engulfed Egypt. This time, Pharaoh did not enjoy such ease and comfort. He was beset by countless croaking and biting frogs.[103]

The plague of frogs buried Egypt under a blanket of deafening noise. The noise was so loud and painful that the Egyptians thought they would die.[104] Children and infants were actually dying from the deafening noises.[105] The Egyptians could not hear one another over the horrendous croaking.[106] They could not sleep, because of the incessant pounding on their eardrums.[107] Frogs clambered into the bellies of the Egyptians, but the sounds of their croaking were barely muffled by the stomach walls of the Egyptians. In a way, the infernal sounds were more horrible than the pain.[108]

---

100) וארא ח-ב, שמו"ר י-ד 101) מלבים וארא, ברכת פרץ שם, סנהדרין סז: ברש"י, זוה"ק, תנדב"א רבה ז, שמו"ר
י-ד, תנחומא וארא יד, תוס' עה"ת וארא ח-ב, וע' מאורי אש בתדב"א שם מה שנראה לו בפי' 102) מדרש הגדול וארא
ז-כו וכו' 103) זוה"ק שם, שפתי כהן שם 104) אוה"ח וארא ח-ד 105) זוה"ק שם 106) שם 107) שם, שכל טוב שם
108) זוה"ק שם, תנחומא בא ד, שמו"ר י-ו וביפ"ת, ילקו"ש קפ"ב, זקוקין על תדב"א שם, ראה גם ישעי' כח פסוקים

The Jewish people were ignored by the frogs, but the Egyptians were under siege. They fled for their lives, seeking some shelter where they would be safe from the frogs.[109] Some Egyptians ran into their homes and barricaded the doors and windows against the frogs.[110] Others hid in sealed underground caves.[111] When the frogs reached these fortified places, they found miraculous strength and smashed the barriers to smithereens. Then they swarmed over the Egyptians hiding in the houses and the caves.[112]

The situation for the Egyptians was hopeless. The frogs were everywhere, inescapable and unavoidable. Frogs were being created by the thousands every second.[113] The moisture of an Egyptian's sweat produced a swarm of frogs.[114] Any place that had dirt with liquid moisture surrounding it produced frogs.[115] An Egyptian fetching water found it infested with frogs, which would then jump into his body and kill him.[116] If an Egyptian tried to walk in the street, he would step on a frog and become injured in the process.[117]

י-יג 109) זוה״ק מובא בילקוט ראובני 110) אלשיך, שפתי כהן וארא ז-כח 111) בעה״ט וארא ח-ב 112) שמו״ר
י-ג, כצינונים 110-111 113) זוה״ק 114) ספר הישר 115) שמו״ר י-ג ברד״ל ויפ״ת 116) שם, מדרש מובא בתורה
שלמה נה 117) ר' אפרים וארא ז-כז

The Egyptians were unable to escape the fearsome onslaught of the frogs who attacked every part of their bodies—hands, feet, even the hidden parts. The frogs climbed into their clothing and burrowed into their armpits.[118]

In the fields, the frogs ripped apart the trees and left the landscape desolate.[119] They attacked the animals as well, clambering into their bodies and killing them.[120]

In the cities, they infested every corner of the Egyptian homes. They sought out the women in the bedrooms and injured them so severely that they could no longer bear children—in retribution for the Egyptians having prevented the Jewish people from having children.[121] The frogs crawled into the bathrooms and bit them, totally demoralizing them.[122]

The frogs reached the dining rooms, where the Egyptians were trying to fortify themselves against their terrible situation by having hearty meals. But it was no use. The frogs got into all the beverages. When an Egyptian would drink something, he would ingest frogs along with it. The frogs would then crawl through his internal organs, biting and nipping everywhere. And croaking. Always that loud and maddening croaking. Even frogs not swallowed by the Egyptians pierced and gnawed into the bellies of the Egyptians.[123*]

The frogs invaded the kitchen and jumped into the cooked dishes without fear of injury.[124] They jumped into the bowls in which the Egyptian women were kneading their dough and buried themselves in the dough. When the women placed the frog-filled dough into the ovens, the fires occasionally went out; the coldness of the frogs had extinguished the flames and saved their lives.[125]

Many of them, however, were burned in the ovens, baked into the bread. When the Egyptians ate this bread, an amazing thing happened.

---

* Some suggest that the frogs jumped into their glasses from on top of the table. Others suggest that the sediment rather than the liquid turned into frogs. Each granule of sediment turned into a frog, which was promptly swallowed by the unsuspecting Egyptians. (*Seichel Tov*) Others suggest that although the frogs had the miraculous ability to break through the marble and stone walls of the buildings in Egypt, they were unable to penetrate the stomachs of the Egyptian people. Thus, the Egyptians lived, but were in incredible pain. (Alshich, *Tehillim* 78)

118) תוס' וארא ז-כט 119) שפתי כהן וארא ז-כח 120) שם 121) שמו"ר טו-כז, י-ג במתנ"כ ועץ יוסף
122) ילקו"ש קפב, תנדב"א שם 123) שמו"ר שם י-ג ובמפרשיו, תנחומא יד, לקח טוב שם ז-כט, ילקו"ש קפ"ב,
זוה"ק 124) ספר הישר 125) שמו"ר י-ב וברד"ל, מהרש"א פסחים נג:

The frogs suddenly came to life in the bellies of the Egyptians. They began to croak and cavort in the bellies of the Egyptians, while the Egyptians became ill. Blisters and rashes erupted on their skin, often leading to a painful death.[126]

These frogs set an important example for the future. A thousand years later, the Babylonian emperor Nevuchadnezzar erected a statue of himself and commanded his subjects to bow down and worship it. Three righteous Jews named Chananiah, Mishael and Azariah refused.

The emperor gave them an ultimatum, "Bow to the statue, or be thrown into the furnace!"

"The frogs in Egypt were not servants of Hashem in the same way we are," they said. "They could not expect rewards in the World to Come as we can. And yet, the frogs went into the ovens of Egypt to fulfill the Will of Hashem. Certainly, we who are true servants of Hashem must glorify His Name by going into the ovens! And just as the frogs were saved from death, so will we survive."

And that was indeed what happened. Nevuchadnezzar had these three righteous men thrown into the furnace. And not only were they saved, the walls of the furnace fell away to reveal the great miracle to all the world.[127]

Ironically, the plague of frogs helped to settle a border dispute between Egypt and neighboring Kush. The extent of the presence of the frogs was now used to define the borders of Egypt, since the frogs never stepped an inch out of Egypt.[128]

Worse than the frogs, who stopped short of killing for the most part, were the other amphibious creatures that came up onto land.[129] The snakes that slithered across the land were not so kindly, biting and killing whatever Egyptians they encountered.[130] The crocodiles were not any better.[131] The plague of blood had deprived the crocodiles of the fish they normally ate, and now they were ravenously hungry, eating children, animals and everything in sight. The land was littered with rotting carcasses, and the atmosphere was corrupted.[132]

During this whole plague, Pharaoh sat on his throne dressed in his royal robes and covered with swarming frogs. His face was

---

126) שכל טוב, שפתי כהן, זוה"ק וארא 127) פסחים נג:, סנהדרין צב:, ר' אפרים, הדר זקנים, תוס' וארא ב-כט, ראה גם רש"י ויקרא כב-לב 128) שמו"ר י-ב, רבנו בחיי וארא ז-כז 129) מדרש הגדול שם 130) בעה"ט בא י-יז 131) אברבנל וארא 132) שם וחלקו עליו באב"ע, ע"ש במלבים שם

contorted with excruciating pain as the frogs pranced in and out of his body and his clothing, biting him at will.

From deep in his stomach, he could hear the conversation of two frogs. "When do we get out of here?" asked one of them. "When [Moshe] the son of Amram prays for our release," the other responded.[133]

Pharaoh Summons Moshe

After six awful days of suffering from the frogs,[134] Pharaoh finally acted. The problem he addressed, however, was not how to stop the plague ravaging his kingdom. Rather, it was how to convince the Egyptians that the plague had not been sent by Hashem. Pharaoh called in his magicians and commanded them to duplicate the feat accomplished by Moshe and Aharon.[135] The Egyptian magicians chanted their incantation and went through their routines, and—lo and behold!—there were frogs. Again, they used their tricks and illusions to convince the Egyptian people that they could do the same things, and therefore, Moshe and Aharon were only highly skilled magicians.[136] But all they were able to do was create the illusion that they could duplicate the plague. There was nothing they could do to stop it.

Frustrated by the failure of his magicians and his own unbelievable pain, Pharaoh finally began to suspect that there might be more than magic to the powers displayed by Moshe and Aharon. They might actually be agents of Hashem.[137] Afraid that the frogs in his belly were endangering his life, Pharaoh summoned Moshe and Aharon to the royal palace.[138] He could no longer wait for other solutions to present themselves.[139]

"Please, I beg you," Pharaoh said to Moshe and Aharon as soon as they entered his presence. "Pray to your God. Ask Him to rid me and Egypt from these frogs. If you can accomplish this, I will send out your nation and you will be able to sacrifice and celebrate your holiday to Hashem."[140] How ironic! Pharaoh who had once denied Hashem was now asking Moshe and Aharon to pray to Hashem.[141] The first crack had appeared in Pharaoh's armor of disbelief in Hashem.[142]

---

133) מדרש הגדול ז-כו , ח-ד שם, שמו"ר י-ב ובמתנ"כ 134) שמו"ר י-ה במהרד"ו ויעו"ש ברש"ש 135) שמו"ר י-ד 136) מדרש הגדול שכל טוב וספורנו וארא ח-ג 137) אב"ע וספורנו שם 138) שמו"ר י-ה, אב"ע אוה"ח ואר ח-ד, מעם לועז 139) פענח רזא ואר שם 140) תרגום יונתן שם 141) לקח טוב שם 142) הגדה זכר יהוסף

"I can safely say that I can get my requests answered at any time," Moshe replied. "Go ahead! Test me! When should I ask Hashem to rid you and your home of the frogs?[143] Whatever you ask I will do—to prove that everything is in Hashem's hands. Unlike your magicians who cannot do things part way, I will leave the frogs in the water to show I can keep them alive and not get rid of them totally.[144] Those that did not yet come up from the river to plague the Egyptians will remain there, and bring you no harm."[145]

I'm still not quite sure this is a plague from Hashem, Pharaoh thought. There is a little thought niggling in the back of my mind that, after all is said and done, they may have fooled me. Perhaps Moshe and Aharon are just two very clever magicians. But if Moshe can really get rid of them, I will believe it is an act of Hashem.[146] Still, why is Moshe so eager to get rid of the plague for me? Perhaps he knows that the magic is wearing off, and he wants to take credit for bringing it to an end.[147] Yes, I still have my doubts. Therefore, since magic can only be done from noon to midnight, I will ask Moshe to get rid of the frogs in the morning.

"Get rid of the frogs tomorrow morning," Pharaoh finally said, to make sure Moshe wasn't using magic.[148] He was also too proud to show he was suffering unbearable pain.[149]

"I will do exactly as you say," Moshe replied. "I will prove to you that all this is the work of Hashem, and there is none like Him.[150] I will pray that the frogs remain in the river. If you are indeed a god as you claim, your majesty, you should be able to get rid of the frogs yourself."[151] Hashem also wanted the Egyptians to smell the dead remains even after the plague was over. Furthermore, it proved that it was not done by magic, because magic would have removed the frogs from the water as well.[152]

Moshe Prays to Hashem

Moshe and Aharon immediately left the idol-infested districts of Egypt and went to the designated place for prayer to Hashem.[153]

---

143) רש"י וארא ח-ה, תרגום יונתן שכל טוב ואב"ע שם, ראה גם רמב"ן שם 144) מדרש הגדול, ר' יהודה החסיד, ספורנו אוה"ח ומלבים שם 145) שמו"ר י-ה ברד"ל, מדרש הגדול, ריב"ש ואב"ע ח-ה 146) מלבים וארא ח-ד 147) רבנו בחיי אב"ע אוה"ח שפתי חכמים ומלבים ח-ה וכו' 148) רבנו בחיי אוה"ח ומלבים שם 149) מושב זקנים ור' אפרים שם, בהדר זקנים ופענח רזא כתוב דהכוונה היתה שלמחר יצאו ממצרים 150) מדרש הגדול ומלבים וארא ח-ה וכו', בשמו"ר י-ה איתא דלמחר היה יום האחרון של המכה 151) מנחה בלולה וארא ח-ה 152) ספורנו מאור ושמש שם, באברבנל ושפתי כהן איתא שנשארו שם למזכרת נצח וכל פעם שיביטו עליהם יזכרו ויראדו 153) לשכל טוב וארא ח-ח

The Egyptian magicians heard Moshe's voice ring out in prayer, loud and clear above the croaking frogs.[154]

"You told me I will be a master over Pharaoh," Moshe cried to Hashem. "I have promised him that the plague would stop tomorrow. Since I always speak to him in Your Name, please make my words come true. Otherwise, I fear Your Name will be desecrated in the eyes of the Egyptians."[155]

Hashem answered Moshe's prayer. The next day, all the frogs in the houses, courtyards and fields of Egypt suddenly died. The frogs that had glorified Hashem's Name by risking death in the ovens of the Egyptians were allowed to live.[156] The frogs in the bellies of the Egyptians were also allowed to live since their death would have killed the Egyptians in whose bellies they sat.[157] All the other frogs died, because they had fulfilled the purpose for which they had been created—the plague of frogs.[158] The frogs that did not die were returned to the river, as Moshe had promised.

Pharaoh Hardens His Heart

It should have been a day of celebration for the Egyptians. After seven dreadful days, the plague of frogs had finally ended. But the Egyptians had no time or stomach for rejoicing. Egypt lay devastated, its waters polluted, its land covered with an endless carpet of frog carcasses.[159] The entire population was mobilized to collect the dead frogs, and even the slowest workers managed to collect tons of dead frogs.[160]

The atmosphere was contaminated by the stench of the dead frogs.[161] Many Egyptians were overcome by the awful smells,[162] and epidemic diseases also swept across the land.[163]

Little by little, however, a measure of normalcy began to return to Egypt. The smell began to recede, and the land and the water began to recover. It was now time for Pharaoh to make good on his promise to let the Jewish people go. But Pharaoh stubbornly refused.[164] The land was returning to normal, and Pharaoh no longer felt the pressure.[165] Besides, Pharaoh rationalized to himself, Moshe

154) ר' אפרים שם 155) שכל טוב שם 156) ילקו"ש קפב, פענח רזא, ספורנו ומלבים כתבו דרק אותם שהיו על הארץ מתו ולא שבבתים 157) תוס' עה"ת שם ח-ט 158) פענח רזא שם משא"כ בערוב שחזרו כולם למקום מושבם 159) ריב"ש ואר"א ח-י 160) שכל טוב ובעה"ט שם 161) לקח טוב ואר"א ז-כח 162) שכל טוב שם 163) ר' אברהם בן הרמב"ם ואר"א ח-טו 164) רשב"ם ותוס' ואר"א ח-יא 165) ספורנו וכל"י שם

had promised to remove all the frogs from Egypt, and the land was still covered by dead frogs. Surely, he should have removed the dead frogs as well as the live ones.[166] Following the typical behavior pattern of wicked people, Pharaoh cried out for help when he was in trouble but forgot all his promises when his life returned to normal.[167] He even forgot that he had ever made such promises.[168] It was time for another plague.

The Plague of Lice

The first two plagues of the first set of three were over. Pharaoh had been warned and, by his failure to heed the warnings, had brought horrible suffering upon himself and his kingdom. The third plague would come without warning, punishing him for ignoring the warnings as well as enslaving the Jewish people.[169]

The land of Egypt would be struck by a plague of lice, a result of the contamination of Egypt by the decomposing frogs and the next logical plague in the progression of proofs of Hashem's existence.[170] The plague of blood could have been attributed to magic, because it affects only water. The plague of frogs affected land, but it originated in the water. The plague of lice, however, was entirely unrelated to water.[171] They came from the dust of the earth.

Why the dust of the earth? There were several reasons. For one thing, it interrupted the terrible labors of the Jewish people.

The Egyptians used to send the Jewish people into the fields to replenish the dwindling supplies of dirt for the bricks. When all the dust of the earth would turn to lice, there would be no more dirt to gather, and they would finally rest. The Egyptians would also make the Jewish people sweep the dirt from the streets and market places of Egypt. This, too, would stop when all the dirt became lice.[172] There was also an element of measure for measure in this plague. The Egyptians had prevented the Jewish people from bathing, causing them to become infested with lice. Now the Egyptians would get a taste of living with lice.[173] Moreover, it was as though Hashem was cursing the earth for being the cause of Jewish suffering.[174]

---

166) מלכים שם 167) שמו"ר י-ו 168) מדרש מובא בתורה שלמה קכ 169) מושב זקנים וארא ח-יב, הגהות מיימני בהגדת הרמב"ם 170) אברבנל וארא ח-יג 171) הגדת ראשית ביכורים וכעי"ז בכמה רשעי העולם כהמן וטיטוס 172) שמו"ר י-ז ובעץ יוסף, תנדב"א שם, מדרש הגדול וארא ח-יב 173) לקח טוב, בעה"ט, מדרש הגדול וארא ח-יב, ח-טו 174) הגדת זבח פסח, שפתי כהן וארא ח-יב וכו', עוללות אפרים מוסיף טעם בזה דע"י יראו כולם איזה אלוה הוא, אפילו כינה קטנה אינו יכול לברוא על אחת כמה וכמה שלא יצר יצר את עצמו!

The Plague Begins

Hashem instructed Moshe to tell Aharon to take his staff and hit the ground, turning all the dust of Egypt into lice. Once again, because of gratitude, Aharon was to administer the plague and not Moshe. The Egyptian soil had protected Moshe when he had killed the Egyptian by keeping the Egyptian's body hidden among its clumps of sod for a long time.[175] It would now be inappropriate for Moshe to strike the land and cause its dust to turn to lice. Therefore, it was Aharon who waved his staff in all directions over the land of Egypt and struck the dust of the earth.[176]

On impact, a cloud of lice arose from the earth and spread across all of Egypt.[177] In addition to the ordinary lice, worms and fleas that thrive on poor sanitation and decay,[178] new strains of lice sprang miraculously from the minuscule grains of dust that covered the ground. All in all, Egypt was infested by fourteen species of huge miraculous lice,[179] ranging in size from a hen's egg to a goose's egg.[180]

The dust that lay on the ground of Egypt became a carpet of lice two *amos* (four feet) deep.[181] Their fields, grains, fruits, all of their crops and their animals grew mantles of lice. Even dirt and dust inside the houses turned into lice.[182] Even Goshen was infested by lice, but only its cultivated land, in retribution for the earth's contributing to the suffering of the Jews. Virgin soil in Goshen, however, was free of lice. Centuries earlier, Yaakov had asked not to be buried in Egypt, because he knew that all graves, not being virgin soil, would be covered with lice.[183]

The lice attacked the Egyptians viciously, crawling into their clothing and attaching themselves to the hair and skin on their faces, their nostrils, inside their ears and all over their bodies. There was so much lice on them, nearly thirty pounds worth, that their vision was blocked and they could not see where they were going.[184] The lice dug their tentacles into the Egyptians and feasted on their flesh and blood, causing them excruciating pain.[185]

The Egyptians tried to flee the lice, but there was no escape.

---

175) שמו"ר י-ז במתנ"כ ומהרד"ו 176) העמק דבר וארא ח-יב, כתב האלשיך שנטיית המטה הביאם על האנשים והבהמות, והכאת הארץ המשיכו את הכינים מן העפר 177) רשב"ם ואב"ע וארא ח-יב 178) רשב"ם ריב"ש ורוקח וארא, תנדב"א שם 179) תנדב"א שם, שפתי כהן מעיר דהיו כמנין "יד" ולא כהודאת החרטומים שאמרו שאצבע אלקים בלבד 180) ילקו"ש וארא קפב 181) שכל טוב וארא ח-יב, ספר הישר 182) מדרש הגדול ח-יב, זוה"ק ח"ב ל 183) מדרש הגדול שם ובשפתי כהן 184) רוקח, ר' אפרים, בעה"ט שם, מדרש מובא בתורה שלמה סז 185) מדרש הגדול שם, תנחומא בא ד, ע"ע רמב"ם אבות ה וברבנו יונה שם, הגדת ריטב"א, שפתי כהן וארא

Wherever they ran, clouds of lice pursued them.[186] They plunged into the river, but the lice plunged right in after them.[187] The Egyptians squirmed and scratched and writhed in pain, rubbing their ravished backs against the wall until the blood flowed freely, but it was no use. The pain and the bleeding continued unabated.[188] Hashem was repaying them measure for measure for causing the Jews to bleed and suffer the torments of lice infestation.[189]

The Magicians Fail

Pharaoh summoned his magicians to the palace and commanded them to use their sorcery to put an end to this maddening plague.[190] The Egyptian magicians soon returned.

"Your majesty," one of the magicians said. "We most humbly beg your pardon, but there is nothing we can do about this plague. We cannot duplicate it, and we cannot make these lice disappear. They are much more difficult than the blood and the frogs.[191] There is simply nothing we can do that will affect these lice in any way."

"Why not?" asked Pharaoh angrily. "Have you tried everything in your arsenal of sorcery?"

"Oh, yes, your majesty," replied the magician. "We've tried all sorts of incantations, potions and brews, but they accomplish nothing, I'm afraid. Believe me, we are deeply embarrassed that we cannot duplicate the magical feats of Aharon, the old Jew. This plague is just too difficult!"[192]

"What makes this plague different?" grumbled Pharaoh in a nasty temper.

"Because we are only able to conjure up demons if we are working with items at least the size of a barley or lentil. But lice are by nature much smaller than that, and our magic doesn't work on them, even these overgrown ones.[193]* Also, we use the powers of *tumah*, defilement, to effect our magic, and *tumah* also requires something the size of a barley."[194]

"There is another reason," a second magician offered. "In order

---

* Although these lice were larger than barley, since the normal size was smaller, they were unable to duplicate the plague. (*Yefei To'ar*)

186) תוס׳ וארא ח-יב 187) בעה״ט וארא ח-יד, מעם לועז וארא ח-יד 188) מעם לועז וארא ח-יג 189) מעם לועז שם 190) שם ר׳ יהודה החסיד ורשב״ם וארא ה-טו 191) רש״י אב״ע חזקוני ושפתי כהן וארא ח-יד וכו׳ 192) חזקוני ומלבים ח-יד 193) שמו״ר י-ז וביפ״ת, סנהדרין סז:, ילקו״ש וארא קפב, הדר זקנים 194) גור אריה וארא ח-יד

for us to be able to work our magic, we have to have our feet firmly planted on the ground. This is simply not possible now, because the lice cover the entire ground. Your majesty, we are not standing on the ground. We are standing on lice!"[195]

"Perhaps I can add one more reason," said another of the magicians. "It may be a little dangerous for me to say this in public, but we all know that a great part of our magical powers lies in our ability to create illusions. To accomplish this, we have to work with forms that already exist on the earth. But these lice, your majesty, are some kind of species that has never been seen before. We cannot do anything with them."[196]

"If I may add just one final word," said another magician with a wry look on his face. "There is a very simple and practical reason why we can do nothing, your majesty. We are too busy scratching! How can we work our magic if we are being eaten alive by these horrible lice that are all over us?"[197]

"I'm afraid we must concede defeat, your majesty," said the first magician. "Moshe and Aharon are much greater magicians than we are."[198]

"Nonsense!" shouted Pharaoh. "No one is greater than the Egyptians in magic, sorcery and witchcraft! If Moshe and Aharon can do it, why can't you?"

"Ahem, your majesty," said the first magician. "I was only being diplomatic by calling them greater magicians. In truth, I do not believe that they are practicing magic here. As you say, your majesty, no one is superior to us in magic. No, we believe that there is a different phenomenon at work here." He drew a breath to bolster his courage. "We believe that we are seeing the Finger of Hashem."[199] They had recognized the Finger of Hashem, the same Finger that had created Adam from the dust of the earth.[200]

For lack of an alternative, an awareness of Hashem had finally been admitted by the Egyptians, and an acknowledgment that the plagues were designed to prove His existence.[201] But in their arrogance, the magicians belittled Hashem's wonders as being small things, the kind which come from one finger.[202] However, they also

---

realized the further implications of their words.

"Your majesty," the magicians said. "If this is the work of His Finger, can you imagine what He could do with His whole Hand?" Clearly, the magicians were coming to the realization that every-thing happening in Egypt—the serpent, the blood, frogs and now the lice—had all come directly from Hashem.[203]

Pharaoh Hardens His Heart Again

Pharaoh was now stripped of the support of his magicians, who readily admitted they were no match for Moshe and Aharon.[204] From then on, Pharaoh would never again call on his magicians to duplicate or coun-teract the "magic" of Moshe and Aharon.

There was no longer any question that Hashem ruled the world and held everything and everyone in His power.[205] And yet, amaz-ingly, Pharaoh still hardened his heart, as Hashem had told Moshe he would do.[206] Pharaoh never felt that his own life was threatened by the plague, and therefore, he was able to shut his eyes to the obvi-ous truth and continue in his obstinate refusal to give in.[207] Sitting in the palace with its dirt-free marble floors, he felt distant from the lice that had generated spontaneously on the dirt-covered grounds and floors of the rest of Egypt. The thought of his people being infested with lice did not disturb him so much, since it was quite common for peasants to have lice.[208]

Having decided to be stubborn and harden his heart, Pharaoh rationalized to himself. Why hadn't he been warned about this plague as he had been warned about the first two? Surely, Moshe had not been aware of the coming of this plague, which proved that everything that had happened was caused by natural phenomena controlled by the gods and the stars, not the God of the Jews.[209]

And yes, there was another puzzling point. If Moshe and Aharon were indeed responsible for these freakish lice, why hadn't they made them small, like lice are supposed to be? The answer lay with the explanation of the magicians. Magic required a minimum

---

202) שפתי כהן וארא ח-יב 203) שכל טוב, מדרש אגדה וארא ח-טו, שמו"ר י-ז ובעץ יוסף 204) רבנו בחיי וארא ח-יד 205) רמב"ן ורבנו בחיי וארא ח-טו 206) וארא ח-טו וברש"י 207) אוה"ח וארא ח-ד 208) ריב"ש וחזקוני וארא ח-טו, בספר הישר מסופר שגם פרעה ואשתו נפגעו בה ואי נלמוד דרק כיני הגוף עלו עליו ולא של העפר אז יתכן שחשב שאין זה נס אלא שאויר מצרים מוזהמת ע"י המכות שעברו ועיין באברבנל 209) אב"ע ומלבים וארא ח-טו

size, and normal lice were just too small. So why couldn't the magicians do anything with the lice? Simple. Moshe and Aharon were better magicians. There was no way around it, much as it was painful to admit. They were just too good. But there was still no reason to release the Jewish people from bondage.[210]

And so Pharaoh hardened his heart once again and refused to let the Jewish people go.

The plague ran its course and was finally over. But the lice on the bodies of the Egyptians remained with them until the day they died.[211] Their ravaged bodies were the "signs" about which Hashem had told Moshe. The "wonders" were the obstinate refusal of the Egyptians to allow the Jewish people to leave, even though their country was being destroyed right in front of their eyes.[212]

The first set of three plagues was complete. It had served its purpose, proving to all of Egypt that Hashem existed—even though Pharaoh himself continued to live in a self-induced fantasy world. The next set of plagues was about to begin.[213]

---

210) חידא וארא ח-ט,טו, אוה"ח שם ט-יד 211) מלבים ומעם לועז וארא ח-יד 212) דברים רבה ז-ט 213) מלבים וארא ז-יד

Beasts, Epidemics and Boils

14

The new set of plagues began where the first had left off—with a destructive invasion of living creatures.[1] Hashem told Moshe to go and warn Pharaoh that if he did not let the Jewish people out of Egypt, mixed hordes of wild animals and birds of prey would attack him, his slaves and his entire kingdom.[2] Among these animals would be many timid creatures who generally avoided human contact and lived in the seclusion of the deep forests, caves and catacombs. Now, however, they would all abandon their timid natures and become ferocious predators intent on the destruction of Egypt.[3]

The wild animals would not attack Goshen, the homeland of the Jewish people, demonstrating conclusively to Pharaoh the clear distinction between Egypt and Goshen.[4] The Jewish people, Hashem's

---

1) אברבנל וארא ח-ט-טז   2) וארא ח-יז ברש"י ואב"ע, תוס' עה"ת שם, שמו"ר יא-ב
3) אברבנל מלבים ומדרש הגדול וארא ח-יז   4) לקח טוב, תרגום יונתן וארא ח-יח

precious flock, would be protected from the wild wolves.[5] Although the plagues of blood and frogs had also not affected Goshen, Pharaoh and his advisors denied that it was in order to spare the Jewish people. Both of these plagues originated from the Nile River, and therefore, it was logical that the central areas of Egypt, which were closest to the river, would be most affected. But animals and birds are not restricted to any habitat, and they could easily have penetrated Goshen. But they did not! Moreover, they actually passed through Goshen on their way to Egypt—without causing any harm or damage to its Jewish inhabitants.[6]

For the previous plague, Hashem had told Moshe to warn Pharaoh in front of his entire royal court. This time, however, Hashem instructed Moshe to confront Pharaoh on his early morning excursion to the river to tend to his bodily needs. Tired of hearing about all the plagues that would descend on Egypt, Pharaoh had begun to linger at the riverside so as to avoid Moshe's visits to the palace.[7] But to his chagrin, Moshe would be waiting for him to tell him about the plague of wild beasts and show him that Hashem controls the entire universe.[8]

Moshe was to tell Pharaoh that the plague would arrive on the following day, and in the meantime, the animals would begin to gather from great distances where their habitats lay and travel across Egypt.[9] The peaceful but ominous sudden migration of animals into the population centers of Egypt would convince the Egyptians that this was more than just coincidence. It was clearly an act of Hashem![10] And as the messenger of Hashem, Moshe was to command the animals to begin their assault on Egypt.

"But how?" Moshe asked Hashem. "Can anyone confront a lion and not be torn apart?"

Hashem reassured him and told him not to be afraid. He was to go out to the fields and announce to the beasts, "Hashem has ordered you to attack Egypt. From the day you were created, you were all designated for this task. Make peace among yourselves, and unite against the common enemy—Egypt!"[11]

---

5) רוקח וארא שם, ע"ע שמו"ר יא-ב וברד"ל 6) רמב"ן רשב"ם מושב זקנים ומלבים וארא ח-יח וכו' 7) שמו"ר יא-א ובמהרז"ו, אב"ע וארא ח-טז 8) לקח טוב רש"י רבינו בחיי ומושב זקנים וארא ח-יט, בתוס' עה"ת מובא דקיום האמיתי של ושמתי פדות בין עמי ובין עמך למחר וגו' אעולם הבא קאי (ע"ד שאמרו היום לעשותם ולמחר וכו') כלומר ע"י שיתלבשו באופן משונה ועי"י אות ברית קודש הנחתמת בבשרם יזכו להתנהגות מיוחדת בעלמא דקשוט, וכבר הבאנו בפרק א' שאכן בזכות זה נגאלו 9) מלבים וארא ח-יט, וע' שמו"ר יא-ב ובעץ יוסף 10) רשב"ם וארא שם 11) מדרש הגדול וארא ח-יז

Measure for Measure

Once again, the plague brought upon the Egyptians was designed to punish them measure for measure. The Egyptians had sent Jewish laborers deep into the forests to capture wild beasts for their sporting events and idolatrous rituals. In the process, many Jews were killed, and even those that survived were separated from their families and unable to have children. Now, the Egyptians would suffer from the wild beasts.[12] The Egyptians had forced the Jewish laborers to tend to their animals. Now, Hashem would use animals to punish the Egyptians.[13] The Egyptians were immoral and promiscuous people, whose lineage was mixed and confused by adultery. Now, they would be punished by mixed hordes of animals.[14]*

Furthermore, the Egyptians forced the Jewish people to spend endless hours nursing Egyptian babies and taking care of large groups of Egyptian children. The wild beasts would devour these children and bring a small measure of freedom to the Jewish people.[15]

Wild Beasts Are Coming!

Early the next morning, Moshe went down to the riverside to confront Pharaoh, as Hashem had instructed him to do.[16] When he arrived, Pharaoh was in the middle of tending to his bodily needs.

"Your majesty," Moshe called out. "I have a message from Hashem."

"Leave me alone," Pharaoh responded. "Can't you see that I'm attending to my needs?"

"Attending to your needs?" Moshe asked. "I thought you claimed to be a god. Do gods move their bowels?"

"So I'm not a god," Pharaoh replied with a shrug. "Right now, I

---

* They also wanted to dilute the genealogy of the Jewish people by killing the males and marrying the females. In retribution, Hashem sent the mixture of animals. (*Midrash Tehillim*) In addition, the Egyptians were subjected to attack by wild beasts in retribution for having fed male Jewish children to the fish and wildlife of the sea. (*Rokeach; Sifsei Kohein, Shemos Rabbah*)

12) תנדב"א רבה ז, שמו"ר יא-ג, תנחומא יד ובעץ יוסף, ילקו"ש קפב, הגדת תימן מובא בתורה שלמה עא
13) דברי הימים למשה, הגדת זבח פסח 14) שמו"ר טו-כז, ילקוט ראובני 15) מדרש ויושע, זבח פסח, ילקו"ש קפב, מדרש הגדול וארא, באברבנל כתוב שגם ילדי מצרים סבלו והיה מדה כנגד מדה על שהטילו צער השעבוד גם על ילדי ישראל 16) לקח טוב וארא ח-טו

have to attend to my needs. Anyway, what I say to my people doesn't really mean anything. They're all a bunch of fools. They believe whatever I tell them, and if believing I'm a god will keep them in control, so be it. The truth doesn't really matter. Only what people believe matters."

"Well, you'd better believe what I'm telling you now," Moshe said. "Hashem has sent me to you with a message."

"What? Another one?" asked Pharaoh.

"Another one indeed," Moshe replied. "And this one is going to be even worse than the others. In exactly one day, Egypt will be overrun by mixed hordes of wild animals and birds of prey. No one has ever seen anything like it. But unless you let the Jewish people out of Egypt, you're going to see it tomorrow. Today, they're going to start gathering. Tomorrow, they attack."

"All right, I heard the message," Pharaoh grunted. "Now leave. I need my privacy."

Moshe turned and walked away, but privacy did not help Pharaoh with his bowel movements. While sitting there his intestines ruptured and protruded. Suddenly, rats came scampering from every direction and sank their sharp little teeth into Pharaoh's exposed intestines.

Pharaoh shrieked in agony, and his cries awakened his household and his court. People rushed to the sound of their king's voice—and discovered him in the midst of his very human functions. Some god, their eyes said with derision, although they remained silent. Disgraced and humiliated, Pharaoh returned to his palace, his heart hardened in a stubborn determination not to set the Jewish people free.[17]

The next day, the mixed hordes of wild beasts overran Egypt—as Moshe had promised. They attacked the palace first and then the rest of Egypt.[18] Pharaoh, who had been the first to attack the Jews, was once again the first to suffer the consequences.[19]

The animals converged on Egypt from every corner of the world.[20] Animals from the tropical rain forests ran side by side with animals from the frosty polar regions, no leader, no followers, all equal and united to fulfill the command of Hashem.[21] Lions, bears, leopards, panthers, hyenas, wolves, pigs, donkeys, oxen, kangaroos, foxes, wild goats, cats, hedgehogs thundered across the trembling ground of Egypt. Rats, mice, weasels, lizards, turtles, snakes, scorpions, leeches, worms scrambled through the dust. Eagles, vultures ravens, owls, pelicans, ostriches, wild birds, flies, fleas, mosquitoes, bees, hornets soared, swooped and buzzed overhead.[22] In fact, the skies in Egypt were so abundantly filled with birds and flying creatures that the sun could not be seen during the day, nor the moon at night.[23] Even the pesky frogs, the old nemesis of the Egyptians, joined the attacking hordes of wild beasts.[24]

The animals rampaged all over Egypt, through all the cities, the towns, the vineyards and the fields.[25] The predators and the normally tame animals all became ferocious beasts intent on ripping apart every Egyptian in sight.[26] Flies and fleas flew into the eyes of

---

17) משנת ר' אליעזר יט, מדרש אגדה ומדרש הגדול ח-טז 18) מדרש הגדול, מלבים וארא ח-טז ואילך 19) שמו"ר יא-ג 20) חידוש נפלאות בהגדה מגדל העדר 21) שפתי כהן שם ח-כ, העמק דבר שם, מעם לועז 22) ע' שמו"ר ג-יא, ילקו"ש קפב, מדרש הגדול, מדרש החפץ, ספר הישר, רש"י, ריב"ש, רד"ק, שפתי כהן, אברבנל ישעיה לד-יא וכו', מדרש תהלים עח 23) מדרש תהלים עח-יא 24) מלבים תהלים עח-מה 25) לקח טוב וארא ח-יז 26) מדרש הגדול וארא ח-יט ובאברבנל

the Egyptians and the hornets sprayed venom into their eyes, blinding them and leaving them immobilized, at the mercy of the larger animals. The Egyptians fled into their homes and barricaded themselves against the prowling beasts.[27]

The Sea Monster

To their great delight, the Egyptians discovered that the animals were unable to break into their barricaded homes. They breathed a collective sigh of relief and settled into the security of their homes. True, they would not be able to step out into the open as long as the hordes prowled everywhere, but at least they were safe in their homes. But it was not to be.

Out of the water, a great sea monster (called a *silonis* or, according to others, a *sironis*) emerged. It had numerous arms each of which was over fifteen feet long. The sea monster ambled through the streets of Egypt, reaching into all the houses through the roofs and ceilings and breaking open their locks. The animals were now able to push open the doors of the Egyptian houses and burst in. While this was happening, the snakes and insects had already burrowed their way through the ground and into the houses from underneath. They chased the fleeing Egyptians from room to room, and attacked babies in their cradles and bit them to death.[28]* When the doors finally were pushed in by the predators, the houses were filled with a seething mass of ferocious animal flesh. Predatory birds and other flying creatures flew in through the wide open doors and filled the air with the angry flapping of their wings and their screeches as they swooped down to attack.[29]

Nowhere to Turn

For days, Egypt was ravaged by the invasion of the animals. Only those people who fled to Goshen or who barricaded themselves in fortified castles and towers were able to escape the animals.[30] Otherwise,

---

* There is much question regarding the identity of this creature. Most authorities believe it to be a mermaid, half human, and half fish. Rav Aryeh Kaplan translates it as a squid, perhaps because of the mention of long arms in *Sefer Hayashar*. See *Yalkut* in *Vayikra* 537 and Malbim, *Shemini* ch. 11, note 80. See Rashi, *Bechoros* 8a. See Yavetz on *Perek Shirah*. See also Radak on *Shmuel I*, 5:4-5.

---

27) שמו"ר יא-ג, ספר הישר   28) ספר הישר, דברי הימים למשה, שכל טוב, מלבים וארא ח-יז וכו'   29) רוקח
וארא ח-יז   30) ריב"ש וארא ח-יט וכו'

the onslaught of the wild beasts was without respite. The animals settled into the land as if they had lived there all their lives.[31] When the
animals slept at night, the nocturnal animals came out to take up
where they had left off. Owls and wolves patrolled Egypt, ready to
strike the moment they saw an Egyptian.[32] The Egyptians dared not
sleep.[33]

"Help us," the Egyptians would beg the Jews. "Walk us home.
Protect us from these beasts!" But it was to no avail. The animals
mauled the Egyptians but ignored the Jews accompanying them.[34]

Nor did the presence of the Jews offer any protection for the
Egyptian children in their care. The Jews in charge of caring for the
children of their Egyptian masters would take the children along
with them wherever they went, sometimes taking as many as five or
ten children. But lions, bears, leopards, wolves and eagles would
accost them, each predator taking one Egyptian child—until there
were none left.

"Where are the children?" the Egyptians would ask.

The Jews would simply point at the animals and shrug.[35]

The animals vented their fury not only on the people of Egypt
but on the land itself. They uprooted trees and devoured crops. The
venom-bearing creatures contaminated everything with which they
came into contact.[36] The plague of blood had destroyed the fish in
the water and thereby deprived many animals of their food supply.
These starved animals now rampaged through Egypt eating everything in sight.[37] One particular type of animal attacked the very soil
of Egypt. This rare species had an umbilical cord through which it
drew nourishment from the soil, and now a horde of these animals
depleted the Egyptian soil of its richness.[38]

Negotiating with Pharaoh

In the heavily fortified royal palace,
Pharaoh cowered under siege, afraid to step
into the open where he could be torn apart
by the wild animals. The realization began
to sink into his mind that he could not continue to ignore Moshe and
Aharon, the messengers of the God of the Jews. It had become perfectly clear that he could not win against them by ignoring them.

---

31) שפתי כהן וארא ח-כ 32) ר' אברהם בן הרמב"ם, רשב"ם וארא ח-יז 33) ספורנו וארא ח-יז 34) אלשיך שם
35) ילקו"ש וארא קפב, תנחומא בא ד, מדרש הגדול וארא ח-יז, מדרש ויושע, שפתי כהן שם 36) שכל טוב,
אברבנל וארא ח-כ 37) אברבנל שם 38) חידוש נפלאות בהגדה מגדל העדר, דברי אליהו, חנוכת התורה וארא
ח-יז, ע' איוב ה-כב וירושלמי כלים ח-ה

Instead, he would have to try to outsmart them in direct negotiations. But first, he had to meet Moshe and Aharon, and there was no way a palace courier from the palace could get through the streets without being eaten alive. Finally, the royal summons was sent with a Jewish messenger.[39]

When Moshe and Aharon arrived, Pharaoh was waiting for them in the throne room.

"Your majesty," said Moshe. "You have summoned us, and we are here."

"Listen well," said Pharaoh. "I have been giving this whole business a lot of thought, and I've come to the realization that you are not impostors and adventurers. It is amazing how these terrible animals have come through Goshen without harming any of the Jews. I have come to the realization that there is indeed a God of the Jews, and I must deal with Him."

"We are very pleased to hear this, your majesty," said Moshe. "Does this mean that you are prepared to allow the Jewish people to leave Egypt?"

"Well, let's talk about it," said Pharaoh. "You said you wanted to leave to go into the desert and sacrifice to your God, correct?" said Pharaoh.

"Yes, your majesty," said Moshe. "We want to take a three-day journey into the desert to sacrifice to our God."

"Yes, that is what I thought I remembered," said Pharaoh. "Well, you will be happy to hear that I have agreed to let you sacrifice to Him.[40] I have really come to respect your God. He is very powerful indeed."

"We are happy to hear this, your majesty," said Moshe.

"In fact," said Pharaoh, "I respect Him so much that I am now convinced His presence is everywhere. You know, originally I thought that if this God of yours existed He must be a God of the desert. You see, I thought that was why you wanted to go into the desert—because that was where your God lived. But now I am convinced He lives everywhere, and therefore, there is no need for you to leave Egypt and go into the desert. Do you understand what I am saying?"

"I think so, your majesty," said Moshe.

---

39) רוקח וארא ח-כא (40 אב״ע וחזקוני שם

"I'm sure you do," said Pharaoh triumphantly. "I hereby give you permission to sacrifice to your God right here in Egypt. Isn't that generous of me?"[41]

"That is indeed very generous of you, your majesty," said Moshe. "However, it is just not practical for a number of reasons. For one thing, Egypt worships animals, particularly sheep and images of sheep. All animals in Egypt are used for work and not for food. How could we sacrifice animals in your own country in front of your eyes?"

"That is no problem whatsoever," said Pharaoh. "I hereby give you my full permission to sacrifice in Egypt."

"That is very kind of you, your majesty," said Moshe. "But it is very disrespectful for us to do so. We cannot do something disrespectful. It is against our nature."

"Against your nature, pah!" said Pharaoh. "A very minor problem. We will deal with that later. You mentioned other reasons. What are they?"

"The other reasons also involve the Egyptian worship of animals," said Moshe. "It is a simple matter of safety. If we sacrifice animals in Egypt, the Egyptians will undoubtedly retaliate against us, whether or not we have royal permission."[42]

Pharaoh glowered at Moshe but could not contradict him.

"No, your majesty," said Moshe. "I'm afraid we have no choice in the matter. We must take a three-day journey into the desert to Mount Chorev and sacrifice to Hashem there. Once we arrive, Hashem will tell us which animals to sacrifice, and how many."[43] The purpose of the three-day journey was, of course, to mislead the Egyptians and lure them into giving chase. In the end they would all drown in the sea.[44]

"Very well," said Pharaoh. "I cannot argue the point. You have to travel into the desert. However! However, it is not necessary to take a three-day journey. One day is much more than enough. Furthermore, I will only let you go on the condition that you first pray to your God to get rid of all these wild beasts."[45]

Pharaoh was not only being evasive, he was also being deceitful

---

41) רש"י וארא ח-כא, מלבים ושפתי כהן שם 42) שמו"ר יא-ג, רש"י רשב"ם הדר זקנים ומלבים וארא ח-כב 43) לקח טוב, אב"ע וארא ח-כג 44) שמו"ר יא-ג וברד"ל 45) שכל טוב, מלבים וארא ח-כד

and dishonest. The "you" he intended to release was the same "you" who was to pray to Hashem in his behalf—namely Moshe and Aharon. Moshe saw through Pharaoh's charade but he chose not to reveal that he understood that Pharaoh was trying to play him for a fool.[46]

"I will immediately pray to Hashem," said Moshe. "I will pray that the wild beasts begin to leave right now so that by tomorrow they will all be gone.[47] And I trust you will keep your part of the bargain and allow my people to leave and sacrifice to Hashem. In the meantime, as a show of our good faith, I will pray that the wild beasts go away even before you send us out."[48]

Pharaoh Breaks His Word

Moshe left Pharaoh and went to his designated place of prayer. He implored Hashem to withdraw the beasts so that they would be gone by tomorrow, as he had promised Pharaoh, and to make sure that no more Egyptians died, so that Pharaoh could not claim he had not kept his part of the bargain.[49]

Hashem heeded Moshe's prayer, and the following day, all the wild beasts were removed from Egypt. Not a single one remained.[50] Hashem did not want to have the animals die in Egypt, as the frogs did, because He did not want the Egyptians to benefit from the plague by using the hides of the animals. The plagues were for punishment only.[51] Moreover, the frogs had been created for the plague, and therefore, once the plague was over they had to die. The wild beasts, however, were living before the plague, and now that the plague was over, they were allowed to return to their former lives.[52]

After the plague was over, however, Pharaoh did not keep his word. Once again, not fearing the consequences, he hardened his heart and refused to set the Jewish people free.[53] He did not bother to call in his magicians, because they had already been discredited during the plague of lice.[54] Nevertheless, the plague of wild animals did bring Pharaoh a little closer to facing the truth. The previous plague had elicited an admission of the power of Hashem's finger.

46) שפתי כהן וארא ח-כה 47) וארא ח-כה 48) מלבים שם 49) ספורנו וארא ח-כו 50) וארא ח-כז תרגום יונתן ומלבים שם

51) שמו"ר יא-ג, רש"י רמב"ן ורבנו בחיי וארא ח-כז 52) תוס' עה"ת שם 53) אב"ע תוס' וספורנו שם ח-כח, אברבנל מבאר דפרעה תלה גם זה בהמזלות ועפי' גזירתם פגעו במצרים ולא בישראל 54) רבנו בחיי שם, וע' פרדר"א מח וברד"ל

This time, Pharaoh had begun to discuss the possibilities of serving Hashem. The redemption was just a few months away.[55]

Pharaoh Is Warned

Hashem now instructed Moshe to address Pharaoh harshly and reprimand him for going back on his word. Once again, Moshe was to demand that Pharaoh send the Jewish people out immediately or else Egypt would suffer another plague.[56] This would be Pharaoh's final warning. If he ignores it, the plague will strike quickly and devastatingly. There would be no opportunity for a last-minute reprieve once the plague began.[57]

The next plague would be an epidemic, a pestilence that would strike the animals of Egypt. Nevertheless, although the people of Egypt would not be affected by the pestilence, Moshe was to point out to Pharaoh that this plague should not be taken lightly. The horses that pulled his chariots were going to die. The donkeys that carried the heavy loads were going to die. The camels that carried travelers on long journeys were going to die. The cattle that pulled the plows through the fields were going to die. The goats that gave milk for the young children were going to die.[58]

Only the livestock of the Jewish people would survive intact. Pharaoh would see the wondrous miracle of an epidemic differentiating between Egyptian and Jewish animals even as they grazed together in the same pastures,[59] and he would understand that Hashem was watching over the Jews.[60]

The stench of the dead frogs and the decomposing victims of the wild animals would now be followed by pestilence—the logical next step in the systematic demolition of Egypt.[61] And it would serve the Egyptians right! The Egyptians forced the Jewish laborers to take the Egyptian flocks to faraway pastures and thus be separated from their families. Now, those precious flocks of the Egyptians would all die.[62] To make matters worse, while the Jews were tending the Egyptian flocks, the Egyptians would steal the animals of the Jews.[63] Sometimes, the Egyptians actually harnessed Jews to plow the fields so as not to overwork their animals.[64]

55) הגדה זכר יהוסף 56) רוקח ואב"ע ואראט-א 57) שפתי כהן שם ואילך ופליג על מש"כ באב"ע 58) מלבים שם (ע' דבריו ח-כב) שלא השתמשו עם שום דבר שנעשתה מבהמות 59) רמב"ן רבנו בחיי אברבנל ושפתי כהן שמות ט-ד 60) ר' אברהם בן הרמב"ם שם 61) אברבנל שם 62) תנחומא וארא יד, שמו"ר יא-ד, תדב"א רבה ז, מדרש הגדול שם 63) הגדה זבח פסח, ילקו"ש קפב 64) הגדה זבח פסח

Hashem instructed Moshe to tell Pharaoh that the plague was set to begin the very next day. The exact prediction would ensure that there could be no claims of coincidence. There could be only one explanation for the plague—a punishment for Pharaoh's refusal to set the Jewish people free.[65] After the plague of frogs, Pharaoh had said he would set the Jewish people free "tomorrow." And he had broken his word. After the plague of wild animals, Pharaoh had also said he would set the Jewish people free "tomorrow" and let them sacrifice to Hashem. And he had again broken his word. Well, there would be a sacrifice "tomorrow," but it would be the animals of the Egyptians that would die.[66] Pharaoh had only until tomorrow to free the Jewish people. If he failed to do so, all the animals would die.[67]

The Plague of Pestilence

The next day, as Hashem had promised, the plaintive howling of the dogs signaled that a great epidemic had struck Egypt.[68] Instantly, all the animals in Egypt that did not have at least partial Jewish ownership died.[69] Every animal grazing in the pastures died,[70] kosher and non-kosher alike.[71] Animals that had survived the plague of the wild beasts in the fortified towers and houses now dropped wherever they were.[72] It was a wondrous miracle that healthy animals in the best condition should suddenly keel over and die.[73]

Although the plague was directed primarily at animals, some Egyptian people also died as a secondary effect of the epidemic. People who worked in close contact with animals caught the highly contagious infection and died. Others were crushed when the animals they were riding suddenly fell over dead.[74]

The Jewish people, on the other hand, suffered no ill effects during this plague. On the contrary, if a Jew owned a sick or weak animal on the verge of death, it did not die during this epidemic—simply to keep a sharp distinction between the animals of the Egyptians and the animals of the Jews. In fact, the distinction was so clear that

---

65) מדרש הגדול, רשב"ם וארא ט-ה 66) ריב"ש ושפתי כהן שם 67) מלבים וארא ריש פרק ט' 68) שפתי כהן שם ט-ד 69) אברבנל שם ט-ו, יש נידון אי כולם מתו ע' רש"י רמב"ן אב"ע רלב"ג ובספר הישר, חזקוני כתב שאע"פ שעצם המכה היתה לא לרגע לא התחילה מכת שחין עד חודש אח"כ, בשו"ת רדב"ז ח"ג סימן תח"י איתא שנתארך המכה כשאר המכות מתחילה היו חולים ונחלשו לאט לאט עד שמתו ועי"ע שמר"ר יא-ד 70) תדב"א רבה 71) הגדת הרוקח 72) רמב"ן ורי"ב וארא ט-ג 73) מושב זקנים, ר' אברהם בן הרמב"ם ט-ג 74) ספר הישר, מדרש הגדול, הגדת השל"ה ועי' בלקח טוב שחולק

ownership disputes between Egyptians and Jews were settled during the plague. If the animal survived it clearly belonged to the Jew.[75]

Moreover, any Jewish connection was enough to ward off the epidemic. If a Jew had agreed in principle to buy a particular animal from an Egyptian, it was protected from the epidemic, even though it was still owned by the Egyptian.[76] But the ownership of the Jew had to be real. Animals in the care of Jews, however, were not protected.[77] Some cunning Egyptians, aware that the plague was coming, went through the motions of selling their livestock to Jews without actually doing it, only to see their livestock die along with all the rest of the animals of the Egyptians.[78]

There was no way around it. Only genuine Jewish livestock was protected. All others died. And when the plague was over, the Egyptians could only replenish their stock by buying from the Jews. And thus the Jewish people became very rich.[79]

Pharaoh Hardens His Heart

This time, Pharaoh did not attempt to summon Moshe and negotiate with him. There was nothing to be negotiated. The animals all died the instant the plague began.[80] Pharaoh had not suffered any personal pain because of this plague.[81] Neither did he consider the epidemic so devastating, since he could replenish his livestock through purchases from the Jews.[82] Besides, it didn't seem appropriate to release the Jewish people because of a plague that was over seconds after it began.[83]

He told himself that perhaps the plague was not from Hashem after all. Perhaps it had been caused by a confluence of astrological signs that affected only Egyptian livestock, or perhaps Egyptian livestock was fed differently from Jewish livestock.[84]

Furthermore, Pharaoh thought, not all Jewish livestock was protected. There were reports about a Jewish man whose entire livestock had died. These reports were, indeed, true, but the man was actually an Egyptian. He was the son of Shlomis bas Dibri, who had been violated by an Egyptian, the Egyptian that Moshe had killed many years earlier. This man was considered an Egyptian, because his father was an Egyptian. The Egyptians, however, considered him

---

75) שמו"ר יא-ד, מדרש הגדול וארא ט-ד וכו', שפתי כהן 76) שכל טוב וארא ט-ד 77) חזקוני שם ט-ג 78) אוה"ח שם ט-ז 79) אברבנל שם 80) ריב"ש שם 81) שפתי כהן שם 82) תוס' עה"ת שם 83) הגדה זכר יהוסף 84) אברבנל וארא ט-ז

a Jew, because his mother was a Jew, and therefore, according to their reasoning, his animals should not have died.[85*]

As a result of this sort of reasoning, Pharaoh decided to harden his heart and refuse to free the Jewish people.

The Plague of Boils

The second set of plagues was now close to completion. It was time for the plague of boils. As the final plague in its set, it came without warning.

Hashem instructed Moshe and Aharon that each of them should collect two handfuls of furnace soot. Then Aharon was to give his two handfuls to Moshe. Moshe was to take his own two handfuls plus Aharon's two handfuls in one of his hands and throw all the soot up towards the sky.[86**] All of this was to be done in Pharaoh's presence, so that he could not claim that this new plague was really a lingering aftereffect of the other plagues. It was important that he witness all the miracles of the new plague.[87]

As Pharaoh watched, the air would become foggy with dust, as during a sandstorm. The dust cloud would spread across all of Egypt, and whenever one of these particles of dust would come into contact with human or animal flesh, it would create boils—very painful boils.[88]

The furnace soot Moshe would throw towards the sky symbolized the devotion of the Jewish people to Hashem—to the extent of throwing themselves into a furnace to sanctify His Name. Avraham had been prepared to die in this fashion at the hands of Nimrod, as were Chananiah, Mishael and Azariah at the hands of Nevuchadnezzar.[89]

The boils that the Egyptians would suffer were an appropriate punishment for some of the torments to which they had subjected the Jewish people. They had forced the Jewish people to be bath atten-

---

* Before the Torah was given, lineage was through the father. This child, however, would be considered Jewish after the giving of the Torah, when lineage would be traced through the mother. (Rashi, *Emor*, 24:10)

** R' Avraham ben Harambam suggests they took smoke, which turned to dust when released.

---

85) מלבים שם   86) שמו"ר יא-ו ובעץ יוסף, ע"ע בראשית רבה ה-ז, ויקרא רבה י-ט במתנ"כ   ומהרז"ו, לקח טוב
ורש"י שם ט-ח, מלבים שם   87) ספורנו שם ט-ח, אברבנל באר   דהיה כדרכי הטבע שאחר הדבר יפגעו הנשארים
שם בשחין   88) אברבנל שם, ע' ר"ש נגעים ט-א   89) ילקו"ש וארא קפב

dants, warming up the cold water and cooling off the scalding water, but the pleasures of the baths had been reserved for the Egyptians only. But with the Egyptians covered with boils and unable to use the baths, the Jewish people would have the baths all to themselves.[90]

In addition, the Jewish people were overloaded with work and unable to treat the wounds inflicted on them by the Egyptians. The Egyptians would now be made to suffer from untreatable boils.[91] The Jewish people, driven mercilessly in their labors, suffered from the relentless heat of the sun. Now, the Egyptians would suffer from the hot soot that produced hot boils on their skins.[92]

Finally, the endless labor of the Jews kept them from their wives as if they were afflicted with boils. Now, the Egyptians would be afflicted with real boils and be separated from their wives.[93*]

Following Hashem's instructions, Moshe and Aharon took two handfuls each of furnace soot. Aharon then placed his soot in Moshe's hand, and Moshe threw the entire four handfuls of soot towards the sky. Miraculously, it reached the heavens.[94] Hashem caused the soot to turn into a thick dust that spread over the entire land of Egypt and created boils on the skin of the Egyptians and their animals.[95] The cloud of dust was so pervasive that there was no room for escape. It reached into every corner of every place.[96]

Four wondrous miracles had taken place before the eyes of Pharaoh. One, Moshe was able to hold four handfuls of soot in his one hand. Two, a weightless substance like soot had been thrown into the sky with such force that it reached the heavens, when an arrow shot from a powerful bow can only travel some two hundred feet. Three, the soot Moshe threw spread over an area equal to four hundred *parsangs*, some eleven hundred miles, when normally such a weightless substance will not scatter more than eight feet. Four, the soot that turned into dust raised boils on contact with Egyptian flesh.[97] All these miracles were designed to serve only one purpose—to show Pharaoh the power of Hashem and His ability to create something from nothing.[98]

---

* Others suggest that the boils from the soot of the furnace were in retribution for the bricks which the Jewish people had to bake in furnaces. (*Tosefos al Hatorah*)

---

90) שמו״ר יא-ו ובעץ יוסף, תנדב״א רבה ז, הגדה זבח פסח ע׳ פרדר״א מח, מעם לועז מביא שנענשו על שאנסו את בנ״י לרחוץ אותם בבתי מרחציהם 91) מדרש אגדה וארא ט-ח, תולדות אדם בהגדה מגדל העדר 92) שפתי כהן וארא, הגדה ע״פ עוללות אפרים 93) הגדת זבח פסח 94) שמו״ר יא-ה 95) שם א-ו, שכל טוב ואברבנל וארא 96) רמב״ן שם ט-ט 97) שמו״ר שם, מכילתא בשלח, מדרש הגדול, רש״י ורבנו בחיי שם ט-ח וכו׳ 98) ר׳ אפרים

The Effects of the Boils

The magicians, who were the main supporters of Pharaoh's resistance, were the first to suffer the agonies of the plague of boils.[99] But the rest of the Egyptians were not far behind. Animals acquired by the Egyptians after the plague of pestilence were also afflicted with boils.[100]

The boils developed into infectious blisters that destroyed the skin of the Egyptians like a flame and spread across their bodies.[101] Some of these boils were moist on the outside and dry on the inside.[102] The clouds of dust from the hot soot attacked the entire bodies of the Egyptians, burning the skin and raising blisters.[103] Air entered the cavity created between the flesh and the raised skin.[104] The cavity then became a breeding ground for germs and filled up with pus,[105] causing bleeding sores and swelling of their bodies.[106] Besides the blisters, the dust also created *tzoraas* all over the bodies of the Egyptians.[107] The infected flesh began to peel away, causing the exposed limbs to decay and shrivel.[108]

Altogether, Hashem sent twenty-four different kinds of boils and lesions on Egypt, some dry, some liquid, some hot, some cold. They may have included mange, which destroyed their body hair, tumors, eczema, lichen, scurvy, skin ulcers, ringworm and other inflammations and skin diseases.[109] All these boils had opposite remedies, so that remedies used to heal one, caused the others to be so inflamed that death resulted. It was, therefore, impossible for the Egyptians to do anything to alleviate their pain.[110] In fact, even after the Jewish people left Egypt, the boils remained with Pharaoh and the Egyptians. They suffered from them for the rest of their lives.[111]

The Egyptians could not stop rubbing and scratching from the constant itching of their blisters. The worst of the blisters were called *rasan*, a skin disease resulting from an infection in the brain.[112*] This

---

* It would appear that *rasan* was part of the plague. *Tzoraas* came along with the boils, in retribution for the Egyptians having kept the Jewish men from their wives, like people stricken with *tzoraas*. We find that Pharaoh was afflicted with *rasan* when he took Sarah and that the *rasan* forced him to separate from her. Therefore, it would seem that *rasan* was the type of skin disease that would have been part of the plague of boils.

---

99) עה"ת שם כל"י ז-יז 100) אברבנל, רש"י מביא מהם הניסו מהם הניראים את מקניהם בבתיהם ולא נפגעו (101
ספר הישר, רש"י אברבנל וארא ט-ט וכו' 102) ב"ק פ:, בכורות מא. 103) ריב"ש ור' אברהם בן הרמב"ם שם
104) פיה"מ לרמב"ם מקואות י-ד 105) לקח טוב ורש"ם וארא שם 106) מעם לעז שם 107) שמו"ר יא-ו
ובמהרזו"ו 108) ספר הישר 109) תורת חיים מהרב אריה קפלן, ויקרא כ-כא וכב-כב ע' תוס' בכורות מא. ובתוי"ט
על מתני' שם 110) מדרש הגדול ט-י, שמו"ר ט-ו ובעץ יוסף 111) בכורות מא., שפתי כהן וארא ט-יא 112) רש"י

disease caused a running nose and eyes, incessant drooling, loss of blood and such weakness that the afflicted person was unable to stand. Hornets would settle on the running sores and then carry the disease to other Egyptians.[113]*

The End of the Magicians

The plague of boils marked the end of the influence of the magicians in the royal court of Egypt. The magicians were unable to duplicate the plague of boils, because they could not find any healthy Egyptians upon whom to try it.[114] But even more, they hadn't the faintest idea of how to create boils from furnace soot.[115]

Earlier, they had also been unable to duplicate the plague of lice, but they had still continued to advise Pharaoh against letting the Jewish people go free, suggesting all sorts of alternative rationales for the plagues.[116] During the plague of boils, however, they were unable to exert any influence on Pharaoh simply because they were unable to get to him.[117] The magicians were so beset with boils that they could not even stand up.[118] The boils had also caused their faces to become deformed beyond recognition,[119] so that even had they been able to walk they would have stayed home to hide the shame of their appearance[120] and the embarrassment of their inability to do anything about it.[121]

The magicians had advised Pharaoh to throw the Jewish children into the water. They had also advised Pharaoh to kill Moshe when he removed Pharaoh's crown as a little child.[122] Now, they were made to suffer the worst of the plague. They never recovered from their boils, and many of them died a short time later. It was the end of the magicians.[123]

---

* The *Gemara* identifies it as a fly. However, R' Yaakov Emden in *Perek Shirah* identifies the flies in the *Gemara* as hornets.

גיטין ע,, שם כתובות ע"ז) 113: רש"י נדה יז., שם בראשית רבה מא-ב, ערוך רש"י ומהרש"א כתובות ע"ז: (114
שכל טוב ומלבים וארא ט-י"א) 115 וארא ט-י"א) שם, במלבים איתא שבב' מכות שעברו נעדרו כי לא נעשית אלא
ע"י הקב"ה   ועתה שחזרו משה ואהרן להיות שלוחיו ית' חזרו גם הם והשתדלו להתדמות להם
117) וארא ט-י"א, בפרדר"א מח ובילקו"ש קפד כתוב בפנים אחרת 118) ר' אברהם בן הרמב"ם וריב"ש וארא ט-
י"א 119) גבורות ד' נז 120) רמב"ן שם 121) תוס' עה"ת שם 122) שמו"ר יא-ו ובעץ יוסף 123) ילקו"ש קפד, מעם

Pharaoh Hardens His Heart

Hashem had told Moshe that He would harden Pharaoh's heart after the first five plagues, and this is what He did now. Otherwise, Pharaoh would have been unable to withstand the boils, the worst of all the plagues to date.[124]

No human being could have withstood the pain and agony caused by the boils, and if Hashem had not hardened Pharaoh's heart, he would certainly have agreed to let the Jewish people go free.[125] But Hashem wanted Pharaoh to give in because he recognized Hashem's power and authority, not because he could no longer stand the pain. Therefore, Hashem hardened his heart and gave him the strength to resist if he so chose.

The plague of boils would remain for all future times as a symbol of the eventual fall of the wicked. Just as the weightless soot was scattered all over Egypt and turned into dust,[126] so will Hashem one day destroy the wicked and scatter them like dust in the wind.[127]

Hailstones, Locusts and Darkness

15

The first two sets of plagues were now complete. Pharaoh was now convinced that Hashem existed and that His authority extended all over the world. However, he was not yet convinced that Hashem was the sole divine power in the universe and that no other gods existed. The third and final set of plagues would prove this to Pharaoh beyond the shadow of a doubt.[1]

By this time, Pharaoh had abandoned his charade of pretending to be a god and going to the riverside to perform his bodily needs in secret. In order to avoid meeting Moshe, he had taken to staying in the privacy and seclusion of his palace.[2] Hashem, therefore, instructed Moshe to go and confront Pharaoh early in the morning in his palace.[3] He was to give Pharaoh another chance to repent and allow the Jewish people to leave.[4] If Pharaoh refused, he would be subjected to a new

א-יב ר״מש (4 םש ע״בא (3 גי-ט אראו ןהכ יתפש ,א-בי ר״מש (2 די-ט אראו םיבלמ (1

plague which would be the equal of all the first six plagues combined.[5] This plague would have the potential of destroying everything in Egypt, its people, its animals, its crops, everything.[6]

Fire and Ice

The two weapons Hashem uses most frequently
against the wicked are fire, as in Sedom, and water,
as during the Great Flood in the time of Noach.[7] The
next plague, Hashem told Moshe, will feature a
miraculous combination of these two mutually exclusive elements.
Hailstones will fall with a deafening noise, an intermingling of ice
and fire, sulfur and smoke.[8] The ice will not cool the fire, nor will the
fire melt the ice. They will be like two generals that do not get along
but join forces to fulfill the will of the king. Michael, the angel who
controls water, and Gavriel, the angel who controls fire, will join
forces to bring the next plague upon Pharaoh and Egypt.[9]

The fire-and-ice hailstones will bombard Egypt. Trees will be
uprooted from the ground. Grains and fruits will be destroyed.
Grass and all other greenery will be shorn from the earth. Houses
and buildings will be shattered.

All living creatures, men or animals, not secluded in underground shelters will be killed.[10] And even those people who survive
the bombardment in their shelters will not escape this plague
unscathed. They will cower in fear in their miserable shelters, their
hearts disintegrating with terror as all their senses are assaulted by
the noise of the explosions and the trembling of the earth.[11]

When Pharaoh sees a plague that is so totally against the course
of nature and so totally devastating, he will surely realize that
Hashem is the sole authority and power of the world.[12] He will
know that this plague could in no way be attributed to sorcery or
magic,[13] only to the unlimited power of Hashem, who alone rules
the world.[14] Pharaoh and the Egyptians will also remember this long
after the plague is over. The evidence of the devastation will remain
in the form of sickness everywhere.[15*]

---

* This sickness was due to the changing weather patterns.

---

5) מדרש הגדול וארא ט-יד וע׳ באברבנל דמפרשו על ארבע מכות האחרונות שהיו שקולים כבולהו 6) ריב״א תוס׳
רי״ד ורש״י וארא ט-יד, שפתי חכמים כלי יקר ובאר יצחק באר דברי רש״י, ראה גם ברבנו בחיי שם 7) שפתי
כהן שם 8) אב״ע ורשב״ם שם 9) רבנו בחיי שם 10) רבנו בחיי וריב״ש שם 11) ריב״ש ותוס׳ עה״ת שם 12) ר׳
אברהם בן הרמב״ם ואברבנל שם 13) אוה״ח שם 14) אברבנל שם 15) ספורנו ט-יד

The Egyptians had sent the Jewish people out to plant and seed the fields and tend to the orchards, thus keeping them away from their families. Now, Hashem would send a hailstorm to destroy all the trees and crops.[16] The Egyptians had not allowed the Jewish laborers to rest on the grass of the fields and cool themselves in the shade of the trees. Now, the hailstorm would deprive the Egyptians themselves of the grass and the trees.[17] The Egyptians had beat the Jewish people with stones and berated them with vile and abusive language. Now, the Egyptians would be pelted by the hailstones and be deafened by the terrifying sounds of the storm.[18]

A Lesson for Pharaoh

Hashem instructed Moshe to make sure that Pharaoh would not lull himself into a false sense of security. His survival through all the previous plagues was no indication of his durability. Hashem could have destroyed him and his nation during any of the previous plagues in the blink of an eye. The only reason he survived was to demonstrate to the entire world the punishment Egypt would suffer for enslaving the Jewish people.[19] Pharaoh was like an acacia tree which is only useful when it is cut down for its wood. Pharaoh's only purpose for existence at this point was to bear the punishments administered to him.[20]

Pharaoh continued to be influenced by people like Bilam, who advised him not to let the Jewish people go.[21] Hashem would now further harden Pharaoh's already stubborn heart, making it as hard as an overcooked liver, so that He could continue to inflict His signs and wonders on Egypt.[22] As long as Pharaoh does not repent of his own free will, he would be kept alive to watch as the miraculous plagues destroy his kingdom.[23] And after everything is over, he would be granted many more years of misery during which to lament the loss of his kingdom and to tell the world of the might of Hashem. He had once declared, "I don't know Hashem." Now, he would say, "Hashem is righteous."[24]

Ultimately, Pharaoh survived the splitting of the sea and lived to tell of the great miracle he had witnessed. Disgraced, he did not

---

16) תנחומא וארא יד, תדב"א רבה ז, דברי הימים למשה 17) שפתי כהן וארא, ע' בילקו"ש ובכל"י מה שמוסיפים בזה 18) ילקו"ש ואברבנל שם 19) שמו"ר יב-א, מדרש הגדול, רש"י ט-טו, אברבנל שם 20) תנחומא וארא ב ובעץ יוסף 21) בעה"ט וארא ט-יז 22) לקח טוב בא י-א, שמו"ר יג-ג 23) רמב"ם עה"ת וארא ט-טז, ספורנו שם 24) מכילתא בשלח, רשב"ם וארא ט-טז

return to Egypt. Instead, he went to Assyria and became the king of Ninveh for many, many years. Eventually, the people of Ninveh became very corrupt and immoral, committing murder and robbery without remorse. Hashem sent the prophet Yonah to exhort them to repentance and warn them that Hashem was prepared to destroy the city.

When Pharaoh heard this, he descended from his throne and tore his garments. Then he took off his royal robes, dressed in sackcloth and put ashes on his head. He made a public outcry about the threat to the city and decreed a three-day fast for everyone in the city; whoever defied the decree would be burned at the stake. He ordered the men, women and their children to be separated from each other. Animals, too, were separated from their offspring. Altogether, one hundred and twenty thousand people raised their voices in bitter lament and sincere repentance. Hashem heard the outcry of the repentant people, and he spared the city of Ninveh.[25]

Save Your Livestock!

Hashem instructed Moshe to tell Pharaoh that at this time tomorrow a very heavy hailstorm would strike Egypt, a phenomenon unlike any that had occurred in the world since the day it was founded.[26] And wonder of wonders, the land of Egypt on which rain never falls would be pelted with rain and hail.[27]

Moshe was to warn Pharaoh and tell him to gather his livestock into a safe place, because any livestock and people remaining in the open would be killed by the hail.[28] This plague was specifically to show the might of Hashem's Hand by destroying the land, not the living creatures. Therefore, all who heeded this warning could save themselves and their livestock.[29] Unlike a mortal king who does not reveal his battle plans to the enemy, Hashem warned the Egyptians of what was in store and gave them the opportunity to save themselves.[30] Furthermore, Hashem wanted some of the Egyptians' livestock to survive so that they would have horses with which to chase the Jewish people into the Red Sea and drown there.[31]

As Hashem had commanded, Moshe went to Pharaoh early in the morning and warned him about the forthcoming plague.[32] He

---

25) פדר"א מג, ילקו"ש ח"ב תק"נ   26) וארא ט-יח   27) רמב"ן וארא ט-יב   28) ספורנו וארא ט-יט, ע"ע ברבנו
אפרים עה"ת   29) רמב"ן וספורנו ואוה"ח וארא ט-יט ואילך   30) שמו"ר יב-ב, מדרש הגדול וארא ט-יט   31) שפתי
כהן וארא ט-כ, אלשיך שם   32) רמב"ן שם ט-יט

described the dreadful effects to be expected from the hailstorm, and then he carved a notch into the wall and pointed to it.

"Your majesty, please take note of this notch," he said. "When the sun reaches this notch tomorrow morning, the plague of hailstones will begin. Those who fear the word of Hashem would be well-advised to bring their livestock in from the fields. If you leave them there in the open, they will be killed by the hailstones. There will be no survivors."[33]

An agitated murmur spread through the assembled advisors and courtiers in the palace. Moshe's warning had made them very nervous. Many considered taking Moshe's advice and bringing their livestock into shelter. After all, what was there to lose by doing so?[34]

"Your majesty," said Iyov, one of Pharaoh's chief advisors. "I have decided to tell my herdsmen to bring in my livestock from the fields. I think it is foolishness to take a risk. I would suggest that everyone else do so as well."

Bilam, another of Pharaoh's chief advisors, disagreed. "If I may be so bold, your majesty," he declared. "I am against this act of faintheartedness. Are we going to concede that this Moshe represents an all-powerful God of the Jews? Or do we stand strong in our position that the Jews are our slaves and no one can take them from us? This is a time for courage, not cowardice. I say we leave the livestock in the fields—as a matter of principle!"

True to his word, Bilam did not bring his animals in before the plague, and many of Pharaoh's advisors followed Bilam's example.[35]

The Plague of Hailstones

Early the following morning, Hashem lifted Moshe up to the heavens.[36] Moshe stretched out his hand, and the plague began. The air filled with jagged stabs of lightning and the harrowing crash of thunder. The earth began to quake.[37] Gentle raindrops began to fall from the sky, but as soon as it entered the lower atmosphere, the winds seized the raindrops and turned them into hailstones.[38]

---

33) שמו"ר יב-ב, רש"י וארא ט-יח, עץ יוסף כתב שזה האות דמאת ד' היתה זאת ולא ע"י כוחות הטומאה, אברבנל מביא שזה היה מלבו הטוב ולא נצטווה ליעץ כן 34) אברבנל שם 35) תרגום יונתן וארא ט-כ וכו', ע' שמו"ר יב-ב 36) מעם לועז, ע' רש"י ושפתי חכמים שם ט-כב 37) מדרש הגדול שם ט-כג, ע' מדרש שוח"ט עח 38) ילקו"ש וארא קפו

Some hailstones were like transparent ice balls with bright flames flickering inside. Others were coated by a mixture of fire and ice, so that the skies were streaked with fire as they fell to the ground. The ice did not cool the fires, nor did the fires melt the ice.[39] When the hailstones struck the ground, they burst open, releasing tongues of flame. The flames also burst open, releasing yet another destructive ball of ice hidden inside.[40]

The hailstones were the size of bricks, and when they came crashing down on the land of Egypt, they pulverized the trees down to their roots, and completely destroyed the grass, crops, fruit and orchards throughout Egypt.[41]

The noise of the thunder and the crashing hailstones was deafening, carrying to the ends of the earth.[42] There was no modulation as there is with normal thunder. Instead, each clap of thunder exploded with the same deafening crash.[43] It was in the merit of the Jewish people, who would soon receive the Torah amidst thunderous noise, that Hashem afflicted the Egyptians with thunderous noises.[44]

---

39) ע׳ שמו״ר יב-ד, במדבר רבה יב-ח במתנ״כ מהרז״ו ועץ יוסף, פרקי דרב כהנא דף ג, ילקו״ש שם, רבנו בחיי ט-לג 40) מדרש הגדול וארא ט-כג 41) רד״ק תהלים עח-מז, ספר הישר, מדרש הגדול ט-כה 42) תוס׳ עה״ת וארא ט-כג 43) שכל טוב וארא ט-כח 44) ילקו״ש וארא קפו

The hailstorm struck with a sudden fury. The thunder and lightning did not warn of coming rain or hail. Rather, they both came together in the same instant, allowing no time or opportunity for escape to safety into caves and shelters. The heavy hailstones killed whatever was in the open.[45]

It's Too Late!

In the first moments of the hailstorm, the Egyptian people were overcome by a whole range of emotions—disorientation because of the horrendous noise, fear for their lives, concern for the survival of their livestock. They did not know what to do first. Some Egyptians tried to bring their livestock to safety even at this late hour, but it was useless. Great barriers of hailstones trapped the animals that had not yet been killed, and it was impossible to move them out of the fields. Hoping to salvage something of value from their doomed livestock, the owners slaughtered the animals for food, and carrying the slabs of meat on their backs, they began to run. But this too was useless. Birds of prey swooped down from the sky amid the falling hailstones and devoured all the slaughtered meat.[46] Hashem would not allow the Egyptians any gain at all from the doomed livestock.[47]

With every passing minute, the carnage increased. All people or animals caught in the open perished. The wicked Egyptians were being punished by the fires of Gehinnom.[48] Those sitting on the ground were scorched and roasted by the eighteen-inch tongues of flames that burst from the hailstones on the ground. Those standing were scorched by the shooting flames of fire that emanated from the falling hailstones. Others froze to death from the icy hail, and their bodies were then consumed by the fire that erupted from within the ice.[49] The force of the pounding hailstones pulverized any property or valuables left outside.[50]

Miraculously, Goshen was free of hailstones,[51] and those few Egyptians caught in the open who had not yet perished from the hailstones tried to flee to the safety of Goshen. A few of them actually got there, but there was no safety for Egyptians in Goshen either. The hailstones followed them into Goshen and killed them there, while the Jews standing nearby were completely unaffected.[52] Similarly,

---

45) מלבים שם ט-כה 46) מדרש הגדול שם, שמו"ר יב-ד שמו"ר יב-ד בעץ יוסף ומתנ"כ 47) ידי משה בשמו"ר שם, ומוסיף שהביאו הסכינים לבנ"י שישחטו הם בחשבם אולי עי"ז יופלטו כמו שאירע במכת דבר 48) שמו"ר שם 49) שמו"ר יב-ד ביפ"ת ומהרז"ו, מדרש אגדה, מעם לועז 50) מלבים תהלים עח-מז ואילך 51) אברבנל 52) מדרש הגדול וארא ט-כו

any Jew who happened to be in Egypt during the hailstorm was also unaffected.[53]

Some Egyptians had anticipated that this would happen, based on the record of the previous plagues, and they tried to secure safety for themselves by buying property together with a Jewish partner. Even this did not help them. The hailstones struck the portion of the property used by the Egyptian but avoided the portion used by the Jewish partner.[54]

The miraculous nature of the plague of hailstones was overwhelming. That Egypt, a land on which rain never falls, should experience an ice storm was shocking. That a land in which cool moist air did not exist should produce thunderclouds and lightning was incomprehensible.[55] That fire and ice could be mixed together, that they did not sap each other's strength, that water could live in a shell of fire, that fire did not encroach on the space of the water, these were four amazing miracles that went against the laws of nature.[56]

A Call for Help

Stubborn and arrogant as he was, Pharaoh could not bear to see what the plague of hailstones was doing to his kingdom. Nor could he bear the horrendous sounds of the crashing thunder and the impacting hailstones.[57] He was convinced that the enormous thunder was actually the wrathful shouts of Hashem who had been angered by the Egyptians.[58*] Swallowing his pride, Pharaoh sent messengers to bring Moshe to the royal palace.[59]

"I've had enough," Pharaoh pleaded. "The noise and hail are making me lose my sanity. Please put an end to it right away. I cannot take any more."

"You know the arrangement, your majesty," Moshe replied.

"Yes, yes, I know," said Pharaoh. "I let the Jewish people leave Egypt, and you stop the trouble. Right?"

"Yes, your majesty," said Moshe.

"Very well," said Pharaoh. "I agree."

---

* Some suggest that Pharaoh thought the hailstorm could lead to a flood like the one in the time of Noach.

53) שכל טוב שם 54) תוס' עה"ת שם 55) אברבנל שם 56) רש"י שם ט-כד ובתולדות יצחק 57) רבנו בחיי שם
כט 58) מלבים שם ט-לד 59) לקח טוב ותרגום יונתן ל-כז וכו', אב"ע ט-יד, שפתי כהן בא י-ג

"But if you pardon my saying so, your majesty," Moshe responded, "how do we know you will do as you say? During the previous plagues, you did not fulfill your promises to the Jewish people."

"Why do you always have to bring up old complaints?" said Pharaoh. "Whatever happened before doesn't matter. This time it's going to be different. You'll see. I am a changed man. I confess that I have sinned against Hashem and your people. I admit that Hashem is righteous, and that I and my nation are the wicked ones."[60]

This was indeed a major change for Pharaoh. Hashem created thunder to put fear in the hearts of the wicked,[61] and the thunder of the hailstorm had certainly put some real fear into the heart of Pharaoh. He had actually acknowledged Hashem's authority.[62*] He recognized the power of Hashem through the breathtaking miracle of the combined fire and ice.[63] He recognized the righteousness of Hashem in warning him of the impending destruction and offering him the opportunity of saving his livestock.[64] He admitted his own guilt in ignoring Iyov's advice and taking Bilam's, thereby causing untold numbers of Egyptians and Egyptian livestock to perish needlessly.[65] In this mood, Pharaoh also humbled himself by admitting that he had indeed sinned in harming the Jewish people.[66]

In spite of Pharaoh's continued broken promises, his admission that Hashem was righteous earned the privilege of a proper burial for those Egyptians who drowned in the sea at the Yam Suf.[67] It also earned Pharaoh himself a reprieve from death at the Yam Suf.[68] The immediate benefit of his admission was that Moshe agreed to pray for him.

"Very well, your majesty," Moshe said. "I shall extend my hands in prayer to Hashem and ask Him to bring an immediate end to the thunder and the hailstorms. However, I will first have to leave the city and go to my designated place of prayer. As you know, I cannot speak to Hashem in a place full of idols."[69]

---

* According to some opinions, Pharaoh was employing a clever play on words, saying, "Hashem is righteous and I . . . my nation is wicked."

---

60) תנחומא וארא טז 61) ברכות נט. 62) שפתי כהן בא י-א 63) מדרש הגדול וארא ט-כז 64) שמו"ר יב-ה, תנחומא ישן וארא כ 65) שמו"ר שם וביפ"ת, דעת זקנים, פענח רזא וארא ט-כז, מלבים שם 66) ריב"ש וארא ט-כז 67) מכילתא בשלח 68) דברי הימים למשה 69) שמו"ר יב-ה

"Why are you telling me this now?" asked Pharaoh. "Don't you do this all the time? Haven't you done this with the previous plagues?"

"Indeed, I have," said Moshe. "However, since I told you the plagues would stop the next day, it was not necessary for me to point out where I am going in between. But since I told you that the hailstorm will stop immediately, I want you to understand the reason for the slight delay. It will take me a little time to get to my designated place of prayer. As soon as I get there, though, I will pray that the hailstorm ceases instantly."[70]

"Fine," said Pharaoh. "Go ahead and leave. Don't waste precious time. Don't you want the Jewish people to leave Egypt as soon as possible?"

"I most certainly do, your majesty," Moshe replied, "but I know the time has not yet come. I realize that you are still not sufficiently fearful of Hashem and that you will go back on your promise to let the Jewish people go. You are all repentance and cooperation right now while the hailstones are smashing your kingdom to bits, but as soon as calm returns to Egypt, you will quickly forget your promise."

"If that's what you believe," said Pharaoh, "why are you going to pray for me?"

"I will pray for you," said Moshe, "because Hashem wants you to witness the greatness of His miracles.[71] And I also want you to realize that the fields that were destroyed, such as the flax and barley that were already ripe and full-grown, will not return to their former state. All I can tell you is that those fields that the hailstorm did not yet destroy, such as the wheat and spelt which were still unformed, flexible and able to bend under the hailstones, will be spared.[72] This is what my prayer will accomplish for you."[73]

It was indeed a miracle that the wheat and spelt withstood the hailstorm thus far. The softness and flexibility of the immature shoot would have protected them somewhat from the impact of the hailstones, but they should have been destroyed by the freezing cold of the ice or the burning heat of the fires within.[74] Nevertheless, they

---

70) רמב"ן ושפתי חכמים וארא ט-כט, דעת זקנים מבאר שהוצרך לצאת מן העיר כי היה מלאה בהמות שנעבדו
לע"ז, בדרך כלל רעו חוץ לעיר ועתה טמנו אותם בבתיהם שלא יוזקו בברד וכדלעיל 71) שמו"ר יב-ה, רש"י
רמב"ן ואוה"ח וארא ט-כט, אוה"ח כתב שכבר ידע משה שלא יקיים פרעה את הבטחתו כי כבר אמר לו ד' שלא
יגאלם עד שימותו בכוריהם 72) רש"י וארא ט-לא וכו' 73) מדרש הגדול, ר' סעדיא גאון וארא ט-ל 74) שמו"ר
יב-ו, רש"י וארא ט-לב, פענח רזא ותולדות יצחק שם

survived, because Hashem wanted to ensure that there would be something left to be destroyed by the next plague.[75]

The survival of some of the grains did little, however, to alleviate the desperate condition of the once rich and prosperous Egypt. The trees and crops were destroyed. Although there was still wheat to be bought, the prices had risen to astronomical levels. Those who could afford it ate. The others starved.[76]

Hailstones in Suspension

As Moshe left the city and passed into the fields, he saw the devastation wrought by the hailstorm,[77] and out of compassion for the land, he decided not to wait till he had placed a full *techum* of two thousand cubits between himself and the idol-filled city.[78] Instead, as soon as he was seventy cubits out of the city, he spread his hands out in prayer. Before he could utter a word, however, Hashem had already put an end to the plague, because Hashem responds to the prayers of the righteous immediately. Hashem also did it so quickly because He dislikes being praised by the wicked. Hashem knew that Pharaoh would cease his praises as soon as the plague ceased, and therefore, Hashem hastened the end of the plague.[79]

As the plague came to an end, the entire hailstorm froze in place. The rains also stopped, because Hashem did not want Egypt to enjoy any residual benefits from the plague.[80] The thunder ceased, the rain stopped, and the falling hailstones were suspended in midair.[81] The angel Gavriel, who is in control of fire, and the angel Bardael, who is in control of hail, descended from the heavens along with myriad other angels and seized the falling hailstones, holding them in readiness until they would be released again in the time of Yehoshua, forty-one years later.[82] The sounds were also suspended and held in readiness until the time of Yehoram, some five hundred years later.[83]

When Yehoshua was conquering Eretz Yisrael, the people of Giveon deserted the defensive confederation and, through subterfuge,

---

75) רמב"ן שם ט-ל (76) ספרי זוטא בהעלותך לא (77) ריבא וארא ט-כט (78) רוקח וארא ט-כט, ע' נדרים נו: שמו"ר
יב-ז, אברבנל מביא מביא שהיה למשה אהל מיוחד לתפילה (79) תנחומא ישן וארא כב, מדרש הגדול וארא ט-לג, ע'
תענית יז. בנוגע תפלת חוני המעגל (80) תולדות יצחק ואברבנל וארא ט-לד, אוה"ח ושפתי כהן בארו שכאן היה
צורך מיוחד לחיזוק לבו כי היא הזיקה יותר מכולהו ע"ש (81) ברכות נד. ובירש"י, וברש"י, ראה רלב"ג וארא ט-לג (82
מדרש מובא בתורה שלמה קיג, ע' מדרש הגדול שם (83) מדרש הגדול שם

gained the promise of protection from Yehoshua. The five leading Amorite kings besieged the city of Giveon to show that desertion could not be tolerated. The Giveonites appealed to Yehoshua for assistance. "Do not fear, Yehoshua," Hashem reassured him. "I have delivered them into your hands." Confident of victory, Yehoshua marched through the night to Giveon and mounted a surprise attack against the besieging armies. As the enemy fled Yehoshua's armies, Hashem sent the suspended hailstones of Egypt down upon them. The hailstones killed more men than the swords of the attackers.[84] When the battle of Giveon was over, the hailstones were again held in suspension until the time of Gog and Magog.[85]

Pharaoh Breaks His Promise

As Moshe had predicted, Pharaoh's resolve to release the Jewish people disappeared along with the last of the hailstones.[86] When Moshe came to demand the fulfillment of Pharaoh's promise, he encountered the arrogant Pharaoh of old.

"I have had a change of heart," said Pharaoh. "Our agreement is void."

"Indeed?" asked Moshe. "And why?"

"I asked for an end to the thunder and hail," Pharaoh explained. "But I did not want an end to the rain. Egypt needs the rain. You did not keep your end of the bargain, and I am released from mine. I have come to the conclusion that if this plague was the work of Hashem, He would certainly have done exactly as I asked. Therefore, I have decided that this hailstorm was nothing more than a freak of nature. Thankfully, it is over, and normal climate conditions have returned to Egypt."[87]

Pharaoh had behaved in a manner typical of wicked people. In times of trouble or peril, wicked people humble themselves, but when the crisis is over, they quickly forget. The Jewish people, on the other hand, are different. When they are in pain, they cry out to Hashem, and when Hashem grants their request, they remain righteous, offering words of praise and gratitude to Hashem for His salvation.[88]

---

84) יהושע י, יפ"ת כ' דודאי יכול הקב"ה לברוא חדשות רק מאחר שכבר ירדו לא רצה שיאבדו ללא טעם, ויתכן עוד עפ"י כללא הידוע דקוב"ה ממעט בניסא ולא עושהו בכדי 85) שמו"ר יב-ז, ועיין במלכים ב ז-ו 86) לקח טוב וארא ט-לד וכו' 87) אברבנל ותולדות יצחק שם 88) שמו"ר יב-ז, מדרש הגדול וארא ט-לד

The Warning of Locusts

Moshe left Pharaoh's palace, disappointed but not surprised.

Each day, Moshe and Aharon would appear at the royal palace to request permission for the Jewish people to leave Egypt. Each day, Pharaoh would tell them to come back the next day, when perhaps he might agree. But invariably, he did not agree the next day. Instead, he simply told them to come back again the next day.[89]

Finally, Hashem instructed Moshe to go to the royal palace and warn Pharaoh, Bilam and Iyov about the upcoming three plagues.[90] In spite of his broken promises, he was to receive yet another warning.[91] Hashem had hardened the hearts of Pharaoh and his advisors.[92] Otherwise, they would have agreed out of fear to let the Jewish people go.[93] This warning would give Pharaoh and his advisors and servants yet another opportunity to repent out of their own free will in honor of the power and authority of Hashem.[94]

Because of their hardened hearts, Hashem's wondrous signs and plagues would be publicized and the Jewish people would tell and retell for all future generations the spectacular story of the plagues Hashem sent upon Egypt to force them to let the Jewish people go.[95] These signs had not yet been completed. The plagues showing Hashem's power over the winds, light and darkness had not yet appeared.[96] The Jews of future generations needed to know about these as well, so that they will properly proclaim Hashem's Name and power to all the world.[97] For this alone, it would have been worthwhile for the Jewish people to leave Egypt.[98]

Following Hashem's instructions, Moshe and Aharon went to warn Pharaoh about the forthcoming plague of locusts.[99]

"Your majesty, we will not be giving you any more warnings after today," Moshe said. "If you do not send the Jewish people out today, Hashem will send a new plague against you tomorrow. It will be a plague of swarming locusts.[100] You still refuse to humble yourself before Hashem.[101] Only on account of the plagues have you humbled yourself at all before Hashem, and even then only out of

89) אברבנל בא י-ג 90) רש"י באר היטב, מנחה בלולה בא י-א, שם מרומז בא ר"ת בלעם איוב 91) ספורנו בא י-
א 92) ריב"ש שם 93) מלבים שם 94) ספורנו שם 95) רבנו בחיי, ר' סעדיא גאון שם 96) אוה"ח בא י- א
97) רבנו בחיי וספורנו שם י-ב 98) מדרש תהלים מד 99) רמב"ן בא שם, יי"מ שאף שלא כתוב ודאי ששמע כן
מפומיה דקוב"ה, וי"מ (ע' מדרש תהלים שם ובדרש זקנים על אתר) דלא צוהו וידעו משה ממה שהיה נחקק על
מטהו כדהבאנו במקומו, ע' לקח טוב בא י-ג 100) אברבנל שם ומביא עוד שנתן לו ד' עוד יום שיוכל לשלחם
דהיינו מחר, ע' שמו"ר יג-ו וביפ"ת 101) רש"י בא י-ג, ע' ראשית חכמה ענוה א

fear and pain.[102] You still think you are a god, and therefore, you refuse to submit to Hashem.[103]

"You have been deceitful with us. After the plague of frogs, you asked me to pray for their removal, and I did. After the plagues of wild beasts and the hailstorms, you promised to let us go, but then you claimed you meant only Aharon and me, not all the Jewish people. Your constant attempts to mislead Hashem have not gone unnoticed. Hashem has taken heed of all your actions, and He will be sending you a plague of swarming locusts."[104]

The importance of humility is clearly demonstrated in Tanach. When the wicked King Achav was told by Eliyahu Hanavi that he and his household were doomed, Achav humbled himself before Hashem. He put on sackcloth and went into mourning, and Hashem took pity on him. He was spared the terrible tragedies destined to befall his household. Instead, they befell Achav's son for the great sins he had committed. Nevuchadnezzar, on the other hand, did not humble himself before Hashem when he was reprimanded for his sins. Instead, he placed himself above all men and declared himself a god. Hashem punished him by making him an animal for seven years.[105]

Pharaoh's lack of humility, Moshe explained, would now bring upon him the plague of locusts.

"If you refuse to let the Jewish people out of Egypt," Moshe said, "Hashem will send a swarm of locusts that will look like an attacking army.[106] The swarm of locusts will be made up of many species,[107] and they will make you as humble as the smallest creatures on earth.[108] The swarm of locusts will be so great in number that it will cover the land and blot out the sun entirely. Clouds of locusts will intercept the rays of the sun[109] and obscure the colors of the land.[110]

"The locusts will devour the wheat and spelt left over from the hailstorm.[111] They will destroy all greens and flowers that have blossomed and grown back from the roots left undamaged by the hail.[112] They will eat ceaselessly, but they will not be satisfied. Just as a blind person is never fully satisfied because he cannot see his food, the

---

102) כלי יקר שם 103) מלבים שם 104) שפתי כהן שם, חזקוני מביא שהיות והחטה והכסמות לא נכו והיה לו עדיין מה לאכול, לא ראה סבה שיכריחו אותו לשלחם מיד, ע' שמו"ר יג-ו ובפי"ת 105) רבנו בחיי שם 106) לקח טוב שם י-ד 107) שכל טוב 108) מלבים בא י-ד 109) אונקלוס רש"י גור אריה ומלבים בא י-ה, לקח טוב, אברבנל שם 110) רלב"ג שם 111) לקח טוב שם 112) ספורנו שם, רוקח שם, רשב"ם ומלבים שם

locusts will never be fully satisfied because the sight of the food will be obscured by the sheer numbers of the locusts. Ever hungry, the locusts will swarm over the land of Egypt and into the homes of the Egyptians in search of the tiny bits of food that may still be left.[113] The swarm of locusts will be so great that it will be something your fathers and grandfathers have not seen from the day they came on to the earth till today.[114]

"Once again, the borders of Egypt will be defined by the plagues it suffers. The locusts will not attack the neighboring lands of Canaan, Kush and the like. They will stay only within the borders of Egypt, and they will fill the land up to the very borders.[115] However, Goshen will not be completely free from locust attack. Anything the Jewish people planted on behalf of the Egyptians, whether seeds, fruits, plants or trees, will be destroyed. The Egyptians will not benefit in any way from the labor they forced upon the Jewish people.[116]

"Beware! This is your last warning. Tomorrow, the locusts arrive!"

As Moshe was completing his words, he noticed Pharaoh's courtiers and advisors deep in serious discussion. Apparently, they had taken Moshe's words to heart and were considering proper courses of action.[117] Before Pharaoh could respond negatively and break the mood of cooperation, Moshe and Aharon immediately left, walking backwards respectfully and not turning their backs to the king.[118] Better to let them discuss this matter in private, thought Moshe. There was a chance that rather than suffer the attack of the locusts they would agree to let the Jewish people go.[119]

Pharaoh Negotiates

Moshe had been right in his assessment of the situation. As soon as he and Aharon left, the discussion became heated and intense. The courtiers and advisors had not wanted Moshe to see their fear of the new plague, but once he and Aharon left, talk flowed freely.[120]

"Your majesty," one of the advisors spoke up. "How long will you allow Moshe[121] and the Jewish nation[122] to be a menace to us?

---

113) כל"י שם 114) בא י-ו 115) שמו"ר יג-ד במהרז"ו 116) מעם לועז 117) שמו"ר שם ובאברבנל 118) אב"ע
בא י-ו, ע' רש"י בשמו"ר יג-ד 119) רמב"ן ואברבנל שם 120) ריב"ש שם י-ז 121) לקח טוב שם 122) רוקח שם

The plagues have destroyed our beautiful Egypt.[123]* And now the attack of the locust swarms will bring such a famine that we will all die![124] Our fields are battered and burned by the hail. All that remains is raw stubble."[125]

"What are you waiting for, your majesty?" shouted another advisor. "A plague may soon come without warning, as the lice and boils did, only this time it will wipe us out. We will not be prepared for it!"[126]

"Your majesty, let us face reality," said a third advisor. "There will be no end to this until we are all dead or until we send the Jews away. Why wait until we are all dead? Let us face the inevitable and get rid of these Jews once and for all. Apparently, there is nothing we can do to keep them."[127]

The plagues had finally penetrated the hearts of Pharaoh's courtiers and advisors. They had finally come to believe in Hashem, and they wanted the Jewish people out of Egypt—fast![128]

In view of the prevalent opinion, Pharaoh sent messengers to bring Moshe and Aharon back to the royal chamber and begin negotiations.[129] Perhaps something could be worked out that would satisfy all parties concerned.[130] Moshe and Aharon were just leaving the palace when the messengers caught up with them.[131] The messengers begged Moshe and Aharon to return, and Moshe and Aharon finally relented.[132] Pharaoh was waiting for them.

"I have made a decision," said Pharaoh. "You can go and serve your God. Who will be going, and who will be sacrificing?"[133]

"Those same Jews that have served you all these years are those that will serve Hashem," Moshe replied. "The youngsters and the elders. Our sons and daughters. Our flocks and our cattle."[134]

"I don't see the need for that," Pharaoh said. "It seems to me that it would be quite enough for your leaders to go and no one else. Just send some of the men. You know, leaders, officers, elders. Why do you need the others?"[135]

"That is impossible," Moshe answered. "Everyone is needed! We need the animals for sacrifices to celebrate our holiday.[136] The

---

* The plagues of pestilence and hail, in particular, destroyed both the land and the animals of Egypt.

123) רשב"ם שם 124) רוקח שם 125) תוס' שם ורמז עוד דתבת מוקש נוטריקון למו קש 126) מלבים בא י-ז (127

128) שפתי כהן שם 129) רלב"ג שם י-ח 130) רש"י ואברבנל שם 131) שפתי כהן שם 132) אברבנל

שם 133) רוקח שם 134) לקח טוב שם 135) רמב"ן שם 136) אברבנל שם י-ט

elders, of course, will conduct the sacrifices.[137] The women will play the music.[138] The youngsters are needed to do chores and carry what is needed. But even babies, who can do nothing useful, share in our festival.[139] Our festivals are for everyone.[140] We want to celebrate the festival of Shavuos to Hashem at Mount Sinai."[141]

For a few more minutes, Pharaoh continued to haggle with Moshe and Aharon, like a businessman trying to negotiate a good price on some merchandise.

"Moshe, you want all the Jewish people to leave," Pharaoh finally said. "I want only some of the men to go. Let us reach a compromise. Let us allow all the men to go but none of the women and children."

"That is not good enough," Moshe responded. "All the Jewish people must leave, because they are all needed to share in the celebration of our festival."[142]

"Don't be so eager to leave Egypt," Pharaoh said ominously. "Evil awaits you in the desert. Baal Tzefon, my god, will hurt you and prevent you from leaving Egypt.[143] And do not feel so secure in your own God. He is evil and will do great harm to you.[144] Yes, I see great evil waiting for you in the desert. My astrological calculations—did you know I was an expert astrologer?—reveal the constellation *Maadim-Raah* hovering above you in the desert. It is a fearful star, a star that causes much destruction. Yes, I can see it clearly. Blood, there will be blood! You will experience great death in the desert.[145] Remember the evil that befell the tribe of Ephraim thirty years ago? They also wanted to escape Egypt, and what happened to them? That's right, most of them perished. Beware! You will also suffer in the end."[146]

When words of Pharaoh's ominous warning reached the Jewish people, they trembled—with good cause. Tragic death did indeed await the Jewish people in the desert after they committed the sin of the Eigel, the Golden Calf. At that time, Hashem was prepared to wipe out a great part of the Jewish people, but Moshe came to their defense. "What will the nations of the world say?" Moshe prayed to

---

137) רוקח שם 138) בעה"ט שם 139) רוקח וחזקוני שם 140) רלב"ג שם 141) רבנו בחיי שם, בפשטות אחג השבועות קאי, בתוס' שם כתוב דחג ד' לנו אפסח קאי, במדרש (המובא במסלות חיים פ' בא) כי חג ד' לנו זו חג סוכות (ע' בספר הנ"ל ביאור נעים בזה) וא"ש עפ"י המבואר בפוסקים דזמן הראויה לזכר עני הכבוד היא בניסן ורק משום שלא יאמרו דלהנתו יוצא חוצה קבעתו תורה בתשרי ודו"ק 142) אברבנל בא י-י 143) חמאת החמדה מובא בתורה שלמה ט 144) רלב"ג בא י-י 145) רש"י ורבנו בחיי שם 146) רוקח שם

Hashem. "They will say Pharaoh, the great astrologer, was right all along in his visions of blood in the desert, in his predictions of Jewish death." Hashem accepted Moshe's argument and changed the blood foreseen by Pharaoh from a symbol of death to a symbol of the *mitzvah* of *bris milah*. On the doorstep of Eretz Yisrael, Hashem commanded Yehoshua that every Jew must have a *bris milah* before entering the land.[147]

Having made his dire predictions, Pharaoh continued. "As far as your argument itself goes," he said, "I beg to differ. Didn't you once tell me you wanted to leave for three days to offer sacrifices to your God? How can you claim that all of you must go when in fact only men offer sacrifices?[148] If you really intended to leave for only three days, you would leave the children who are certainly not capable of offering sacrifices.[149]

"It seems clear to me that you want the little children to go with you because you intend to run away for good. I see only evil in your mind. I would agree to send the men if you leave the children as a surety for your return.[150] But do you really expect me to allow all of you to leave? Who will be left here in my control?[151] The whole thing is preposterous! I will not send any!"[152]

As Pharaoh reached the end of his speech, he rose to his feet in a self-induced rage. Bilam obligingly chased Moshe and Aharon out of Pharaoh's presence and sent them away.[153]

One must stop and wonder at Pharaoh's amazing obstinacy. Granted that Hashem had hardened his heart, but still how could Pharaoh be such a fool as to allow his kingdom to be so utterly and systematically destroyed? As far as he knew, Moshe had said that the Jewish people only wanted to leave for three days, so why didn't he accept it at face value? Why did he insist on not letting them leave? The answer is, Pharaoh always had the suspicion, because of his disbelief in Hashem, that the Jewish people were planning to leave for good. He was only willing to consider the possibility of their leaving because of the awesome plagues. But when he saw Moshe insisting that they must all leave, he was once again convinced that they had no intention of returning.[154]

---

147) רש"י שם, ילקו"ש שצ"ב 148) לקח טוב, רבנו בחיי שם (וכו') 149) שמו"ר יג-ה 150) שכל טוב, חזקוני בא
יא-י 151) ר' אברהם בן הרמב"ם שם י-י 152) שמו"ר שם 153) מדרש מובא בתורה שלמה י 154) אוה"ח בא י-ז

The Plague of Locusts

Moshe had given Pharaoh sufficient warning of the coming plague of the locusts and the opportunity to repent. Hashem now instructed Moshe not to persist in negotiating with Pharaoh but to go right out and bring down the plague of locusts on Egypt. Moshe was to extend his staff over Egypt, causing a powerful morning east wind to blow all day and night. Tomorrow, the locusts would arrive on that wind.[155]

The plague of locusts was an appropriate punishment for the Egyptians. The Egyptians had forced the Jewish people to plant wheat, barley, beans and lentils and to pick the fruits off the trees, all in order to keep them away from their families and prevent the further growth of the Jewish people.[156] Then they had taken crops from the fields in which the Jews had toiled. Now, the locusts would devour all the crops in the land of Egypt.[157]

Furthermore, the Hebrew word for locust is *arbeh*, a variation of the word *harbeh*, many, since locusts usually arrive in great numbers. Hashem had given the Jewish people the blessing of *"arbeh,"* of becoming a nation of *"many"* people. The Egyptians had tried to crush this nation and prevent its growth, and therefore, they were punished with *"arbeh,"* locusts.[158]

Moshe tied a locust onto his staff and extended it over the land of Egypt in a summons to the locusts to the northeast of Egypt.[159] Hashem sent an east wind that blew all day and all night.[160] The wind carried locusts who reproduced in the warm air currents.[161] By morning, the wind had transported a host of locusts into Egypt.[162]

The locusts descended on the land of Egypt on *Shabbos* morning.[163] They came from Babylon (Bavel) and Assyria (Ashur),[164] and miraculously, they covered the entire land of Egypt as soon as they arrived.[165] In the blink of an eye, Egypt was thoroughly congested with the locusts of the neighboring countries, which had all crowded into the Egyptian airspace.[166] Altogether, seven different species of locust descended upon Egypt. Whatever one species of locust left

---

155) אברבנל שם י-יב 156) תנחומא וארא יד, תדב"א רבה ז, שכל טוב בא י"א 157) אברבנל וארא 158) שפתי כהן וארא, ע' מלבים בלק כב-ה 159) אוה"ח בא י"ב, ר' יהודה החסיד מביא שהטה מטהו על המלאך הממונה על הארבה 160) בא י-ב וכו' 161) פענח רזא שם 162) בא י"ג, רבנו בחיי שם דהקב"ה דן הרשעים בבקר, במכילתא בשלח ובמדרש אגדה י-יג דהקב"ה מביא פרעניותם ברוח קדים כדחזינן כאן, במי נח, ובסדום 163) בעה"ט שם י"ד 164) מלבים שם י"ג 165) מעם לועז שם י-ו 166) שפתי כהן שם י-טו

over, the other species consumed.[167] The devastating effects of locust infestation are described in great detail in the prophecy of Yoel during the reign of King Yehoram. In Egypt as well, the locusts destroyed everything that grew. They left nothing.[168]

The swarms of locusts were so numerous that they formed a dense cloud impenetrable to the rays of the sun.[169] A gloomy darkness settled over Egypt,[170] obscuring the new green foliage struggling to emerge in the wake of the hailstorm.[171] It was almost as if a total eclipse was taking place over Egypt.[172]

These locusts were unlike any ever seen before. They had teeth like iron. Their claws were sharp, like those of a lion. Their horns were destructive, like those of an ox. Their necks were sturdy, like those of a horse. Their wings were powerful, like those of an eagle. Their shape resembled fish and snakes. Their saliva was poisonous, and those Egyptians unfortunate enough to have locusts alight on their faces died from the poisons in their saliva.[173]

167) מדרש הגדול שם י-יד, ע׳ יואל א-ב, בשכל טוב מובא שהיו ח׳ מאות מיני ארבה! 168) יואל שם וברד״ק, רי״מ שהיה בזמן מנשה בן חזקיה 169) מדרש הגדול, אברבנל ומלבים שם י-טו 170) אב״ע שם 171) שכל טוב ורלב״ג שם 172) מנחה בלולה שם 173) מדרש הגדול בא י-יז, מדרש באוצר המדרשים תקמ״א

Their bodies were sheathed in armor, and inscribed over their hearts was the letter *ches*, a sign that these locusts were Hashem's *chayil*, His army. And what an army they were! They had been lying dormant, waiting to receive the call to arms from Hashem. And when the call came, they surged forward to fulfill the will of their Master. This army did not need provisions and generals. The locusts swarmed over mountaintops and into any structure they encountered.[174]

The locusts devoured the corn and fruits in the field.[175] They felled trees with their sharp teeth,[176] peeling away any edible portions they could find. Ravaged tree trunks lay scattered in the fields like dried white bones.[177] The locusts gnawed through the roots of all that grew, until Egypt was denuded of all foliage and greenery.[178] Not a single part of Egypt was spared the attack of the swarming locusts.[179] Nevertheless, if a tree on Egyptian land was owned by a Jew, the locusts devoured everything around the tree but did not touch the tree itself.[180]

The Egyptians had been hoping to scavenge for fallen fruit and other edibles amid the debris left by the hailstorm, but the attack of the locusts destroyed all such hope. Nothing edible escaped their voracious hunger.[181] In a very short time, there was no more food left for the locusts in the fields. Normally, when this happened, the locusts would leave, seeking greener pastures elsewhere. This time, however, they invaded the homes of the Egyptians.[182] Like a plundering army, the locusts ransacked the houses of the Egyptians, eating whatever they managed to find. Clothing, jewelry, nothing was considered inedible to these locusts.[183] The starving Egyptians resorted to capturing and preserving some of the locusts for food. They salted them and stored them in barrels. Although they had never been allowed to reap any benefit from the earlier plagues, they were too crazed by hunger to take this into consideration.[184]

The Egyptian people were also attacked and killed by the locusts. The locusts stung the Egyptians like bees and injected deadly venom into their veins. They pounded into the faces and eyes of

174) שכל טוב בא י-ד, ע' מפרשי נ"ך ריש יואל 175) מעם לועז שם י-יג 176) מדרש הגדול בא י-טו 177) יואל שם, ובפנים הצגנוה כשיטת מדרש הגדול ושכל טוב דבמצרים היה ממש כדוגמת המסופר ביואל 178) רש"י בעה"ט ומלבים שם 179) רבנו בחיי שם 180) מעם לועז שם 181) מדרש הגדול שם י-יב 182) מעם לועז שם י-ו 183) מדרש הגדול שם י-טו, מעם לועז מביא שבמכה זו גם גושן נפגע וטעמא שיעקרו כל הנטיעות שנטעו ישראל בעבורם שלא יוכלו המצריים להנות מהם אחר יציאתם 184) שמו"ר יג-ז ובעץ יוסף, תנחומא וארא יד

the Egyptians, injuring and blinding them.[185] They worked their ways into the mouths, noses, ears and other orifices of the Egyptians.[186] Some of the locusts were even able to kill with the vapors of their exhalations.[187] To make matters worse, the swarming locusts were accompanied by poisonous snakes who attacked the Egyptians simultaneously and took a heavy toll.[188]

Never had the world seen a swarm of locust of this magnitude. Never had there been locusts of such fearsome physique and demeanor. Never had locusts invaded the homes of people.[189] Never again would there be a plague such as this. Only in Eretz Yisrael during the time of the prophet Yoel would there be anything even close.[190] And even then, there would be only one species at a time, not a convergence of many species as had attacked Egypt.[191]

Pharaoh Begs for Mercy

In front of Pharaoh's horrified eyes, Egypt was disintegrating. Soon there would be nothing to eat, and all Egyptians would die of hunger. But before they could die of hunger, they would probably be killed by the venomous locusts who had invaded their homes.[192] In desperation, Pharaoh sent messengers to summon Moshe and Aharon to the palace immediately.[193]

"Oh, what a fool I've been," Pharaoh lamented tearfully as soon as Moshe and Aharon arrived. "I have sinned to Hashem, and to you. I have sinned to Hashem in not letting the Jewish people go. I have sinned to you for expelling you from my palace and wishing you evil.[194] Please forgive me, and remove the horrible locusts from whatever is left of my kingdom.[195] Please pray for me. You will see, this will be the last time I will have to ask you to pray for me, because this time, I will truly let the Jewish people go.[196] Just do me one favor. Some of the Egyptian people have preserved locusts in barrels for food. Please let them keep these preserved locusts. Otherwise, they will starve to death."[197]

Moshe left the capital city of Egypt. He went to his designated place of prayer and begged Hashem to withdraw the locusts.[198]

185) מדרש הגדול בא י-יז, רבנו בחיי, מושב זקנים 186) ר' ויינא מובא בתורה שלמה דף יד 187) מדרש החפץ
בא י-יז בהנדפס כתוב שארס הארבה הרגם, אבל בכתב יד בתורה שלמה כתוב שהבל פיהם הרגם 188) בעה"ט
שם 189) מעם לועז שם י-יג 190) ברטנורה רלב"ג ואברבנל שם י-יד 191) דעת זקנים שם, ע' רמב"ן מזרחי
ושפתי חכמים שם 192) אברבנל ומלבים שם י-טו, ע' כל"י בא י-ה 193) אב"ע בא י-טז 194) שמו"ר יג-1 195)
אברבנל בא י-טז 196) רבנו בחיי בא י-יז, ראה רמב"ן ומזרחי שם 197) מהרז"ו בשמו"ר יג-1 198) אב"ע בא י-יז

Hashem caused a powerful wind to rise in the west.[199] The wind was cold, and as such, it brought a stop to the rapid reproduction of the locusts engendered by the warm east wind.[200] The wind carried every single locust east to the sea so that not one locust remained in Egypt.[201] The locusts would await the Egyptians by the sea, and when the Egyptians would pursue the Jewish people to the sea, the locusts would torment them once again.[202]

Pharaoh's request that his people be allowed to keep the locusts preserved in barrels was refused. There would be absolutely no gain to the Egyptians from the plagues. The live locusts lifted the dead locusts onto their backs, and the winds carried them out of Egypt.[203]

Moshe's prayer to Hashem to withdraw the locusts from Egypt was so strong that it continues to affect Egypt until this very day. Throughout history, locusts have never again eaten any of the crops of Egypt. Moshe had not prayed that the *tzfardeia* leave Egypt, only that the plague of *tzfardeia* should come to an end. The plague did indeed come to an end, but the *tzfardeia* remained in Egypt. Moshe did pray that the locusts withdraw from Egypt, and consequently, they have withdrawn and never returned.[204*]

The final result of the plague of locusts, however, was no different from that of the earlier plagues. Pharaoh had capitulated under extreme pressure. Hashem now hardened the heart of Pharaoh and gave him the courage and the strength to break his promise, if he so chose. Pharaoh so chose. As soon as the land of Egypt returned to a semblance of normalcy, Pharaoh reneged on his promise to let the Jewish people go.[205]

The Plague of Darkness

Without sending another warning to Pharaoh, Hashem now instructed Moshe to extend his staff over the heavens and bring the plague of darkness on the land of Egypt.[206]

Early in the morning,[207] Moshe miraculously stretched out his

---

* The Nile crocodile is still considered the most dangerous of all alligators and crocodiles in the world.

---

199) מלבים שם י-יט 200) פענח רזא שם 201) רוקח שם 202) ואמרי נועם שם 203) שמו"ר יג-ז, ילקוט מעין גנים בא י-יט, ע' תורה שלמה טו 204) רבנו בחיי שם מרבנו חננאל, הבאנו שהשם ארבה היה סימן לבנ"י המתברכים בארבה את זרעך, שפתי כהן מוסף דג"ז שירדו כולם תוך המים היה סימן לבנ"י שכל עצמותיהם ירדו לתוך הים כדי שלא יתפללו להם כדרך עו"ז 205) רבנו בחיי שם י-יט 206) אב"ע שם י-כא, בא שם 207) תרגום יונתן ורבנו בחיי שם

staff over the heavens, as Hashem had instructed him,[208] and prayed
that the plague of darkness descend on Egypt.[209] He removed the
natural darkness of night from Egypt so that the light of the sun
would not be able to penetrate it.[210] Clouds brought by the west
wind that had removed the locusts hovered over Egypt. A dense
mist descended from the sky and obscured the sun.[211] The mist was
solid and thick as a coin or a wall,[212] and it totally blocked out the
rays of the sun.[213] Ibn Ezra writes that he once traveled to the Ocean
Sea (Atlantic Ocean) and found a fog so dense that it was impossible
to say if it was day or night. These fogs sometimes lasted as long as
five consecutive days.[214*]

There were many reasons and explanations for the plague of
darkness. There was, of course, the element of measure for measure.
The Egyptians had tormented the Jews by making them balance
candles on their heads, under threat of death, to provide illumination for Egyptian meals. Now, the Egyptians themselves would be
forced to sit in darkness.[215] The Egyptians had imprisoned the Jewish people in dark cells. Now, the Egyptians themselves would be
trapped in the darkness.[216] The Egyptians had forced the Jewish
people to work late into the night and in the predawn darkness.
Now, the Egyptians would sit in darkness while the Jews enjoyed
the light.[217] The Egyptians brought the darkness of exile upon the
Jewish people. Now, the Egyptians would be made to suffer the
agonies of darkness.[218]

Furthermore, the significance of light is that it allows clear dis-
tinctions, whereas darkness does not. The Jewish people are compared to light, because they are distinct from all other nations. The
Egyptians had tried to annihilate the nation of light, and therefore
the plague of darkness was particularly appropriate to the Egyptians.[219] In addition, the Egyptians were sun-worshippers, and the

---

* A similar darkness can be found in the Harei Choshech, "the Mountains of Dark-
ness," a geographical area (mentioned in *Masechet Tamid* regarding the story of
Alexander the Great) of dense foliage that allows no light to penetrate. (Ramban,
Minchah Belulah, Abarbanel)

---

208) תוס' עה"ת שם 209) שם י-כב 210) שם י-כב 211) ספורנו שם י-כא) רמב"ן ואברבנל בא י-כג, ע' מדרש חדש בא י-כא,
אוה"ח שם, שמו"ר יד-ב ובעץ יוסף שבארו ב' חלקי החושך וענייניהם והוסיפו שהאיר שהאור במושבי בנ"י היה אות
על התורה שהיו עתידים לקבל הנקראת אור כש"נ כי נר מצוה ותורה אור, ראה גם בשפתי כהן 212) שמו"ר יד-א
וברש"ש, רוקח בא י-כב 213) אברבנל בא 214) אב"ע שם י-כב 215) מדרש הגדול, לקח טוב בא י-כא 216) תנחומא
בא ד 217) מעם לועז, שפתי כהן בא י-כב 218) זבח פסח, הגדה ע"פ עוללות אפרים 219) ילקו"ש וארא קפ"ב

plague of darkness demonstrated the ineffectiveness of the sun.[220]

There were also practical reasons for the plague of darkness. Among the Jews, there were some people who were undeserving of redemption. These were affluent people who enjoyed close relations with the Egyptians and were not subjected to the torments of their Jewish brethren. They enjoyed comfortable lives in Egypt and did not really want to leave. Their lifestyles made it perfectly clear that they had no interest in accepting the Torah. They did not want to risk the dangers of the desert or face the possibility that there might be no food or water. Clearly, these people did not deserve to be included in the exodus, and therefore, Hashem decreed that they should die. However, Hashem did not want the Egyptians to see the Jews bury their dead. He did not want them to say, "You see? We are not the only ones suffering from plagues!" Therefore, Hashem brought darkness to Egypt so that the Jewish people could bury their dead under cover of darkness.[221]

Finally, Hashem would instruct Moshe to make sure the Jews "borrowed" jewels and clothing from the Egyptians before leaving Egypt. During the plague of darkness, the Jews had the opportunity to search out the hidden treasures in the homes of the Egyptians. Later, when they asked to "borrow" their treasures, the Egyptians would claim that they had nothing. But the Jews would remind them of the whereabouts of their treasures.[222]

Meanwhile, as the plague of darkness took effect, all of Egypt was plunged into pitch blackness.[223] Over Goshen, however, there was a great gap in the cloud cover, allowing the Jewish people to enjoy normal light.[224]

The plague of darkness had begun in broad daylight so that the Egyptians should understand that it was a completely miraculous manifestation, not an extension of the night.[225] Even more miraculous, a splendid spiritual light had earlier appeared in Goshen while it was still dark to let the Jewish people know that the plague of darkness was on the way and that they would not be affected.[226]

For the Egyptians, however, the darkness was intense, much more so than the normal darkness of night. An Egyptian who held his hand up in front of his eyes still could not see it.[227] In fact, the

---

220) מעם לועז בשם ילקוט ראובני 221) תנחומא וארא יד, פדר"א רבה ז, ספר הישר, תוס' על הגדה, מעם לועז,
במדרש הגדול כג מובא שחלק מאותם שמתו היו מוסרים, דהיינו שהיו מגידים למצרים מקום מטמוני ישראל
222) רש"י בא י-כב, זבח פסח 223) לקח טוב שם י-כא 224) אברבנל שם 225) תרגום יונתן שם ובפי' יונתן,
רבנו בחיי שם 226) שפתי כהן שם שהיה שם מאור שנגנז לצדיקים לע"ל 227) ספר הישר

darkness was so dense it could actually be touched and felt, as one touches and feels a coin.[228]

This darkness lasted for three days. During this time, the Egyptians were able to move about in their homes,[229] but they were unable to see each other or leave their homes. They were trapped.[230] Some Egyptians tried to light candles or torches, but they were useless.[231] The flames were smothered by the thick darkness.[232] The darkness also gave off toxic fumes, forcing the Egyptians to cover their noses and mouths when breathing.[233]

For these three days straight, the Jewish people had light in their homes, and the Egyptians were engulfed in total darkness.[234] Nevertheless, these were not pleasant times for the Jewish people. During these days of darkness, the Jews unworthy of being redeemed perished.[235] Fully four fifths of the Jews between the ages of twenty and sixty died during this time.[236] Therefore, while the Egyptians sat unaware and blinded by darkness, the Jewish people were busy burying their dead.[237] Strangely enough, Dassan and Aviram did not perish during this time. For all their wickedness, they believed in the exodus of Egypt, and therefore, they did not die.[238]*

After the three days of darkness, the plague actually intensified for another three days. On the fourth day, a much thicker darkness descended on Egypt,[239] a darkness four times greater than the darkness of the first three days.[240]** This new darkness had a brutal effect

---

* Dassan and Aviram remained in Egypt until right before the miracle of the splitting of the sea. (*Targum Yonasan, Beshalach* 14:3) According to another view, they owed their survival indirectly to Moshe. When Moshe saw that so many Jews were dying in the plague of darkness, he asked Hashem why this was happening. Hashem explained that these people were wicked and deserved to die. Moshe asked Hashem to allow someone from this group to live. Hashem chose to allow the two great sinners Dassan and Aviram to live. They would cause great distress for Moshe and the Jewish people in the future. (*Midrash Hachefetz, Shemos* 2:13)

** The first three days of the plague were meant to obscure the vision of the Egyptians and prevent them from seeing the Jewish people bury their dead. The next three days were meant to immobilize the Egyptians and allow the Jewish people to search the homes.

---

228) לקח טוב ורש"י שם, שמו"ר יד-א 229) שמו"ר יד-ג 230) אב"ע בא י-כג 231) מדרש הגדול שם י-כא (232
רמב"ן ואברבנל שם י-כג 233) רלב"ג ומעם לועז שם 234) מדרש הגדול שם, ברוקח וכן בתוס' עה"ת מובא
שהיתה בי"ג באדר המן בחר בהאי יומא מפני שראה חשכותה ומיתת רבים מישראל בה, ונעלם ממנו שאז היה
אור בהיר במושבי בנ"י, וגם בימיו כתיב ליהודים היתה אורה וגו'. 235) שמו"ר יד-ג, תוס' עה"ת שם י-כב, אלשיך
ומעם לועז שם 236) מכילתא בשלח, מדרש הגדול, רש"י בשלח יג-יח, תוכן הדברים דיש ג' פירושים בתבת
וחמושים אחד מחמש, אחד מחמשים, ואחד מחמש מאות 237) שמו"ר יד-ג 238) רוקח בא י-כב 239) שמו"ר שם
ובעץ יוסף 240) מעם לועז שם

on the Egyptians, making them physically ill.[241] Moreover, the darkness was so thick that the Egyptians were frozen in place. Any Egyptian standing was unable to sit down. Any Egyptian sitting was unable to get up. The Egyptians could not shift positions or straighten their bodies. The exact position they were in when the fourth day arrived was the exact position in which they remained for the next three days.[242] In this position, they were, of course, unable to take precautions against inhaling the toxic fumes. Miraculously, however, they were able to survive for the duration of the plague.[243]

During the first three days of the plague, the Egyptians were able to move about their homes but nothing else. The Jews used this time to bury their dead without the knowledge of the Egyptians. During the second three days of darkness, the Egyptians were totally immobilized, and the Jews used this time to go into the homes of the Egyptians and seek out their hidden treasures.[244] Later, when the Jews asked to "borrow" them, the Egyptians would not be able to deny having hidden treasures.[245]

In the middle of the dense darkness, the Jewish people entered the homes of the Egyptians, accompanied by a miraculous light that allowed them to see everything. What a wondrous miracle this was—that Hashem could create a light seen only by some people and not by others![246] The Jews searched out all the hidden treasures of the Egyptians, such as gold, silver and costly garments, but they touched nothing. The plague of darkness, being the third of its set, had come without warning. This had worked to the benefit of the Jews in that the Egyptians did not have the foreknowledge and opportunity to hide their treasures in places that would be more difficult to discover.[247] Now, when the Jews entered the Egyptian homes to search for treasures, they were invariably successful.

When the Egyptians eventually discovered what had happened, they were amazed by the integrity of the Jewish people. "How wonderful is this nation!" they exclaimed when they discovered that nothing had been taken during the days of darkness. Later, when the Jewish people returned to "borrow" these hidden treasures, the Egyptians gave them more easily, knowing that the borrowers were people of integrity.[248] How ironic that the Egyptians

---

241) ספורנו ט-יד 242) שמו״ר שם, מדרש הגדול י-כא ואילך, רבנו בחיי שם 243) רלב״ג ומעם לועז שם י-כג
244) אלשיך ומעם לועז שם י-כב 245) פענח רזא שם 246) משנת ר׳ אליעזר יא 247) מושב זקנים שם י-כא, אמרי
נועם שם 248) שמו״ר יד-ב, מדרש הגדול בא י-כג, ר׳ אפרים עה״ת שם

who had refused to give the Jewish people straw for their bricks would now lend them their most treasured possessions.[249]

Although the Egyptians were engulfed in total darkness, Hashem created clear visions in their minds of the Jewish people rejoicing in Goshen, eating and drinking in celebration of their good fortune. These visions of the celebrating Jews added greatly to the frustration of the Egyptians as they sat trapped in darkness.[250]

After the second three days of darkness, the plague stopped. Unlike the other plagues which lasted seven days, the plague of darkness lasted only six days. The seventh day of darkness would be inflicted on the Egyptians at the Yam Suf, when the Egyptians would chase the Jewish people into the sea.[251]

Pharaoh had been greatly disconcerted by the plague of darkness. The agony of being immobilized for six days was more than he could bear. Afraid of what future plagues were in store for him, he sent messengers to bring Moshe and Aharon to the royal palace.

"I have a new offer for you," said Pharaoh. "I have made a new analysis of the situation, and this is what I can offer you. Take the men. Take the women. You can even take the children. Even the infants. But the animals stay.[252] You certainly don't need all your animals with you, and you have so many thousands.[253] They are your livelihood and your wealth, and if you leave them here, I will feel sure that you will return after the promised three days."[254]

"I'm afraid this is not a deal, your majesty," Moshe replied. "Not only will we take all our animals, but you, your wife and your servants will contribute additional animals as offerings to Hashem. Furthermore, we will take your treasures with us.[255] We will take all kosher animals and any animal that has even partial Jewish ownership."[256]

"But why do you need so many animals?" asked Pharaoh.

"We have no idea at this point what our needs will be," Moshe replied. "We don't know which animals Hashem will require and how many of each.[257] He may want us to replace all the sacrifices we missed for the last two hundred and ten years. That would be a lot

249) ר' אפרים שם 250) מדרש הגדול שם 251) שמו"ר שם, רוקח כתב דנמשכה לששה ימים בלבד דהיה אות על הגהינום המיועד להם ואש הגהינום אינו מעניש בשבת 252) אברבנל בא, ע' רמב"ן שפתי כהן ומלבים מש"כ בזה 253) מדרש הגדול בא י-כה 254) רמב"ן ורבנו בחיי שם י-כד, בשפתי כהן מוסבר שרצה פרעה שאלוהיהם (כלומר הבהמות) יהיו תחת שליטת מצרים ולא עם בני"י 255) מדרש הגדול, לקח טוב, רש"י בא י-כה וכו', ילקוט ראובני 256) לקח טוב בא י-כו, שמו"ר יח-א 257) אב"ע בא שם

of animals![258] I know you would like to worship our animals, but I'm afraid there will be none available to you. Not even a solitary hoof."[259]

"Aha! Now I know you are a liar," Pharaoh declared triumphantly. "It is not possible that you need all these animals for a three-day journey. You are obviously no messenger of God, just a dishonest adventurer.[260] Get out of my sight at once! Do not ever come here before me again, for the day you do, you will die!"[261]

"You have spoken properly, and at the right time as well," Moshe replied. "It is quite true that I will never come to see you again in your palace. But you will soon come to my house to see me, and your servants will bow before me.[262] It will happen one midnight in the future.[263] I have completed my mission from Hashem. I will bring no more plagues upon Egypt. But you are not finished, your majesty. The next plague—and there will indeed be one!—will be administered directly by Hashem Himself."[264]

Revelation in the Palace

Moshe was about to leave the royal palace for the last time, as he had assured Pharaoh. But Hashem wanted Moshe to give one last message to Pharaoh before he left the palace never to return. Therefore, Hashem decided to communicate with Moshe right then and there in Pharaoh's palace. Ordinarily, Hashem did not appear to Moshe in the capital city of Egypt because of all the idols that infested the city. This time, however, Hashem decided to communicate with Moshe in the palace itself so that he could warn Pharaoh about the tenth and final plague before he left.[265]

Hashem elevated Moshe ten *tefachim* (about five feet) off the ground to extricate him from the contaminated domain of the idols.[266] Hashem then revealed to Moshe that He was about to bring the tenth and most severe plague upon the Egyptians, a plague which would guarantee that Pharaoh would release the

258) שמו״ר יח-א, רמב״ן שם 259) שפתי כהן שם 260) אברבנל שם 261) אברבנל שם 262) כציון 262 שמו״ר שם, שם יד-ד ובענף יוסף, ע׳ רמב״ן בא י-כט 263) רמב״ן שם יא-ד 264) בעה״ט שם י-כט, בשפתי כהן מובא שראה משה שיהיה עוד מכה על מקלו ואי״ל הקב״ה שיעשנה כביכול בעצמו יען והקריב אברהם אבינו את בנו בכורו לד׳ (ישמעאל לא זכה להיות הבכור אף שנולד קודם) 265) שמו״ר יח-א, רמב״ן בא י-כט, אברבנל שם, במושב זקנים ואוה״ח איתא באופן אחר 266) דעת זקנים שם יא-א, י״מ דרק לתפלה יצא אבל קבל נבואתו במקומו, פענח רזא מביא דבמכת ברד כשהוצדה פרעה שאכן חטא, זרק כל ע״ז חוץ לעיר ונתאפשר המקום לגלוי אלקי, אחרים פרשו שלא דבר אליו ד׳ כאן וידעו משה מנבואתו במדין

Jewish people once and for all.[267] Not only would he allow the Jewish people to leave, he would actually push them to get out of Egypt as quickly as possible.[268] Men, women, children, animals, all would be released.[269] No one would remain.

The exodus from Egypt would take place amid great confusion and bedlam. The Egyptians would be in such a hurry to drive out the Jewish people that there would be no time for instructions and an orderly departure. The time to give the Jewish people instructions was right now, before the last plague is administered. Moshe was to tell the Jewish people quietly to borrow the gold, silver and costly garments of the Egyptians in a discreet manner, so that no panic resulted among the Egyptians.[270] The Jewish people were instructed to empty Egypt of its treasures to fulfill Hashem's promise to Avraham that his descendants "would go out with great wealth." Hashem had fulfilled the decree of enslavement. He would also fulfill the decree of enrichment.[271]

Moshe was to be prepared for some reluctance on the part of the Jewish people to obey this commandment. Some of them might be under the impression that the promise of wealth was contingent on four hundred years of slavery, not two hundred and ten. These people would be willing to forego all the great wealth as long as they could leave immediately and not wait for the entire period of four hundred years to run its course. Moshe was to reassure these people that, regardless of their calculations, they would be leaving very shortly—with the great wealth.[272]

Other people might object to gathering all this wealth because of a fear that their escape would be hindered by too many possessions. Moreover, if they took the wealth of Egypt, the Egyptians would have that much more incentive to pursue them and try to bring them back.[273] Better to take nothing and be free forever, than to take all this wealth and be forced to return after three days.[274] Moshe was to assure these people as well that their fears were groundless. Hashem would cause the Egyptians to look kindly upon the Jewish people. They will be happy to lend them whatever they wish, or they will even offer additional treasures of their own free

---

267) מעם לועז בא יא-א ולכן נקראת עם התואר "מכת" בכורות 268) לקח טוב שם 269) רשב"ם ורבנו בחיי שם
270) מנחה בלולה ואברבנל שם יא-ב ושאלו עתה ע"מ לקחתם אחר המכה, אלשיך כ' שגם לקיחתם היה אז דאינו
דרך ארץ לעשות כן בשעת הקבורה והאבל, וע' במלבים על אתר 271) עפ"י ברכות ט:, רש"י בא יא-ב 272) מלבים
שם יא-ג, עיון יעקב ברכות ט: 273) שם, ע' רי"ף והכותב בעין יעקב 274) ענף יוסף שם

will.[275] They will feel pangs of conscience for the torments to which they subjected the Jewish people during all this time, and they will acknowledge that they deserved the punishment of the plagues.[276]

Hashem then told Moshe everything that would occur during the plague of the firstborn, and He instructed Moshe to convey this information to Pharaoh.[277]

Thus ended the only revelation of Hashem to Moshe in the royal palace or anywhere else in the capital city.

The Last Warning

Moshe was overjoyed that Hashem had appeared to him in Pharaoh's palace, allowing Moshe's promise never to return to hold true. Now that Hashem had given Moshe the message to Pharaoh about the next plague, there would certainly be no reason for him ever to return.[278]

"Your majesty," Moshe said. "I have just received a final message for you from Hashem.[279] On the eve of the fifteenth day of Nissan, at the midnight hour, the time for the redemption of the Jewish people will arrive.[280] On that night, Hashem will pass judgment on the wicked and punish Egypt.[281] Hashem will send a plague that will strike at the exact midpoint of the night.[282] This plague will be equal to all the plagues that have come thus far. It will kill all the firstborns of Egypt."[283]

According to some views, Moshe was not so exact in his prediction. Rather, he told Pharaoh it would happen approximately at midnight. There was a possibility that the calculations of the Egyptian astronomers would be slightly inaccurate, making it seem that midnight came earlier. If the plague did not strike at the moment they considered midnight, they would think Moshe was mistaken and not fully credible. Therefore, Moshe only promised that the plague would strike near midnight.[284]

"The plague will strike on a Wednesday night," Moshe continued, "when the constellation *Maadim* dominates the sky. This constellation is a sign of disaster for you, not for us, as you predicted.[285]

275) ר' אברהם בן הרמב"ם ורשב"ם בא יא-ב 276) שכל טוב, מנחה בלולה ורמב"ן שם יא-ג, ר' יהודה החסיד
מוסף שהתנו להקנות להם כל נכסיהם אי כי לא ישובו, ע"ע מלבים בא יא-ב ושם יב-לה (277 רמב"ן שם יא-א (278
שמו"ר יח-א ובעץ יוסף 279) שמו"ר שם 280) ברכות-ג:, לקח טוב ורשב"ם שם יא-ד (281 לקח טוב שם 282)
רש"י שם 283) מדרש הגדול שם יא-ט (284 רש"י ברכות שם, ע' רבנו בחיי שם 285) רבנו בחיי ומלבים שם יא-
ד, בתורה שלמה מובא ילקוט מעין גנים גנים שיש לו חשבון אחרת ומוסיף שיושפך מהם דם כי אז ישליט כוכב שבתאי

Hashem will leave His Abode, so to speak,[286] and go out into Egypt, where He will kill the firstborn of the Egyptians because of His love for His own firstborn children, the Jewish people.[287]

"You are undoubtedly aware, your majesty, of Hashem's covenant with Avraham because of which the Jewish people were enslaved. Well, the time of bondage has run out. The next stage has arrived. Do you know what that is, your majesty? It is the time to pass judgment on the tormentors of the Jewish people.[288]

"Listen well, your majesty, as I describe the tenth plague, the horrifying tenth plague. Every Egyptian firstborn shall die, from the most prominent princes in line to succeed to the throne of Egypt[289] down to the lowliest slaves who are behind the millstone and imprisoned.[290] If there is a household with no living firstborn, the head of the household will die. Firstborn animals will also die.[291]

"There will be a dreadful outcry in Egypt, cries of pain louder and more agonized than any that were ever heard before or will ever be heard again. This night will be the worst of all.[292] All the people will cry out in pain and call for an uprising against you, because your stubborn refusal to let the Jewish people go has led to the deaths of their firstborn.[293]

"A great miracle will occur in Egypt during this plague, your majesty," said Moshe. "The Angel of Death will stalk Egypt, and the dogs, who always sense his presence, will be barking in great fear. Yet the sounds of terrified barking will be heard only in Egypt. Among the Jews, however, the dogs will not bark or cause any people or animals to become frightened.[294] What a miracle this will be, that dogs who normally bark in the night will now fall silent even though they sense the presence of the Angel of Death.[295] The sight of Jews moving swiftly through the night with staves in their hands will also not induce the dogs to break their silence.[296] They will not so much as move their lips to cause any harm to the Jewish people. This goes for other animals as well.[297*] In Egypt, however, the dogs

---

* Moshe would even silence the statues of dogs that barked by magic whenever they detected anyone trying to escape Egypt. (*Yalkut Reuveni*)

---

286) רוקח בא יא-ד 287) אוה"ח שם ובפסיקתא חדתא באוצר המדרשים תצז, שפתי כהן מפרש "אני יוצא" שאצא 288) מהנהגת רחמים ואתלבש בהנהגה של דין 289) מנחה בלולה שם 289) אונקלוס, לקח טוב, אב"ע שם יא-ה 290) אב"ע וספורנו שם, מנחה בלולה שם, ע' רש"י וברטנורה בביאור בכור השבי 291) בעה"ט שם 292) ריב"ש ורוקח שם יא-ו 293) מלבים שם יא-ז 294) לקח טוב, אב"ע, דעת זקנים, שפתי כהן שם 295) חזקוני שם 296) מושב זקנים, ריב"א ותולדות יצחק שם, וע' שפתי כהן שמביא שהכלבים לא אכלו את חלליהם כדי שיראו כולם הנס הגדול, וגם מהאי טעמא זכו למדאה"כ לכלב תשליכון אותו 297) ר' סעדיא גאון שם

will bark very loudly, more loudy than they ever barked before."[298]

Hashem does not begrudge any creature its reward. Because the dogs did not bark among the Jews during the plague of the firstborn, Hashem later commanded that carcasses unfit for Jewish people to eat should be thrown to dogs. If Hashem is so meticulous about rewarding a dog, there must certainly be great rewards in store for the righteous who sanctify His Name in the world.[299]

"This is how it will all end, your majesty," continued Moshe. "All your firstborn ministers and advisors will die, and those who are not firstborn will come to beg me for mercy."[300]

Moshe turned to the distinguished ministers surrounding Pharaoh.

"You over there are a firstborn," Moshe called out. "You will die, and I will never see you again. You over there are not a firstborn. You will come down to me, to my house.[301] That general, this duke, you will all come down to me and plead.[302] But we will not leave, your majesty. We will only leave when you yourself emancipate us and personally command us to leave Egypt.[303] Only then will we leave. From that point on, Egypt will fall to second-class rank as a nation, never to recover its former glory."[304]

Once again, Moshe had shown his great respect and deference for the king of Egypt. Moshe knew full well that Pharaoh himself would come plead with the Jewish people to leave Egypt, but Moshe honored Pharaoh by not making public mention of it.[305]

"Are you finished, Moshe?" asked Pharaoh.

"Yes, your majesty," Moshe replied. "I have nothing else to say."

Pharaoh laughed mockingly. "Do you really think you've frightened me?" Pharaoh asked. "How bad can this plague be? There are probably no more than a few hundred firstborns in all of Egypt."

"Not quite, your majesty," Moshe replied. "The criteria for first-born are the first child of either the father or the mother. Therefore, your average promiscuous Egyptian may have fathered as many as ten firstborn children by ten different women. You may also have one woman who bore ten firstborn children to ten different fathers.

Moreover, these firstborn will die no matter if they are male or female. So you see, your majesty, I don't think you should take this matter so lightly."[306]

An old woman in attendance at the royal court spoke up. "You are a liar, Moshe," she said. "You say that there will be a great outcry among all the people of Egypt. Well, how about me? I am an old woman. I have no mother or father, no brother or sister, no son or daughter. Why would someone like me cry out?"

"Just wait and see," Moshe replied. "You will be the first of all the people to cry over this plague."[307]

There was nothing more to say. The time had come for Moshe to leave. Moshe had not forgotten Pharaoh's offensive behavior towards him, the messenger of Hashem, expelling him from the royal court. During his entire address to Pharaoh and his ministers, Moshe had contained his anger.[308] But now, Moshe felt some reaction was in order. He lifted his hand in anger to show Pharaoh that he was worthy of being hit for his disrespectful behavior.[309]* Then rather than backing out respectfully, as he usually did, Moshe turned his back on Pharaoh as a sign of insolence.[310] Then he strode out of the royal palace for the last time.

After Moshe left Pharaoh, Hashem told him that the tenth and final plague would indeed take place. Pharaoh should be frightened to death of the imminent plague, but he would still not relent. Hashem had hardened Pharaoh's heart.[311] Pharaoh would refuse to let the Jewish people out of Egypt, and therefore, he would witness the death of the firstborns, the splitting of the sea and the drowning of the Egyptian army.[312]

---

* Moshe actually hit Pharaoh. (Rashi)

---

306) מדרש הגדול שם יא-ה, דברי הימים למשה 307) מדרש הגדול שם יא-ו 308) מנחה בלולה, רש"י שם יא-
ח 309) ר' יהודה החסיד שם 310) בן יהוידע זבחים קב. 311) רמב"ן בא יא-ט 312) רש"י ומלבים שם.

The Korban Pesach

16

The last encounter with Pharaoh in the palace was over. Moshe and Aharon would never again return. As they left the palace, they went directly out of the capital city to the designated place of prayer, and Hashem appeared to them. This time there were no more messages for the stubborn Pharaoh. Instead, Hashem gave them the *mitzvah* of *kiddush hachodesh*, sanctification of the new month.

The sun was about to set, and Hashem instructed Moshe and Aharon to look for the new moon. When they would see the moon in its state of renewal they should declare the new month. Moshe was perplexed. He was unsure of the correct appearance of the new moon and its proper position. Hashem, therefore, showed him an exact image of the appearance of the moon which required the sanctification of the new month.[1]

---

1) רש״י ממכילתא בא יב-ב, מושב זקנים שם

Hashem instructed Moshe to sanctify the coming month of Nissan, which from that time on would be considered the first month of the year. Originally, the first month of the year had been Tishrei, the month during which Adam was created. The month in which the Jewish people would be liberated from slavery in Egypt would now supersede Tishrei in greatness, and it would become the new first month of the year. All the months of the year would, therefore, be ranked in relation to the exodus of the Jewish people from Egypt, e.g. the second month after the exodus, the third month after the exodus, and so forth.[2]

The names by which we know the months are not mentioned in the Torah. They are Persian names given to the months during the Babylonian exile after the destruction of the first Beis Hamikdash, and they signify the particular characteristics of each month.[3] In the Torah, however, the months are identified by their number in relation to the month of the exodus, as a constant reminder that Hashem took us out of Egypt.[4] Nissan is a good month for the Jewish people, the month in which we became one of the leading nations of the world.[5]

Hashem told Moshe to sanctify the moon, because the Jewish calendar year follows the lunar cycle of 354 days, rather than the solar cycle of 365.[6] The *mitzvah* of sanctifying the new moon each month bears witness that Hashem is constantly renewing the world.[7]

MONTH	MEANING	SIGNIFICANCE
NISSAN	miracles	miraculous plagues and splitting of the sea
IYAR	light	Hashem's *mann* enlightened the people
SIVAN	like Sinai	the Torah was given at Mount Sinai
TAMMUZ	name of idol	a reminder of the Eigel
AV	father	sin of the *meraglim*, "father" of Jewish suffering
ELUL	high	creation of the world makes this month high
TISHREI	release	forgiveness and release from sins
CHESHVAN	brought upon	Shlomo completed the Beis Hamikdash
KISLEV	*ksil*, rain sign	rainy season begins
TEVES	goodness	Moshe killed Sichon and Og
SHEVAT	stick	rains come down with the force of a stick
ADAR	mighty	birth of the great Moshe

2) רש״י ממכילתא שם, שמו״ר טו-יז, חזקוני שם, ע׳ ר״ה יא., תוס׳ שם כז., מלבים 3) רמב״ן ורבנו בחיי בא יב-
ב, ירושלמי ר״ה א-ב 4) שמו״ר טו-ז, רמב״ן ורש״ש בא שם 5) אוה״ח שם, ראה גם רש״י תענית כת. ד״ה משנכנס
6) מכילתא ואב״ע בא שם 7) רבנו בחיי שם, עיין ויק״ר כט-ח

What Is the Korban Pesach?

Having told Moshe and Aharon to sanctify the new moon and to establish Nissan as the first month of the year, Hashem now entrusted them with the central *mitzvah* of this sanctified and illustrious month—the *korban pesach*.[8]

Hashem commanded the Jewish people to sacrifice a lamb or goat on the fourteenth day of Nissan and eat it that night, on the fifteenth day of Nissan (on the Jewish calendar, a day begins at nightfall and ends with the following nightfall). On that night, Hashem would kill all the firstborn of Egypt, but the firstborn of the Jewish people would not be affected. The *korban pesach* symbolized this distinction. Hashem would "pass over" (*pesach* in Hebrew) the homes of the Jewish people and bring death only to the Egyptian homes.[9]

The fifteenth of Nissan would forever be remembered as a day of festivity, celebrating the plague of the firstborn and the exodus of the Jewish people from Egypt.[10] It would signal the beginning of Pesach, a seven-day festival ending on the twenty-first of Nissan, the day the Jewish people would actually cross the sea, the climax of the exodus.[11] This festival would commemorate the new nationhood of the Jewish people[12] and celebrate it with special festival offerings. It would always be a source of hope and encouragement to the Jewish people, even in the worst of times.[13]

The animal chosen for the *korban pesach* was the lamb, the astrological sign of the month of Nissan and the animal the Egyptians worshipped. By sacrificing the lamb, the Jewish people would be declaring that the Egyptian gods were powerless. To emphasize this concept, the lamb was to be sacrificed in the middle of the month when the astrological sign was at its highest point of ascendancy and the god was supposedly at the height of its powers. Ironically, the act of symbolically slaughtering the Egyptian god, which should supposedly bring great danger of Egyptian reprisal, would be the very act that protected the Jews from the plague of the firstborn.[14] As such, the *korban pesach* would remain as a reminder for all future generations that Hashem performed great miracles for the Jewish people when he took them out of Egypt.[15]

---

8) מדרש החפץ שם 9) רש"י שם יב-יא 10) לקח טוב ורש"י שם יב-יד 11) רבנו בחיי ואב"ע שם יב-טו ואילך 12) משך חכמה 13) אוה"ח בא יב-יד 14) צרור המור שם יב-ו, ע"ע שמו"ר טז-ג, מו"נ ח"ג מו, רמב"ן בא יב-ג 15) חינוך מצות ו-ז

The Laws of the Korban Pesach

All the Jewish people—both men and women[16]—were required to take a lamb or goat on the tenth day of Nissan.[17] Each household was to share one lamb or goat, which was to be a one-year-old male without a blemish.[18] The animal was to be tied to the bedpost and kept under observation for four days, until the fourteenth of the month, to ensure that it was free from blemishes.[19]

A household too small to consume an entire lamb on its own could form a group with other households, as long as each individual would be assured of at least a *kezayis* (an olive-sized piece) of meat from the *korban*.[20] Only those who joined the group before the *korban* was slaughtered could eat from its meat.[21]

The actual slaughtering of the *korban* could be done by either the owner or by a community appointee.[22] After the lamb is slaughtered, its blood is collected in a basin. A bundle of three hyssop roots is dipped into the blood three times. The first time the blood is applied to one doorpost, the second time to the other doorpost and the third to the crossbeam of the doorway.[23]*

The lamb must be roasted whole over a fire, its head, legs and organs included, until it is well done. It may not be cooked in a pot of water. It should be eaten after nightfall with *matzah* and bitter herbs called *marror*, and all meat must be consumed before daybreak;[24] any meat left over after daybreak should be put aside and burned on the sixteenth (the first day of *Chol Hamoed* in Eretz Yisrael).[25] It is forbidden to break any bone that has a *kezayis* of meat on it.[26]

The members of the group should all remain together and not break up into smaller groups to eat the *korban*.[27] They should not exit the house designated by the group as the eating place until they finish

---

* Rashi and others suggest (based on the opinions cited in the *Mechilta*) that the inner portion of the door was touched with blood.

---

16) רמב״ם ריש הל׳ קרבן פסח   17) מכילתא בא   18) רש״י ממכילתא בא יב-ג   19) רש״י שם יב-ו, בתכלת מרדכי

ממהרש״ם שם   מבואר מדוע נקשרה למטתם בפרט   20) רש״י ממכילתא שם יב-ד   21) רמב״ם הל׳ ק״פ ב-א

22) שם א-ד, רש״י ממכילתא בא יב-ו   23) מכילתא תרגום יונתן רש״י בא יב-ז וגם יב-כב, ספרי חקת פרק יט-ו ושם יט-

ח ובמלבים שם, ע׳ ברוקח, מבואר במלבים שלא היו דיני דיני קדימה בסדר נתינת הדם, וזולת הזריקה וקשירתה למטה

אין בין פסח מצרים לפסח לדורות   24) רש״י ממכילתא בא יב-ח וכו׳, ר׳ סעדיא גאון כ׳ דלא נאסרה אא״כ לא היה

צלוי כלל   25) בא יב-י, חזקוני מוסיף בזה   תבלין דאם היה נא לא היה נעים לחכם ויבואו לידי נותר   26) ע׳ רש״י

בא יב-מו   27) רש״י ממכילתא בא שם

eating the *korban*.[28] The *korban* should be eaten in a hurried rather than a leisurely manner, with a full understanding of its significance. They should understand that while they are eating the *korban*, Hashem is passing over the Jewish homes marked by the paschal blood and killing all the firstborns of the Egyptians.[29]

No uncircumcised Jew, nor an uncircumcised convert to Judaism, may eat from the *korban*.[30] Any gentile or apostate Jew, such as one who has turned to idolatry, may not join the group eating the *korban*, nor may even a morsel be offered to him.[31] A gentile who is officially a resident of Eretz Yisrael, or a gentile worker hired or belonging to a Jew, may not eat from the *korban*.[32] Any circumcised slave of a Jew may eat of the *korban*.

Matzah is eaten for a period of seven days. On the evening of the fifteenth day of Nissan, it is mandatory. For the next six days, through the twenty-first day of Nissan, it is an optional *mitzvah*.[33]

Beginning the afternoon of the fourteenth, all *chametz* (leaven) should be cleared from Jewish property through the end of the seven-day festival.[34] The *matzah* should be supervised carefully, from as early as when the wheat is cut, so that it does not become *chametz*.[35]

No labors may be done on the first and seventh day of the festival, other than those required for the preparation of food.[36]

Moshe Instructs the Jewish People

When Hashem had finished telling Moshe the laws of the *korban pesach*, Moshe had one question.

"Master of the universe, how can I possibly tell the Jewish people to do this?" he asked. "Sheep are the idols of Egypt! If the Jewish people slaughter the idols of Egypt, the Egyptians will massacre them!"

Hashem, however, reassured Moshe on this point. Before the Jewish people left Egypt, it was essential that they publicly slaughter the Egyptian gods to demonstrate once and for all that their gods are worthless.[37]

28) מדרש הגדול שם 29) ע׳ בא יב-יא ואילך 30) בא יב-מח 31) רש״י (וגור אריה עליו) ומדרש הגודל שם יב-מג, רמב״ם ק״פ ט-ז, רלב״ג יב-מג 32) מדרש הגדול בא יב-מה 33) בא יב-טו ואילך, אונקלוס ומכילתא שם 34) בא יב-טו, שם יב-יט, רש״י ממכילתא שם, פסחים ד:, שם יא: 35) שם יא: בא יב-יז ובאב״ע 36) בא יב-טז ובמכילתא 37) שמו״ר טז-א וכו׳

Thus reassured, Moshe went to convey all that he had learned to the Jewish people. First, he went to the elders and explained the laws of the *korban pesach* to them. Then he told them to inform the Jewish people about the laws of *korban pesach* and to assemble them in front of Moshe to hear his teachings. The elders earned the privilege of telling the Jewish people about the *korban pesach* because they had believed Moshe's tidings of exodus when he had first come to Egypt.[38]

The elders assembled the Jewish people, and Moshe told them about the *mitzvah* of sanctifying the new month and the new role of the month of Nissan as the first of all months.[39] Then he spoke to them about the *korban pesach*.

"Draw yourselves away from idol worship," Moshe told them. "Take the very idol you worship and slaughter it for a *korban pesach*.[40] Go out to your stables and get a lamb or a goat.[41] If you have neither, go to the marketplace and buy one. Each household must have a *korban pesach* so that you will all share in the celebration of these miraculous events.[42] Take the *korban pesach* on the tenth of this month. Tie it to your bedpost and supervise it carefully for four days to ensure that it has no blemishes. Then sacrifice it on the fourteenth of the month."[43]

Moshe then told the Jewish people about the laws of slaughtering the *korban pesach*, the application of blood on the doors and the reasons for it, and the laws of *chametz* and *matzah*.[44] He told them not to fear the screaming Egyptians who will be enraged by the death of the firstborn. Hashem would protect all the Jewish people whose doorposts are marked by the blood of the *korban*.[45]

The Jewish people followed Moshe's instructions, and the head of each household went to get a sheep for a *korban pesach*. When the tenth of Nissan arrived, they tied their sheep to the bedpost, as Moshe had told them. By tying the sheep to their bedposts on the tenth of Nissan, the Jewish people were deemed worthy of crossing the Jordan River into Eretz Yisrael on the tenth of Nissan as well.[46]

38) שמו"ר טז-א (39 בא יב-כא וברמב"ן, שמו"ר טז-א (40 מכילתא ומדרש הגדול שם יב-כא (41 רמב"ן שם יב-כא (42 רש"י ממכילתא, לקח טוב ורבנו בחיי שם (43 רמב"ן שם (44 שם (45 אב"ע שם יב-יג (46 לקח טוב בא יב-ו, ע' דעת זקנים יב-ג דהיה יב-ג כדי שלא יצטרכו לצאת תוך ג' ימים אחר המילה

Civil Unrest in Egypt

The tenth of Nissan fell on a Shabbos. The firstborn Egyptians heard the wailing sounds of the lambs tied to the Jewish bedposts and decided to investigate.

"What is going on here?" they asked.

"We are preparing this lamb for an offering called the *pesach* sacrifice," the Jew responded. "After the sacrifice is brought, Hashem will pass over the Jewish homes and kill all the firstborn in the Egyptian homes."

The memories of the first nine plagues Hashem had brought upon Egypt were still fresh in their minds, and the news that all the Egyptian firstborns were about to die caused them all to fall faint to the ground. When they regained consciousness, they were consumed with a tremendous hatred of the Jews who were humiliating their gods and would soon cause the death of their firstborn. In their anger, they decided to kill the Jews, but Hashem instantly made them ill. Their bodies were wracked by excruciating pain, and they were totally incapacitated. The sight of their beloved gods bound to the Jewish beds and about to be sacrificed was more agonizing to them than all the plagues they had endured. Helpless, they began to weep uncontrollably, as if they themselves were tied to the beds.

The firstborns realized they could do nothing to prevent the sacrifice of the sheep. If that came to pass, they were sure to die in the next plague. They had only one alternative left. They ran to their fathers and begged them to set the Jewish people free so that the Egyptian firstborn would be spared.

"All of the plagues Moshe has predicted have come true," they said to their fathers. "If the Jews are not sent out of Egypt, we will all be killed!"

"Even so," their fathers replied. "We will never allow the Jews out of Egypt. If you have any complaints, take them to Pharaoh. He himself is a firstborn."

Desperate, the firstborns ran to the palace and sought an audience with Pharaoh.

"You must allow the Jewish people to leave Egypt," they pleaded. "We will all die in the next plague that Moshe has foretold!"

"Who sent you to me?" Pharaoh responded.

"Our fathers," they replied.

"What an outrage!" Pharaoh screamed. "How dare they tell you to do this! I will never let the Jews go. We must risk our own lives rather than let them leave our land. I want your fathers killed!" Pharaoh turned to his guards. "Expel these people at once! I want them out of here!"

Overcome by fear and frustration, the firstborn Egyptians fled the palace and turned their wrath on their own insensitive fathers. Six hundred thousand fathers of firstborn Egyptians died on that fateful day. As a last resort, the firstborn decided to circumvent the government and go directly to the people, but they too refused. The firstborn then revolted, and civil strife broke out in Egypt. But in the end nothing changed.

Many miracles had taken place. The firstborn could not stop the Jewish people from going ahead with the *korban pesach*. The forthcoming plague of the firstborn could not be stopped, and in the interim, many other Egyptians died in the turbulent time that preceded the plague. In commemoration of the many miracles that occurred on the Shabbos of the tenth of Nissan in that year, the Shabbos before Pesach would always be known as Shabbos Hagadol, the great Shabbos.[47]*

A number of other reasons are also given for this Shabbos being called Shabbos Hagadol. On this Shabbos, the Jewish people began the performance of their first *mitzvah*, the preparations for the *korban pesach*.[48] On this Shabbos, for the first time, all the Jewish people believed that Hashem created the world in six days and rested on the seventh.[49] On this Shabbos, the Jewish people as a whole repented for their sins and turned away from *avodah zarah*.[50] On this Shabbos, the Jewish people realized that they were forever free from Egyptian labor.[51] Significantly, the numerical value (*gematria*) of the Hebrew letters of "Shabbos Hagadol" is equal to the numerical value of "on the tenth of Nissan."[52]

It is a custom in many Jewish communities around the world

---

* Many others suggest that this incident did not happen on Shabbos Hagadol but as soon as Moshe informed Pharaoh about the upcoming plague.

47) פסיקתא דרב כהנא ז (דף נה), תנחומא ישן בא, זוה״ק פנחס רנא, מחזור ויטרי דף רכב, תוס׳ שבת פז:
ובמהרש״א, דעת זקנים בא יב-ג, לקח טוב בא יב-ו, שמו״ר טז-ג, דברי הימים למשה, מדרש הגדול שם יא-ה, ע׳
ילקו״ש תהלים קל״ו וטור וב״ח או״ח סימן ת״ל 48) חזקוני בא יב-ג 49) מעם לועז בא 50) חת״ס 51) צפנת פענח,
מעם לועז 52) רבנו אפרים עה״ת

for the rabbi to lecture on the laws of Pesach on the Shabbos before
Pesach. This lecture draws many people to *shul* for long periods of
time, and this, according to some views, gave rise to the name Shabbos Hagadol.[53]

Last Minute Instructions

On the fourteenth day of Nissan, as the time
of sacrificing the *korban pesach* drew near,
Moshe explained the laws to the Jewish people, not only as they applied to them but as
they would apply to all future generations. No uncircumcised people could participate in the *korban pesach*. The blood of the *bris milah*
would protect the Jewish people from the plague of the firstborn
along with the blood of the *korban*.[54] Therefore, the blood of the *bris
milah* should be placed on the door together with the blood of the
korban.[55] Moshe had not instructed them previously to circumcise
themselves, because Hashem wanted the Jewish people to acquire
the merit of circumcision on the fourteenth, the time of their
redemption.[56]

Moshe also told the Jewish people to eat the *korban pesach* in the
hurried manner of a person about to embark on a journey.[57] In other
words, they should eat it with their belts buckled, their feet shod and
their staffs in their hands.[58] The symbolism of a people in a hurry to
leave is obvious, but there was also a practical purpose in this
instruction. By eating the *korban pesach*, each person would be protected from the death of the firstborn. By eating in a hurried manner,
they would be ensured of coming under the protective umbrella
before the attack would begin.[59]

The Angels of Destruction

On the night after the fourteenth of Nissan,
Hashem would personally execute judgment on Egypt. He would pass through the
land, and in one instant, every Egyptian
firstborn would die.[60] Hashem would come Himself, because only

---

53) שבלי הלקט כה, צדה לדרך   54) רש"י בא יב-מג, שמו"ר יט-ה, במדבר רבה יא-ג   55) פרדר"א כט, תרגום
יונתן בא יב-יג, במדרש ויושע מובא ששמו את דמו על כותלי בתיהם   56) ע' דעת זקנים שם   57) רש"י בא יב-יא
ובשפתי חכמים, ספורנו שם 58) אב"ע שם, אברבנל כתב שהיה אז הדרך שהאוכל במתינות עושה כן שמקלו מונח
ואין נעליו על רגליו וקשר חגורתו מותר, וכל הני היו פרטים בהלכות חפזון וכ"ה במלבים 59) אב"ע בא יב-יב
60) רש"י בא שם, במכילתא אי' שלא אמר בחצות לילה כי אי לא יארע באותו רגע לפי חשבונם יתרופפו כל
אמונתם וע"ש

He could identify which Egyptian was truly a firstborn.[61] Moreover, only He could distinguish between Egyptian and Jew. A messenger could easily mistake a Jew who had sinned for an Egyptian.[62]

Hashem would kill all the firstborn of the Egyptian people and animals. He would also destroy the Egyptian gods. Those made of wood would rot. Those made of stone would crumble or dissolve. Those made of metal would melt or rust.[63]

During this terrible night, the blood on the doorposts of the Jewish people would protect them.[64] The blood would show that the Jewish people have done the *mitzvos* that Hashem commanded them to do, and thus they will be protected from the angels of destruction let loose over the land of Egypt.[65] All Jews are considered the first-born of Hashem, and all of them would be protected by the sign of the blood.[66] And as long as the sign of the blood is on the eating places of the *korban pesach,* the protection will extend to all dwellings and places, even if not marked by the sign of the blood.[67] Neverthe-less, the Jews should not venture out during this night, since the forces of destruction will be let loose on the land. Only indoors would they be protected.[68] The exodus would thus have to wait until morning. Furthermore, Hashem did not want the Jewish people to leave Egypt like thieves in the night. He wanted them to leave in the morning in full view of the Egyptians.[69]

One might wonder at the presence of angels of destruction if Hashem had promised to administer the plague of the firstborn by Himself. There are a number of explanations for this. According to some views, the angels of destruction accompanied Hashem but did not actually administer the plague.[70] Furthermore, the angels of destruction were let loose on Egypt after midnight, when the plague had already been administered.[71] According to some views, the angels of destruction had no power over the Egyptians and could only harm Jews who had not participated in the *korban pesach*.[72] In

61) זוה"ק וירא קח 62) רבנו בחיי בא שם ומוסיף שהיה מלאך מטט' 63) רש"י ממכילתא בא שם, לקח טוב שם, שמו"ר טו-טו, הגדת שבלי הלקט 64) ע' בא יב-יג ואילך, אוה"ח יג, זבח פסח מסביר דלולא פסיחת ד' על בתי ישראל היה אותו מזל הממונה על הבכורים ממית גם בכורי ישראל ע"ש 65) תרגום יונתן, אברבנל, מעם לועז בא יב-יב, שם יג-כג, זוה"ק מקץ ר"א, בהגדה ע"פ מעשה נסים מובא דשאר המכות נעצרו ע"י כח התפילה, לא כן מכה זו שעשה ד' בעצמו לא היה עצה להמלט זולת מצות הללו 66) גבורות ד' לז 67) מכילתא ולקח טוב בא יב-יג רש"י ממכילתא שם יב-כב 69) מנחה בלולה כג 70) רבנו בחיי וחזקוני שם, ע' רמב"ן ודעת זקנים שם יב-יב 71) שפתי חכמים, ראה שם בגור אריה 72) זוה"ק בא מא

fact, some commentaries explain that the destroyer from which the Jews were protected did not refer to angels of destruction but to the plague itself.[73] Some commentaries claim that the angels of destruction were only empowered to cause injury, not death.[74]

According to other views, the angels of destruction were responsible for killing the oldest in each household, while Hashem Himself killed the true firstborns.[75] In variations of this view, the angels of destruction were responsible for killing the obvious firstborn, while Hashem Himself killed the unidentified firstborn born of Egyptian adultery. The angels of destruction killed the firstborn who ventured outside, while Hashem killed the firstborn in their homes.[76] The angels of destruction killed firstborn children still in the womb, while Hashem killed those who were already born.[77]

The End of the Message

"Listen carefully," Moshe told the Jewish people in the Name of Hashem. "When the plague strikes, the Egyptians will try to send you away as quickly as possible, because they will fear for their very lives. Do not listen to them. Although you will have eaten the *korban pesach* in the hurried manner of a person about to embark on a journey, you must wait until the morning to leave. In the morning, you will indeed leave Egypt with great haste, in such haste that you will have no time to take provisions for the journey.[78]

"Remember this day forever! It will always be a day of celebration, a holiday for all the generations to come, according to the eternal laws of Hashem. The laws of *korban pesach*, *chametz* and *matzah* are also eternal laws of Hashem which you will observe when you enter Eretz Yisrael.[79]

"Someday, your children may ask you, 'Why does this holiday involve so much effort?[80] Why does this holiday, unlike other holidays, have the numerous laws of *chametz* and *matzah*?[81] Why on this holiday, unlike other holidays, is the sacrifice roasted and brought on the day before the holiday?'[82] On that day, you shall tell your children

73) הגדת שבלי הלקט, אברבנל מפרש ד"משחית" קאי אמצרים 74) אמרי נועם שם יב-כג, ע' חזקוני שם יב-יב
75) אמרי נועם שם יב-יב, יב-כג, יב-כג, עיין רוקח יב-כט 76) ע' תוס' ומושב זקנים שם יב-יב, הגדה ע"פ חסד לאברהם
77) שמו"ר יז-ד וביד' משה 78) ברכות ט. וברש"י, מכילתא, מעם לועז מביא שהוצרכה החיפוו שלא ישקעו
בשער הנון דטומאה (הבאנו במבוא ע"ש) 79) מכילתא בא יב-יד, שם יב-כד, ורע' מושב זקנים 80) רוקח שם יב-
כו 81) רשב"ם שם, ר' אפרים עה"ת שם 82) חזקוני וספורנו שם

that it is because Hashem passed over the Jewish homes when He killed all the firstborn in the land of Egypt.[83] All the special laws of this holiday are to commemorate that event.[84] These are the words of Hashem to you."

When Moshe finished addressing the Jewish people, many of them nodded in joyous acceptance of the laws of Hashem.[85] They bowed and prostrated themselves on the ground, while singing the praises of Hashem. Moshe had just told them in the Name of Hashem that they were about to go free, that they would have children and that they would inherit Eretz Yisrael.[86] Their joy knew no bounds.

The Fourteenth of Nissan

On Wednesday afternoon, the fourteenth of Nissan, the elders were appointed to be the messengers of the Jewish people in the sacrifice of the *korban pesach*.[87] They meticulously followed the instructions Moshe had given to them, and by doing so, they showed all the Jewish people how to bring the *korban pesach* properly.[88]

However, a serious problem developed that day. Moshe had instructed the Jewish people to circumcise themselves on that day, because the blood of *bris milah* would protect them in the night. He also told them that an uncircumcised Jew could not participate in the *korban pesach*. Many of the Jewish people responded with great joy. They immediately ran to Moshe, Aharon and Yehoshua and requested a *bris milah*, which was duly performed.[89] There were, however, other Jewish people who were somewhat reluctant to circumcise themselves, either because they feared the smell of blood or because they still wanted to curry favor with the Egyptians.

In order to induce these reluctant Jews to circumcise themselves and participate in the *korban pesach*, Hashem told Moshe to sacrifice his *korban* immediately. Then He caused the scent of Gan Eden to cling to the *korban pesach*, and all of Egypt was filled with the heavenly odor of the *korban pesach*. A pleasant odor began to permeate all across Egypt. The Jewish people who had not yet joined a group for the *korban pesach* came running to Moshe.

---

83) רש"י שם יב-כז 84) ראה ר' אפרים ורוקח שם 85) ריב"ש וחזקוני שם 86) מכילתא ולקח טוב שם 87) חזקוני שם יב-כא עפ"י שבת פז: וע"ש בתוס' 88) אברבנל שם 89) שמו"ר יט-ה, מדרש ויושע בפסוק ימינך, בדרשת אבן שואב מובא שהיה אז יהושע בן נ"ה שנים

"Please, can we have some of your *korban pesach*?" they pleaded.

"I'm afraid I cannot share it with you," Moshe replied. "Hashem has commanded that only those that have a *bris milah* may partake in the *korban pesach*! So if you want to partake of the *korban pesach* you must circumcise yourselves. And besides, whoever doesn't partake of the *korban pesach* will die in the plague tonight. Therefore, it would seem highly advisable that you circumcise yourselves immediately."

They did not need any more convincing, and within a short time, Moshe, Aharon and Yehoshua circumcised all the Jewish people.[90] The preparation was now complete. All the Jewish people were circumcised and included in a group for the *korban pesach*.[91]

The heavenly aroma of the *korban pesach* also attracted the attention of many Egyptians. The smells, however, led them to a sight which disturbed them profoundly. In the Jewish homes, they saw wailing lambs tied to the bedposts. They saw other lambs already

90) שמו"ר יט-ה, לקח טוב בא יב-ו, במדבר רבה יא-ג, שיר השירים רבה א-יב ובעץ יוסף אות נ"ז, שמו"ר טז-ג, ע"ע רד"ל שם ואוה"ח בא יב-מג, ע' רש"י יהושע ה-ב, כריתות ט., משכיל לדוד ברש"י יד-ו ובחידושי הגרי"ז הלוי עה"ת שם. 91) רוקח בא יב-כח

slaughtered and being roasted whole right before their eyes. They saw Jewish people applying the blood of the lambs to the doorposts and lintels of their homes. The lambs represented the gods of Egypt, and what was happening was blasphemous in Egyptian eyes. The sight of their gods being slaughtered and skewered was more painful to the Egyptians than the worst of the plagues. The Jewish people were making a mockery of the Egyptian gods, and there was nothing the Egyptians could do about it.[92]

At night, the Egyptians witnessed the Jewish people eating the *korban pesach* and singing praises and melodies to Hashem in celebration of the long awaited exodus.[93] The tantalizing smells of the *korban* made the Egyptians salivate with hunger. They begged the Jewish people to share it with them, but they refused, in accordance with the laws they had been taught. For many years, the Egyptians used to torment the Jews in a similar fashion. They would have the Jews hunt and prepare food for them, but the Jews themselves were never allowed to share in the banquets they had helped prepare. Now, the tables were turned. The Egyptians wanted to share in the *korban* of the Jews, but they could not.[94]

Some Egyptians went to Moshe and asked to be given a share of the *korban pesach*.

"Impossible!" Moshe told them. "Hashem has forbidden a gentile or a stranger to eat from the *korban pesach*."

"Yes, we understand," the Egyptians replied, "but we are not followers of His, and His laws do not interest us. We just want to have some of that wonderful meat."

"It is still impossible," said Moshe. "We do follow the laws of Hashem, and Hashem has forbidden us to give any part of the *korban* to a gentile or a stranger. I must honor the law, and I cannot give you any of it."[95]

There were some virtuous Egyptians who came to Moshe during the day and asked to be converted to Judaism so that they could join in the great redemption of Hashem's people. These Egyptians were converted to Judaism and given a *bris milah*, and consequently, they were included in the *korban pesach*. These converted Egyptians came to be known as the "Erev Rav."[96]

As the Jewish people were eating the *korban pesach*, they realized

---

92) זוה"ק פנחס רנא, תוס' עה"ת, חזקוני, יוסף מקנה, וע' הגדת השיר והשבח 93) שמו"ר יז-ה, רבנו מיוחס בא, ראה ערכין י: 94) שמו"ר טז-ד 95) שמו"ר יט-א, רלב"ג בא יב-מג 96) שמו"ר יח-י

they were completely healed from their *bris milah*. At the same time the Egyptians were to be killed the Jews were to be healed.[97] Indeed, any Jew who was sick and dying recovered that night and remained alive, so that the Egyptians should not say, "This plague has stricken the Jews as well."[98]

The Laws of Pesach

The *korban pesach* was more than just a symbolic slaughtering of the Egyptian god in full view of the Egyptians. It had many meanings and significances for the Jews themselves. The Jewish people were in a low state, having no *mitzvos* to their credit which would make them worthy of being redeemed. Hashem, therefore, gave them the two *mitzvos* of *korban pesach* and *bris milah*. He commanded the Jewish people to draw away from the *avodah zarah* of the Egyptians and use it for a *mitzvah* instead.[99]

True, the Jewish people had been careful to avoid *lashon hara* and immorality. They also kept their Jewish names and language, but that alone was not enough. They needed to do a positive act to make them worthy of being redeemed from Egypt. The *korban pesach* provided that positive act.[100]

In yet another sense, the *korban pesach* was connected to the plague of the firstborn. Hashem said, "You slaughter the *korban pesach*, and I'll slaughter the firstborns of Egypt."[101]

Characteristics of the Korban

The *korban pesach* was to be a lamb or goat, symbolizing the destruction of the Egyptian gods. It was to be a male, symbolizing the impending plague of the firstborn. It was to be unblemished, symbolizing the perfection of Hashem's sovereignty over the world. All in all, it was a symbol that Hashem was going to kill the firstborn of Egypt.[102]

Furthermore, by taking a one-year-old unblemished male, which is premium quality, the connection to the idol in the minds of

---

97) וכן היה בכל המכות, זוה"ק בא לו ע"פ ישעיה יט-כב, בהגדת ה"ר צדוק הכהן מלובלין נתבאר בכמה אנפין נהירין 98) גר"א 99) רש"י ממכילתא בא יב-ו, מושב זקנים ורבנו אפרים שם, בגור אריה מבאר דאחר הברית מילה ונעשו עבדי ד' הוצרכו להראות בפועל שהם מבוטלים לרצונו ית' לכן הקריבו את הפסח, אחרים פרשו שהוקרבו תחתיהם כי גם הם מכונים כן כש"נ שה פזורה נדחה 100) שפתי כהן בא יב-ו, אף שהיו להם זכויות אלו עכ"ז אחז"ל שגואלם הקב"ה בזכות דם פסח ודם מילה ואולי זכיות הנ"ל רק מהרו את הקץ 101) שמו"ר טו-יב 102) שם ובאברבנל

the Egyptians was reinforced.[103] And since every Jew was represented in the slaughter of the korban pesach by appointed messengers, every Jew was taking a demonstrable part in the destruction of the Egyptian gods.[104]

The lamb was also reminiscent of the patriarchs, in whose merit the Jewish people would be redeemed. Avraham replaced Yitzchak on the Akeidah with a ram, and Yaakov had a dispute with Lavan regarding the rightful ownership of sheep.[105]

Cattle are generally also acceptable for Jewish sacrifice. In this particular case, however, cattle were not used because of their association with the unfortunate incident of the Eigel the Jewish people would worship in the desert.[106]

The blood from the korban pesach that was applied to their doors would be an atonement for their sins.[107] The blood on the doorposts and crossbeams symbolized a red letter "ח," a symbol for חיים, life. Anyone putting the blood on the door, would be "passed over" and given life when Hashem passes through Egypt to kill the firstborn.[108] The blood placed on the door was also a reminder of Avraham's bris milah, which took place on Pesach. This was another reason the blood offered protection for the Jewish people during the plague.[109]

In yet another sense, the blood on the doors served as a barrier between the purity of the Jewish homes and the idolatry and witchcraft that permeated and defiled the Egyptian environment.[110]

The blood was to be applied with hyssop roots, which are the lowliest of grasses. This signified that although the Egyptians considered the Jews a lowly people, they are precious in the eyes of Hashem.[111]

The korban pesach was to be eaten in a hurried manner for a number of reasons. A hurried meal is demeaning to the food, which in this case symbolized the Egyptian gods.[112] The degradation of the Egyptian gods was only intensified by the tying of the lambs to the Jewish bedposts for four days[113] and by the use of the lowly hyssop to apply the blood of the lambs to the Jewish doorposts.[114] Another reason for eating the korban in haste is to commemorate the haste with which Hashem destroyed the firstborn of Egypt.[115]

---

103) חזקוני בא יב-ה 104) שם יב-ו 105) ר' אפרים שם יב-ג 106) תוס' עה"ת שם יב-ה 107) שמו"ר טז-ב, מו"נ ח"ג מו, ע' רש"י בא ג-מו 108) חזקוני בא יב-ז, ראה מדרש ויושע בפסוק ימינך 109) שמו"ר יז-ג, ר' אפרים עה"ת בא יב-כב 110) זוה"ק בא לה: 111) שמו"ר שם 112) חזקוני בא יב-יא 113) שם יב-ו 114) רלב"ג שם יב-כב 115) שכל טוב שם יב-יא

The requirement of roasting is based on the need for haste, since roasting is the quickest way to prepare meat.[116] The requirement to remain inside the house while the *korban* is being eaten is also based on the need for haste. People who are truly in a hurry stay in one place and eat quickly until they are finished.[117]

The celebration of the *korban pesach* was a joyous occasion to be shared by all Jews. If a Jew could not afford to buy his own lamb, his more fortunate brethren were to acquire one for him.[118] The *korban pesach* was to be eaten by everyone together as one cohesive group, because the only true joy is shared joy.[119] It was to be roasted in a manner fit for kings and people of distinction, because this was a time of freedom, when every Jew was as free as a king.[120]

GENERAL SYMBOLISMS OF THE KORBAN PESACH	
FUNCTION	SIGNIFICANCE
slaughtered in afternoon	exile revealed to Avraham in afternoon[121]
roasted over fire	Avraham went through Nimrod's furnace
eaten with *matzah*	Sarah gave *matzah* to the visiting angels
eaten with *marror*	Yaakov's pain by Eisav and the loss of Yosef[122]
roast on open flame	draw attention of the Egyptians[123]
roasted whole	symbolize Egyptian idol being burned[124]
nothing left over uneaten	Hashem left no Egyptian firstborn alive[125]
no bones must be broken	not kingly to break bones for last morsel[126]
leftovers must be burned	not kingly to eat leftover food[127]
wear shoes while eating	Avraham didn't take a shoelace of booty[128]
korban pesach itself	protection from death of the firstborn
matzah	the beginning of freedom
marror	bitterness of slavery[129]
no *goyim*, uncircumcised	*milah* blood mixed with *korban*[130]
no delay in *matzah* dough	Hashem did not delay in killing firstborn[131]

116) רשב"ם מנחה בלולה וחזקוני שם יב-ח ואילך 117) חזקוני שם יב-מו 118) שמו"ר שם 119) ריב"ש יב-ג, ראה
רבנו בחיי יב-כא, אברבנל, ספר החינוך מצוה טו 120) ספר החינוך מצוה ז 121) זוה"ק בא 122) שמו"ר טו-יב
123) זוה"ק פנחס רנא, דעת זקנים וחזקוני בא יב-ח 124) זוה"ק שם, דעת זקנים, חזקוני 125) שמו"ר טו-יב 126)
ספר החינוך מצוה טז, דעת זקנים 127) ספר החינוך מצוה ח' 128) תנחומא לך לך יג 129) חזקוני, ע' צל"ח
פסחים קטז: דבאר דאע"פ שמצה מורה על החרות שהיה אחר הגלות שהמרור רומז עליה, עכ"ז בליל הסדר
מקדימין המרור להמצה יען וע"י צער השעבוד יצאו קודם זמן הקץ (כמו שנביא בס"ד לקמן) נמצא שהיה התחלת
הישועה 130) תוס' בא יב-מח 131) אוה"ח בא י ב-יז

The Death of the Firstborn

17

The tenth plague—the death of the firstborn—
was a direct retribution for what the Egyptians had done to the Jewish people for so many
years. By their harsh labor decrees, the Egyptians
had caused the death of countless Jewish people.
They had also killed Jewish children for their
warm, fresh blood. They had killed Jewish children
and plastered them into the walls of new buildings. They had thrown Jewish children into the
river. They had mounted a mortal attack on the
Jewish people, the firstborn of Hashem. But now,
the tables would turn on the Egyptians, and all
their firstborn would die.[1] Moreover, the Egyptians
used to dedicate their firstborn children to their
idols, and therefore, their firstborn children perished in the overall destruction of the idolatrous
cult of Egypt.[2]

---

1) שמו״ר אליהו רבה, אברבנל, שפתי כהן, בשכל טוב מובא שהיה מדה במדה למה
שרחץ פרעה בדמם של בכורי ישראל 2) מלבים בא יא-ה

A Fateful Night in History

The night of the fifteenth of Nissan has been an auspicious time for the Jewish people and an inauspicious time for their enemies since the beginning of creation. Adam, the first man, told his sons Kayin and Hevel that this particular night was suited for sacrificing to Hashem because the Jewish people would bring the *korban pesach* on this night. Kayin, the older son, brought an unworthy sacrifice of parched barley and flax seeds, while Hevel, the younger son, brought a fine sacrifice from the firstborn of his flocks still in its virgin wool. Hashem accepted Hevel's sacrifice but rejected Kayin's.[3]

The day on which Yitzchak chose to bless his son Eisav was the fourteenth of Nissan. Yitzchak told Eisav that on that upcoming night, the night of the fifteenth of Nissan, his future descendants would celebrate the holiday of Pesach. Moreover, the gates of blessing of the falling dew are opened on that night. Therefore, it was an auspicious time for Yitzchak to bless his son. "Go bring me a dish so that I can bless you in return," Yitzchak said to Eisav.

However, the great hunter Eisav was not successful in finding game to feed his father. Hashem had kept the animals away from him in order to detain him.

In the meantime, Eisav's mother Rivkah was preparing her younger son Yaakov to capture the blessings of Yitzchak for himself. "Tonight the gates of blessing are opened," Rivkah said to Yaakov. "Tonight the angels in Heaven will say Shirah on the occasion of our future children being redeemed from slavery. Go and bring your father a tasty dish so that he will bless you in return." Yaakov secured two kid goats, one to serve to his father and one to represent the future *korban pesach*. Yaakov was successful, and he received his father's blessings.[4]

During the Period of the Judges, Midian oppressed and caused great suffering to the Jewish people. On the night of the fifteenth of Nissan, Gideon took an army of three hundred picked men and destroyed the large and powerful Midianite army.[5]

During the Period of the Kings, the armies of Assyria (Ashur) oppressed the Jewish people and, under King Sancheriv, besieged the city of Jerusalem. On the night of the fifteenth of Nissan, an angel

---

3) פרדר״א כא וברד״ל 4) שם לב וברד״ל 5) שופטים ז-ט וברש״י, ע׳ ילקו״ש אסתר תתרנח

of Hashem came down into the Assyrian encampment while the Assyrians slept and killed one hundred and eighty-five thousand Assyrian soldiers. Sancheriv returned to Assyria without his armies and was killed by his own family.[6]

After the destruction of the First Beis Hamikdash, when the exiled Jewish people were living in the Persian Empire, Haman prepared a great tree upon which to hang Mordechai, the leader of the Jews. On that same night, the night of the fifteenth of Nissan, King Achashverosh's sleep was disturbed and a chain of events was set into motion that brought about Haman's downfall and the rise of Mordechai and the Jewish people.[7]

Many other great events happened on that night. Hashem had destroyed Sedom. Avimelech dreamed that he had sinned in taking Sarah to his palace. Sisra and his Canaanite armies were annihilated that night. Daniel emerged unharmed from the lion's den that night. Belshazzar, the Babylonian king, drank from the vessels of the Beis Hamikdash and died later that same night.[8]

Midnight, on the night of the fifteenth of Nissan, was long destined for the death of the firstborn Egyptians. Avraham went to war on the night of the fifteenth of Nissan with the four kings who had abducted his nephew Lot. Yet he fought them only during the first half of the night. The second half of the night was reserved for the slaying of the firstborn Egyptians, the oppressors of Avraham's descendants.[9]

After two hundred and nine years in Egyptian bondage, Rachel the granddaughter of Shuselach had lost her child on the night of the fifteenth of Nissan. As told earlier, she had delivered while still in the work pit, and the child was mixed into the cement. The painstricken cries of the bereaved mother were so intense that they rose to the heavens. The angel Gavriel placed the brick in which the child had died before the Heavenly Court, and it was decreed that in exactly one year Hashem would punish the Egyptians for their atrocities.[10]

6) מלכים ב יט-לה וברד"ק 7) אסתר ו, פסיקתא דרב כהנא יז (דף קכט), ע' פיוט לליל שמורים ליל ב' דפסח 8) אברבנל בהגדתו, ע' במדבר רבה כ-יא 9) רש"י ותרגום יונתן בראשית יד-טו, בראשית רבה מג, פרדר"א כ"ז, פסיקתא דרב כהנא ז 10) פדר"א מח

The Plague Begins

While the Jewish people ate from the *korban pesach* and celebrated their imminent redemption in the safety and security of their blood-marked homes, the time of judgment for the Egyptian people was drawing near.[11] Hashem convened the Heavenly Court and the sentence of death was decreed on all the firstborn of Egypt. The decree was to be carried out at midnight. Although Hashem alone would kill the firstborn, He nevertheless took "counsel" with His Heavenly Court in order to show the importance of humility.[12]

In general, court sentences are carried out during the daytime. In this case, however, an exception was made. The Egyptians had oppressed the Jews by reversing the normal order of things. They had forced the Jews to work at night rather than by day. They had also forced men to do women's work and women to do men's work. Hashem, therefore, reversed the normal order of things and punished the Egyptians at night.[13]

At the stroke of midnight, at the precise moment when the two halves of the night meet, an amazing phenomenon took place in Egypt.[14] It was at the time of the full moon, when the perception that the heavenly hosts are possessed of divine powers is strongest.[15] Just at that moment, the awesome power of Hashem was revealed. The darkness of the night was suddenly dispelled, and all of Egypt was illuminated as if by the midday sun.[16]* Thunder and lightning rent the skies over Egypt,[17] and a poisonous gas fouled the air.[18] The Egyptian firstborn inhaled the poisonous gas, and gasping for breath, they died. Others of the firstborn were killed by deafening sounds of the thunder,[19] while yet others died without natural causes, simply by the Word of Hashem.[20]

---

* Since this great miracle took place at night, Hashem caused it to become light as day so that it should be noticeable immediately.

---

11) דברי הימים למשה, רשב"ם וספורנו בא יב-כט וע' לקמן ציון 28 ויתכן דתלוי בפלוגתת חז"ל אי נאכל עד חצות או כל הלילה 12) רש"י בא יב-כט, שמו"ר יב-ד במהרז"ו, הדר זקנים ומושב זקנים וירא 13) שמו"ר יח-ט וע"ש במתנ"כ 14) מכילתא 15) מנחה בלולה בא יב-כט, בהגדה ע"פ חפץ חיים מבאר בזה מדאה"כ זכור את יום אשר יצאתם וגו' שגאלנו ד' בחצות ליל אמצע החודש כשמול של מצרים (טלה) בתוקפה 16) זוה"ק לז מובא באוה"ח בא יב-כט, הגר"א כתב דבז דלכן נקראת הלילה "הזה" (לשון זכר) ולא "הזאת" (לשון נקבה) דהיה אז יום ובצדקת יוסף מבאר דזה תוכן תוכן שאלתנו מה נשתנה הלילה הזה "הזה" מכל הלילות ודוק 17) רוק"ח בא יא-ו 18) אברבנל שם 19) רוקח שם 20) תרגום יונתן בא יב-כט

Not all the firstborn Egyptians died right away. One group did indeed die instantly at the stroke of midnight. A second group collapsed and continued to struggle for life until morning, when the Jewish people were permitted to leave their homes and survey the wreckage of the plague. Yet a third group fell mortally ill but managed to cling to life for three days.[21]

Strangely, the poisonous gas and the sounds of the thunder did not harm the other Egyptians who were not firstborn.[22] Hashem's Hand had struck only the firstborn Egyptians. And with Egypt so brightly illuminated, all the surviving Egyptians were able to witness the horrific sight.[23] Faster than the blink of an eye, thousands upon thousands of firstborn Egyptians died before the eyes of each family.[24]

The Death of the Dead

Firstborn people or animals were held in the highest regard by the Egyptians, because they worshipped the lamb whose sign was the first of the zodiac.[25] Whenever a firstborn child died, the Egyptian family would create a sculpted likeness and bury it under the house or else carve an image of the child into the walls of the house. They would then sing and dance before the image or the sculpture as if the child were still alive. On this fateful night, at the stroke of midnight, the Egyptians heard a powerful thunderclap and saw a jagged bolt of lightning strike the land. Suddenly, all the likenesses and images of the dead firstborn were destroyed in an instant. The metal melted, the wood rotted, the stone shattered, and nothing remained of the memorials to the dead firstborn children.

One woman began to scream with even more heartrending cries than all the rest. The woman was alone in the world, with no children or any other family. The only connection she had to another person was the statue memorializing her dead firstborn child. She used to pay homage at his statue and thereby console her broken heart. And now the shrine to her son had been destroyed.

This woman was a highborn lady who often attended the royal court of Pharaoh. When Moshe had warned of the impending

21) ריש מסכת שמחות, פסיקתא דר"כ, ר' אפרים עה"ת, רוקח בא יב-כט, חזקוני ילקוט ראובני נג, ילקו"ש בהעלותך תקכ, ראה במדבר לג-ד 22) אברבנל 23) זוה"ק לז 24) מכילתא בא יב, אברבנל מנחה בלולה ואלשיך בא יא-ה 25) זוה"ק פנחס, אברבנל שם

plague, she had said, "You say that there will be a great outcry among all the people of Egypt. Well, how about me? I am an old woman. I have no mother or father, no brother or sister, no son or daughter. Why would someone like me cry out?"

"Just wait and see," Moshe had replied. "You will be the first of all people to cry over this plague."[26] And now, his prophecy had come true.

Not only the enshrined and venerated firstborn were exhumed. Even firstborn Egyptians long buried in graveyards and under the homes were not spared. The dogs ran wild over Egypt, digging up old corpses in caves, graves, and burial chambers and ripping them to pieces. Families watched in horror as the dogs scattered the bones of their dead relatives in the streets of Egypt. In this way, grief and mourning visited the homes of all Egyptians, even those in which there were no firstborn to die. If a family did not have a child that died, it had an ancestor whose body was exhumed and defiled by the rampaging dogs. All of Egypt was grief-stricken.

One woman thought she could save her child by hiding him on the roof. But right after midnight, a dog climbed onto the roof and snatched the child. When the woman went to check on her child, she found only emptiness. In a panic, she looked down into the street and saw a dog dragging away her half-eaten child. She screamed with such anguish that all of Egypt virtually trembled at the sound.[27]

Some Egyptians, fearful of Hashem's wrath, tried to save their firstborn children by sending them to sleep in the homes of the Jewish people. These same Egyptians had brought their animals indoors from the fields before the plague of hail. But their attempts were to no avail. Just as Hashem passed over the Jewish homes to strike the Egyptian homes, He also passed over the Jews in their own homes to kill the Egyptians who were there. An Egyptian firstborn died even as he slept in the same bed as a Jew. And the Jews slept so deeply that they did not hear the outcry of the Egyptians.[28]

Other Egyptians, in anticipation of the plague, tried to conceal their firstborn children in the supposed safety of the temples of the Egyptian gods. But it was the worst of all places. During the plague, Hashem destroyed the Egyptian temples' gods as well. Metal idols melted to the ground, wooden idols rotted, stone idols crumbled, and everything associated with the idols disintegrated. The Egyptians were so devoted to the gods that their destruction caused greater grief and sorrow than the death of their firstborn children.[29]

The only idol not destroyed was Baal Tzefon. Hashem allowed this idol to remain standing so that Pharaoh and the Egyptians would delude themselves into thinking that at least one of their gods had some real power. This would encourage them to chase the fleeing Jews from Egypt and then be drowned in the sea.[30]

So Many Firstborn Egyptians?

As the casualty count mounted, the Egyptians were astounded at the great number of people dying in the plague. "Can there have been so many firstborn in Egypt?" they wondered.

In fact, Hashem was killing all Egyptians who could be construed as firstborn in any way whatsoever, male or female. Many Egyptians were firstborn to their mother but not their father. Others were firstborn to their father but not their mother. If there were no firstborn in a particular home, the oldest person in the house was honored with the title of firstborn and killed. Guardians of homes were also considered firstborn and killed.[31] People who were not firstborn but represented themselves as firstborn because of the honors involved were also given honorary firstborn status and killed.[32] Mothers carrying a firstborn child miscarried and died along with the unborn child.[33]

Not only Egyptians residing in Egypt died during the plague. Some firstborn Egyptians, fearful of Moshe's warning, fled to neighboring Cham, but they perished nonetheless. Firstborn foreign visitors who happened to be in Egypt during the plague also perished, so that the Egyptians should not be able to attribute the plague to the gods of other nations.[34] Indeed, the neighboring nations related to the Egyptians, such as Cham, Kush, Put and Lud, were all stricken by the plague, as were the Egyptians.[35] All their firstborn perished, and all their idols were destroyed.[36]

---

29) מדרש הגדול, מכילתא, מדרש החפץ בא יב-ל, פסיקתא דרב כהנא ז, דעת זקנים, מושב זקנים ורוקח בא יא-ה וכו', שמו"ר טו-טו, דברי הימים למשה, מדרש ויושע, שבלי הלקט 30) מכילתא יב-כט, ילקו"ש רח, שמו"ר טו-טו, מדרש החפץ בא יב-יב 31) מכילתא, מדרש הגדול בא יב-ל, פסיקתא דרב כהנא ז, משנת ר' אליעזר יט, חזקוני בא יא-ה 32) פנים יפות בא יב-כט 33) שמו"ר יז-ה בידי משה ורד"ל 34) רש"י שם יב-כט ממכילתא, מנחה בלולה, פענח רזא יא-ה וכו' 35) מכילתא, מלבים בא יב-יב, כולם היו יוצ"ח של חם 36) מדרש הגדול בא יב-יב

All in all, no less than six hundred thousand firstborn died during the plague.[37] But among the Jewish people there were no deaths. Even extremely ill Jews who by all right should not have survived the night were kept alive by Hashem on that night. Otherwise, the Egyptians might have said that the plague was affecting the Jewish people as well as the Egyptians.[38]

Maidservants, Captives and Animals

The plague of the firstborn struck every family without exception, from the firstborn son of Pharaoh to the firstborn children of his relatives, ministers and servants to the firstborn children of maidservants and captives sitting in the Egyptian dungeons.[39] The only firstborn Egyptians spared from death were those who converted earlier in the day in order to participate in the *korban pesach*.[40]

These captives included princes of other nations who had been captured and imprisoned in the dungeons of Egypt. The firstborn among these captives also perished in the plague. Even as they sat in their dungeons, they had gloated over the fate of Egypt and said, "Our gods have done this to the Egyptians for imprisoning us and treating us so savagely." Hashem, therefore, caused the firstborn among them to die as well, in order to prove the plague was only from Hashem.[41]

The maidservants in the dungeons whose firstborn died were of two kinds. One was really a captive who worked at the millstones during the day and was locked up for the night in the dungeon. The other maidservants who found themselves in the dungeons were ordinary housemaids who tried to find safety for their children in the dungeons. It did them no good, however, and all their firstborn children perished.[42] Although these people were themselves oppressed, they were still liable to the plague. In spite of their lowly status, they looked upon the Jews with malice and were in favor of their continued bondage. "We would rather be imprisoned for the rest of our lives," they would say, "than to see the Jewish people

37) שם יב-ל, משנת ר' אליעזר ט 38) הגדת הגר"א, לקוטי ריצב"א ועד"ז הבאנו במכת דבר 39) מדרש ויושע פסוק ימינך, רש"י בא יב-כט) 40) שמו"ר יח-י ששונא ישראל אמתיים מתו גם אי לא היו בכורים 41) רש"י ממכילתא שם, מדרש הגדול ומלבים 42) רש"י אב"ע ומדרש הגדול בא יב-כט, תרגום יונתן רש"י חמדת הימים ורבנו בחיי שם יא-ה

leave Egypt." Furthermore, they would participate in all sorts of magical rites intended to prevent the exodus of the Jewish people from Egypt.[43]

In addition to all this, there was also an element of measure for measure in the affliction of the captives and maidservants. Many of the captives and maidservants of the Egyptians were Jews. Serach, the daughter of Asher, the only surviving child of the Shevatim, was put to work on a millstone and imprisoned during the night. Indeed, when Sarah had come to Egypt centuries before, she too was put to work on a millstone.[44] Therefore, Hashem afflicted the Egyptians through their captives and maidservants.

The firstborn among the animals of the Egyptians, both domesticated and wild, also perished in the plague.[45] The Egyptians worshipped animals as gods, and they were likely to say that their own gods had brought this plague upon them. Therefore, Hashem caused all the firstborn animals to die as well to prove that the plague was only from Hashem.[46] In fact, even idol-statues of animals were destroyed for this very reason.[47]

The Only Surviving Firstborns

In the middle of the night, Pharaoh arose and went out to inspect the palace. Through the windows, he could hear the screams and lamentations of countless bereaved families in the stillness of the Egyptian night. In the palace itself, Pharaoh was shocked to see how many of his family had perished in the plague. Only his daughter Basya, who was a firstborn child, had survived. Pharaoh began to worry for his own safety, for he himself was a firstborn. Indeed, Egypt only accepted the venerated firstborns as kings.[48]

As he surveyed the carnage, Pharaoh became furious with himself for having heeded those of his councilors who advised against capitulating to Moshe. In his rage, he sought a scapegoat, and he drew his sword and killed his councilors and courtiers. It seemed that there was no end to the carnage caused by the plague of the firstborn. In the prelude to the plague, the firstborn had turned on

---

43) רש"י ממכילתא שם, שם יב-כט, שמו"ר יח-י, זוה"ק לז, פסיקתא רבה יז, שפתי כהן יב-כט (44 מדרש הגדול שם, פסיקתא דרב כהנא ז, פסיקתא רבתי יז, ילקו"ש קפו (45 מדרש הגדול יב-יב (46 רש"י ממכילתא בא יא-ה, שם יב-כט, פסיקתא דרב כהנא ז, זוה"ק לו והלאה (47 זוה"ק שם, שפתי כהן בא יב-כט (48 רש"י ממכילתא ורמב"ן יא-ה, שם יב-ל, ספר הישר, מלבים בא יב-כט עיין ספר הישר שהיא אחותה מן האם

their own fathers and slaughtered them. During the plague itself, innumerable firstborn had died. And in the aftermath, Pharaoh had killed many of his own best people.[49]

As Pharaoh wandered half-crazed around his palace, he was consumed by a dread that he was about to die, the last firstborn to be stricken. Then he heard an ominous rumble from outside the palace drawing closer by the second. As it drew closer, the sounds of angry shouting could be heard. The Egyptian people had had enough, and they were storming the palace!

Pharaoh fled for his life. There was only one place to turn. Moshe! Pharaoh took his daughter Basya, and together, the only two surviving firstborns in Egypt went off to find Moshe and ask him to pray for their survival.[50]

It was still night as they set off for Goshen.[51] The miraculous light that had illuminated the night during the plague had now faded away, and the full darkness of night had returned.[52]

As soon as they reached the Jewish settlements, Pharaoh began to shout at the top of his lungs, "Moshe and Aharon! Get up and leave my country at once." An angel caused Pharaoh's voice to be broadcast over a distance of four hundred *parsangs* so that it was heard all over Egypt.[53]

Moshe and Aharon heard Pharaoh yelling, but they ignored his cries, waiting instead until he approached them in person.[54]

"Where could Moshe possibly live?" Pharaoh asked Basya.

Jewish people looked outside and recognized the exalted Pharaoh wandering through the Jewish streets.

"Excuse me, sir," Pharaoh called to the Jews. "Do you perhaps know where Moshe and Aharon live?"

"Certainly," the Jew would reply. "Down that block over there."

"No!" some of the mischievous children interjected, pointing to a dark alley. "He lives over there in that alley."

Pharaoh followed the directions he was given, but he could not find Moshe and Aharon. The Jewish children were playfully sending him on wild goose chases, causing the frustrated Pharaoh to run in endless circles all over Goshen.[55]

---

49) זוה"ק מה, דברי הימים למשה (50 זוה"ק לו והלאה, שמו"ר יח-ח ובעץ יוסף, שם יח-ג וכו', ספר הישר, מדרש ויושע פסוק ימינך פרעה זה שני לאביו אבל ראשון לאמו (51 חלק זה של סיפור יציאתם נעתק מספר הישר ומדרש ויושע פסוק ימינך (חוץ מהפרטים שנסממנו בציונים, ראה תרגום יונתן אבי"ע ורמב"ן בא יב-לא (52 אוה"ח שם יב-ל (53 ירושלמי פסחים ה-ה, מדרש אגדה ותרגום יונתן בא יב-לא וכו', ילקוט ראובני נ"ד (54 ילקוט ראובני שם (55 רש"י ממכילתא שם, תנחומא ישן יט

Finally, Pharaoh managed to stumble across Moshe's home. When he got there, all he heard was joyous singing and rejoicing over the good fortune Hashem had given the Jewish people.

At the last minute Pharaoh was overcome by a wave of self-doubt. "Oh, how foolish I have been!" he said to Basya. "Moshe has always dealt honorably with me. He never deceived me in all the time I have known him. During the plagues, when I asked him to pray for our welfare and put an end to the plagues, he did it. But I did not appreciate his integrity, and foolishly, I drove him away. I told him never to return to the palace, for the day he returns would be the day of his death. Oh, I am such a miserable wretch. How I wish I had let the Jewish people go!" Pharaoh sighed deeply and burst into tears.

"Knock on the door, Father," said Basya. "It will be all right."

Pharaoh knocked cautiously on the door.

"Who is it?" Moshe asked from within.

"It is a humble and defeated man," said Pharaoh. "It is I, Pharaoh."

"What are you doing up so late at night?" asked Moshe. "Does a king knock on doors in the middle of the night? And where are your attendants, your great entourage?"

"Please, my friend Moshe," Pharaoh pleaded. "Come out and speak with me. I need you to pray for me and for Egypt. Soon there will be nothing left of my great kingdom, no people, no land."

"I cannot come out," Moshe replied. "Hashem has forbidden all Jews to leave their homes before morning."

"Then come to the window," Pharaoh pleaded. "At least I will be able to see you face to face."

"Moshe, it is I, Basya!" Basya interjected. "Is this the gratitude you show after all I have done for you? I raised you as an infant, and now look at what has befallen my entire family!"

"Has any of the previous nine plagues affected you?" Moshe asked.

"No," Basya replied.

"Exactly," said Moshe. "You have nothing to worry about, Basya. Although you are the firstborn of your mother you will not die. The kindness you have shown me will protect you."[56]

---

56) שמו"ר יח-ג רש"ש וכו', פסיקתא רבה יז ויש מפרשים שירד עם עבדיו כמו שאמר משה כבר

"But what good will it do me to survive," said Basya, "if my entire family perishes?"

"Well, what did you expect?" said Moshe. "Of course, they have perished. They have disobeyed Hashem. But you are not like them, and that is why you will live. As for you, Pharaoh, what can I say to you? You told me never to see you again. I cannot speak with you."

"But it is dark," spluttered Pharaoh. "Look, I cannot see you clearly. Can you see me? Of course not. It is so dark. We cannot really see each other, can we? So why can't we talk? It won't violate any vows."[57]

"Let me ask you," said Moshe, "are you coming to me, or am I coming to you? Do you by chance remember what I said in your palace? I said your servants would come bow down to me. I wasn't talking about your servants, of course, but about you. I only mentioned the servants out of respect for your royal office."[58]

"Very well," said Pharaoh, "I have come to you. Explain to me what is going on here. You said the firstborn would perish, yet countless more have died!"

"I assure you they are all firstborn in one way or another," Moshe answered. "As for yourself, there is still time to save yourself. I want you to proclaim publicly, 'Nation of Yisrael, you are no longer slaves of Pharaoh! From this moment on, you are the servants of Hashem![59] You are no longer under my dominion but under your own. Leave my nation and go on your three-day journey.'"

Moshe had only told Pharaoh to make this statement one time, but Pharaoh kept repeating it over and over again.

"Why are you straining yourself like this?" Moshe asked Pharaoh.

"You don't understand," Pharaoh stammered nervously. "I am a firstborn. I may die at any moment." Pharaoh fell to his knees and raised his hands in supplication.[60] The rest of his words poured out in a jumbled torrent. "Please pray for me, Moshe. I beg you. I'll do anything you ask. Leave Egypt! Take everything, your families, your livestock. You don't have to leave anything behind. Even the Erev Rav can go with you.[61] Go on your three-day journey, as you've requested all along.[62] Just pray for my life.[63] I will even participate in your sacrifices, you'll see. I'll give you some of my own animals, the animals of my ministers. Only bless me, I beg you. Pray for me that I survive this terrible time."[64]

"Do not worry," Moshe reassured him. "You will remain alive. Hashem has something greater in store for you. In just a short time, you will witness the power of Hashem's Hand and the wonders and miracles He has yet to show you."[65] This was, of course, a reference to the greatest of all miracles—the splitting of the sea.

"I want you to leave Egypt at once," said Pharaoh. "This very minute!"

"That is impossible," Moshe replied. "We are not thieves in the night that we should leave Egypt in such a fashion. Hashem has commanded that we leave in broad daylight in full view of all the Egyptian people—with Hashem's mighty Hand manifest to all!"[66]

The Exodus Begins

As Moshe had promised, the exodus of the Jewish people from Egypt had finally begun. Although they remained in their homes all night, that was by their own choice. Pharaoh had told them to leave, and thus, they were free at last![67] The Jewish people sang and rejoiced amidst the grief and devastation of Egypt.[68]

As Hashem had commanded, the Jewish people did not break the bones of the korban pesach. Instead, they took the "unbroken bones" and threw them into the streets of Egypt. The dogs immediately smelled the roasted bones and pounced on them, breaking them, sucking them dry and dragging them through the streets. The Egyptians watched their hallowed god being disgraced by dogs in the street, and they could not stand it. They wrested the mutilated bones from the jaws of the dogs and buried them deep underground. The dogs conceded defeat and forgot about the bones.

A wondrous miracle had just taken place. There was no longer any trace of animalistic idol worship in Egypt (except for Baal Tzefon). The only remnant had, ironically, been the bone of the korban pesach, and now even that was gone, buried deep underground by the Egyptians themselves. Hashem now stood alone in the eyes of the Egyptians as the true God, the sole Creator of the Universe.[69]

---

64) מכילתא, אב"ע רלב"ג ריב"ש ומלבים שם, משנת ר' אליעזר 65) תנחומא ישן יט 66) מכילתא, תנחומא ז, מדרש הגדול בא יב-לא, ספר הישר 67) רמב"ן, פענח רזא בא שם 68) פדר"א מח 69) זוה"ק בא מא ומוסיף שם דלכן אסרה רחמנא לשבור עצמות הקרבן כדי שיתרבה כבוד השי"ת כשהעובדים בעצמם ימצאם ויצטרכו לקוברם

Ever since the six days of creation, Hashem had already prepared this great night for the fulfillment of His promise to take the Jewish people out of Egypt.[70] Throughout all the years of their enslavement, Hashem had protected and sustained the Jewish people for this night.[71] This night, the fifteenth of Nissan, was a night of protection for the Jewish people from all harm.[72] And in the future it would remain so for *tzaddikim*. On this night, Gideon would be victorious in battle. On this night, Sancheriv's army would be destroyed and Jerusalem would be saved. On this night, Chananiah, Mishael and Azariah would be saved from the burning furnace. On this night, the process of the downfall of Haman would begin. On this night, Daniel would emerge unharmed from the lions' den. On this night, the final redemption through Mashiach and Eliyahu Hanavi will begin.[73]

In commemoration of the special character of this night, it is customary to open the doors to the street during the celebration of the *seder* on Pesach—as a sign of faith that Hashem is watching over us. By the merit of this faith, we hope Hashem will "pour out His wrath" on the nations that oppress us and send us our deliverance through the good tidings of Eliyahu Hanavi. For this reason, we set aside a cup of wine for Eliyahu Hanavi at the *seder*. This is meant to show that just as Hashem delivered us from Egypt, so will He send Eliyahu Hanavi to redeem us from our present exile.[74]

There is also a custom to stay awake this entire night of watchfulness and recount the wonders and the miracles Hashem performed for the Jewish people.[75]

Sanctifying the Jewish Firstborn

When Hashem "passed over" the firstborn of the Jewish people, a consecrated bond was created between them. The *mitzvah* of *pidyon haben* memorializes this bond as well as the overall concept that the entire world belongs to Hashem, who allows us to enjoy it through His kindness.

---

70) בא יב-מב, ר"ה יא: ר' אפרים עה"ת כתב דת"ל שנות הגלות מרומזות בדברי התורה במעשה בראשית כי "תהו ובהו" בגימטריה תל 71) מלבים בא יב-מא 72) רש"י ממכילתא בא יב-מב 73) שמו"ר יח-יב, רוקח תרגום יונתן אוה"ח בא יב-מב 74) שו"ע או"ח סי' ת"פ ובנו"כ, שם סי' תפא ובספר המנהיג לראב"ן, בכלי יקר ושמחת הרגל לחיד"א אי' שאי ישמרו מצות הלילה אזי ח"ו שמורים הוא ואם לאו ח"ו תוכל הקערה להתהפך על פיה וכעניין תשעה באב שנופלת תמיד באותו יום בשבוע שחל יום א' דפסח 75) אב"ע וחזקוני, שו"ע שם, הזוה"ק מפליג בגודל מצות סיפור יצ"מ באותו לילה ועי"ש, בתוספתא פסחים י-ח מבואר דגם לימוד הלכות הפסח בכלל החיוב, רשב"ץ כתב דגם בכל השנה נמשכת המצוה (בשדי חמד ערך זכור מביא שדין הדיבור בזכר יצ"מ דכל השנה

Hashem commanded Moshe that every Jewish male firstborn to his mother must be sanctified to Him. The choice of the mother was to symbolize Hashem's love for the Jewish people, which is as great as the love of a mother for her child. The consecrated firstborn child would dedicate his life to the service of Hashem, unless his father redeemed him from a Kohein for the sum of five *sela'im*. After the sin of the Eigel, the Leviim took the place of the firstborn in the service of Hashem.

Since the animals of the Jewish people were also spared, the firstborn animals were also consecrated to Hashem. A firstborn kosher domesticated animal, such as an ox, sheep or goat, was to be given to the Kohein. If the animal was free of blemishes, it would be sacrificed, and the meat would be eaten by the Kohein to whom the animal had been given. If it was blemished, the Kohein could slaughter it and eat its meat right away.

In this set of *mitzvos*, we find the only instance of a non-kosher animal being consecrated to Hashem. The Torah deems a firstborn donkey consecrated until it is exchanged for a sheep. The inclusion of the non-kosher donkey in this *mitzvah* is to remind us of the first-born Egyptians, who are *am hadomeh lichamor*, a nation compared to donkeys. The donkey also reminds us of the donkeys that were used as pack animals by the Jewish people during the exodus.[76]

נובע מכתוב דוהגדת לבנך הנאמרת בליל זה) ע׳ רמב״ם סה״מ קנ״ז, הלכות חמץ ומצה ז, ספר החינוך כ״א, מדרש שוח״ט תהלים מד. 76) עיין בא יג א-יג ורש״י שם. עיין תנחומא רבינו בחיי רמב״ן ספורנו רשב״ם וריב״ש. ועיין ספר החינוך מצוה י״ח.

The Exodus from Egypt

18

Having made the decision to let the Jewish people go, the Egyptians wanted them to be gone right away. The Egyptians were afraid they would all die before the killing night was over. Moshe had said the firstborn would die, but it seemed every household had already suffered between five and ten fatalities. They did not realize that Hashem was revealing the fruits of Egyptian adultery and that all the dead were indeed firstborn in one way or another.[1] To the Egyptians it seemed that every single one of them was in danger as long as the Jewish people remained in Egypt. But the Jewish people had been commanded by Hashem to wait until morning, and nothing the Egyptians could do would make them leave one moment sooner.[2]

The morning of the fifteenth day of Nissan could not come quickly enough for the Egyptians,

---

1) רש״י ממכילתא, מדרש ויושע 2) מכילתא, מדרש ויושע, תנחומא ישן

and as soon as dawn broke, the Egyptians were already running through the streets and exhorting the Jewish people to leave. The Jewish people emerged from their homes in the light of the new day and were astounded at the spectacle that awaited them.

Egyptian bodies, dead or on the verge of death, were strewn all over the streets. Hashem had kept some of them alive so that the Jewish people could witness the last remnants of the great miracle of the plague unfold before their own eyes.[3] The Egyptian people, with Pharaoh himself at their head, were shouting at the Jewish people to hurry and leave. Some Egyptians left carts piled high with bodies standing in the street while they ran off to hurry the Jews on their way.[4] Presently, one side of the street was filled with Jewish people being escorted from their homes, while the other side was piled high with Egyptian corpses.[5]

Leaving with Great Wealth

In their mad rush to leave, the Jewish people had little time to accumulate the wealth Moshe had promised them. In truth, at this point, the Jewish people did not have much interest in the accumulation of wealth, which would only delay their departure and encumber them on their journey.[6] Nevertheless, Hashem had commanded them to strip Egypt of its wealth and take it with them, and this was what they had to do.

They spread out all over Egypt, going from house to house to borrow gold, silver and precious garments.[7] It was an unpleasant task for the Jewish people, because the Egyptians were all in mourning. But this was what they had been commanded to do, and this was what they did.[8]

The Jewish people had explored the Egyptian homes during the plague of darkness, and they were able to assist the Egyptians in remembering where their valuables were hidden.[9] Even when the Jewish visitors had not been able to locate the Egyptian treasures

---

3) זוה"ק בא לו ואילך, רוקח בא יב-כט 4) תנחומא ישן בא יט, מדרש הגדול בא יב-לג, ע' מכילתא בשלח, שמו"ר כ-ג, זוה"ק מה, ומפורש שהכוונה ב"ויהי בשלח" שלווה אותם פרעה (ולכן נאמר ויהי צער דע"י לווה מתחבר המלווה עם המתלווה כמ"ש מהר"ל וכמ"ש הפעם ילוה ולוה וגו') וזכו בזכות לוויה זו למ"ש דברים לג-ח דבדור שלישי מותרים לבא בקהל משא"כ בעמון ומואב 5) זוה"ק בא לח 6) ברכות ט: 7) שמות ג-כב, בא יא-ב וכו', שם יב-לה וכו' ברש"י ממכילתא, שמו"ר יח-י במהרז"ו, לעיל הבאנו מש"כ האלשיך שגם עצם הלקיחה היתה לפני מכת בכורות וכאן מוסיף דכמה דכמה מהם לא האמינו 8) אלשיך בא יב-לה, מדרש הגדול שמות ג-כב, לקח טוב יא-ב, שמו"ר יד-ג.

during the plague of darkness, its presence was now revealed. Miraculously, the treasures themselves called out from their hiding places asking to be given to the Jews. The Egyptians had no choice but to give away all their treasures.[10] In fact, the Egyptians were so eager for the Jews to leave that they gave them even more treasure than they requested.[11] Even if it happened that an Egyptian had a change of heart and wanted his treasures returned, he wouldn't dare ask for it, because he did not want to delay the departure of the Jews.[12]

The Jewish women "borrowed" things from the Egyptian neighbors who had oppressed and enslaved them just a short time earlier. Now, however, the Egyptian women were suddenly friendly and accommodating, begging the Jewish women to accept their most treasured possessions.[13] Those Jewish women who could not leave their young children to visit their Egyptian neighbors asked their friends to gather treasures for them. In general, the Jewish people cooperated with each other selflessly in these matters.[14] Those who needed clothing were given clothing, while those who needed other articles were helped as well.[15] Furthermore, every Jew asked for and received clothing suitable to his social standing.[16] All Jews, however, received some sort of beautiful garments so that they would feel proud as they traveled among other nations.[17] Besides gold, silver and rich clothes, the Jewish people also took the bars and sheets of precious metal made from the melted Egyptian idols.[18]

Hashem's promise to Avraham—that his descendants would leave Egypt with wealth and riches—was clearly fulfilled.[19] Egypt was stripped of its treasures. So great was the wealth carried off by the Jews that each individual Jew needed ninety donkeys to bear his personal fortune, in addition to other livestock such as cattle, horses and camels. In fact, each individual Jew was wealthy enough to build an entire Mishkan just from his own resources.[20]

Egypt had lost everything—its idols, its riches, its honor, its

13) וכו' יב-לג בא וחזקוני זקנים הדר יב-לו, בא ומכילתא רש"י 11) יא-ב בא עה"ת תוס' 10)
שמות הגדול מדרש 15) יא-ב בא שמות ראה עה"ב תוס' 14) ראובני ילקוט ג-כא, שמות אב"ע ג-יא, שמו"ר
ברור היה בלבד וזהב כסף שאלו דאילו מסביר אליהו חופת במהרז"ו, ג-יא שמו"ר 17) יב-לה בא אב"ע 16) ג-כב
לו, ישן תנחומא ח, בא תנחומא 18) לחוג אלא הלכו שלא נראה היה שמלות גם וכששאלו לנצח לצאת שרצונם
שמספר מעיר יעקב עיון הגדול, מדרש ה:, בכורות 20) יב-לח בא הגדול מדרש הישר, ספר מכילתא 19)
דאות כו' לא גדול ברכוש יצאו כן ואחרי וגו' וענו ועבדום "צדיק" אותו יאמר שלא חז"ל למ"ש רומז החמורים
צדיק) שנקרא איתא דר"ע באותיות צדי, נכתבת ס"ך שבש אף) תשעים בגימטריה "צ"

pride. It is comparable to a servant of a king who was given a great sum of money to buy a fish in the market. The servant returned with a spoiled fish. The master allowed the servant to choose his own punishment, giving him three choices.

"Eat the spoiled fish," said the king, "or suffer one hundred lashes or pay one hundred gold coins."

The servant chose to eat the fish. However, after just a few bites, he could no longer bear to take another piece of the foul fish into his mouth. He decided to suffer the lashes instead. After sixty lashes, he could bear no more. Having no other choice, he paid one hundred gold coins to the king and was set free.

How foolish was this servant! If he had offered to pay the coins from the beginning, he could have avoided the agony of the other two punishments. As it was, however, he received all three punishments.

Pharaoh, too, could have avoided much pain and sorrow for himself and his kingdom had he been farsighted from the beginning. He could have allowed the Jewish people to leave and not suffered any punishments. As it was, he put Egypt through a long series of brutal plagues and impoverization, and in the end, he let the Jewish people go anyway! The Egyptians, who took pride in their great wisdom and intellect, had shown themselves to be quite foolish indeed![21]

finding Yosef's Remains

While the Jewish people were collecting the treasures of the Egyptians, Moshe was attending to two last-minute tasks. He was arranging for the transportation of the cedar wood Yaakov had brought to Egypt for the construction of the Mishkan, and he was looking for the remains of Yosef which were to be taken along to Eretz Yisrael for burial.[22] The Jewish people felt it appropriate for Moshe, who was their leader, to take care of the remains of Yosef, who had been a king. It would be an honor to Yosef, and to Moshe as well.[23]

Many years before, Yosef had insisted that his brothers take an oath upon themselves and their descendants that when the Jews

---

21) רבנו בחיי בא יב-לג, פרקי דרב כהנא דף פא, מכילתא בשלח יד-ה 22) שמו"ר יח-י ובמתנ"כ, שמו"ר כ-יט

23) מכילתא, שפתי כהן בשלח יג-יט

return to Eretz Yisrael they would take the remains of Yosef along with them.[24] To ensure that this would happen, each of the brothers accepted this responsibility individually.[25] Yosef had felt he had a right to demand this from his brothers, because they had caused him to be brought to Egypt in the first place.[26] The Midrash compares this to a thief who stole a barrel of wine and drank it all up. When the thief was caught, the owner reproached him, "It is bad enough that you drank up all my wine, but at least you could have returned the empty barrel when you were done."[27]

As the time of departure drew near, Moshe searched for the coffin of Yosef, but he could not find it. The Egyptians had obviously hidden Yosef's coffin, knowing full well that the Jewish people were bound by oath not to leave Egypt without it.[28] Moshe then went to seek the assistance of Serach the daughter of Asher, the only surviving member of the children of the Shevatim. He felt certain she would know the whereabouts of Yosef's coffin.[29] And indeed she did. She told him that the Egyptians had sealed Yosef's remains in a metal coffin and lowered it to the bottom of the Nile River. The Egyptians believed that the weight of the metal would keep the coffin on the riverbed and prevent its discovery and that its permanent presence on the riverbed would bring blessings to the Nile.[30*]

Armed with this information, Moshe stood by the riverside of the Nile. He took a sheet of gold and carved the Name of Hashem upon it. He also wrote the Hebrew words עלי שור (Arise, O ox!). Then he threw the sheet of gold tablet into the waters of the Nile.[31**]

---

* Some suggest that the coffin was made of lead. In retribution for hiding the remains of Yosef in a lead coffin under the Nile, the Egyptians would sink like lead in the Yam Suf. (*Hadar Zekeinim, R' Ephraim al Hatorah, Beshalach*)

** Some suggest that he threw a rock or clay. Others say that this very sheet of gold was used again when Michah threw it into the fire, and the Golden Calf came out. The calf and the comparison of Yosef to an ox went hand in hand. (*Tosefos, Beshalach*; Rashi, *Sanhedrin* 103b)

---

24) רש"י ממכילתא בשלח יג-יט, אוה"ח פ' בשלח כ' שהוצרך להשביעם שחשש אולי ישכחוהו בעסקם בביזה 25) מדרש מובא בתורה שלמה בשלח דף יז 26) סוטה יג., שמו"ר כ-טיט 27) שמו"ר שם 28) שמו"ר שם יא-ז (דברים רבה יא-29 שמו"ר שם, בבראשית רבה צב וכן בדברים רבה יא-ז איתא שחפש לעצמותיו שלשה ימים שלימים, ע' תוס' סוטה שם, י"מ ששאל אמו יוכבד שלפי כמה שיטות היתה אז יותר מבת מאתים 30) מכילתא, ע' תרגום יונתן בשלח ומהרש"א סוטה שם 31) מכילתא, דברי הימים למשה, תוס' בשלח יג-יט, שמו"ר כ-יט, פסיקתא דרב כהנא ובה"ג"ה שם

"Yosef Yosef!" Moshe called out. "The time has arrived for our exodus from Egypt. Hashem has fulfilled His oath to the Jewish people, and now it is time for the Jewish people to fulfill their oath to you. We cannot leave until we find your remains and take them with us. As of now, the Jewish people, and indeed the Shechinah, are being delayed because we cannot find you. We cannot wait any longer. If you come up now, we will take your coffin with us. If you do not, we are absolved from our oath."

Suddenly, the surface of the river began to ripple, and the shape of a metal coffin materialized in the water. Despite its heavy weight, it floated on the surface. Moshe reached out, took hold of the coffin and drew it out of the water.[32]

The coffin weighed the equivalent of five hundred *kikar* of gold. Inside the coffin lay the remains of the twelve Shevatim as well. When he had elicited the oath from his brothers, Yosef had also insisted that his coffin be carried only by people and not by animals. Moshe, therefore, lifted the heavy coffin onto his shoulders and carried it with him.[33]* All around him the Jewish people were carrying their own heavy loads of jewels and other valuables taken from the Egyptians.[34]

In another version of this story, Yosef's coffin was kept in the royal burial chamber in the palace. The burial chamber was protected by golden statues that were built in such a way that they barked like dogs when trespassers appeared. When Moshe entered the burial chamber, he was able to stop the statues from sounding the alarm.[35] With the alarm system incapacitated, Moshe began to search for Yosef's coffin among the coffins of the kings of Egypt. It did not take him long to find it, however, since a heavenly aroma emanated from it.[36]

---

* This measure of gold weighs approximately thirty-two thousand pounds, and therefore, it could only have been lifted through a miracle, just as the *aron hakodesh*, the holy ark, carried itself miraculously. Moshe wrote Hashem's Name on a piece of parchment and wrapped it around the bones of Yosef. From then on, the casket carried itself.

---

32) שמו"ר שם, מיכלתא, תנחומא בשלח ב, בזוה"ק וישלח כתוב דיוסף נקרא שור ומצרים חמור ונצטוינן שלא לחבר הני יחד 33) פענח רזא יג-יט, מדרש החפץ בשלח יג-יט, ע' דברים רבה יא-ז ובשפתי כהן ויחי דמבארים דודאי מעוצם קדושתו של אותו צדיק היה כל גופו בריא ושלם רק שלפני פטירתו בקש מד' שיעשה לו כן על אשר חטא לפניו ית', במכילתא (מובא בהדר זקנים וגם בשפתי כהן בשלח) איתא דבנסעם כשראו ארונו על יד ארון הקודש שאלו ע"ז ונענו קיים זה מה שכתוב בזה 34) דברים רבה יא-ז 35) שמו"ר כ-יט, מכילתא בשלח 36) ילקו"ש שה"ש תתקפא, צרור המור, ר' אפרים מרמז שנטמן שם ד"יוסף" בגימ' "נילוס"

Hashem does not let the righteous go unrewarded. When the righteous Yaakov passed away, only Yosef, viceroy of Egypt, was deemed worthy enough to bring his remains to burial. When the righteous Yosef passed away, only the exalted Moshe, leader of the Jewish people, was deemed worthy enough to bring his remains to burial. Forty years later, when the righteous Moshe would pass away, no one among the Jewish people was worthy enough to bring his remains to burial, and therefore, Hashem Himself took care of Moshe's burial.[37]

It was fortunate for the Jewish people that they had Yosef's coffin with them, because this helped them merit the miracle of the splitting of the sea. The sea only split upon the appearance of the remains of the righteous Yosef who resisted the temptations of Potiphar's wife. In his merit, all the Jewish people were able to cross in safety.[38]

Unleavened Bread

Being pressed by the Egyptians to leave as soon as the day of the fifteenth of Nissan dawned, the Jewish people had no time to prepare properly for the journey into the desert. The fresh dough was still in their kneading bowls when the Egyptians pushed them to leave.[39] They took the leftover *matzah* and *marror* from the previous night, wrapped them in their garments and carried the bundle on their shoulders. Although they had beasts of burden, the Jewish people loved their newly-given *mitzvos* of *matzah* and *marror*, and they insisted on carrying them personally.[40]

The dough and the kneading bowl were also wrapped and carried on their heads as they were leaving Egypt, and as they were walking, a miracle occurred.[41] Because of the hasty departure, the

---

37) שמו"ר שם, מכילתא בשלח, בשפתי כהן פ' קרח מובא ששבט לוי לא נטל חלק בביזה יען ולא נכללו בגזירת וענו אותם, וא"כ קשה למה הפליגו חז"ל בגדלותו שבשעה שעסקו כולם בביזה הלך לטפל עם עצמות יוסף, וע' הגדה מגדל העדר בפי' משנה למלך דכתב (מה שכבר הבאנו) דגם אותם שלא שאלו קבלו מרוב תשוקת מצרים ליתן להם כמ"ש שנתן ד' חן העם במצרים ובזה יכלו ליטול ואעפ"כ הוא לא עשה כן, ע' במפרשים בסוטה שם דבארו מדוע לא היו ישראל פטורים מדינא דהעוסק במצוה פטור מן המצוה דלקחו הביזה עפ"י צווי ד' 38) ע' סוטה יט:, בראשית רבה פז-ח 39) רש"י ממכילתא בא יב-לד, שם יב-לט, לקח טוב שם, ראה שבלי הלקט, גבורות ד' לז, גור אריה ומלבים על אתר דיש פלוגתא אי היה בדעתם לאפותם טרם יציאתם שלא יחמצו או לא דהאיסור חמץ כל שבעה אינו אלא לדורות ע' פסחים צו, שם קטז בר"ן ובתוס' רי"ד, רמב"ן כאן כתב שהיה להם איסור חמץ ונאפו על הדרך כי בחפזון יצאו, י"מ שלשעו אותם כל שעה שלא יחמצו, ע' שפתי כהן, ובהגדת שלמה קצה- רא) ר' אפרים עה"ת מוסף שגם שביתת שביתה בהמה לא היה אז אלא לדורות עולם 40) רש"י ממכילתא, תרגום יונתן, רלב"ג בא יב-לד וברבנו בחיי דמבאר המחלוקת, ע' אב"ע מנחה בלולה וחזקוני ותוך דבריו די"מ שנטלו הנותר מקר"פ כדי לשרפו כאשר נצטוו וי"מ שבהתמתם היו מלאים כסף וזהב וכו' ובחרו זה לשאת על שכמם 41) שמו"ר יח-יא, רד"ל אב"ע וחזקוני כתבו שלא נאפו על הדרך כ"א בסוכות

dough had not risen or been baked, but now, the sun above their heads baked the dough as if it had been placed in an oven.[42] The newly-baked bread was unleavened, and for this reason, Jewish people for all future generations are commanded to eat unleavened *matzah* on Pesach.[43] The unleavened *matzah* the Jewish people carried as they left Egypt was a clear sign of the haste in which they were leaving.[44] The widespread custom of wrapping the *afikomen* on Pesach and hiding it commemorates the wrapped dough the Jewish people carried with them when they left Egypt.[45]

Leaving Egypt without adequate provisions for the journey into the desert[46] was a great act of faith on the part of the Jewish people.[47] But their faith in Hashem was well-placed. Miraculously, the small amount of *matzah* they carried with them lasted for thirty days, from the fifteenth of Nissan until the fifteenth of Iyar, when they received the *mann*.[48]

The Exodus Begins

Although the bulk of the Jewish people lived in Goshen, many of them were scattered all over Egypt. The arrangement, therefore, was that all Jews would assemble at Ramses and leave together from there. There was a poetic justice to the choice of Ramses, the site of the worst enslavement of the Jewish people, as the staging point for their exodus from Egypt.[49] Miraculously, the assembly of the entire Jewish population of Egypt, which should have taken forty days, was accomplished in an hour.[50]

The Jewish people were escorted in their travels by seven cloud pillars, also known as clouds of glory. There was one cloud pillar in front of them, one behind and one on each side. One cloud pillar was above them to protect them from the rains and the heat, and another was below them to protect them from reptiles and insects. The seventh cloud pillar traveled ahead of them to flatten the roads and

---

42) תרגום יונתן ורוקח בא יב-לט 43) הגדה ע״פ שבלי הלקט שנצטוו לאכול מצה ביודוע ית׳ מה שיארע בצאתם, בבית הלוי פ׳ בא מבואר הענין ביתר העמקה, ע׳ פסחים קטז, ובהגדות זבח פסח, ליל שימורים, ומעשה נסים, והאופן הכי פשוט שיש ע׳ סבות נפרדות, א׳ הנאכלת עם הפסח ונקראת לחם עוני זכר לעבדותם, ב׳ הנאכלות בכל דור ודור זכר למה שנאפו על שכמי אבותינו כאשר נגרשו, ע״ע הגדת שלמה קצה-רא 44) גור אריה בא יב-לד, גבורות ד׳ לז 45) חזקוני בא יב-לד 46) רלב״ג ורי״ש בא יב-לט, במדרש הגדול מובא שלא היה להם כלום ואפילו אגוזים להאכיל את טפם 47) רש״י ממכילתא 48) מכילתא, לקח טוב בא יב-לט, ע׳ רש״י בשלח טו-א, שפתי כהן מביא שלא קבלו את המן עד שהתרעמו יען והתחברו עם הערב רב 49) חזקוני בא יב-לז ילקו״ש מסעי תשפו, מדרש אגדה בשלח, ע׳ ילקוט ראובני סוף ויגש ורלב״ג בראשית מז-ג, י״מ שגושן היה שכונה בעיר רעמסס, פרטי הנס מבוארים ברש״י ומפרשיו יתרו יט-ד

ease their journey. Enclosed in this cocoon of cloud pillars, the Jewish people traveled from Ramses a distance of one hundred and twenty *mil* to a place outside Egypt called Succos in ease and comfort, as if they were being carried on the wings of an eagle.[51] Miraculously, a journey which should have taken three days was accomplished in an hour.[52]

As the journey began, the full realization of what was happening began to sink into the consciousness of the Jewish people. After all the years of slave labor and oppression, they were free at last. All the pent-up strains were suddenly released, and they were overcome by weakness and serious illnesses. Just as a person under tremendous strain labors with his last ounce of strength but collapses when the crisis passes, so did the Jewish people succumb to illness as soon as they were set free. Nevertheless, Hashem sent a spiritual wind through the clouds of glory. This wind penetrated the bodies of the Jewish people and healed them.[53]

When the Jewish people arrived in Succos, they took the opportunity to rest and recover from the great panic and nervousness of their hasty departure from Egypt. Then they regrouped and took a head count.[54] The result of the census was that 599,999 men between the ages of 20-60 had left Egypt. Hashem who had been in exile with the Jewish people, so to speak, included Himself in the count of the emancipated and thereby completed the number to 600,000.[55] This great number did not include women, of whom there must have been at least an equal number, nor did it include men under twenty or over sixty. It also did not include the entire Shevet Levi.[56*] The

---

* Some suggest that there were a ratio of at least five to one between the women and children and the men. Accordingly, there would have been three million Jews, including men below the age of twenty and above the age of sixty. Others suggest that there were eight hundred thousand Jews besides the six hundred thousand mentioned. (*Me'am Lo'ez, Targum Yonasan*) Therefore, it would seem that the total Jewish population at the time of the exodus was between 1. 4 million to 3 million, not including Shevet Levi. (*Shir Hashirim Rabbah* 3:7, 6:9; *Midrash Hagadol*) Assuming that only one fifth of the Jewish people left Egypt while the other four fifths perished during the plague of darkness, there were between fifteen and twenty million Jews in Egypt prior to the plagues. Others suggest due to the high rate of Jewish reproduction the number was probably even greater. (*Rokeach*)

---

51) תרגום יונתן בא יב-לז, מעם לועז 52) רש"י ממכילתא, מעם לועז, ע' הגהות הגר"א על המכילתא 53) זוה"ק בשלח מה 54) העמק דבר בא שם וי"מ שנמנו לראות אי היו אלו שחזרו 55) רש"י ורבנו בחיי בא שם ומקורם בפרדר"א לט, ע' תרגום יונתן שם, שה"ש רבה ג-ו, מדרש הגדול, ובמבוא הבאנו דחז"ל אמרו דגם בשבעים נפש שירדו נמנה הקב"ה בתוכם 56) רש"י ממכילתא, אב"ע בא שם, מעם לועז

small group of seventy people who had come down to Egypt with Yaakov had grown to a populous nation of several millions.[57] Hashem had promised Yaakov that his children would grow into a great nation in Egypt, and it had come to pass.[58]

The exodus of the Jewish people also included Basya and her household[59] as well as over two million last-minute Egyptian converts known as the Erev Rav.[60] These Egyptian converts also brought large numbers of cattle and livestock with them from Egypt.[61]

The Erev Rav was composed of those Egyptians who converted to Judaism after seeing Hashem's miracles and wonders. Among them were leading Egyptian magicians, including Ianus and Iambrus, who had acknowledged the limitless power of Hashem. Hashem advised Moshe against accepting them as converts. Moshe pleaded for them, arguing that they would tell the world about Hashem's greatness and omnipotence. Hashem allowed Moshe to accept them into the Jewish fold. Ultimately, however, the Erev Rav instigated the worship of the Golden Calf.[62]

free at Last

In the year 2448 after creation, the Jewish people were free at last. Four hundred and thirty years had elapsed from the time Hashem foretold the exile of the Jewish people to Avraham.[63] Hashem had told Avraham that his descendants would be in exile for four hundred years, but in fact, the actual sojourn of the Jewish people in Egypt lasted only two hundred and ten years. The count of four hundred years began thirty years after the prophecy with the birth of Yitzchak as a stranger in a foreign land. One hundred and ninety years later, the Jewish people went down to Egypt.[64]

---

57) חזקוני שמות א-ה 58) רלב"ג בא שם 59) רוקח בא יב-לח 60) אב"ע בא יב-לח, זוה"ק כי תשא קצא, תרגום יונתן ולקח טוב שם, ע' רש"י ושפתי כהן, בילקוט ראובני אות גרים מובא שהיו מאותם שנמלו עפ"י צוואת יוסף מלך מצרים בשנות הרעב, ע' מכילתא, מדרש הגדול, רלב"ג, ותוס' בנדה יג: 61) ספרנו בא שם, וע' שפתי כהן כי תשא (והבאנה כבר) שלא נטלו הערב רב מביזת מצרים כי לא עבדו 62) זוה"ק כי תשא, רלב"ג ושפתי כהן בא שם 63) רש"י תרגום יונתן מוסיף ששלושים דקאמר אמנין השמיטות קאי כי שלושים שמיטות עולה לרד"ו שנים, סדר עולם ג 64) רש"י בא יב-מ, מושב זקנים בראשית טו-יג, האחרונים שו"ט לייישב ולהתאים מנין השנים ונציין כאן כמה מהם רש"י מביא מהמכילתא כך, בברית בין הבתרים היה אברהם אבינו בן ע' שנה, ל' שנה אח"כ נולד יצחק, כשהיה יצחק בן ששים נולד יעקב, יעקב היה בן ק"ל כשבא למצרים ונולדה אז יוכבד בין החומות, כשהיתה בת ק"ל נולד משה, כשהיה בן פ' שנה יצאו א"כ ת"ל שנים והחשבון האידך מתחיל מלידתו של יצחק א"כ ת' שנים ע"ע שבלי הלקט וסדר עולם בבראשית רבה סג-ג (וביפ"ת, כ"ה במכילתא, וע"ע הגדה באוצר התפילות) באר דלפני כניסתם למצרים גרו בני ישראל בפלשטים שהיה ממשפחת מצרים וג"ז נכלל מלבים כ' דקאי ארץ גושן שהיה מיוחד לבנ"י בגלותם והנקבע ת"ל שנים לפני יצ"מ בפדר"א איתא שאפרים ומנשה נולדו ה' שנים לפני כניסתם, וכשתצטרף אלו עם שנות השעבוד כפול שתים מרוב קשוי השעבוד תמצא ת"ל שנים (ומובא גם בהדר

On the fifteenth of Nissan, Avraham received the prophecy about the future exile of his descendants. On the fifteenth of Nissan, exactly twenty-nine years later, the angels informed Avraham that he would have a child. On the fifteenth of Nissan, exactly one year later, Yitzchak was born. On the fifteenth of Nissan, exactly four hundred years later, the Jewish people went out of Egypt.[65] Hashem did not hold back the redemption of the Jewish people for even a second.[66]

The exodus was accomplished. The Jewish people had gained their freedom, and the Egyptians had rid themselves of the Jews whose presence had caused them untold misery and destruction. Which of the two peoples was the happier? Was it the Jewish people who were free at last? Or was it the Egyptians who would no longer be subjected to plagues? This question is best answered with a parable.

There was once a heavyset man riding on a little donkey. The ride was extremely painful for the man, and the load was extremely heavy for the donkey. The man could not wait to reach his destination so that he could get off the donkey, while the donkey could not wait to reach his destination so that the rider could dismount. Finally, they arrived at their destination, and the heavy man got off. They were both happy to be rid of each other. In the case of Egypt as well, the Egyptians were as happy to see the Jewish people leave as the Jewish people were to be free.[67]

The exodus from Egypt was complete. The Jewish people were a free nation, no longer slaves to Pharaoh. Hashem had done the unthinkable: Pharaoh had once said, "Who is Hashem?" But at the end, he said, "Hashem is righteous." Pharaoh had once said, "I don't know Hashem." But at the end, he said, "Pray to Hashem." Pharaoh had once said, "I will never let you go." But at the end, he personally escorted the Jewish people out of Egypt.[68]

זקנים) עד״ז מובא בפרשת דרכים (דף כז) דנקצר מספר השנים מרוב הכמות וכמ״ש ששים בכרס אחד וגם שעבדו יום ולילה רמב״ן כ' שהוסף ד' ל' שנים על שחטאו במצרים ריטב״א בהגדתו כ' שקצרו ד' שלא יפלו ממדרגתם שם כ' שגם האבות סבלו וג״ז בכלל מעם לועז מביא שעצם השעבוד היה פ״י שנה ואחד מחמש יצא נמצא דהיה שקול לחמשה פעמים פ״ו שהוא ת״ל רא״ש עה״ת (ע״ע פענח רזא ריש וארא) מביא שאמר יצחק לפני הקב״ה שיקטין את שמו מישחק (כמ״ש ושבועתו לישחק) ליצחק ועי״ז הוריד ד' הנ״מ משין לצדיק משנות גלותם לכן היה רק רד״ו בלבד ר' יונתן אייבשיץ כתב דבשבת לא עבדו וזה היה לרדו שנה נמצא שלושים שנות שבתות והיינו השלושים שהוצרכה להתוסף על הד' מאות ואכן היה גלות אבל לא עבדו ולכן אומרים בשבת זכר ליציאת מצרים.

65) רש״י ממכילתא בא יב-מא ובבאר יצחק שם   66) רש״י ממכילתא שם   67) מדרש שוח״ט תהלים קה 68) מכילתא, מדרש הגדול בשלח, פסיקתא רבה יט.

Travels in the Desert

19

Hashem had finally brought the Jewish people out of their bondage in Egypt, but some unfinished business remained. It is comparable to the story about a young prince who was attacked by robbers and beaten severely. The king hunted down most of the culprits who attacked his son and had them executed. Meanwhile, the lad told his father about his terrible ordeal in great detail, and the king's rage knew no bounds. He sent his police to hunt down the rest of the culprits and to persist in their search until every last one had been captured and executed.

In the case of the Jewish people as well, Hashem had punished Pharaoh and Egypt severely through the ten plagues and secured the freedom of His beloved people. Hashem, however, was not satisfied. The Egyptians would have to die as punishment for the atrocities they had committed against the Jewish people. Their fate was sealed. Within days, they would be lying dead at the bottom of the sea.[1]

The exodus of the Jewish people also produced ambivalent feelings in another sense. It is comparable to the story of a father who had once lost a child but was now making a wedding for his other child. At the wedding feast, the father was overcome with mixed feelings of sadness and happiness. He was filled with joy for the child who was getting married, but that very happiness had reminded him of the child who had passed away and made him sad.

Hashem rejoiced, so to speak, at the redemption and exodus of His beloved Jewish people But that very joy recalled the tragedy of the people of Ephraim who had attempted to leave Egypt thirty years earlier and perished at the hands of the Philistines.[2]

The Indirect Route

Now that the Jewish people were out of Egypt, the foremost question was which route to take to reach Eretz Yisrael. The direct route would have taken them through the lands of the Philistines[3] and brought them directly into Eretz Yisrael within three days. Moshe had told Pharaoh that the Jewish people wanted to take a three-day journey into the desert. By the time the three days were over, they could all have been in Eretz Yisrael. However, Hashem wanted the Jewish people to be in the desert at the end of the three days so that Pharaoh could not accuse Moshe of having lied.[4]

Moreover, the time had come for the Egyptians to receive full retribution for their crimes. At the end of the three days, therefore, the Jewish people had to be in the desert near the sea so that the Egyptians would be lured there and drown.[5] Hashem could have, of course, drowned the Egyptians by making the Nile River overflow its banks, but He wanted the Jewish people and all the world to witness the great miracle of the splitting of the sea.[6]

Even after the splitting of the sea and the death of the Egyptians, Hashem did not take the Jewish people through the lands of the Philistines, because he wanted to protect them from encounters

1) שמו"ר כ-יב ובעץ יוסף, ילקו"ש רכו 2) מדרש אבחיר, ילקו"ש רכ"ו 3) שמו"ר כ-יג, במהרז"ו כתוב שהיה אורך י"א יום ע"ש וברד"ל, אב"ע בשלח יג-יז 4) אברבנל בשלח יג-יח 5) ילקו"ש רכז ובזית רענן, ראה גם ברי"ש, רבנו בחיי, חזקוני, ושפתי כהן 6) תדב"א רבה ז

with the warlike peoples of the region who were waiting to pounce on them.[7] As a shepherd leading his flock through the land of the wolves, so did Hashem take the Jewish people on a circuitous route to avoid their enemies.[8]

Should the Jewish people try to pass through the land of the Philistines they ran the risk of provoking a war. Since many of the Jewish people were still weak in their faith, the prospect of war might have caused them to abandon their quest for Eretz Yisrael and return to Egypt.[9] Furthermore, the Philistines were the most intimidating enemy the Jewish people would face. They were ethnically related to the Egyptians, and therefore, they were likely to seek a battlefield confrontation with the Jews.[10] To make matters worse, the bodies of the people of Ephraim who had fallen in battle with the Philistines thirty years before were still strewn in the fields alongside the road that passed through the land of the Philistines. This gruesome sight would certainly frighten the Jewish people and cause them to lose heart.[11]

In addition to consideration for the sensitivities of the Jewish people, Hashem also wanted to avoid the Philistines out of deference to their grandfather King Avimelech. Avraham and Avimelech had made a treaty of non-aggression, a pact that was to remain in effect for three generations. At the time of the Jewish exodus from Egypt, the king of the Philistines was a very old man who was the grandson of Avimelech.[12] Therefore, the pact was still in effect.

In actuality, it was to the benefit of the Jewish people themselves not to enter Eretz Yisrael but to spend some time in the desert. They needed to receive the Torah at Mount Sinai and to spend time studying the laws and practicing the *mitzvos*, especially those *mitzvos* that pertained to living in Eretz Yisrael, such as *terumos* and *maasros*.[13] If they entered Eretz Yisrael right away, they would spend most of their time with reclaiming the land, planting trees, building homes and the like, and they would not devote sufficient time to the study of the Torah. In the desert, however, their main occupation would be studying the Torah, while Hashem Himself fed and clothed them.[14]

---

7) שמו"ר כ-יא ומת"כ (8 שמו"ר כ-יח (9 רש"י ממכילתא, שמו"ר כ-יד, רמב"ן בשלח יג-יז מוסיף שגם עמלק וכנען ילחמו אתם אלא שאז יהיו רחוק ממצרים ויצטרכו ללחום בטחונם בו ית' (10 דעת זקנים ורוקח בשלח יג-יז (11 שמו"ר כ-יא, ילקו"ש רכא, מדרש החפץ, תוס' בשלח יג-יז, בילקוט שמעוני איתא בנוסח אחרת (12 מכילתא, לקח טוב בשלח יג-יז (13 שמו"ר כ-טו ובמהרז"ו (14 מכילתא, שמו"ר שם ובזית רענן, בילקו"ש רכו מובא שהמלחמה עם הפלשתים הי' דוחה את מעמד הנבחר המיועדת להם מתחילת היצירה

THE JOURNEYS OF THE JEWISH PEOPLE
FROM THE EXODUS UNTIL THE SPLITTING OF THE SEA

YAM HAGADOL
(MEDITERRANEAN SEA)

YERUSHALAYIM

EGYPT

BEERSHEVA

PISOM

RAMSES

CANAAN

GOSHEN

PHILISTIA

NAHAL MITZRAYIM

❶

MIGDAL

SUCCOS

❷

ETHAM

MOUNT SEIR

NILE RIVER

YAM SUF

BAAL TZFON

❸

PI HACHIROS

ETHAM DESERT

NAHAL MARAH

SINAI DESERT

THE PATH THROUGH THE SEA

MIGDAL

EXIT

ENTRANCE

ETHAM

BAAL TZFON

PI HACHIROS

YAM SUF

MOUNT SINAI

A long time spent in the humbling desert would also give the Jewish people the opportunity to adjust psychologically to their newfound freedom and develop intestinal fortitude and a strong mental attitude. After witnessing the great miracles Hashem would perform for them in the desert, such as the *mann*, the victory over Amalek and Miriam's miraculous traveling well, the Jewish people would have the full confidence needed to fight for and conquer Eretz Yisrael.[15] At the same time, the nations of the region would marvel at how the great multitude of the Jewish people had survived in the desert for such a long time and they would be awed by the miracles that sustained them. Afterwards, when the Jews invaded Eretz Yisrael, the nations would be overcome by fear and would not have the heart to mount a powerful resistance.[16]

There was also another benefit in spending some time in the desert before entering Eretz Yisrael. When the Philistines heard that the Jewish people had left Egypt with the intention of coming to Eretz Yisrael, they went on a destructive rampage through the land, uprooting trees, demolishing buildings and wreaking all sorts of havoc in order to make the land uninhabitable for the large Jewish population. A long stay in the desert would also give the land a chance to recover.[17]

The Jewish people, however, were unaware that their travels would take them on a route that avoided confrontation.[18] They armed themselves with bows and arrows, lances, swords, spears and fighting staffs and prepared to defend themselves.[19] Armed and confident, the Jewish people set off into the desert for their rendezvous with destiny on the shores of the sea.[20]

The Cloud Pillars

The fifteenth day of Nissan, the first day of the exodus, came to an end. The Jewish people had congregated in Ramses from all over Egypt and, all together, had traveled south to Succos, and now they encamped for the night.[21] The next day was Friday, the sixteenth of Nissan, the second day of Pesach. On this

---

15) מו״נ ח״ג ד, רבנו בחיי יג-יז, ע׳ באברבנל 16) שמו״ר כ-טז, שה״ש רבה ג-ה ברש״ש ורד״ל 17) מכילתא, שמו״ר כ-טו 18) רמב״ן בשלח יג-יח, אוה״ח שם, רבנו בחיי מבארו עפ״י כללא הידוע דאין הקב״ה עושה נס בכדי ע״ש היטב 19) מדרש הגדול, בעה״ט בשלח יג-יח 20) ר׳ סעדיא גאון, אב״ע רלב״ג בשלח שם 21) רש״י בשלח יג-כ, ראה רלב״ג בראשית מז-ג

day, the second day of their freedom, they left Succos and traveled to Etham, at the edge of the desert.[22]

Hashem lavished loving care on the Jewish people during their travels, tending to their needs as a servant tends to his master's needs. He made sure they were never hungry and that even in the desert they had a spring from which to draw water.[23] He provided them with the cloud pillars to lead and protect them along the way, like a shepherd protects his flock.[24] The cloud pillar in front of them served to point out the direction in which they were to travel.[25] It was like a vertical beam that reached from the sky to the ground.[26]

At Succos, the Jewish people came to the realization that they were being treated with special honor by Hashem.[27] They realized that the Shechinah was present in the cloud pillars, and that Hashem was personally escorting them.[28] The Jewish people were deemed worthy of this great honor in the merit of Avraham who, in his great hospitality, personally escorted the angels out of his home.[29]

In the future, the amazing honor of a personal escort by Hashem would continue to have astonishing effects. Onkelos, the great convert to Judaism and author of *Targum Onkelos*, was the nephew of Caesar, the Roman emperor. When Caesar heard of his conversion he sent emissaries to summon him to Rome. Onkelos would tell these emissaries passages from the Torah and thereby inspire them to convert as well. After several attempts, Caesar instructed his emissaries to refrain from any religious discussions with Onkelos.

Onkelos, however, was not to be thwarted. "I have a riddle for you," Onkelos told them. "A private soldier carries a torch to light the way of his sergeant. The sergeant lights the way for the general. The general lights the way for the king. For whom does the king light the way?"

"For no one!" they declared. "The king serves no one."

22) רש"י, ריב"ש, חזקוני ושפתי כהן בשלח יג-כא, פענח רזא מביא שביום זה הפריד משה עצמותיהם של השבטים מעצמותיו של יוסף והפרישם ממנו ולא לקח עמו כ"א ארונו של יוסף (23 מכילתא, פסיקתא דרב כהנא י, שמו"ר כ-יא (24 מדרש תהלים (25 שפתי כהן בשלח יג-כא (26 אב"ע ואברבנל שם (27 תרגום יונתן שם, רמב"ן שם יג-יז, ספורנו שם יג-כא, במדרש החפץ מובא באופן אחר (28 רש"י ממכילתא, רמב"ן בשלח יג-כא, ע' זוה"ק מו, רשב"ם כתב שהיה ע"י מלאכים (29 מכילתא, שמו"ר טו-יא ובעץ יוסף, ע' תדב"א רבה יב, מעניין דבהדר זקנים עה"כ והוא עומד עליהם תחת העץ ויאכלו מתפרש מלת "תחת" במובן ובמקום "במקום" שהגין להם מן הצל כי ענק היה וא"כ לישנא דקרא כי בסוכות "הושבתי" ולא כתיב "ישבו" דאע"פ שהיה עץ לאברהם אבינו עכ"ז רצה להגן להם בעצמו ולכן זכו בניו לישב בצילא דקוב"ה

"Indeed," said Onkelos. "Witness therefore the greatness of Hashem, the Master of the Universe. When the Jewish people traveled in the desert, He personally escorted them in with cloud pillars and a pillar of fire."

Caesar's emissaries were duly impressed and converted to Judaism.[30]

Indeed, the personal escort of Hashem continued day and night without interruption. As night fell, a pillar of fire joined the cloud pillars and took its position in front of the encampment.[31] As the cloud pillars protected them from the heat of the sun,[32*] so did the pillar of fire protect them from the cold at night.

The cloud pillars did not relinquish their watch until the pillars of fire were in place, just like the palace guards do not relinquish their watch during the changing of the guard until the new guards are in place.[33] The transition was smooth, and it always took place at the moment day changed into night or night changed into day. In fact, the pillars obscured the sky to such an extent that the changing of the pillars was the only way the Jewish people could differentiate between night and day.[34] During the day, they saw only clouds, and during the night, they saw only fire.[35]

The pillar of fire was a barrier between the Jewish people and the surrounding desert, protecting the Jewish encampment from attack by nocturnal animals.[36] It illuminated the entire camp with a uniform light equal to the brightness of day.[37] However, all the illumination was inward. From the outside, the darkness of night prevailed.[38]

The travels of the encampment did not stop at night, and the cloud pillars that served as the guide remained on duty around the clock. This was because the enormous size of the encampment made progress very slow, and the nighttime hours were needed to cover

---

* The Erev Rav, however, were not worthy of being protected by these pillars. They had to stay beyond the clouds and fire. (*Sifsei Kohein, Ki Sisa, Chukas*)

---

30) ע״ז יא. 31) רש״י, מושב זקנים בשלח יג-כב, ע׳ שבת כג:, הופעתה הראשונה היתה בכניסת השבת כי אותו יום ע״ש היה 32) אוה״ח בשלח יג-כב 33) רש״י בשלח יג-כב ובבאר יצחק שם, בברייתא דמלאכת המשכן (באוצר המפרשים ח״ב דף רפה) וכן במושב זקנים ואב״ע הקצר איתא דשניהם נמצאו תמיד רק שביום נראה עמוד הענן ובלילה עמוד האש 34) ברייתא דמלאכת המשכן (באוצר המדרשים ח״ב דף רפה) 35) פענח רזא בשלח יג-כא 36) מדרש תהלים 37) אלשיך בשלח יג-כב 38) לקח טוב שם יג-כא

ground. The Jewish people had forty-nine days from the time of their exodus to reach their rendezvous at Mount Sinai for the giving of the Torah. Moreover, the news that the Jewish people were traveling through the night would convince Pharaoh that they did not intend to return, and he would give chase with his armies. This would lead to the spectacular miracles at the splitting of the sea.[39]

The ceaseless traveling, however, did not present a hardship for the Jewish people. The cloud pillars that enfolded them not only protected them but actually carried them. The Jewish people were able to stand still, and the cloud carried them along to their destination, like passengers on a boat.[40]

Reversing Direction

The travels of the Jewish people took them eastward, away from Egypt. After traveling from Ramses to Succos on Thursday the fifteenth of Nissan, they traveled from Succos to Etham, circumventing the Yam Suf, on Friday the sixteenth of Nissan. The seventeenth day of Nissan, the third day of Pesach and third day out of Egypt, fell on Shabbos, and the entire encampment rested. On Sunday, the fourth day out of Egypt, the Jewish encampment again prepared to travel in an eastward direction, taking it further and further away from Egypt.[41]

In the Jewish encampment there were a number of Egyptian soldiers who had been sent along by Pharaoh to monitor the movements of the Jews. As the Jewish people prepared to continue their travels for a fourth day, these soldiers raised a protest.

"Halt! You cannot go further!" they shouted. "It is your fourth day out of Egypt. You only had permission from Pharaoh to go on a three-day journey. The time is up! Return to Egypt without further delay. Right now!"

"Nonsense!" the indignant Jews shouted in response. "Why should we return? Pharaoh was only too eager to see us go. He declared us free people and gave us permission to leave. No, he actually begged us to leave."

---

39) מנחה בלולה שם, ע״ע שכל טוב, אב״ע, רבנו בחיי, ומלבים 40) שפתי כהן בשלח יג-כא, ע׳ פסיקתא דרב כהנא יב, ויקרא רבה ט-ט ובמהרז״ו שם דנתיגעו ונתיעפו מן הדרך לכן התרעמו, בפרדר״א מב מפורש שלולא זה היו ראויים לקבל את התורה מיד 41) כ״ה במכילתא יד-א וכו׳ לפי גירסת הגר״א כל הראשונים גורסים שהיה ביום ג׳ ונתעכבו בפי החירות ולדידהו רק ביום ד׳ הגיעו המצריים לפרעה להגיד לו שאין רצונם לשוב

"We are not interested in getting into debates with you," the soldiers replied. "These are our instructions. Pharaoh sent us along with you to make sure you return. You have no choice in the matter. You must return!"

Enraged, the Jewish people fell upon the soldiers and began beating them, killing some and wounding several others. The rest fled back to Egypt.[42]

In the aftermath of the skirmish, Moshe sounded a call to assembly on a trumpet, a practice that would become commonplace during the years in the desert. All the Jewish people gathered to hear Moshe's announcement.

"Listen carefully," Moshe began. "Hashem has commanded all the Jewish people to turn around and travel back in the direction of Egypt. Pharaoh must not think we lied when we told him we were going on a three-day journey. He must not think we are trying to escape."[43]

The announcement caused much consternation and confusion among the Jews. Some Jews whose faith was still weak began to pull at their hair and tear their clothes in terror and anguish.

"Do not worry," Moshe reassured them. "Trust in Hashem. He has assured me that you will all remain free. There is a purpose in these instructions, although we may not understand it at the moment. Hashem is doing this to bring Pharaoh and Egypt to their final downfall."

Moshe's words calmed the fears of the Jewish people, and with renewed faith in Hashem, they set out in the direction Moshe had indicated.[44]

"Pi Hachiros" Although the Jewish people had nervously agreed to follow Moshe's instructions, Hashem placed wild beasts, lions, snakes and scorpions on their eastward path to ensure that they would turn in the direction of Egypt.[45]

At the end of their travels on the fourth day, the Jewish people encamped at a place called Pi Hachiros, not far from the Yam Suf.

---

42) מכילתא, ילקו״ש רל 43) שם 44) רש״י ממכילתא בשלח יד-ד, ר׳ אברהם בן הרמב״ם מבאר דבעצם נסעו תמיד על פי ענני הכבוד רק שאילו ראו שהם מכוונים אותם למקום יגונם ועבודתם היו מהררים בלבבם על נאמנותם, לכן הגיד להם משה מקודם, ראה מש״כ בשפתי כהן ע״ז. 45) ע׳ שמו״ר טו-טו, שמו״ר כא-ה, אלשיך יד-ג

This place had once been called Pisom, but it was not the Egyptian slave city. Over time, it came to be the point of no return for people trying to escape Egypt. If they reached this place, they could consider themselves free. Therefore, it came to be known as Pi Hachiros, "the Opening of the Free."[46] Furthermore, Pi Hachiros was situated in a narrow valley between two stone pillars which looked like a mouth. The temple of Baal Tzfon, the only surviving Egyptian idol, was situated in this valley, to the south of the Jewish encampment. The sea lay to the east, and the desert to the west.[47]

The two great stone pillars that stood astride the entrance to the valley of Pi Hachiros had the shape of a man and a woman, and each one also seemed to have two round eyes. The stone formation was natural and not the work of human hands, and for this reason, it was chosen as the site for the temple of Baal Tzfon. The idol was made entirely of copper and had the form of an angry dog on it.[48] The temple stood in the center of a great plaza, a place of exceptional beauty and splendor, the pride of Egypt. Underneath the temple, one third of the treasures accumulated by Yosef for the royal coffers lay concealed. These treasures were destined to be taken by the Jewish people as part of Hashem's promise to Avraham.

To the north of Pi Hachiros stood a fortified tower known as Migdal. This tower was used by the Egyptian military for reconnaissance and to mount ambushes on enemy forces during wartime. It was an intimidating structure.[49]

Once the Jewish people returned to Pi Hachiros they were hemmed in on all sides, and this was exactly what Hashem intended. The dangerous beasts moved into the desert to the west of the Jewish encampment. The east of the encampment was blockaded by the sea. The northern route was cut off by the military tower at Migdal. The southern route was blocked by the temple of Baal Tzfon. There was no avenue of escape.[50*]

---

* Some suggest that they went there because the downfall of Egypt would begin at a place of idol worship, just as the plagues had begun with blood on the Nile, which was also a place of idol worship. (*Midrash Hachefetz*)

---

46) רש"י ממכילתא, מעם לועז יד,ב מביא דפיתום מלשון סתימת הפה שנסתמו ונסגרו שם בעבודתם ופי החירות מלשון חרות מעבודתם 47) מכילתא, ילקו"ש רלג, מעם לועז, מלבים שם יד-ב כתב שממגדול והים היו לב' הצדדים, מצרים עמדה לאחריהם והמדבר לפניהם, ועמדו ישראל בפי החירות במקום בעל צפון 48) מכילתא, תרגום יונתן, ואב"ע בשלח יד-ב, ילקוט ראובני 49) מכילתא, ילקו"ש קל, אברבנל ומלבים בשלח שם, שפתי כהן מפרש "צפון" ששם נצפנו ונגנזו האוצרות שאסף יוסף 50) שמו"ר טו-טו, שם כא-ה ובעץ יוסף, מכילתא, מדרש אגדה

With the Jewish people in place as the bait, it was now time to draw out the Egyptians in pursuit and lure them to their doom. The return of the Jewish people in the direction of Egypt was puzzling, but their proximity to the temple of Baal Tzfon offered a solution. Pharaoh would assume that the Egyptian idol had stalled the escape of the Jews and forced them to turn back towards Egypt. Pharaoh would further assume that Baal Tzfon had placed the wild beasts in the desert to steer the Jews back towards Egypt.[51] Based on the evidence, he would assume that the Jewish people had been trying to escape, traveling day and night.[52] But in their haste and through the intervention of the idol, they had lost their way and returned to Pi Hachiros.[53]

With his courage bolstered by the new evidence, Pharaoh would have a change of heart. He would come to the realization that he had erred in allowing them to leave. Clearly, the Jews still had a slave mentality, unable to think and act as free people. The Jews were there for the taking. All Pharaoh had to do was capture them and bring them back to Egypt as slaves.[54]

Hashem now informed Moshe that He would once again harden Pharaoh's heart to allow him to follow his evil instincts.[55] In spite of all the indications that the Jewish people could be easily recaptured, Pharaoh would not forget the plagues so quickly. Fear would hold him back from giving chase. But once Hashem would harden his heart, these considerations would be forgotten, and he would give chase. As a result of this ill-advised chase, the Egyptian army would perish by drowning in the sea—as punishment for throwing Jewish children into the river.[56] When this entire episode would reach its conclusion, it would be so clear to the Egyptians that Hashem, the God of the Jewish people, was the all-powerful Master of the Universe that they would never again attempt to enslave the Jewish people.[57]

"The Jews Are Escaping"

On the fifth day after the Jewish exodus from Egypt, an uneasy calm descended on the region. The Jewish people were encamped in Pi Hachiros, seemingly

---

51) נצי"ב על מכילתא, שמו"ר טו-טו, אברבנל 52) רבנו בחיי בשלח יד-ב, חזקוני מוסיף שטענו דבמעמקי שכלם של ישראל אכתי עבדים הם לא רק שחוזרים אלא שגם הולכים למקום שהתחילו להשתעבד, פיתום 53) מכילתא, אב"ע בשלח יד-ג 54) מכילתא, חזקוני יד-ב 55) מכילתא 56) אב"ע, רמב"ן, ע' מדרש אגדה בשלח יד-ד 57) אב"ע ורלב"ג שם

boxed in on all sides and awaiting further instructions from Hashem. In Egypt, a semblance of normalcy was returning to the land. All the firstborn who had died on the night of the plague and during the three-day aftermath were buried. The Egyptian thoughts now turned to the Jews in Pi Hachiros and the intriguing reports about their travels in the desert.[58]

Pharaoh now assembled all the evidence and came to the conclusion that the Jewish people were trying to escape. The Egyptian soldiers who had escaped the wrath of the Jews in their encampment on the fourth day returned to report that the Jewish people intended to escape.[59] Amalekite agents also appeared in the Egyptian court with similar reports.[60] Torch and flag signals from the high places in the vicinity of Pi Hachiros also confirmed these reports.[61]

In addition, members of the Erev Rav who had decided to return to Egypt told Pharaoh of the intentions of the Jewish people. These last-minute converts to Judaism were disillusioned with their new status as Jews and did not relish the incessant travels in the desert.

After three days, these reluctant Jews approached Moshe and demanded that the entire encampment return to Egypt in order to keep their word to Pharaoh. Moshe told them not to be concerned, for they would never again see the Egyptians. The former Egyptians, however, insisted that they return. Otherwise, they were prepared to fight the Jewish people.

Realizing what he was up against, Moshe led the Jewish people into battle against these elements and killed many of them. But some of them survived and returned to Egypt. They sought an audience with Pharaoh and told him that they had not sacrificed to the Jewish God, and that from the beginning they had regretted their conversion to Judaism. Having ingratiated themselves with Pharaoh once again, they told him that the Jewish people had no intentions of ever returning to Egypt.[62]

More important than anything else, Hashem miraculously implanted the thought in Pharaoh's head that the Jewish people were escaping.[63]

---

58) עיין לעיל (59 רש"י ממכילתא בשלח יד-ה, ע"ש ברכנו בחיי, בהדר זקנים נרמז "כי ברח" בגימטריה "עמלק"
60) מכילתא, שפתי כהן בשלח (61 מכילתא בשלח, מעם לועז, ע' פירוש המשניות לרמב"ם יומא סוף פ"ו
62) דברי הימים למשה, מדרש החפץ, אברבנל בשלח יד-ה (63 שמו"ר כט-ה וע"ש בעץ יוסף, רבנו בחיי מביא
שידע פרעה דמספר שנות הגזירה היה יותר מר"י שנה ובע"כ שברחו לפני קצם, רמז לדבר "ברח" עולה ר"י

Thoroughly convinced that the Jews were escaping, Pharaoh turned to his officers, and to Dassan and Aviram, two Jews who had remained behind during the exodus. "Gentlemen," he said. "I think we may recover our lost property. The Jews are lost in the desert. Baal Tzfon has protected my interests. He has thwarted the attempt of the Jews to escape Egypt. Now, it is time we did something about this fortunate state of affairs."[64]*

A Change of Heart

In spite of his strong inclination to pursue the Jewish people and bring them back to Egypt as slaves, Pharaoh could not bring himself to make the final decision to set the process into motion. The painful memories of the plagues were still vivid in his mind, and he could not bring himself to make a firm decision. [65] He called a gathering of the councilors, sages and magicians still remaining in Egypt and asked for their advice.

"Your majesty," one of his advisors said. "I think the departure of the Jews is a great loss to Egypt. And I'm not even talking about all those treasures and jewels they managed to borrow before they left. All those women, children, livestock, sages, magicians, craftsmen. How valuable they could have been to the kingdom!"

"Your majesty, I agree," said another advisor. "And let us not forget that millions of the best and finest of our own Egyptian population also converted and left with them. That is a great loss indeed."

"The arrogance of the Jews!" a third advisor called out. "I can still see them in my mind's eye, leaving tribe by tribe with those colorful flags fluttering in defiance."

"Your majesty," a fourth advisor added soberly. "I think we may not have managed the Jews as well as we could have. Had we treated them better and not enslaved them, they would not have left Egypt, and we all would have been very much enriched by their presence. Now we are just another nation, and a severely battered one at that."[66]

---

* Dassan and Aviram remained in Egypt, not wanting to leave. They would later join the Jewish people at Krias Yam Suf. It is of no surprise that these wicked Jews acted in this manner. (*Targum, Midrash Hachefetz, Shemos*)

---

64) מכילתא, תרגום יונתן, רוקח בשלח יד-ג, שכל טוב שם יד-לא (65 מכילתא, מדרש אגדה בשלח יד-ד

66) שה״ש רבה ד-יב, שמו״ר כ-א וכו׳ ביפ״ת ומתנ״כ ורש״ש, ע׳ מכילתא ותנחומא ישן בשלח ה

"Your majesty, there is another point," the first advisor continued. "Even since the days of the Jewish viceroy Yosef,* the Egyptian
empire has controlled all the nations in this part of the world. We
gained this control in exchange for the food Yosef was able to stock-
pile. The governments are appointed with Egyptian approval and
pay heavy tribute to the Egyptian treasury. If we let the Jews leave,
how can we expect to maintain control? All the nations will laugh at
us. Mighty Egypt is unable to hold onto its slaves. Mighty indeed!
We will lose our power and prestige. We will lose our empire."

Pharaoh sighed. "How true! What's more, I could have avoided
all the plagues and pain and the loss of prestige if I had let the Jews
go of my own free will. Egypt could have remained powerful even
without the Jews." This was, in fact, not true. Hashem had caused
Egypt to become a powerful empire out of respect of the Jews. It
would have been more demeaning to the Jews to be enslaved to a
second-rate power.[67]

Pharaoh thought for a while longer, and then he spoke. "It
seems clear to me that the Jews have no intention of returning. The
manner in which they left—the banner, the music, the singing—are
not quite fitting for slaves taking a short vacation.[68] Furthermore,
they said they wanted to sacrifice to the Jewish God, but they have
not done so. Nevertheless, they seem to be lost and wandering, and
they are now back in Pi Hachiros, closer to Egypt.[69]

"I have erred in not consulting with Baal Tzfon during my trou-
bles, but he has been kind to me. He has obviously caused the Jews
to become lost and wander back to Pi Hachiros. Baal Tzfon will help
me get the Jewish people back. I will put my trust in him, and then
I will be successful.[70]

"And besides, there is more than the Jews at stake here, as one
of you pointed out so aptly. How about all the Egyptians who were
duped into converting to Judaism and leaving with the Jews? I never
intended that they should leave, and I want them back. They are my
people!"[71]

---

* Yosef ruled the world during the Great Famine. (*Pirkei d'Rabbi Eliezer* 11)

---

67) מכילתא, שמו"ר כ-א וכו', שמו"ר טו-י, שפתי כהן בשלח יד-ה ואילך, מעם לועז 68) רמב"ן בשלח יד-ה, ע'
מנחה בלולה מש"כ עפ"י דרכו 69) רמב"ן שם יד-ד, אברבנל שם יד-ה 70) ספורנו שם יד-ה 71) מעם לועז שם, באלשיך
מבואר שחשב פרעה לעצמו שהיות ואינו רואה עזר אלקי ישראל בנסיעותם, סימן הוא שלא רצה שיגאלם, ומה
שהביא המכות לא היה אלא על שחטא באמרו מי ד' וכו'

Still, in spite of the convincing arguments of his advisors and his own strong feelings on the matter, Pharaoh was too traumatized by the experience of the plagues to take action. He simply did not have the emotional fortitude to move against the Jews.[72]

At this point, Hashem began to harden his heart. The memory of the plagues began to fade from Pharaoh's mind, and his old audacity and ruthlessness began to return. Suddenly, he was determined to give chase, not only to bring back his own wayward Egyptians but all the Jewish people as well.[73]

Hashem now caused Pharaoh to focus his mind on the manner in which the Jewish people left Egypt. The image of the former slaves, fully armed, marching off with banners and song incensed Pharaoh.[74] What an affront to the honor of Egypt! It was as if they had scored a victory over the glorious Egyptian kingdom.[75] Intolerable!

"I have made up my mind!" Pharaoh declared with his old resolve and obstinacy. "We *will* pursue those renegade slaves. We *will* capture them. And we will bring them back. I have spoken!"[76]

Pharaoh's decision to pursue the Jewish people is considered one of the fifty miracles Hashem performed for them. Indeed, Pharaoh had been so shocked and humbled by the plagues that his decision to risk further punishment was nothing short of miraculous.[77]

Preparing the Reluctant Egyptians

Pharaoh had decided to pursue the Jewish people, but things were no longer as simple as they used to be. The days when Pharaoh's commands had been followed blindly by the Egyptian populace were over. The Egyptians had suffered too much on account of the Jews, and they were not prepared to risk further injury by attempting to bring them back.[78] They were willing to accept the loss of money the Jewish people had carried out of Egypt. It was a small price to pay for safety.[79] Pharaoh needed a cunning plan to cajole the Egyptians into pursuing the Jews. He had one.[80]

---

72) מכילתא, מדרש אגדה בשלח יד-ד 73) אב״ע, רמב״ן, מעם לועז בשלח שם 74) מכילתא, אב״ע רשב״ם, ריב״ש, רלב״ג, רוקח, ומלבים בשלח יד-ח 75) ספורנו שם 76) אברבנל, מעם לועז בשלח יד-ד 77) מעם לועז בשלח טו-א, ראה רמב״ן יד-ד 78) מדרש אגדה, אוה״ח בשלח יד-ה 79) מכילתא עפ״י גירסת הגר״א בשלח טו-טו 80) מכילתא ותרגום יונתן שם יד-ו

"I call upon all Egyptians to join me in a major campaign," Pharaoh proclaimed in public. "We must ride forth and recapture our fleeing Jewish slaves. All who participate in this campaign will, of course, be richly rewarded. Just your share of the treasures the Jews are carrying with them will make you wealthy for the rest of your lives.

"But it is more than that. This campaign means a great deal to me, and I will prove it. Ordinarily, the king is preceded into battle by his army for the sake of his protection, but I will ride at the head of the columns. Ordinarily, the king takes the greatest portion of the booty, but I will share equally with all of you."[81]

"That is very honorable of you, your majesty," the servants of Pharaoh said. "But why are you doing it? Why is this campaign so important to you?"

"I want to make war on the Jewish God," Pharaoh declared gravely. "It is only fitting that the king takes personal command in such a war."[82] To Pharaoh, this was indeed not just a war against the Jews but against Hashem.[83]

In his mad rush to exact revenge on the Jewish people, Pharaoh himself harnessed his own horse to its chariot. His generals, following his example, ran to saddle their horses and prepare for battle.[84] So great is the power of hatred that the haughty Pharaoh broke all the rules of royal protocol and saddled his own horse![85] This evil diligence was also exhibited by Bilam, who saddled his own donkey when he was called upon to curse the Jews. We also see displays of diligence for the good. Avraham, in his eagerness to obey Hashem's commandment and sacrifice his son Yitzchak on the Akeidah, ran to saddle his own donkey. And Yosef, in his eagerness to greet his father Yaakov after a separation of many years, also ran to saddle his own donkey. Both Pharaoh and Bilam would be unsuccessful in their assaults on the Jews in the merit of the righteous Avraham and Yosef who were diligent in the service of Hashem.[86]

One might wonder where the Egyptians found animals to harness to their chariots after the mass destruction of the plagues. Actually, these were the animals of the Egyptians who feared God and brought their animals indoors during the plague of hailstones. However, in the

81) רש"י ממכילתא בשלח טו-ט, מדרש אגדה שם, שם יד-ו 82) שם יד-ו 83) במדבר רבה ח-ג 83) מדרש אגדה, רבנו בחיי
בשלח יד-ז והלאה 84) מכילתא, מדרש החפץ, אברבנל יד-ו, ע"ע אב"ע ורלב"ג שם 85) מכילתא ולקח טוב בשלח
יד-ו 86) מכילתא

frenzy of revenge generated by Pharaoh, even these more righteous Egyptians were lured into the camp of the pursuers.[87]

As the preparations for battle proceeded, Pharaoh mustered six hundred deluxe war chariots for the expeditionary force. He also commandeered hundreds of other chariots for his auxiliary forces.[88] Although each chariot was normally equipped with a two-horse team, Pharaoh ordered a third horse added to each chariot to increase its speed. By the time Pharaoh finished, every horse in the kingdom had been commandeered for the expeditionary force. Each chariot was also accompanied by a platoon of three hundred heavily-armed soldiers.[89] Pharaoh's six hundred premium war chariots would be crushed in the sea, as retribution for the six hundred bricks the Jewish laborers were required to produce each day.[90]

As Pharaoh continued his preparations, he calculated the size of the force he would need. According to Pharaoh's population records there were three million Jewish men of military age. He did not know that four-fifths of the Jewish population of Egypt had discreetly passed away during the plague of darkness, leaving only six hundred thousand men of military age. Therefore, Pharaoh began to muster an army many times larger than he could possibly need.[91]

The soldiers Pharaoh selected for his special force included men from families who had traditionally practiced circumcision since the days Yosef had demanded that anyone fed from the royal granaries must be circumcised. Pharaoh knew that Hashem defended the Jewish people because of their *bris milah*, and he assumed that circumcised Egyptian soldiers would neutralize this advantage.[92] In addition to his own Egyptians, Pharaoh also recruited battle-hardened mercenaries from neighboring countries.[93]

Having amassed a huge force, Pharaoh organized a strict chain of command, from lieutenants to generals. There were officers who commanded platoons of one hundred troops, officers who commanded one thousand troops and so forth. The common denominator among all the soldiers was their intense desire to pursue the Jews and defeat them.[94]

---

87) רש"י ממכילתא, תרגום יונתן בשלח יד-ז 88) רש"י ממכילתא, ר' יהודה החסיד בשלח יד-ז, זוה"ק מו 89)
מכילתא, מדרש הגדול בשלח יד-ז, ילקו"ש ר"ל ובזית רענן 90) מדרש ויושע 91) מכילתא, רבנו בחיי, ורוקח
בשלח יג-יח, שם יד-ז, בשפתי כהן מפורט כל חשבון רכבי מצרים ותדרשנו משם 92) שפתי כהן בשלח יד-ז 93)
מכילתא שם, ספורנו בשלח יד-ז 94) רבנו בחיי, מעם לועז בשלח יד-ז, נצי"ב במכילתא אב"ע, ומלבים שם טו-
ט, ראה פיוט לאחרון של פסח

Pharaoh surveyed the army he had organized and declared triumphantly, "With this army I will smash the Jewish people. I will kill and kill and kill, and those that remain I will take back as slaves. I will take every bit of treasure they have. But the greatest satisfaction I will have will be when I look at my sword and see it dripping with Jewish blood."[95] These evil words would be used against him by Hashem. The Egyptians would eventually die in the sea, and all their wealth would be inherited by the Jewish people.[96]

Among the Egyptian soldiers there were three different groups. One group was not intent on killing the Jews, only on taking their money. The second group had no interest in the money of the Jews but only wanted to kill them. The third group burned with an evil hatred equal to that of Pharaoh himself. They wanted to kill the Jews and take their money. In the end, the Egyptians would drown at sea in three ways. Those who wanted only money would drown as quickly as lead sinks to the bottom of the sea. Those who wanted to kill but did not want to rob would drown as quickly as a stone sinks to the bottom of the sea. The worst Egyptians, the ones intent on murder and robbery, would drown agonizingly, being heaved and tossed in the waves like straw which falls to the bottom of the sea ever so slowly.[97]

The Chase Begins

The reports of the intended escape of the Jews had reached Pharaoh on the fourth and fifth days of the exodus. On Tuesday, the sixth day of the exodus, the Egyptian army was assembled and ready to march. It would take them one day to reach the Jewish people.[98] In order to gain maximum speed, Pharaoh ordered that the mares be hitched to the front chariots and the stallions to the chariots behind them, on the assumption that the stallions would run faster to catch the mares.[99]

Before giving the order to march, Pharaoh distributed gems, jewels, gold and silver from his treasury to all the soldiers in the

---

95) רש״י ממכילתא, ר׳ סעדיא גאון, מדרש אגדה, תרגום יונתן, ואוה״ח בשלח טו-ט 96) ויקרא רבה כא-א במתנ״כ 97) מדרש ויושע, מכילתא בשלח טו-ט אב״ע, רבנו בחיי, מעם לועז בשלח יד-ז, נציב במכילתא, ספורנו טו-ט, ראה פיוט לאחרון של פסח 98) ע׳ רש״י ממכילתא בין המכילתא וש״ח עליו יד-ה, שם יד-ט, בתורה שלמה בשלח יד-ב בהערות ג׳ ומ״ז (וכן שם פרק טו הערה ד) שיש פלוגתא בין המכילתא והסדר עולם איזה יום בשבוע היה, בסדר עולם גופא יש ב׳ נוסחאות, לא׳ מהם י׳ ניסן היה ביום א׳ (ולא כמקובל בטעם שבת הגדול), ע״ע שבת פז. וכו׳, לקח טוב, מדרש הגדול 99) זוה״ק מו, מדרש תהלים יח

army. The horses were also adorned and outfitted with the most precious stones and finery. The mood was festive.[100] In the end, every adult Egyptian male had joined the vast army of pursuit, leaving only women and children in Egypt.[101]

Pharaoh gave the signal, and the chase began. True to his word, Pharaoh himself led the charge, staying at the head of his troops. The Egyptian army was a unified, cohesive force with one common goal. No Egyptian entertained thoughts of fatigue, discouragement or illness. No one was distracted by injury or private affairs. All minds were focused on the Jews who were trying to escape. All they could think about were the Jews. As they sped across the desert they shouted curses and expletives against the Jews into the hot desert winds.

In sharp contrast to the venomous force hurtling through the desert, the Jewish people were celebrating their freedom with food and drink, singing praises and offering thanks to Hashem for their deliverance from Egypt.[102] They were no longer in Pi Hachiros, however. They had moved to a new encampment to the northeast, in the direction of the sea.[103]

Meanwhile, the Egyptian army of pursuit arrived in Pi Hachiros, but the Jewish people had moved towards the sea. When the reports of the new Jewish position reached Pharaoh, he was ecstatic. The Jews were boxed in with no means of escape. Clearly, Baal Tzfon had maneuvered the Jewish people into this hopeless position, Pharaoh thought. Gratefully, Pharaoh offered sacrifices to his beloved idol.[104*] It did not cross Pharaoh's mind that Hashem was setting a trap for him and that the chase would end at the bottom of the sea.[105]

---

* Although Pharaoh would have liked to have his slaves back, his empire would not suffer severely if they were killed. It would suffer severely if they escaped and the booty was not recaptured. The prestige of Egypt would suffer a mortal blow from which it could never recover.

---

100) תנחומא שופטים יג, תנחומא ישן בשלח ד"ה אשירה 101) תנחומא שופטים ט, מכילתא מדרש הגדול, ספר הישר, מעם לועז טו-א 102) רש"י ממכילתא, אב"ע בשלח יד-י, במדבר רבה ח-ג, ספר הישר, שפתי כהן בשלח יד-ח 103) מלבים שם יד-ט 104) מכילתא בשלח יד-ט 105) לקח טוב בשלח יד-ט

Fear in the Jewish Hearts

On the sixth day of the exodus, the Jewish people saw the Egyptian army approaching in the distance, and a shiver of fear went through their hearts.[106] But what struck even greater fear into their hearts was the sight of Uzah, the ministering angel of Egypt, hovering in the air over the Egyptian army. He seemed intent on the annihilation of the Jews.[107]

Earlier, when the Jewish people had left Egypt, the angel Uzah who represented the interests of Egypt in Heaven went to Hashem and demanded a hearing against the angel Michael who represented the interests of the Jews.

"Master of the Universe," said the angel Uzah. "You decreed that the Jewish people be exiled in Egypt for four hundred years. The time of the exile has not yet been fulfilled. I request permission to bring the Jewish people back to Egypt."

The angel Michael did not respond. But Hashem Himself came to the defense of the Jewish people. The decree had never intended that there be four hundred years of servitude to the Egyptians. It had been a decree of exile, of being a stranger in an alien land. This began when Yitzchak was born, and from that time, fully four hundred years had passed. The time had come for the exodus, and the angel Uzah was denied permission to bring the Jewish people back to Egypt. Having lost his case, Uzah was expelled from Heaven, but although forbidden to assist the Egyptians, he did escort them in their quest to recapture the Jewish people.[108]

The Jewish people had good reason to be frightened. Pharaoh and his army were bearing down on them as one cohesive unit, filled with fury, intent on revenge for the plague of the firstborn and hungry for the treasures the Jews carried with them.[109] The incident in which the Egyptian soldiers were killed in the Jewish encampment did not help matters either.[110]

Doubt seeped into the hearts of some of the Jewish people. Perhaps the plagues and miracles in Egypt had only come because

---

106) רש"י בשלח יד-ה, שם יד-ח ואילך, ראה רשב"ם שם יד-ח 107) שמו"ר כא-ה, רבנו בחיי, בעה"ט בשלח יד-י, בתולדות נח איתה דשם שרו של מצרים כשם המדינה ולעת עתה נקראת עוזה ע"ש המאורע, ע' רש"י ומפרשיו יד-י, שמו"ר טו-טו, שם כב-ב 108) מדרש ויושע פסוק דבר, הדר זקנים בשלח יד-י, שפתי כהן מביא דשרו של מצרים נתגלה בצורת בכור כי רצה לנקום למה שנעשה לעמו, בתוס' עה"ת מובא שרעדו על שראו מצרים בן חם שכבר מת מזמן רב ובראאותם שעמד מקברו יראו ולכן מצינו שאמרו אח"כ המבלי אין קברים במצרים וכו', ע"ע בהדר זקנים 109) שמו"ר כא-ה, אברבנל בשלח יד-י, רש"י ממכילתא שם, מעם לועז שם 110) מכילתא שם

Pharaoh had failed to honor Hashem. Perhaps now that he had repented Hashem would not take the side of the Jewish people. After all, Hashem had allowed them to be trapped between the sea and a charging army.[111]

Prayers and Complaints

Hashem had, of course, not abandoned the Jewish people by any means. The Jewish people had been put in this situation so that they should be stimulated to pray to Hashem. While slaves in Egypt, the Jewish people had prayed for their redemption, but now that they were free, they neglected to pray. Hashem wanted them to pray, to approach Him with the sweet sounds of their prayer.[112]

And this was exactly what happened. Cut off in all directions and with the Egyptian army approaching, the Jewish people could turn nowhere but to Hashem.[113] They knew that in times of need prayer was the answer. It had been that way for Avraham, Yitzchak and Yaakov, and it was that way for their descendants.[114] As the Jews began to pray, a feeling of repentance surged through their hearts, the kind of repentance that one hundred fasts could not inspire. At the moment Pharaoh was sacrificing to Baal Tzfon, the Jewish people were being cleansed of their sins.[115]

With great fervor and devotion, the Jewish people prayed to Hashem that Pharaoh and his army return to Egypt without causing them any harm.[116] But Pharaoh and his army did not turn back. Inexorably, they kept coming closer and closer.

Some of the Jewish people, inspired by their prayer into a deep faith in Hashem, channeled their doubts towards the validity of Moshe's words.[117] A great internal debate broke out among the Jewish people as to the best method of dealing with the current crisis. One group recommended surrender and return to Egypt without further resistance. A second group wanted to engage the Egyptians in battle without any further delay. A third group wanted to create noisy diversions and make belligerent moves towards the Egyptians but to stop short of actual combat. A fourth group wanted all the

111) שמו"ר כא-ה, מעם לועז בשלח שם 112) שמו"ר שם 113) שמו"ר שם ובי"ת, לקח טוב בשלח יד-י 114) רש"י ממכילתא שם, ע' ברטנורה עה"ת ובס' זכרון 115) שמו"ר שם, פדר"א מב 116) מלבים שם 117) רמב"ן, לקח טוב, ומלבים בשלח יד-י וכו'

people to throw themselves into the sea rather than face the Egyptians.[118] The fear and confusion of the Jewish people was so great that many began to send signals of surrender to the approaching Egyptians.[119]

There were also some decidedly wicked people among the Jews who bombarded Moshe with complaints.[120]

"Do you know why the Egyptians are chasing us?" they screamed to Moshe. "Because they want their money back! And it's all your fault. You told us to take all their money. Now look where it has gotten us![121] The Jews who died during the plague of darkness are better off than we are. At least we were able to give them a decent burial. But what's going to happen to us? Our corpses will rot in the desert.[122] Is there a shortage of burial grounds in Egypt that you had to bring us to this place to die? We should have stayed there and died![123] And even if we do survive, what are our prospects here in the desert? We will be stranded out here in the desolation, and we will all die of hunger."[124]

This complaint was the first of the ten times the Jewish people angered Hashem in the desert.[125]

Hope and Trust in Hashem

In a display of remarkable wisdom and leadership, Moshe calmed the fears of the Jewish people and brought them under control. He addressed the concerns of all the groups, offering them hope and reassurance.[126]

"So some of you want to throw yourselves into the sea?" he said. "Stand fast, I tell you, and you will witness the salvation Hashem will perform for you. Some of you want to return to Egypt? I assure you there is no need to worry. This is the last day you will ever see the Egyptians. Some of you want to go fight the Egyptians? It is not necessary. Hashem Himself will fight on your behalf.

---

118) מכילתא, ספר הישר, רמב״ן, רבנו בחיי, רוקח, צרור המור, ע׳ ירושלמי תענית ב-ה ובקרבן העדה, ע׳ היטב
בתרגום יונתן ובפי׳ יונתן בספר הישר נקבו שמותם ואלו הן: זבולון בנימין ונפתלי אמרו נחזור מצרימה, יהודה
דן ובני יוסף אמרו נלחום אותם, ראובן שמעון ויששכר אמרו נקפוץ לתוך הים, לוי גד ואשר רצו להפיל אימה
עליהם 119) שה״ש רבה ב-ל, אברבנל מעורר דודאי לא הסתפקו בהבטחתו ית׳ אלא דסבירי להו שכבר קיים
הבטחתו לגמרי ועתה הניחו אותם בהנהגתו ית׳ המלובשת בטבע ולכן נזדעזו 120) ר׳ אברהם בן הרמב״ם ורוקח
בשלח יד-יא, ע׳ תרגום יונתן בשפתי כהן, איתא שהיו הערב רב, וטענתם בפיהם דעל בני״י אין לו טענה יען
ונשתעבדו שם כ״כ ורק מחמתם יוצא לקראתם כי הם לא עבדו כלל 121) שמו״ר כא-ה 122) מכילתא ולקח טוב
בשלח יד-יא והלאה 123) רש״י שם 124) רש״י שם 125) רשב״ם וספורנו שם 125) אבות ה-ד, ערכין טו. 126) מכילתא בשלח
יד-יג, בלקח טוב שמות ב-י אי׳ דלכן נקרא משה בשם יקותיאל כי בהאי שעתא נתן תקוה בלבבי עמו

Some of you want to create noisy diversions? The only sounds that need to concern you are the sounds of prayer.[127]

"You see the Egyptians approaching, but do not worry. Hashem is showing you the Egyptians today for one last look. Look at them, for you will witness their destruction.[128] Hashem will fight the Egyptians for you, as He will fight your battles for you always in all generations to come. All you need to do is stand by silently and watch. Pray to Hashem before and thank Him afterwards, but always trust in Him to deliver you from your enemies.[129]*

"But this you must remember! Complaints and grumbling will not benefit you. If you want to be delivered from the Egyptians, you must be silent and have faith in Hashem. Otherwise, you will fall into the hands of the Egyptians."[130]

Moshe's strong and confident words calmed the Jewish people, but they could not resist asking, "When will Hashem save us?"

"Tomorrow," Moshe replied.

"Tomorrow seems like an eternity," they said. "The tension is unbearable. We are frightened."

"Very well," said Moshe. "Hashem will begin saving you today."

Moshe prayed to Hashem, and suddenly, the divine spirit rested on the Jewish people. With their new insight, they saw an army of ministering angels standing before them.

"Here is the army that will defend you," Moshe told them. "They are all on our side, and there are more of them."[131]

Hashem now spoke to the Jewish people. They had doubted His ability and intention to protect them, but in front of their very eyes, they would see their salvation unfold.[132]

Filled with confidence and joy, the Jewish people raised their voices in songs of praise to Hashem.[133]

---

* Some infer from here that if a person has been wronged he should not attempt to take matters into his own hands. The wisest course is to trust in Hashem to make sure that justice is done. (*R' Ephraim al Hatorah*)

---

127) מכילתא, ספר הישר, רבנו בחיי, ורוקח בשלח יד-יא וכו', בזוה"ק מה נתבאר דנתגיירו הערב רב ושפיר יכלו לראותם 128) ריב"ש ואוה"ח בשלח יד-יג 129) מכילתא, לקח טוב בשלח יד-יד, מדרש תהלים ד 130) רבנו בחיי, מנחה בלולה, חזקוני בשלח יד-יד, רלב"ג מוסיף שתכלית שתווי צווי ואתם תחרישון היתה שלא ישמע אותם פרעה פן יווכח שהם כ"כ קרובים לו 131) מכילתא, מדרש הגדול בשלח ואילך 132) שה"ש רבה א-יט וע"ש ביפ"ת 133) לקח טוב בשלח יד-יד.

The Splitting of the Sea

20

With the crisis behind him, Moshe immersed himself in prayer to Hashem on behalf of the Jewish people. He implored Hashem for guidance and wisdom in dealing with his volatile flock. What was he to tell them? How could he bolster their flagging faith and spirits?[1] In which direction was he to lead them now that they were completely boxed in?[2] With all his heart, he begged Hashem to help the nation He had taken out of Egypt and to show the Egyptians that they were powerless against Him.[3]

Hashem responded to Moshe by telling him there was no need for continued prayer. If anything, Moshe's extended dialogues and prayers were delaying the miraculous salvation of the Jewish people.[4] The outcome had already been determined in the merit of the prayers of the Jewish people themselves[5] and because Hashem had taken

---

1) ספורנו בשלח יד-טו   2) ילקו"ש רלג, ע' פדר"א מב   3) ספר הישר   4) אברבנל
5) מכילתא, שמו"ר כא-א וכו', תרגום יונתן בשלח יד-טו

upon Himself responsibility for the security of the Jewish people.[6]

The sea had been prepared and waiting for this great moment since the six days of creation.[7] All Moshe needed to do was lead the people into the sea, and they would be saved. The sea was awaiting their arrival, and it would not stand in their way.[8] In spite of the few complainers, the Jewish people, at this point, were unified in unquestioning faith, like Avraham when Hashem told him to leave Charan.[9] They would all follow Moshe into the sea, and they would be saved.[10] Only a lack of merits could prevent the destined great miracle from coming to pass, and the Jewish people were not lacking in merit by any means.[11]

The Jewish people had merited the exodus from Egypt for many reasons. The ordained term of exile had expired, but nonetheless they needed to be deemed worthy of redemption. And indeed they were. Their suffering, their anguished outcries to Hashem, their repentance and their familial descent from the Patriarchs all made them worthy of redemption.[12] The kindness and compassion they showed each other in the worst of times also elicited a similar response from Hashem towards them.[13]

Furthermore, the Jewish people represented the three things upon which the world stands—the Torah, which they would accept at Mount Sinai, the divine service, which they would perform through building the Mishkan and sacrificing in it to Hashem, and kindness, which they showed each other in Egypt. This alone made them worthy of being redeemed.[14] The redemption of such a people in such a miraculous fashion as the exodus from Egypt would, of course, bring glory to the Name of Hashem.[15]

By their conduct during the exodus, the Jewish people showed themselves worthy of the miracle of the splitting of the sea. They left Egypt with few provisions on their backs but much faith in their hearts.[16] When the entire encampment, men, women and children, turned back in the direction of Pi Hachiros, the Jewish people again showed their faith in Hashem.[17] The faith of Avraham and his

‎6) רש"י ממכילתא בשלח שם 7) מכילתא שם 8) שם, שמו"ר כא-ב, שם כא-ח 9) שפתי כהן 10) ספורנו בשלח יד-‏
‎טו 11) מלבים שם טו-ה וצ"ל דזכות דם פסח ודם מילה הי' לכפרה או לעצם היציאה אבל להושע בקריעת הים‏
‎הוצרכה אמונתם וכדלקמן ועיין שמו"ר כא-ז 12) ירושלמי תענית א-א 13) שפתי כהן שמות ב-כה, ראה המסופר‏
‎בתדב"א רבה כ"ג וכ"ה 14) מדרש תהלים קיד, מכילתא בשלח טו-יג, רבנו בחיי שם טו-יב 15) שמו"ר א-לו‏
‎וביפ"ת 16) מכילתא 17) שמו"ר כא-ח‏

observance of the *mitzvah* of *bris milah* also worked to the favor of the Jews,[18] as did the merit of the Shevatim.[19]

There is also a specific connection between the merit of the Patriarchs and the splitting of the sea. Avraham split the wood for the Akeidah and Yitzchak allowed himself to be placed upon that wood and sacrificed, thus earning for their descendants the miracle of the splitting of the sea. Yaakov was promised by Hashem that his descendants would spread out in all directions of the world—west, east, north and south. This blessing was symbolized by the splitting of the sea and the spreading out of its waters.[20]

The donations the Jewish people would eventually offer to the Mishkan and the great city of Yerushalayim that they would build and sanctify also added to their merits.[21]

Finally, as with the exodus, the Jewish people would have the sea split for them simply because this spectacular miracle would bring everlasting glory to the Name of Hashem.[22]

The Command to Split the Sea

As the sixth day of the exodus drew to a close, Hashem commanded Moshe to be prepared to part the waters of the sea and lead the Jewish people across on the dry seabed.[23] Moshe alone was worthy of performing such a great miracle,[24]* and he would perform this spectacular feat without the assistance of his supernatural staff. The staff had been created for the sole purpose of inflicting the wonders and plagues on Egypt, as was indicated by the words דצ״ך עד״ש באח״ב engraved upon it, and its mission had been accomplished.[25]

Moreover, Hashem wanted to reaffirm the greatness of Moshe in the eyes of the Jewish people. Some of the more mean-spirited

---

* Moshe had not administered the plagues associated with water because he had been saved by the water. Similarly, he could have thought that someone else should split the sea. (*Yefei To'ar*)

---

18) מכילתא   19) מכילתא, גם במדרש תהלים קיד (וכן בילקו״ש) נצרפו הכתוב דהים ראה וינוס למד״כ וינס החוצה ועז״א מה ראה ארונו של יוסף ראה   20) שמו״ר כא-ח ובמבמדרה״ר, מכילתא, ילקו״ש רלג, יש שרמזו במה שנאמר ביעקב ופרצת וגו׳ דימה רומז על הים וצפונה על בעל צפון וקדמה על הרוח קדים   21) דעת זקנים בשלח יד-טז עפ״י   מכילתא   22) מכילתא   23) מכילתא   24) בשלח יד-טז ויקרא רבה א-ה, בתורה שלמה בשלח טו-כ מובא ילקוט מעין גנים שבתחילה סרב משה לקרוע את הים באמרו לאחיו הגדול והשיבו השי״ת כי כבר נתכבד אהרן בענני הכבוד   25) שפתי כהן בשלח יד-טז

Jews had been heard to grumble, "If only I had Moshe's staff I could perform the same feats. What's so outstanding about him?" At the splitting of the sea, when they beheld Moshe set aside the supernatural staff and part the waters with his hand, they would understand that Moshe was indeed outstanding.[26]

Moshe was to lift the staff towards the sky, and a ferocious wind would come howling from the east. Then as the east wind roiled and churned the waters of the sea, Moshe was to set aside his staff. He was to stretch his bare hand over the waters—and they would part before him! The dry seabed would appear, flanked by two towering walls of water. The Jewish people would pass in safety.[27]

The Egyptians were back to their old denials of Hashem, and therefore, Hashem would harden their hearts for the last time. He would give them the rash confidence to pursue the Jewish people. The Egyptians would drown in the sea, and the greatness of Hashem would be manifest to the entire world for all time.[28] The only reason the Jewish people were in their present predicament was to help set the scene for the dazzling spectacle that would destroy the Egyptians once and for all.[29]

Final Judgment Is Passed

The sixth day of the exodus ended on a note of high drama and expectancy. The Jewish people with their backs to the sea faced the snarling Egyptian multitudes intent on their destruction. Hundreds of years of exile and a year of belligerent confrontation would reach their shattering climax in this desolate place. There was a sense of foreboding and doom in the air, but whose doom would it be?

At this very time, the Heavenly Court was in session.[30] Samael, the prosecuting angel, stood before Hashem together with Rahav, the ministering angel of the sea.

"The Jewish people are not worthy of being saved from the sea," Samael declared. "They are guilty of idol worship!"

Hashem defended the Jewish people. They had never worshipped idols as a rebellious act against Hashem. They had done it under duress of their taskmasters, and they did not deserve to be

---

26) ראה שמו"ר כא-א-ט במהרז"ו, תוס' עה"ת, רבנו בחיי חזקוני בשלח יד-טז, רוקח מביא שנצטווה להכותה אי לא בקע וע' לקמן המסופר בשעת קריעתה 27) אברבנל וספורנו בשלח יד-טז, וע"ע באב"ע 28) לקח טוב, שפתי כהן, ומלבים בשלח יד-יז ואילך 29) אב"ע שם 30) רמב"ן ורבנו בחיי שם יד-טו ואילך

judged as deliberate violators. Hashem, therefore, decreed that the Jewish people would pass through the sea in safety while their Egyptian pursuers perished by drowning.[31]

"But I sense a spirit of judgment not directed at the Egyptians," Samael protested. "This judgment is surely directed at the Jews."

There was indeed another pending judgment related to the events at the sea, but it was not against the Jewish people. It was against Iyov, the former advisor of Pharaoh. Hashem gave Iyov into Samael's hands, not to be killed but to be subjected to a life of suffering. When the salvation of the Jewish people would be complete, Samael would be required to relinquish Iyov.[32]

Uzah, the ministering angel of Egypt, now spoke in defense of the Egyptians. "Hashem, You are a righteous God," he said. "You are fair and incorruptible. Why condemn the Egyptians to death by drowning? The Egyptians paid their debt to the Jewish people. Why punish them further?"

In response to Uzah's words, Hashem gathered all the hosts of the heavens and ministering angels of all the nations of the world. He recounted the events that had led up to the present situation.

The Jewish people had first gone down to Egypt during the Great Famine in the time of Yosef. Arriving in the country as honored guests, relatives of the viceroy who had saved Egypt and made it powerful, they were slowly drawn into forced labor and slavery. They were forced to build cities for the Egyptians, and later, decrees were passed to have all Jewish male children drowned.

The Jewish people wept and cried out in pain to Hashem, and He answered their pleas. He sent Moshe and Aharon as His emissaries to Pharaoh to demand the release of the Jews. Pharaoh rejected their demands and arrogantly stated, "Who is Hashem? I don't know Hashem!" Hashem sent plagues upon Egypt until he finally released them. But now he has become stubborn again. He is pursuing the Jewish people with the intent of bringing them back to Egypt.

Hashem now put the question to the hosts of the heavens and the ministering angels. Did the Egyptians deserve to drown in the sea?

"Yes!" they declared in unison. "Death to the Egyptians."

---

31) ילקו"ש רלד, מעם לועז, ע"ע זוה"ק תרומה קע ושכל טוב יד-כא   32) שמו"ר כא-ז ביפ"ת ומהרז"ו, ע"ע לקח טוב וארא ז-ה

"Please have pity on the Egyptians," Uzah began to plead. "I admit that the Jewish people deserve their freedom, but let the Egyptians live. They will cause no more trouble for the Jewish people."

While Uzah was speaking, the angel Michael sent the angel Gavriel down to Egypt. Gavriel dismantled a wall in a certain building and took out one particular brick. He brought this brick up to Heaven and laid it before the Heavenly Court.

"Look at this brick," Gavriel said. "Within this brick lies the body of a young Jewish baby plastered by the Egyptians into the walls of a building. Does such a nation deserve to be spared?"

The hosts of the heavens and the ministering angels of the nations of the world reaffirmed their judgment against the Egyptians, and their fate was sealed.[33] The death sentence on the Egyptians was ultimately sealed because they were hardened sinners, particularly with regard to eight specific crimes. They were idol worshippers. They were adulterers. They were murderers. They desecrated the Name of Hashem. They had a corrupt court system. They were slanderers. They used profane language. They were arrogant.[34]

"Since the judgment against the Egyptians has been finalized," the angel Gavriel insisted, "they should be destroyed right away."

Hashem, however, did not want to destroy them during the night. He wanted to wait until the early morning hours, the exact time at which Avraham had set out to take Yitzchak to the Akeidah. In Avraham's merit, the power of the Egyptians would be crushed forever.[35]

Now that the matter was resolved, the angels wanted to sing Shirah, a special song of praise to Hashem on the occasion of the destruction of the Egyptians.

"How can you say Shirah when My handiworks are drowning in the sea?" Hashem said. Although the Egyptians deserved to die, what was about to happen was still a tragedy, and the accompaniment of songs was not appropriate.[36]

---

33) רש״י מכילתא שם יד-יט, ילקו״ש רמג, בראשית רבה לה-ג, מעם לועז (34 תדב״א רבה טו, ע״ש בזקוקין דגם במצרים מצינו כולם זולת ג״ע, אף דמצרים נקראת ערות הארץ ואי׳ שהיתה שטופי זימה לא מצינו כן מפורש בסיפור גלותנו ויתכן להחשיב לחטוא זה במה שהמיתו הזכרים בלבד בגלל שרצו לקחת אידך לגרמייהו, ובעצם צ״ע הלא אבי המגדף שבא על שלומית בת דברי עול בזה וצ״ל דלא היה חטא בתור עם (35 ילקו״ש רלה 36) מגילה י:, ע׳ לקמן ריש פרק כ״א

Protection in the Night

Once the Heavenly Court passed final judgment on the Egyptians, the final stages of the drama began to unfold. Moshe stretched out his staff towards the sky, and an east wind began to blow. It would not stop blowing for the rest of this eventful night.[37] This was a supernatural wind, a raging wind Hashem sends to destroy the evil. The evil people of the generation of the Great Flood, the Dor Hahaflagah and Sedom all fell victim to this raging wind. It also carried the plague of locusts into Egypt.[38] For the Jewish people, on the other hand, it presented itself as warm and temperate, a comfortable breeze.[39]* This wind would prepare the waters for Moshe's miraculous feat of splitting the sea.[40] It would also dupe Pharaoh into thinking that the parting of the waters was a natural phenomenon and that there was no reason to fear following the Jewish people onto the seabed.[41]

While the wind blew, angels descended from Heaven and moved the pillar clouds and the pillar of fire from the front of the Jewish encampment to the rear, where they would serve as a barrier against the approaching Egyptians.[42] These pillars would initiate the downfall of the Egyptians.[43]

In their new position, the cloud pillars served as a barrier against the Egyptian attackers[44] and a shield against their missiles and projectiles.[45] Considering the vast numerical superiority of the Egyptians, they could have buried the Jewish people even by throwing clods of earth.[46] The cloud pillars plunged the Egyptians into total darkness, preventing them from seeing the Jews and the Jews from seeing them.[47]

This darkness was really an extension of the ninth plague to which Egypt had been subjected, the plague of darkness. Unlike the other plagues which had lasted for seven days, the darkness had only lasted for six days. The remainder of the plague had been held in abeyance until the nocturnal confrontation between the Jewish people and their Egyptian pursuers on the shores of the sea. Now, as

---

* It was a cold wind that eventually froze the waters. (Malbim 14: 21)

37) ע' אברבנל וספורנו בשלח יד-טז, שם יד-כא, וע"ע דאברהם בן הרמב"ם שם 38) מכילתא 39) לקח טוב בראשית מא-ו, ע' רש"י גיטן לא: 40) ספורנו בשלח יד-טז ואילך, וע"ש ברמב"ן ורלב"ג 41) רמב"ן בשלח יד-כא, ראה ספר החינוך מצוה קל"ב 42) רמב"ן וספורנו בשלח יד-יט, בהדר זקנים כתוב שהיה האש לפניהם 43) בראשית רבה לה-ג ובמתני"כ, וע' אב"ע 44) רש"י ממכילתא יתרו יט-ד 45) רש"י ממכילתא בשלח יד-יט 46) מעם ליעז בשלח טו-א 47) רש"י ממכילתא בשלח יד-יט וכו', שפתי כהן שם

earlier, the Egyptians were immobilized in their positions by the darkness. Those standing remained standing, those sitting remained sitting. They saw nothing, not even the person right next to them.[48]

The pillar of fire also served as a barrier against Egyptian penetration to the Jewish encampment.[49] It also provided bright illumination for the Jewish people, but because of the cloud pillars behind it, it left the Egyptians in total darkness.[50] Nevertheless, in the midst of their inky darkness, Hashem allowed the Egyptians a miraculous glimpse of the Jewish people eating, drinking and rejoicing in their well-lit encampment. This was one of fifty miracles performed by Hashem at the sea.[51]

With the rear of the Jewish encampment secured against attack by the Egyptians, the Jewish people were now ready to cross the sea calmly and safely. Even though it was dark, the pillar of fire gave them more illumination than they would need.[52]

Into the Sea

In the middle of the night, the Jewish people were already preparing to cross the Yam Suf. In reality, they could just as well have circled around the south shore of the Yam Suf and continued on in the direction of Eretz Yisrael, but Hashem wanted the Jewish people to lure their Egyptian pursuers into the sea.[53]

Now, as they stood on the shores of the sea, a new question arose. Who would have the honor of being the first to enter the sea? There was, of course, enough room in the Yam Suf for all the Jewish people to descend at once, but the honorary "first step" was the issue. Who would take it?[54]

"We should be first, because Reuven was the firstborn," said the people of Shevet Reuven.

"No, we should be first," said the people of Shevet Yehudah. "We are the most distinguished among the tribes, the providers of the future kings of Eretz Yisrael."

"No, we should be first," said the people of Shevet Levi. "We have been sanctified to perform the divine service in the Beis Hamikdash."

"No, we should be first," said the people of Shevet Zevulun and

Shevet Naphtali. "We were blessed to inherit our portions in Eretz Yisrael near the sea. Therefore, we should be the first to go into the sea."

A heated argument broke out amongst the tribes, and in the midst of the quarrel Binyamin spoke up.

"Hashem told Moshe to tell the Bnei Yisrael, the children of Yisrael, to go into the sea. Now, who are most appropriately considered the children of Yisrael? Certainly it is Binyamin. When all the other tribes were born, their father's name was still Yaakov. When our ancestor Binyamin was born, however, his name had already been changed to Yisrael. Furthermore, our tribe brought up the rear during our travels, while Yehudah was in front. But when we turned around to go back to Pi Hachiros, we assumed the forward position. Therefore, we should be the first to enter the sea."

Without waiting for a response, the tribe of Binyamin ran to the stormy sea.[55] The other tribes were incensed at the audacity of Binyamin's action, and the tribes of Yehudah, Zevulun and Naphtali actually pelted them with stones. They felt that Hashem had commanded the Jewish people to enter the sea only after it had already split to show that the miracle was intended to punish the Egyptians rather than to save drowning Jews. Binyamin had therefore violated the commandment and deserved to be pelted. A major uproar ensued, and Moshe himself had to intervene.[56]

In the meantime, Nachshon the son of Aminadav from the tribe of Yehudah sprinted ahead of Binyamin and plunged into the gale-driven waters of the sea, so that his tribe should have the honor of being the first into the sea.[57]

Hashem was pleased that this entire controversy was conducted without personal hatred or animosity. Rather, the foremost interest of each tribe was to glorify Hashem and sanctify His Name. Therefore, Hashem rewarded the tribe of Binyamin with the honor of having the Holy of Holies of the Beis Hamikdash in his territory and Yehudah with the hereditary monarchy and the rest of the Beis Hamikdash.[58]

According to another version of this incident, the question

---

55) סוטה לז ובעיון יעקב, מכילתא, מעם לועז, ברי״ף על עין יעקב מפורש שנקודת פלוגדת היתה מי יזכה
להוליך את עצמותיו של יוסף לתוך הים (ע׳ דבר נפלא בגודל הזכות בתפארת שלמה פ׳ בשלח), ראה בתרגום על
בראשית מט-יג וגם על דברים לג-כג, פנים יפות בשלח יד-כב, רד״ל בפדר״א מב, מרכבת המשנה על המכילתא
56) ע׳ מעם לועז 57) ליתר הפרטים ראה במכילתא, פדר״א מב, מדרש תהלים עו-קיד, רש״י תהלים סח-כח, מדרש
הלל, שמו״ר כא-י, רבנו בחיי בשלח יד-טו 58) מכילתא ילקוט בשלח רלד ובתהלים תשצט סוטה רש״י סוטה לז.
במדב״ר יג-ז.

was who would be bold enough to jump into the water first. Some lacked sufficient faith to jump into the stormy waters, while others thought Hashem wanted them to enter the sea only after it split.

While the tribes stood alongside the sea paralyzed by indecision, Nachshon the son of Aminadav from the tribe of Yehudah leaped into the stormy waters.[59] The rest of the tribe of Yehudah immediately followed suit, as did many of the people from the other tribes. They began to walk straight ahead into the Yam Suf until the waters reached their mouths and nostrils and they could not continue to travel any further.

"We are drowning in the sea," the Jewish people began to pray. "We cannot go any further."

The giant waves of the storm-tossed sea were breaking all around them, and some of the less stouthearted were beginning to retreat to the shore.

Moshe began to pray to Hashem, but Hashem told him it was not the time for lengthy prayer. The Jews were on the verge of drowning, and the situation called for decisive action. Moshe was to stretch his hand out over the sea, and it would split open.[60]

Hashem had waited to see an act of faith on the part of the Jewish people, and only then were they deemed worthy of the great miracle of the splitting of the sea.[61*]

The Sea Splits

Moshe approached the sea. "By my authority as a messenger of Hashem, I command you to split at once. Part your waters and open a path upon which the Jewish people can cross through your midst."

"I am not required to obey you," the sea replied. "I am greater and older than you, for I was created on the third day, while you were created on the sixth."[62]

"The sea will not split for me," Moshe cried out to Hashem.

---

* According to *Yefei To'ar*, "all" the Jewish people were now in the sea. According to others, those with insufficient faith waited until the sea split. (*Reishis Chachmah* *ahavah*, 8)

---

59) מכילתא וסוטה שם 60) מכילתא, הדר זקנים יד-טו, במדרש תהלים קיד איתא שרק כף רגלם נכנסו ומיד נבקע, ראה גם רש"י יחזקאל מז-ג 61) מהרז"ו בשמו"ר כא-י, ע' ראשית חכמה אהבה ח 62) שמו"ר יא-ו ובמהרז"ו, מדרש ויושע, ומבואר שעצם הבקיעה נעשתה ע"י פרישת ידיו, והרוח גרם היבשה כשעמדו המים על שני הצדדים

Hashem told Moshe that if the sea refused to obey he should strike like a teacher who strikes an inattentive student. Moshe struck the sea, but it still refused to obey.[63]

"There is an idol worshipper among you," said the sea. "His name is Michah, and he presently has an idol with him. The Jewish people do not deserve that I should part for them if they have idol worshippers among them."[64*]

Moshe used all his powers of persuasion to convince the sea to part. He showed the sea his staff with Hashem's Name engraved on it. But the sea refused to part. He told the sea about the merits the Jewish people had earned through the *mitzvah* of *bris milah*. But the sea refused to part. He showed the sea the casket of Yosef who had overcome human nature and resisted the temptation to sin. But the sea still would not part.[65]

Moshe asked Hashem to help him accomplish this seemingly impossible feat. Hashem placed His right Hand on Moshe's right hand, so to speak, and Moshe once again addressed the sea.

"By the word of Hashem," Moshe said, "He has commanded you to part, because ever since the six days of creation, your existence has been conditional on your parting before the Jewish people on this night. You have no choice in the matter."

Moshe removed his staff from his hand, as Hashem had earlier instructed him to do, and lifted his hand very high in full view of everyone. When the sea saw Moshe standing there with his hand outstretched and the Hand of Hashem resting upon him, it trembled and parted at once.[66]

With a thunderous wrenching sound, an opening appeared in the surface of the sea as it began to spread itself apart. The opening grew deeper and deeper until the sea floor was exposed, and a

---

* Some suggest that the sea refused to part because it was not blocking the way of the Jewish people. They could have gone along the southern shore of the sea and continued on straight to Eretz Yisrael. (*Alshich*)

63) פסיקתא חדתא, מדרש ויושע (64 מעם לועז, במצרים הי׳ אמונת ישראל חזקה ויש להבין מהיכן למד מיכה ככה ומאיפה נטלו, באדרת אליהו האזינו מפורש ש׳׳והמים להם חמה״ קאי אשורש חטאו שכבר היה נטוע בו מחשבתו אז אולם פסל לא היה בידו וי״מ שהיה אתו הכסף לקנותה, ע׳ פדר״א וברד״ל, שמו״ר מא-א וברד״ל, שמו״ר כד-א, תנחומא כי תשא ובעץ יופס ויד יוסף, ירושלמי סוכה ד-ג (65 פדר״א מב, ע׳ תנחומא נשא ל ובראשית רבה פז-י שטען הים לעצמו כשם שהתגבר יוסף על טבעו כך אני אלך נגד טבעי, ברד״ל על פדר״א שם וכב מפורש במדרש תהלים קיד דכשראה משה מטה משה לא רצה לקיים ציווי יען וזה יהיה המטה שיכה את הסלע שאמר לו ד׳ שרק ידבר אליו (66 מדרש הגדול בשלח יד-כז, בראשית רבה ה-ה, זוה״ק בשלח מט, שמו״ר כא-ג, שם כא-י, ע׳ חולין ז., מכילתא ר׳ אפרים, רד״ק על תהלים קיד

tremendous crash was heard around the world. The ear-splitting sound struck terror in the hearts of all who heard it.[67] The displaced waters swelled upwards in two gigantic waves on either side of the exposed sea floor. Then the two waves hardened into solid walls flanking the path that had formed on the seabed.[68]

"Why did you not part for me right away?" Moshe asked the sea after it had finally parted. "I commanded you to part in the Name of Hashem. I told you of the merits of the Jewish people. I showed you the holy staff. And yet you did not part. Why did you part now?"

"I did not flee before you," the sea replied. "I fled and parted my waters when I saw the vision of the Creator of the Universe, the God of Yaakov."[69]

The people around the world not only heard the sounds of the splitting of the sea, but they were also granted an actual view of some of the manifestations of this miracle. For at the moment the sea split, all the waters of the world also split and began to flow towards the sea. Water in springs, lakes, caves, ditches and pits in the ground split into two. Water in barrels, pitchers and glasses split into two. Ships on the water were thrown by the force of the splitting waters.[70]

The Jewish People Enter the Sea

The courageous Jews who had plunged into the sea were now relieved by the splitting of the sea. The less stouthearted Jews now joined them on the dry seabed.[71] All the Jewish people now moved into the sea, with the tribe of Dan bringing up the rear. Michah was the last of the tribe of Dan to enter the sea.[72] Moshe waited at the entrance to the sea, as a symbol of protection against the approaching Egyptians, until every single Jew had entered into the corridor of the parted sea. Only then did he allow himself to join them.[73]

The wind was still blowing ferociously as the Jewish people began stepping into the sea.[74] The sea had only split in front of the

---

67) מדרש ויושע בפסוק אמר, מעם לועז בשלח טו-א 68) ריב"ש ואברבנל בשלח יד-כא 69) מכילתא עפ"י תהלים קיד 70) מכילתא, שכל טוב בשלח יד-כא, בעה"ט שם, בתולדות יצחק מבואר דזה היה מחוקי הנס יען וכל מימי העולם תחת שר אחד בשמים וכידוע ממהר"ל שגם לנסים יש סדר 71) מהרש"א סוטה לז., קול אליהו בשלח יד-כב 72) קול אליהו שם 73) אברבנל בשלח יד-יט 74) אב"ע בשם יד-כא

shore, but as the Jewish people walked further into the sea, it kept opening before them until they reached the point of exit.[75]

The unfolding miracle of the splitting sea also affected the condition of the ground upon which the Jewish people trod. At first, it was still damp and muddy from the wetness of the water, but as the night wore on the situation improved.[76] However, not knowing what was coming, the people of the tribe of Reuven were exasperated that they had to walk in mud.

"Do you see this?" they called out to the people of Shimon. "Hashem can cause the waters to part, but He cannot make dry ground! We have gone from the lime of Egypt to the mud of the sea."

This gross lack of faith could have caused them all to drown, but Hashem forgave them in order to glorify His Name before the entire world.[77]

As the Jewish people trudged down the damp and muddy incline into the sea, the east wind continued to blow, and a change began to take place in the condition of the ground. The stormy waters settled into the depths and were congealed by the wind into a smooth, glassy but not slippery surface.[78] Two thirds of the waters of the sea were contained in this thick floor. The other third formed two crystalline walls on either side.

The total effect was to raise the level of the sea floor on which the Jewish people were walking almost to land level. The Jewish people would walk for a short distance down the incline of the seabed. Then they would walk straight across over the frozen water that filled the deepest part of the sea until they reached the point of exit. By doing this, Hashem had created a comfortable path for the Jewish people. He had eliminated the need for them to descend all the way to the bottom of the sea and then to climb all the way back up to the shore.[79]

The walls of hardened water that flanked the path through the sea rose to greater heights than the highest mountains on the land.[80*]

---

* Some suggest that the sea rose 600 *mil*, while others suggest it rose 1,600 *mil*, over 900 miles. (*Midrash, Vayosha*)

---

75) ע' מלכים בשלח יד-כב, ומעם לעז בשלח טו-א   76) ילקו"ש רלד ובזית רענן, ראה רש"י נח ח-יג ובמעם לועז נס החמישי   77) מדרש תהלים קו, מדרש הגדול בשלח יד-כא   78) ספורנו בשלח יד-טז, שם יד-כא, ע"ע רבנו בחיי וטור עה"ת   79) ע' מדרש תהלים קיד, חזקוני ומלבים יד-כא וכו', מדרש אגדה, דעת זקנים טו-ח, במדבר רבה ט-יד, פיוט לאחרון של פסח, ראה גם מעם לועז בשלח טו-א ובענף יוסף דמבאר שיטת הגר"א מדוע לא נקרע כי אם שליש העליון בלבד   80) תרגום יונתן בשלח יד-כב, ראה גם סוטה לד. מה שאיתא בירדן

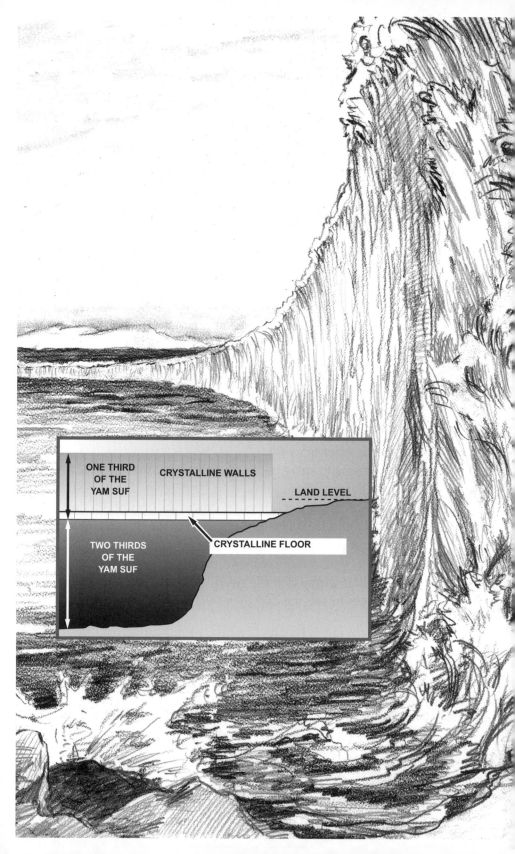

ONE THIRD OF THE YAM SUF

CRYSTALLINE WALLS

LAND LEVEL

TWO THIRDS OF THE YAM SUF

CRYSTALLINE FLOOR

All the world marveled at the magnificent sight of the erect walls of
water standing motionless like mountains of bricks.[81] And the
knowledge that this great miracle had been performed for the Jewish people caused the nations of the world to view them with fear
and respect.[82]

From the very top of the wall of water, the angel Gavriel kept a
protective eye on the Jewish people crossing the sea. He also kept a
wary eye on the water in case the sea, because of its grievance
against the idol-carrying Michah, reconsidered its decision to allow
the Jewish people to pass through in safety.[83]

The Jewish people were surrounded by the sea on all four sides,
and Gavriel exhorted each of the sides to maintain its protection of
the Jewish people. The right side should protect them because they
would accept the Torah from the right Hand of Hashem and because
of the *mitzvah* of *mezuzah* which is affixed to the right doorpost. The
left side should protect them because of the *tefillin* they will wear on
their left arms. The front side should protect them because of the
mitzvah of *bris milah* that is in front of each and every Jew.[84] The rear
side should protect them because of the *kesher shel tefillin*, the knot of
the *tefillin* that lies on the nape of the neck, and because of the *tzitzis*
that are worn on their backs.[85]

Hashem had granted the Jewish people this great miracle
because of these merits, and now the sea as well would control its
wrath and maintain its protection because of these merits.[86]

Therefore, in order to recall the enveloping protection of the sea
in the merit of *tzitzis*, it is customary to wrap oneself in one's *tallis*
when first putting it on.

---

81) מדרש תמורה באוצר המדרשים תקפב, ר' סעדיא גאון בשלח טו-ח 82) מעם לועז בשלח טו-א 83) ילקו"ש
רלד, מדרש תהלים קיד 84) מכילתא, ילקו"ש רלד, ילקוט מכירי קלו, ע' בעה"ט בשלח טו-א דאז בגימטריה ח'
ורומז על זכות המילה, ע' מנחות מג: 85) מכילתא, ילקו"ש רלד, ילקוט מכירי, תוס' ודעת זקנים בשלח יד-כב
וכו' בפרט בפסוק כט 86) מכילתא בשלח יד-כט, רוקח

Many Miracles in One

The splitting of the sea was a many-faceted miracle, full of miracles within miracles. Basically, however, ten major miracles took place in the sea.[89]

First, Hashem caused the sea to split, not all at once but as a receding fissure that kept opening more and more with every step the Jewish people took into the sea.[90]

Second, the floor of the sea, which was composed of thick ice, was not wet or slippery in any way. The Jewish people were able to walk across it as if they were walking on a smooth road clear of any obstacles or obstructions.[91]

Third, the two walls of water that rose on each side of the opening formed an arch over the Jewish people, so that it was as if they were walking through a tunnel of water that kept them warm and protected from the elements.[92]* The tunnel ran in a semicircle rather than a straight line, so that the Jewish people emerged at a far more distant point on the same shore from which they had entered the sea. They did not cross over to the opposite shore.[93]

Fourth, the water did not just split in half, leaving one path for all the Jewish people. Rather, it split into twelve different lines, with each tribe having its own separate tunnel through which to pass as a family.

Fifth, the walls and floors of each of these tunnels were not just blocks of raw ice. Rather, they were formed in decorative patterns and mosaics of great beauty to give the Jewish people pleasure as they passed through.

Sixth, the frozen walls of salty seawater provided sweet drinking water for any of the Jewish people who were thirsty. Children found trees in the water, as well as honey, oil, apples and pomegranates whenever they felt hungry. Animals also found greenery sprouting from the walls upon which to graze.[94]

---

* It was miraculous to be completely surrounded by formations of ice and still feel warm.

---

89) מכילתא, להמסופר מכאן עד סוף הפרק ימצא המעיין במכילתא ותנחומא בשלח י עפ״י עץ יוסף, שאר כל הפרטים הצגנו קו לקו 90) מלבים בשלח יד-כב 91) מלבים, רבנו בחיי בשלח יד-כא וכו׳ 92) מכילתא בשלח טו-ח, פיה״מ לר״מ אבות ה, גוזי קדם ד 93) פיה״מ לר״מ שם, אב״ע בשלח יד-יז, שם יד-כב, ראה מעם לועז שם טו-ח, פיה״מ לר״מ שם, ילקוט מכירי תהלים עח, מדרש שוח״ט תהלים קיד
א 94) שמו״ר כא-י, ע׳ אדר״נ לג, פיה״מ לר״מ שם,

Seventh, whenever a thirsty Jewish person finished drinking, the walls again solidified, like a flask that was closed after it was used.[95]

Eighth, the ice walls were crystalline and transparent, allowing the people in each tunnel to see into the neighboring tunnel. There were also openings in the walls to allow them to converse with the people in the adjoining tunnels if they found it necessary. The openings also allowed people in different tunnels to sing praises to Hashem together and to feel more secure and relaxed.[96]

Ninth, the dry ground under the Jewish people turned back into boiling mud as soon as the Egyptians arrived.

Tenth, the ice walls disintegrated as soon as the Egyptians arrived, showering them with ice pellets as heavy as stones.

War with Hashem

While the Jewish people were walking through the tunnels in the sea, Pharaoh and the Egyptians were trying to mount an attack from the rear. All through the night, however, the cloud pillars had shielded the Jewish people from the Egyptians. This was about to change.

Pharaoh had been riding a stallion, but as the expected confrontation drew closer, he chose a mare instead. He explained to his officers that he was afraid the stallion, being male, might be too powerful, and in a melee, it might inadvertently kill its rider. He was also afraid, he further explained, that the stallion would be more difficult to control than the female mare, and if the situation became exceedingly dangerous, the stallion was more likely to bolt and run.

However, these were not his true motives in changing horses. Pharaoh had declared war on Hashem, and while riding his stallion, he had seen a vision of Hashem on a stallion. This seemed to signify that he would have no advantage in the battle. Pharaoh, therefore, decided to ride a mare, but he immediately saw a vision of Hashem on a mare. Pharaoh then tried a red, a black and a white horse, but each time, the vision showed Hashem on a similar horse.[97]

Forgetting about his choice of horses, Pharaoh began to shoot arrows at the Jewish encampment. Hashem intercepted the arrows

---

95) ע' מכילתא, שכל טוב בשלח טו-ח, אדר"נ לג 96) פדר"א מב, ילקוט מכירי קלו, מדרש תהלים קלו, מדרש
ויושע בפסוק וברוח וגו' 97) מדרש תהלים יח, שה"ש רבה א-ט ובעץ יוסף, מדרש הגדול בשלח יד-כג

with the cloud pillars and hurled them back at Pharaoh. Pharaoh threw stones and missiles, but these too were intercepted and returned. He had his trumpeters make a loud commotion intended to frighten the enemy camp, but the sounds were absorbed by the cloud pillars. In return, Hashem bombarded the Egyptians with thunder and lightning. Whatever Pharaoh tried was neutralized or intercepted and turned against him. The time had come to teach Pharaoh and the Egyptians a final lesson.[98]

The Eleventh Plague

The Egyptians had already endured ten plagues in Egypt, and now, by the sea, they would be subjected to many more plagues and wonders. Altogether, there were fifty miracles performed against the Egyptians.[99] The fifty plagues visited on the Egyptians by the sea all fell into the general categories of the ten plagues visited on Egypt, just as the darkness which affected the Egyptians in the beginning of the night was reminiscent of the plague of darkness in Egypt.[100]

In a certain way, however, all these fifty plagues were different facets of one final, spectacular plague, the eleventh plague which was, by far, the greatest of them all.[101]

According to some opinions in the Talmud, the number of plagues is greater than fifty, but only because additional subdivisions are included.[102] Rabbi Yosi derives the number fifty from the phrasing of the Torah. The plague lice was said to have been administered by "the Finger of Hashem," while the wonders by the sea are attributed to "the Hand of Hashem." Therefore, since a hand is five times a finger, the miracles by the sea were five times those in Egypt—in other words, fifty.[103] Rabbi Eliezer agrees with this reasoning. However, he considers each plague to have been fourfold, since it originated from four different attributes of divine wrath and affected the four fundamental forms of matter—fire (energy), air (gasses), water (liquids) and earth (solids). According to this calculation, there were forty plagues in Egypt and two hundred by the sea.

98) מדרש תהלים יח 99) מכילתא, מדרש תהלים עח 100) פיה"מ לר"מ אבות ה 101) פיוט לאחרון של פסח 102) כ"ה בהגדה וגם במדרש תהלים 103) מדרש תהלים, בבעה"ט וארא ז-טז איתא בפנים אחרת, ע' כל בו, בתרגום יונתן בראשית טו-יד איתא שהיו ר"נ מכות, מפיוט לאחרון ש"פ ג"כ מבואר שהחמשה היו כלולים במכה אחת במלואים לתורה שלמה בשלח ו מפורטות כמה חשבונות לחלק מכה אחת מהשי"ת לכמה מכות כלפי אותם שהוכו בהן

Rabbi Akiva takes Rabbi Eliezer's reasoning one step further by adding an attribute of divine wrath and considering the simultaneous affliction of all four forms as a fifth form. Accordingly, there were fifty plagues in Egypt and two hundred and fifty by the sea. Others calculate two hundred and fifty plagues by adding the two hundred and forty-eight organs which endured the plagues, the coldness of the ice and the heat of the water.[104]

No matter how the calculations are made, however, it seems clear that the affliction of the Egyptians by the sea was greater than the affliction in Egypt. The Egyptians had not learned their lesson. They had witnessed all the miracles and wonders Hashem had performed in Egypt, and still, they insisted on rebelling against Him. For this they deserved the greatest punishment.[105]

The Egyptians Enter the Sea

As the night drew to a close, the Egyptians reached the shores of the sea in their pursuit of the Jewish people. They saw before them a straight trodden path, and correctly assuming that this was the escape route of the Jewish people, they plunged into it without much consideration of the consequences.[106]

The morning of the seventh day of the exodus was about to break. The fateful hours during which Hashem punishes the wicked were fast arriving. These hours were also well-suited for the salvation of the righteous who spend the night studying Torah and serving Him.[107] Furthermore, Avraham had risen to travel to the Akeidah during these hours and thereby caused them to become a favorable time for his descendants.[108] The destruction of the Egyptians was about to begin.

As the Egyptians entered the sea, the thundering sounds of their onslaught reached the Jewish people who were walking ahead and frightened them so badly that many fainted away.

In Heaven, a large multitude of avenging angels appealed to Hashem to allow them to destroy the Egyptian armies, but Hashem refused. Hashem wanted to avenge Himself personally on the Egyptians for the suffering they had caused the Jewish people for so many years.[109]

---

104) מעשה ד' עה"ת פרק א 105) הגדת ליל שימרים 106) מלבים בשלח יד-כג 107) ר' אפרים עה"ת שם יד-כז 108) מכילתא, מדרש הגדול שם יד-כד 109) מחזור ויטרי דף רצג, מדרש הגדול בשלח יד-כה, מדרש וישע בפסוק מרכבות וגו', שפתי כהן

Meanwhile, in the lingering pre-dawn darkness, the Egyptian pursuers were still unaware that they had left the relative safety of dry land and were penetrating deeper into the sea. Ahead of them, the fire pillar and the cloud pillars that escorted and directed the Jewish people on their travels drew back and moved towards the Egyptians. The path of the Jewish people was clearly defined by the walls of frozen water, and the pillars could be used for other purposes.[110]

The approach of the pillars frightened the Egyptians.[111] The howling east wind had fallen silent as the night came to a close, but in the shadowy confines of the path beneath the sea, the Egyptians had not grasped the significance of the sudden silence. Now, in the light of the approaching pillar of fire, they looked up at the cliffs of water that rose on either side of them, and couldn't understand where they were.[112]

The thought crossed their minds that they were actually inside the sea, but they rejected it.[113] The thought was simply too horrible to consider. Perhaps they were on an island, they thought.[114] And even if they were indeed inside the sea, perhaps this was all a natural phenomenon caused by the fierce east wind and they would still have time to retrace their steps to safety once their business was done.[115] Even in this perilous situation, it did not occur to the Egyptians to break off their pursuit of the Jewish people. They still remained focused on their objective of destroying the Jewish people and carrying back the spoils.[116]

The foolish reasoning of the Egyptians was nothing short of miraculous. Faced with the prospect of the sea falling on their heads and drowning them, the Egyptians insisted on a grand self-delusion that would lead to their destruction. They had deluded the Jewish people into slavery, and now measure for measure, they would themselves be deluded into rushing recklessly to their destruction in the bowels of the sea.[117]

---

110) ריב"ש וחזקוני בשלח יד-כד   111) רש"י ממכילתא בשלח שם, ע' אב"ע על אתר ולעיל בפסוק יט דהיה מלאך   112) פדר"א מב, לקח טוב בשלח יד-כג   113) אברבנל וחזקוני שם, מלבים בשלח יד-יט ואילך   114) ע' רש"י מכילתא ומלבים בשלח טו-ח   115) רמב"ן ושפתי כהן שם טו-ט   116) מושב זקנים בשלח יד-כה, מדרש אגדה בשלח טו-ט, ראה מכילתא, רמב"ן, וספורנו, כתב הרוקח בשלח טו-ה דגם המצרים חלקו את עצמם לי"ב כתות וכו"א הלך באחד מהי"ב שבילים   117) מכילתא בשלח טו-ט דזה פי' נערמו מים והיא מדה במדה למ"ש הבה נתחכמה לו, ע' מכילתא בשלח טו-ח וגם במעם לועז שם טו-ה

The Destruction of the Egyptians Begins

The pillar of fire that had revealed to the Egyptians that they had entered the sea now began to ensure that they would never leave it. The heat radiated by the pillar of fire began to melt the frozen walls, and icy water showered the stunned Egyptians. Chunks of ice fell away from the crumbling walls and pummeled the Egyptians on their heads.

The Egyptians reeled back in horror as the frozen sea began to disintegrate before them. They reined in their horses and tried to turn back, but another miracle prevented their retreat. The image of a mare appeared in the cloud formation and lured all the Egyptian stallions towards it. The mare then turned and ran into the depths of the sea, causing all the stallions to give chase.[118] The Egyptians were amazed at the strange behavior of their horses, who normally had an aversion to water.[119] They whipped their horses in a frantic attempt to gain control, but it was no use.[120] Against their will, the Egyptians were being hurtled into a dark world punctuated by eerie beams of light and filled with unknown terrors.[121]

Having destabilized the frozen walls, the pillar of fire began to boil the frozen ground of the path beneath the sea, scalding the hooves of the horses and throwing them into a panic.[122] Complete pandemonium broke out. Horses reared up and tumbled to the ground. Other horses toppled over the fallen horses, and the disoriented Egyptian riders were thrown into the churning tangle of human and animal limbs.[123]

Miraculously, hot coals appeared on the floor of the sea and set fire to the chariot wheels, while ministering angels removed a single wheel from each chariot. The unbalanced chariots, with their burning wheels and their panic-crazed horses, careened uncontrollably in all directions. Everywhere, chariots were collapsing, and their riders were thrown free, crushing and breaking their bodies.[124] As the chariots burned, the weapons of the Egyptians were also consumed by the

---

118) לקח טוב בשלח יד-כג, מלבים שם יד-יט, ע' שמו״ר כג-יד, רבנו בחיי בשלח טו-א 119) שכל טוב 120) רבנו
בחיי בשלח טו-א, שמו״ר כג-ד 121) ר' אברהם בן הרמב״ם בשלח יד-כד 122) רש״י ממכילתא בשלח יד-כד
123) רש״י ממכילתא, שכל טוב וריב״א בשלח יד-כד וכו' 124) רש״י ממכילתא, תולדות יצחק, פענח רזא, תרגום
יונתן שם

flames, and the jewels and treasures they had brought with them were scattered on the bottom of the sea.[125]

In this scene of mass confusion, the cloud pillars dissolved the floor of the sea path and turned it into thick, gelatinous mud. The thick mud caused every chariot to become bogged down, and a massive traffic jam ensued.[126] Some enterprising Egyptians attempted to extricate themselves by removing all the wheels of their chariots and converting them into improvised mud sleds. But this did not do them much good, since the path was thoroughly clogged with stalled vehicles. In the rear of the Egyptian column, some of the chariots that were just entering the sea foundered on the mud, and their riders drowned in the shallow water.[127]

Many of the Egyptians who had penetrated into the depths of the sea realized the gravity and desperation of their situation.[128] They decided to abandon their chariots and retreat on foot, but this too was impossible. The mud was so deep that it was impossible to make any progress through it.[129] The Egyptians were being punished severely through mud, as measure for measure, for forcing the Jewish people to labor with bricks and clay.[130]

In their state of utter confusion, Hashem brought additional plagues upon the Egyptians in the sea. Sickness and pestilence immobilized them.[131] The remnants of the fearless locust that had attacked the Egyptians in Egypt were waiting patiently to attack them again.[132]

Thunder and lightning ripped through the somber skies, striking terror into the hearts of the trapped Egyptians. Rain, hail and hot coals pelted the Egyptians from above. The waters of the sea began to percolate, and hot coals fell everywhere. The Egyptians did nothing. There was nothing they could do.[133] The fiery plagues which the Egyptians suffered at the sea and in Egypt were symbolic of the fires of Gehinnom.[134]

Hashem also afflicted the Egyptians and their horses at the sea with five plagues that were distinctly theirs. They were afflicted with numbness of the heart, total confusion, eyes that receded into

125) מכילתא, רבנו בחיי שם 126) רש״י ממכילתא, ספורנו בשלח יד-יט, שם יד-כד 127) ע׳ רש״י, מנחה בלולה, מושב זקנים אלשיך, שפתי כהן, ומלבים בשלח יד-כה וכן טו-ד 128) ריב״ש בשלח יד-כה 129) ר׳ אברהם בן הרמב״ם, רלב״ג, ומנחה בלולה בשלח יד-כה 130) רש״י בשלח טו-ד 131) מכילתא בשלח יד-כד, פיוט לאחרון ש״פ, ספורנו 132) אמרי נועם בא י-יט 133) רש״י ממכילתא, תרגום יונתן, ריב״ש, ורשב״ם בשלח יד-כד וכו׳, ראה גם רש״י ישעיה סד-א 134) אור יחזקאל אמונה דף רלב

their sockets, skin that became consumed and tongues that dissolved in their mouths. Not one limb of one Egyptian was unaffected.[135] The putrid stench of rotting flesh and charred wood filled the Egyptian side of the sea, while the Jewish side enjoyed the most wonderful fragrances.[136]

By this time, a west wind had begun to blow, and the melting walls of the sea trembled under the pressure of the waters they held back. The horses came to their senses and realized that if they continued to chase the receding mare they were all doomed. They began to retreat in the direction from which they had come, but the deep mud and total chaos prevented their progress.[137] The horses also could not become disentangled from their chariots and found themselves being dragged further and further into the depths of the sea.[138]

It finally began to dawn on the Egyptians that their adversary was none other than Hashem and that they were losing very badly. And just as this realization began to sink in, they saw a vision of the ministering angel of Egypt being consumed by flames. Their last hopes were dashed, and they were completely demoralized. All was lost. There was no chance that they would ever overtake the Jews, and their own survival seemed very much at stake.[139]

Among the confused ranks of the Egyptians, many voices called for a retreat at all costs, but a number of diehards stubbornly refused to concede.

"Are we to run from the Jews?" they sneered. "Are we to be defeated by escaped slaves?"

"Fools," the wiser ones replied. "We are not fighting the Jews. We are fighting the Jewish God. It is useless. It is perfectly clear now that this very same God was responsible for all the plagues we suffered in Egypt. It was no magic, as the government wanted us to believe. There is nothing we can do but run for our lives!"[140]

"We must run if we value our lives," others agreed. "There is no one to stop us if we return to Egypt."[141]

---

135) מכילתא בשלח טו-א, ע' זכריה יד-יב ואילך, מעשה ד' תורה פרק א 136) מכילתא טו-ח, מעם לועז טו-א
137) מכילתא, רלב"ג ואב"ע בשלח יד-כז, וכו' 138) מכילתא, מדרש הגדול, שכל טוב, רלב"ג בשלח יד-כד וכו'
139) מכילתא, שכל טוב, אברבנל ומלבים שם, זוה"ק מט 140) מכילתא, שכל טוב, אברבנל, מלבים שם, ע' בעה"ט
טו-ד 141) מעם לועז בשלח טו-א

In Egypt, however, the Egyptians who had remained behind were not faring much better. Miraculously, the sea currents had shifted, and seawater began to spill into Egypt, causing many Egyptians to drown in the comfort of their own homes.[142] Moreover, the Egyptians in Egypt were granted the ability to witness the sufferings of their friends and families at the sea.[143]

The Drowning of the Egyptians

It was now time for the dramatic events at the sea to reach their climax. The Egyptians had thought themselves very clever when they decided to drown the Jews. Hashem, who always punishes measure for measure, had made a covenant with Noach never again to send a flood upon the earth. Therefore, they thought that by drowning the Jews they had outsmarted Hashem and maneuvered Him into a position where He would not be able to avenge Himself on them. But they were wrong. Hashem had promised never again to flood the entire world. He never forswore punishing a single nation by drowning. The time had now come for the Egyptians to suffer the fate to which they had subjected the Jewish people.[144]

Hashem asked the Egyptian horses why they were pursuing the Jews. The horses put the blame on the riders. Hashem then asked the Egyptian riders why they were pursuing the Jews. The riders put the blame on the uncontrollable horses. Hashem, therefore, decided to judge them both together as a unit. As a unit, they would drown for attempting to harm the Jewish people.[145]

Early Wednesday morning, on the seventh day of the exodus, the seventh day of Pesach, Hashem instructed Moshe to stretch out his hand over the sea and return the waters of the sea to their original state.[146]

Moshe did as he was told. He stretched out his hand over the sea. Hashem immediately caused a cool wind to blow on the walls of frozen water and dissolve them. Miraculously, a wind had caused the waters to form into walls, and a second wind caused

---

142) שם 143) מכילתא, מדרש הגדול, שמו״ר כא-י, שם כב-ב, רוקח בשלח יד-כד 144) מכילתא, שמו״ר כב-א
145) מכילתא בשלח טו-א 146) רש״י ממכילתא ושכל טוב בשלח יד-כו וכו׳, ילקו״ש רלו, בנוגע הזמן שחזרו
לאיתנם יעוין בשכל טוב, חזקוני, ופנים יפות

them to dissolve.[147] The melted waters covered the Egyptian chariots and horsemen.[148] At the same time, all the waters in the world, which had also split, returned to their original state.[149] As the reservoirs of the world returned to normal, some of their waters poured into the Yam Suf to participate in the drowning of the Egyptians.[150]

The waters came from everywhere to cover the Egyptians and drown them. The returning waters of the sea itself, the waters of the abyss from the core of the earth, the waters of the heavens, all of these joined together in a stormy union that washed over the Egyptians and drowned them.[151]

According to some commentaries, the last of the Egyptians stepped into the sea just as the last of the Jews were emerging. Therefore, when the sea returned to its original state after the entry of the last of the Egyptians, all the Jews had already emerged safely. The Jews too physically weak to clamber out of the converging waves by themselves were lovingly lifted out of the water by Hashem Himself and gently placed on the shore.[152]

According to other commentaries, however, the Jewish people were still in the sea when the Egyptians began to drown.[153] A great miracle occurred, and part of the sea remained split while the rest returned to its original state. While an east wind blew for the Jews, keeping the waters apart, a west wind blew for the Egyptians, bringing them together.[154] In any case, the speed of the crossing of the entire great multitude of the Jewish people on the floor of the sea in the middle of the night was truly miraculous.[155]

Meanwhile, in the raging sea, the waters flowed straight at Pharaoh and then at the rest of the Egyptians.[156] They came at the Egyptians from all four sides, encircling them like a closed flask and sealing off every avenue of escape.[157] As the waters closed about them, the Egyptians became totally disoriented, and some of them actually ran straight at the soaring waves, which knocked them down to the depths of the sea.[158]

With escape by natural means impossible, the Egyptians tried to rescue themselves through magic and sorcery. Some of them were

147) אב"ע בשלח יד-כט, וע"ש עוד טו-י 148) רש"י ממכילתא בשלח יד-כו, שכל טוב, דעת זקנים, רשב"ם, וחזקוני שם טו-יב 149) מכילתא, שמו"ר כב-ב 150) מעם לועז 151) מכילתא, שכל טוב בשלח טו-ה, ראה מעם לועז בשלח טו-א, פיוט לאחרון ש"פ, ואהלות יח-ו 152) שמו"ר כב-ב ביפ"ת, מדרש תהלים יח-כב, ע' מעם לועז בשלח טו-א 153) שמו"ר שם, מכילתא, ע' מדרש החפץ ורשב"ם 154) אב"ע בשלח יד-כט 155) מעם לועז בשלח טו-א 156) מכילתא בשלח יד-כז 157) ע' מכילתא, שמו"ר כב-ב, תרגום יונתן בשלח טו-ח 158) שמו"ר טו-טו וביפ"ת, רש"י ממכילתא בשלח יד-כז

able to levitate themselves out of the sea and high into the air. The sea beseeched Hashem to return the escaped Egyptians to its waters. "Am I to let the deposit entrusted to my possession escape?" the sea asked. Instantly, a giant wave swept high into the air and plunged the escaped magicians back into the water.[159]

The master magicians Yochni and Mamrai forged magical wings and soared up into the sky. Hashem sent the angel Michael to intercept them. Michael grabbed them by their hair and flung them back into the sea.[160]

Like Food in a Pot

As the waters closed over the heads of the Egyptians, they still were given no respite from their other afflictions. Angels of destruction poured fire and sulfur over them, and they were pelted incessantly by hailstones and arrows.[161] Jagged chunks of ice from the disintegrating walls continued to fall on their heads.[162]

The waters closed around the Egyptians and began to toss them in and out of the water, being stirred like food cooking in a pot.[163] Whirlpools which developed in the swirling waters of the sea added to the effect.[164] The waters tossed the flailing Egyptians in every direction.[165] Repeatedly, the lower waters flung them up, and the upper waters flung them down.[166]

The waves grabbed the horses together with their riders and flung them high into the air, only to have them plunge back into the sea. Miraculously, the horses did not become separated from their riders, not on the way up and not on the way down, no matter if the rider was on top or the horse. Inseparable, as Hashem had decreed, both fell into the sea and drowned.[167]

This process was repeated many times, but Hashem gave the Egyptians the strength to endure these tortures. Every time an Egyptian would extricate himself from his horse, the swirling would toss him back on, and the two would be hurled in tandem into the air.[168]

When the tossing finally came to an end, the Egyptians were plunged with great force to the bottom of the sea, driven by the height from which they had fallen and the weight of their chariots.

---

159) ילקו"ש רלה, מדרש ויושע בפסוק נשפת, ריב"ש ואוה"ח בשלח יד-כז 160) ילקו"ש רלה 161) מכילתא, שה"ש רבה א-ט, רבינו בחיי, הדר זקנים, רוקח בשלח יד-כז וכו' 162) מלבים בשלח יד-כז 163) רש"י ממכילתא בשלח יד-כז 164) מכילתא, שכל טוב בשלח טו-ה 165) שפתי כהן בשלח יד-כז 166) מלבים שם 167) שה"ש רבה א-ט וביפה קול, מנחה בלולה בשלח יד-כז, מעם לועז 168) רש"י ממכילתא בשלח יד-כז, שכל טוב בשלח יד-כז, מעם לועז

At the bottom of the sea, they were thrown into roaring fires and smashed against the remnants of the congealed waters.[169] Then their scorched and shattered bodies were scattered among the rocks on the bottom of the sea.[170]

The speed with which the Egyptians drowned depended on the level of their wickedness. The least evil among Egyptians sank like lead and were drowned instantly. The middle level Egyptians sank like stones, so that their drowning was also fairly quick and merciful. The most wicked of the Egyptians sank like straw—very slowly and painfully.[171]

Many Egyptians had already stripped off their clothes because of the stifling heat, and the force of the water and the wind stripped the clothes from the rest of the Egyptians. The bodies of the Egyptians would be washed ashore naked, symbolizing the judgment of Gehinnom, whereby the wicked are disgraced by the removal of their clothing.[172]

The Sea Surrenders the Bodies

As the Jewish people stood in safety on the shore, they could hear the screams of the Egyptians as they suffered torture and pain under the water. Slowly, the sounds faded as the Egyptians began to expire, and the Jewish people rejoiced at the downfall of their enemies.[173]

But some of them were still not convinced that they had heard the last of the Egyptians. "Who knows?" they complained. "Just as we have come out safely here, perhaps the Egyptians will come out safely somewhere else."

Moshe cried out to Hashem, "They don't believe the Egyptians are dead! I beg You, Hashem, show them that You have taken revenge on the enemies of Your people."

Hashem sent a north wind to split the sea and extract the battered bodies of the Egyptians.

"Hashem," the sea protested. "Does a master take his gifts back from his servant? The bodies of the Egyptians will be food for my fish."

Hashem reassured the sea that one and one half times as many

---

169) ר' אברהם בן הרמב"ם, שכל טוב, אב"ע, מלבים בשלח טו-ד, פיוט לאחרון של פסח 170) רש"י בשלח טו-ח, בעה"ט שם טו-ד, ע' מכילתא ומעם לועז שם טו-א 171) מכילתא, וע' לקמן פרק כא ציון 71 172) אסתר רבה ג- יד וביפה ענף ומהרז"ו 173) רלב"ג בשלח יד-כח

bodies would be returned to the sea during the time of Sisra.

"Does the servant have the effrontery to ask the Master for His due?" the sea asked. "What will happen at the time of Sisra? Will I have to ask for my repayment?"

Hashem thereupon appointed the Kishon River to carry out the promise to the sea, and the sea was pacified.[174]*

The sea now disgorged the Egyptians from its depths.[175] The north wind carried all these Egyptian bodies to the shore near the Jewish encampment.[176] Even those who perished in the muck and mire at the entrance to the sea were carried by the waves to where the Jewish people could see them and how they had died.[177]

The land, however, did not want any part of these wicked Egyptians, and it tossed them back into the sea. The sea disgorged them again onto the land. The Egyptian bodies were tossed back and forth between the land and the sea. Hashem finally intervened and instructed the land to accept the bodies of the Egyptians. They had been created from the dust of the land, and they had lived their lives on the land. The land was obligated to accept them for burial.

"When I originally absorbed the blood of Hevel when Kayin killed him, I was cursed," the land replied. "How can I now accept this great multitude of wicked people without being cursed?"

Hashem swore to the land that it would not be cursed for accepting the dead Egyptians, and the land was pacified.[178]

Bodies and Treasures on the Shore

Many of the Egyptians disgorged onto the land by the sea still clung to a small spark of life. They were on the verge of death, but in the last moments of their lives they would be able to appreciate the full import of what had occurred.

---

* When the Canaanite army led by general Sisra were preparing to attack the Jewish people, Hashem caused the weather to become extremely hot. The soldiers went to bathe and cool off in the Kishon River, and they were swept away by the currents and cast into the Yam Suf. It was then that the fish of the sea sang praise to Hashem for the fulfillment of His promise.

---

174) ערכין טו., פסחים קיח:, מדרש ויושע בפסוק תהומות וגו' ומבואר שהיו תשע מאות רכב במלחמות כנען ואילו במצרים לא היו כ"א שש מאות, וע"ש בתוס' בערכין דכתב דאע"פ דמנין המתים היו יותר במצרים, כאן לא נמנו אלא החשובים 175) תוס' עה"ת בשלח טו-יב 176) ערכין טו., פסחים קיח:, מדרש ויושע בפסוק תהומות וגו' 177) שכל טוב בשלח טו-ד 178) מכילתא, תרגום יונתן בשלח טו-יב, פדר"א מב וברד"ל, ע' פסחים קיח:, זוה"ק מז, מעם לועז טו-א, מרכבת המשנה וקו המדה על המכילתא דהגם דמתחילה רצה אותם לדגים שבים, מאחר שהסכים לפולטם לא רצה שום חלק בהם

As they lay expiring on the shore, these dying Egyptians would be recognized by Jews, who trampled them and encouraged their dogs to mangle them.[179]

"Look!" a Jew would exclaim. "My taskmaster! You have gotten what you deserve."

"I know you," a Jew would say to another of the Egyptians. "You were a minister in the royal palace, and look where you are now."

In the last moments of their lives, the Egyptians suffered the agony of total humiliation in front of their former slaves. Their downfall was complete, and seeing the Jews rejoice only made it more painful.[180]

With all the Egyptians dead and dying cast up on the shore, the Jewish people could now rest assured that the Egyptian threat was finally over. Those Egyptians who still clung to life would also suffer the pain of knowing that only the Egyptians had perished in the sea. They would also suffer the taunts and jibes of their former slaves while their last moments of life were ebbing away. Finally, the wealth washed up on shore along with the Egyptian bodies—gold, silver, gems, pearls—was so great that all the Jewish people became very wealthy. This wealth, which had adorned the Egyptian horses, was far greater than the wealth the Jewish people had carried with them from Egypt. Those treasures had been taken from the common people, but the wealth they acquired by the sea had originally come from the royal treasurehouses.[181]

The wealth the Jewish people amassed at sea was a great miracle. The sea did not hold back any of the treasures carried by the Egyptians and their horses. Everything was disgorged and deposited at the feet of the Jewish people on the shore. Moreover, the Jewish people had not lost any of the treasures they had carried with them, even though they were running from their Egyptian pursuers in the depths of the sea.[182*]

---

* The Erev Rav did not receive a share of the booty, because they had not been subjected to slave labor in Egypt. (*Sifsei Kohein, Ki Sisa* 32)

---

179) מדרש תהלים כב, מדרש אגדה בשלח יד-ל וכו', רוקח בשלח טו-י, עיין תהלים עח-כד 180) מכילתא, תרגום
יונתן בשלח יד-ל, פדר"א מב 181) מכילתא בשלח יד-ל 182) מעם לועז בשלח טו-א

Burial of the Egyptians

All the Egyptians who had not perished in the water died on the shore. Not even one Egyptian from Pharaoh's army was able to escape death on that day.[183] Horses and riders who were ordinarily good swimmers could not survive in the wind-driven waters of the sea.[184] When the Egyptians were all dead, the angels uttered the following blessing, "Blessed are You, Hashem, who humbles the sinners and causes salvation to flourish."[185]

After all the Egyptians had died and their treasures had been collected by the Jewish people, the earth fulfilled its promise to Hashem to accept the dead Egyptians for burial. Great fissures appeared, and all the dead Egyptians were swallowed up and interred in the depths of the earth.

Despite their monumental wickedness, the Egyptians did not suffer the indignity of burial at sea and having their remains devoured by the fish.[186] They had earned this privilege by declaring that Hashem was waging war against them on behalf of the Jewish people. By recognizing and acknowledging the presence of Hashem, they were spared the further indignity of having their bodies eaten by fish, vultures or scavenging animals.[187] Also, when Pharaoh had admitted that Hashem was righteous while he and his nation were wicked, he had earned the right of burial for his armies.[188] Finally, Hashem never begrudges anyone a deserved reward for a righteous deed. Centuries before, the Egyptians had honored Yaakov by allowing him to be taken to Canaan and buried by his children. They had also paid consolation visits to the grieving children. In so doing, they had earned the right to have a decent burial for the army that perished in the sea.[189]

The Patriarchs Return to Life

Hashem had made many promises to Avraham, Yitzchak and Yaakov about their future descendants. At the sea, where the miracles performed for the Jewish people reached their highest point, Hashem brought the Patriarchs back to life and allowed them to witness with their own eyes the redemption and triumph of their children.[190]

---

184) מכילתא, רוקח וספורנו בשלח יד-כח, בספר היובלים איתא שמליון ורבבה אנשים מתו בתוך הים! (183
שם (188 מכילתא שבלי הלקט תפילה יח (186 מכילתא בשלח טו-יב, פדר"א מב וברד"ל (187 מכילתא 185
מכילתא (185 פדר"א יז, לט, מב וברד"ל (190 ראה רש"י תהלים עח-יב, בראשית רבה צב-ב וביפ"ת, מעם לועז בשלח טו-(189
א, פיוט לאחרון ש"פ, זוה"ק בשלח מב:

The remains of Yosef and the twelve Shevatim were being carried by the Jewish people as they left Egypt. At the sea, Hashem brought them back to life as well so that they too could witness the spectacular miracles He performed for their descendants.[191]

The Survivors

Not everyone caught in the stormy sea on that fateful morning died. The foreign mercenaries serving in Pharaoh's army were spared a watery death, although they did suffer miserably before they were washed ashore. Battered and stunned, but alive and conscious, they were eyewitnesses to the spectacular wonders and miracles the God of the Jews performed at sea, and they lived to tell the world about them. In fact, the survival of these mercenaries was one of the more remarkable miracles Hashem performed by the sea, since not a single Egyptian survived.[192] Except for Pharaoh—perhaps.

There are different opinions regarding the fate of Pharaoh after the Egyptian catastrophe at the sea. There is a general consensus that he did not return to the throne of Egypt, but what happened to the man himself?

According to some views, Pharaoh was the first of the Egyptians to drown, since he was personally leading the Egyptian army. Others suggest that Pharaoh was the last to drown, because Hashem wanted him to witness the collapse of his empire and the great miracles He performed for the Jewish people.[193]

According to other views, although Pharaoh was in the thick of the action, he was miraculously rescued at the last moment.[194] As he witnessed the destruction of his army and the disintegration of his empire, Pharaoh had a flash of insight and declared, "Who is like You among the mighty, O Hashem?" Because of these words, spoken in a spirit of true repentance, Hashem allowed him to remain alive and tell the world about His wonders and miracles. He would later reign for five hundred years as king of Ninveh, where he would rebuke his people and make them repent.[195]

Others suggest that when Pharaoh realized what was happening he said, "You, Hashem, are righteous, while I and my nation are wicked. You are the only God. There is no one else but You."

---

191) מעם לועז בשלח טו-א 192) שם 193) מכילתא, רוקח בשלח יד-כח 194) מכילתא, מעם לועז בשלח טו-א
195) פדר"א מג, לקח טוב, שכל טוב בשלח יד-כח

"Wicked man," the angel Gavriel admonished him. "You once uttered the words 'Who is Hashem?' Do you think you can avoid the consequences by praising Him now?"

Gavriel tied a chain around Pharaoh's neck and left him in the bottom of the sea. There he would remain for fifty days of pain, and torture as punishment for his insolent words towards Hashem.

After the fifty days were over, Pharaoh was allowed to live. He was taken to the gates of Gehinnom, and whenever an idol worshipper was brought in, he would castigate him, "Fool! Why didn't you learn your lesson from me? I rebelled against Hashem and was struck by ten plagues. I was still stubborn, and I was cast to the bottom of the sea for fifty days. Do you need all that to happen to you before you become a believer?"

Afterwards, wherever Pharaoh went, he would praise Hashem and guide people to accept Him and follow in His ways.[196] Some suggest that when Pharaoh died his soul transmigrated into the body of the king of Ninveh, and from then on, the king of Ninveh began his mission to publicize the wonders of Hashem.[197]

Fifty Miracles

In all, Hashem performed fifty miracles for the Jewish people after they left Egypt.[198] They were as follows:

1. The cloud pillars and the pillar of fire.
2. Pharaoh's decision to pursue the Jewish people.
3. The changing pattern of the cloud and fire pillars at sea.
4. The cloud pillars shielded the Jews from Egyptian artillery.
5. The parting of the sea.
6. The parting of all the waters in the world.
7. The parting of the waters into twelve parts.
8. The waters formed a tunnel over the Jewish people.
9. The floor of the sea became perfectly dry.
10. The floor of the sea formed a mosaic pattern.
11. The frozen walls were transparent.
12. The frozen walls provided food and drink for the Jewish people.
13. The saltwater walls provided sweet drinking water.
14. The walls that melted to give drinks hardening again.

---

15. The Jewish women did not miscarry during the crossing.
16. The floor of the sea leveled off, with no steep inclines.
17. The speed of the Jewish crossing.
18. The height to which the frozen walls rose.
19. The vegetation that grew on the seabed for grazing animals.
20. The illogical pursuit of the Egyptians into the sea.
21. The floor turned into thick mud when the Egyptians came.
22. The pillar of fire scalded the hooves of the horses.
23. The single wheels falled off each chariot.
24. The Egyptians drowned according to their levels of wickedness.
25. The uncontrolled charge of chariots and horses into the sea.
26. The mud became hard again to break the bones of the Egyptians.
27. The hail, coals and stones falling from the sky.
28. The wrenching sound of the splitting sea heard around the world.
29. The putrid odor for the Egyptians and fragrant odor for the Jews.
30. The frozen sea melted instantly over the Egyptians.
31. The waters of the sea followed the Egyptians wherever they ran.
32. The sea returned to its original state when the Jews came out.
33. The waters and the wind pulled the Egyptians back into the sea.
34. The Egyptians were stirred in the sea like food in a pot.
35. Horsemen and horses bound together while being tossed.
36. The sea waters and the sky waters joined to drown the Egyptians.
37. The height and depth to which the Egyptians were tossed.
38. Falling Egyptians died and were covered by the sea.
39. The Egyptians in Egypt being afflicted at the same time.
40. The sea disgorged the dead Egyptians in full view of the Jews.
41. Egyptians survived the plague at sea until they reached land.
42. Foreign mercenaries in the Egyptian army not dying.
43. Pharaoh surviving the entire storm at sea.
44. The Jewish people not being punished at the sea for their sins.
45. The Egyptian treasures and spoils being washed ashore.
46. The Egyptians swallowed by the depths with also disgorged.
47. The land opening and swallowing (burying) the Egyptians.
48. The Patriarchs and the Shevatim being brought back to life.
49. The Jewish people attaining a high level of prophecy.
50. Young babies and infants in the womb singing the Shirah.

Unconditional Faith in Hashem

After witnessing the miracle of the splitting of the sea, the Jewish people reached such a great level of fear of Hashem and faith in Him that the Shechinah, the Divine Presence, rested upon them. They reached a level of holiness and faith that made them worthy of singing songs of praise to Hashem in the manner of the angels.[199] In addition, since they themselves were saved from the Egyptians, they were required to give formal thanks to Hashem, and this they did by singing the Shirah.[200]

Standing on the shore of the sea, the Jewish people felt as if they actually saw Hashem's awesome right hand strike the Egyptians, and they were filled with a boundless awe and fear of Hashem. At that moment, they achieved a clarity of vision that was prophetic.[201] Indeed, so great was this clarity of vision that a maidservant's vision at the sea was greater than the prophetic vision of a great prophet like Yechezkel. The later prophets were only able to perceive the Shechinah as surrounded by ministering angels, but the Jewish people at the sea saw the glory of Hashem as He Himself destroyed the Egyptians.[202]

Earlier, the Jewish people had also witnessed wonderful miracles performed on their behalf during the time of the plagues in Egypt. Yet only after seeing the dead Egyptians washed up on the shores of the sea did the Jewish people reach the highest levels of unconditional faith and fear of Hashem. Standing by the sea, the Jewish people saw the clear delineation between reward and punishment for the first time. Hashem had rewarded them for their faith, and He had punished the Egyptians for their sins. This tangible demonstration catapulted them to the highest levels of faith.[203] In fact, even the fainthearted and the doubters who had asked if there were "not enough graves in Egypt" now reached these exalted levels of faith.[204]

In the future, the levels of faith of the Jewish people would rise and fall depending on their situation. But the faith awakened in the Jewish people at the sea was so profound, so indelibly inscribed on their hearts that it would forever remain a part of their very being.

---

199) שמו"ר כג-ב, מכילתא, רוקח בשלח יד-לא 200) אגדת בראשית נט, וע"ע סנהדרין צד ובסידור הגר"א עזרת אבותינו וכו' 201) מדרש שוח"ט, ע' מכילתא ושכל טוב בשלח טו-ב 202) מכילתא, שכל טוב בשלח טו-ב, ע' רבנו בחיי, דורשי רשומות אמרו ישיר משה ר"ת יש שפחה יותר ראתה ממה שראו הנביאים 203) אור יחזקאל אמונה דף רלב 204) שפתי כהן בשלח יד-ל

This faith would sustain them through the darkest and most trying times in their history, and ultimately, it would earn them the coming of Mashiach and the eternal redemption from exile of the body and the spirit. May it come speedily in our days.[205]

205) תדב״א רבה

The Song of Praise

21

While the Jewish people were crossing the sea and the Egyptians were drowning, the angels in Heaven wanted to sing Shirah, the song of praise to Hashem, in honor of the miraculous events that were taking place. But Hashem did not allow it. "How can you say Shirah when My handiworks are drowning in the sea?" Hashem said. When the entire event was over and the Jewish people were standing safe and triumphant, the angels again wanted to sing Shirah. This time, Hashem agreed that the singing of Shirah would be appropriate. However, he gave the honor to the Jewish people. The angels had the opportunity to sing Shirah every day, while this might be the only opportunity of their entire lifetimes for the Jews assembled by the sea.[1]

---

1) שמו"ר כג-ח, ע' רמב"ן בשלח טו-יט והלאה דבשעת הליכתם בים אמרו שירה, ע' דבר מעוניין בעץ יוסף על המדרש שם, בישמח משה מובא מדרש שהפסוק ד' ימלוך לעולם ועד שרו טרם כניסתם תוך הים

Moshe composed the hauntingly beautiful lyrics of the Shirah and then taught them to the Jewish people.[2] Once they became familiar with it, Moshe led the recital of the Shirah verse by verse.[3]

The Jews of this generation were the first people in history to sing Shirah, offering praise to Hashem through song. Adam did not sing Shirah upon the occasion of his creation. Avraham did not sing Shirah after being saved in the burning furnace. Yitzchak did not sing Shirah after escaping the knife on the Akeidah. Yaakov did not sing Shirah after surviving the confrontations with Shechem, Eisav and Eisav's ministering angel. Although they did offer praise to Hashem, it was not in the form of song. The Jewish people who witnessed the miracles at the sea were the first to have the honor of singing a song of praise to Hashem.[4] The singing of the Shirah also atoned for the lapse of faith among some of the Jewish people before the sea split open to receive them.[5]

In the future, at the time of *Techias Hameisim*, the Resurrection of the Dead, the Shirah will also be sung. Indeed, so beloved is the Shirah to Hashem that whoever sings the Shirah in this world will earn the privilege of singing the Shirah in the world to come as well.[6]

Everyone Sings Shirah

In this time of great salvation, when every single Jew experienced and benefited from the great miracles at the sea, all the Jewish people sang the Shirah—men, women and even children. Miraculously, babies sitting on their mothers' laps joined in singing the Shirah. Nursing newborns joined in singing the Shirah.[7]* Even embryos in their mothers' wombs joined in singing the Shirah.

Because of the great faith of the Jewish mothers, Hashem had preserved their children in their wombs and did not let them miscarry during the tumultuous events of the crossing of the sea. The women of the Erev Rav, having less faith, did not merit this protection and miscarried.[8] For a brief wondrous moment, the wombs of

---

* The infants did not sing in the same manner as the adults, since they were incapable of speaking. Rather, their souls sang to Hashem through the divine spirit (*ruach hakodesh*), expressing their spiritual attachment (*dveikus*) to Him. (*Iyun Yaakov, Chiddushei Aggados*)

---

2) אב״ע ורלב״ג בשלח טו-א 3) ע׳ משנה סוטה ה-ד ובגמ׳ ל: כמה שיטות בזה ועי״ש בפי׳ המשניות 4) שמו״ר כג-ד ובעץ יוסף, ע״ש עוד במהרז״ו ויפ״ת, בשפתי כהן ג״כ נתבאר דברי המדרש 5) מדרש תהלים יח 6) ע׳ סנהדרין צא, מכילתא, ילקוט המכירי תהלים קלו 7) סוטה ל:, מכילתא 8) צרור המור בשלח טו-א

the Jewish women became transparent, and their embryos were able to point at the Shechinah and say, "This is my God, and I will beautify Him."[9] Some suggest that these embryos came out of their mothers' wombs to sing Shirah and returned when they had finished.[10]

The Women Sing

At first, all the men sang the Shirah, and the women modestly refrained. In the silence that followed, Hashem expressed a desire to hear songs of praise from the "women of valor." And so the women, too, prepared to sing the Shirah.[11] But the angels in Heaven protested.

"We stood by while the Jewish men sang before us," they said. "Now it is our turn. The women can wait."

"No!" Miriam spoke up. "After the men, it is only right that we should sing." Some suggest that Miriam invited the angels to sing with them. Others suggest that Miriam deferred to the angels and agreed to sing only after they had finished.

At last, it was the turn of the women to sing the Shirah.[12] Led by an exuberant Miriam, the women took musical instruments, such as tambourines, drums and flutes, and danced while they sang.[13] So confident were the Jewish women in Hashem's wondrous salvation that they had prepared for the occasion by packing musical instruments in their luggage when they left Egypt.[14]

There was, of course, the problem of how the women were allowed to sing in front of the men. According to some commentaries, the intended purpose of the musical instruments was not only to add to the festivities but also to cover the sounds of their voices in the presence of the men.[15] According to others, this occasion was an exception to the rule. Since the singing was through *ruach hakodesh*, divine inspiration, Miriam and the women were allowed to sing the complete Shirah just as the men did.[16] Others suggest that the women did not sing. Moshe and the men sang, and the women responded.[17] There is also a view that Miriam alone sang only the first verse of the Shirah.[18]

---

9) סוטה ל:, עיון יעקב נותן בזה תבלין עפ"י מש"א חז"ל דלומדים עם העובר כל התורה כולה וכו' הרי דזה דרגא גבוהה ברוחניות וכמו כן שרו לד' ע"ש (10 מעם לעז בשלח טו-א (11 חום' עה"ת בשלח טו-כ (12 רוקח בשלח טו-כא, ריב"א שם (13 מכילתא, ת"א, תרגום יונתן ר' סעדיא גאון בשלח טו-כ, פיוט לאחרון של פסח (14 רש"י ממכילתא בשלח טו-כ (15 צידה לדרך, מעם לועז בשלח טו-כ (16 באר מים חיים בשלח טו-כ, ע"ע במכילתא, חזקוני, נחל הקדמונים בשלח טו-כא (17 ילקוט ראובני בשלח טו-כ (18 רמב"ן בשלח טו-יט

Be that as it may, the role of the women was secondary to that of the men in the singing of the Shirah at the sea, because the divine salvation came through Moshe and Aharon. In the future, when the Jewish people would be victorious over the Canaanite army of Sisra, the prophet and judge Devorah would lead the women in song before the men, because the salvation of the Jewish people came through Yael, who killed Sisra.[19]

🞰 THE SHIRAH 🞰

I will sing to Hashem for He is exalted above all,
the horse and its rider were thrown into the sea.[20]

Hashem is exalted in this world and in the world to come.[21] The lion is king of all wild animals, the ox of all domestic animals, the eagle of all birds. Man stands above them all, and Hashem is exalted above everything, including the man.[22]

Yet people often tend to forget this, and Hashem devastates them with the very thing by which they exalted themselves. The people in the time of Noach denied their need for Hashem's rain, relying instead on ground mist; they were destroyed by the Great Flood.[23] The Dor Hahaflagah joined forces to build a tower and fight Hashem; these united people were dispersed to the ends of the earth. The city of Sedom felt secure in its wealth and turned away the poor and needy; it was obliterated. Sisra, the Canaanite general, felt secure in his host of chariots, and Sancheriv, too, relied on his chariots; the chariots were wiped out. Nevuchadnezzar declared himself a god. Hashem told Nevuchadnezzar, "Because you exalted yourself above people, you will dwell among animals." And so it was.[24]

Pharaoh also declared, "The river is mine. I made it." Hashem destroyed all of Egypt, the horses and their riders, by drowning them in the sea.[25] The name פַּרְעֹה can be reformulated as הִפָּרַע, meaning

19) לקח טוב שם טו-כ, ע' שופטים ד-ה, במגילה יד נמנה בין הנביאות 20) בשלח טו-א 21) תנחומא בשלח יב
22) חגיגה יג: 23) בראשית ב-ו 24) מכילתא, רבנו בחיי בשלח טו-א, ילקו"ש רמג, פיוט לאחרון של פסח
25) מכילתא, רבנו בחיי בשלח טו-א, עיין דעת חכמה ומוסר ח"ג דף מב, תדב"א רבה ז

retribution and punishment. Within his own name, Pharaoh bore the allusion to his future punishment.[26] The most arrogant self-image of a man is of himself riding on a horse. Therefore, Hashem took horse and rider in tandem and hurled them into the sea to show that He reigns supreme and is exalted above all.[27]

A person may take pride in what he does or what he has, but only if he acknowledges that everything comes from Hashem.[28]

Hashem is my strength and song,
He was a salvation for me.
This is my God, and I will beautify Him,
the God of my father, and I will exalt Him.[29]

In these verses, the Jewish people praise the amazing phenomenon that the very same action which punished the Egyptians at sea was an act of pity and salvation towards the Jews.[30] They acknowledge that Hashem was their salvation through the Patriarchs and through Moshe, that he would continue to be their salvation through Yehoshua and that he would be their salvation in the world to come.[31] Particular mention is made of the Patriarchs who were brought back to life to witness the splitting of the sea.[32]

The Jewish people promise to beautify Him by the way in which they perform His *mitzvos*—by making sure to have a beautiful *lulav, succah, tzitzis, tefillin* or *shofar,* and spending as much as an additional third to acquire a *mitzvah* object of greater beauty.[33] They promise to exalt Him by emulating His ways. As He is gracious, so will they be. As He is compassionate, so will they be.[34]

When the Jewish people perceived the glory of Hashem with prophetic clarity, they pointed to Hashem with their finger, as if actually seeing Him, and said, "This is my God, and I will beautify Him."[35] The Jewish people will beautify Hashem by building the Beis Hamikdash to house the Shechinah.

At that time, the nations of the world will approach the Jewish

---

26) שכל טוב שמות ה-כב 27) מכילתא, רבנו בחיי 28) דעת חכמה ומוסר ח"ג דף מג 29) רש"י ממכילתא ואונקלוס בשלח טו-ב 30) מכילתא, רלב"ג, מנחה בלולה, שפתי כהן, מיזוג הנפלאה הלזו של חסד ודין כשבאים לפונדק אחת נקראות תפארת ובזכות הפאר (כלומר תפילין) נקרע ודוק 31) מכילתא, ר' אפרים עה"ת 32) מנחה בלולה, ספורנו 33) ע' שבת קלג:, מכילתא, ילקו"ש רמד וכו' 34) ע' רש"י שבת קלג: 35) רש"י ממכילתא, שמו"ר כג-טו

people and say, "Why are you so devoted to your God that you are willing to accept death and torture for Him? Why are you so loyal to him even when He has forsaken you? You are a proud and mighty nation. Come join us and we will appoint you as our commanders, governors and officers."

The Jewish people will respond by praising Him. "He dresses in white to purify our sins. He dresses in red to bring destruction, punishment and retribution to our enemies. With eyes like a dove, He watches lovingly over the righteous as they pray and study in the houses of worship. His judgment is always righteous, and we honor Him."

The nations will be very inspired by the praise of Hashem. "Let us join you," they will respond. "Let us help build the Beis Hamikdash."

"He is our beloved, and not yours," the Jewish people will say. "We will build His holy sanctuary, not you."[36]

One particular group among the Jewish people said the words "This is my God" with special feeling. During Pharaoh's decree of death on all Jewish male babies, the terrified mothers went out to the fields to give birth. They left their newborn infants in the fields, crying out to Hashem, "We entrust our children to Your care. We have done ours. Please do Yours." Hashem sustained these children with oil and honey, and they survived to join the exodus. These children, now fully grown, stood together and sang, "This is my God."[37]

Hashem is master of war, Hashem is His Name.[38]

When Hashem cast the chariots of Pharaoh into the sea, He was characterized in the world as a master of war.[39] Before the battle, Hashem brings His armor, so to speak, the weapons of war He arrays against the enemies of the Jewish people, but in the end, Hashem does battle only with the power of His Name.[40] The array of weapons is only to frighten the enemies of the Jews and encourage them to desist from their evil designs.[41]

Furthermore, the very Name Hashem, which brings death and

36) מכילתא, שה"ש רבה תתקפ"ח, רש"י שה"ש ה-ט וכו', שם ו-א וכו'   37) מכילתא, שמו"ר כג-ח, תרגום יונתן
וי"מ שבמדבר נגדלו 38) בשלח טו-ג 39) חזקוני ר"ה במלבים 40) ר' סעדיא גאון, רבנו בחיי, מלבים 41) ע' רש"י
ממכילתא, רבנו בחיי מפרש בזה ד' ילחם לכם וגו' וע"ש

destruction in war, also brings kindness and compassion to His loyal followers.[42] A mortal king who fights a war must turn away from the domestic needs of his kingdom, but Hashem listens to the prayers and sustains the inhabitants of the world even while He is fighting a war.[43]

In the war against the Egyptians, myriad angels wanted to destroy Egypt, but Hashem turned down their requests. He alone would fight the Egyptians, and thus, He was called a master of war.[44] A mortal king sends his army to fight for him, but Hashem goes into battle alone.[45]

Hashem is invincible in battle.[46] His power is constant and everlasting.[47] He fought for the Jewish people in Egypt and at the sea, He would fight for them at the Jordan River during the conquest of Eretz Yisrael, and He will continue to fight for them in the future.[48]

Pharaoh's chariots and army were cast into the sea,
and his best officers drowned in the Sea of Reeds.[49]

Hashem destroyed the six hundred prime chariots as easily as if it were only one.[50] Hashem also caused the most powerful chariot drivers to go down in the shallow part of the sea—among the reeds. They stepped into mire and fell straight to the bottom and drowned.[51] Thus, the strongest part of the army perished first, and the weaker part afterwards.[52]

The waters of the abyss covered them.
They sank like stones to the depths.[53]

Those Egyptians who sank like stones were of the middle level in the extent of their wickedness. Because they did not descend to the lowest depth of evil, their deaths were quick and merciful. The comparison to a stone was symbolic of their having wanted to kill the Jewish children on the "birthing stones"[54] and also of their having hardened their hearts like stones.[55]

42) מכילתא, ספורנו, אוה"ח, ע"ע רש"י ואתחנן, ראה לעיל ציון 30 43) רש"י ממכילתא, לקח טוב 44) שפתי כהן 45) שם 46) מכילתא 47) שם 48) שם 49) בשלח טו-ד 50) מכילתא 51) שפתי כהן ומלבים 52) רלב"ג 53) בשלח טו-ה 54) מכילתא 55) שם

Your right hand, Hashem, is glorified with strength,
Your right hand, Hashem, crushes the enemy.[56]

The use of anthropomorphic terms like hand or mouth when referring to Hashem are, of course, purely allegorical. Hashem is pure spirit, without body or form. These terms are simply meant to help convey concepts in a manner to which human beings can relate.[57]

The right Hand of this verse represents the unlimited power of Hashem. This right Hand rescued the weak and slow-footed among the Jewish people who were caught in the sea when the waters closed over the heads of the Egyptians.[58] This same right Hand crushed the enemies of the Jewish people and will continue to do so in the future.[59]

According to some commentaries, Hashem's two Hands, so to speak, are always equal, serving either as two rights or as two lefts. Hashem gave the Torah with His right Hand. If the Jewish people learn Torah and follow His will, inspiring the right Hand of Torah, so to speak, the other Hand will also serve as a right Hand and protect them. If the Jewish people do not follow His will and learn His Torah, then both Hands will serve as left, and the divine protection will be withdrawn.[60] Similarly, if the Jewish people produce the "voice of Yaakov" through prayer and Torah they will be protected from the "hands of Eisav" which try to harm them.[61] If we follow His will, He will be awake for us, so to speak. Otherwise, He will be as if asleep while misfortune befalls the Jewish people.[62]

In another sense, the strength of the right Hand of Hashem is turned inward. He practices extraordinary restraint and provides sinners with ample opportunity to repent. Only after waiting a long time did Hashem destroy the generation of the Great Flood and the city of Sedom. Egypt was subjected to ten plagues over a period of nearly a year without being totally destroyed. Only after they stubbornly insisted on pursuing the Jewish people did Hashem annihilate them.[63] *

56) בשלח טו-ו 57) רש״י בשלח טו-ח, מעם לועז טו-ו 58) שמו״ר כב-ב, רוקח, ע׳ מעם לועז בשלח טו-א, רבנו בחיי מבאר הכוונה ביד ימינך 59) רש״י ממכילתא, זוה״ק, רשב״ם 60) רש״י ממכילתא, זוה״ק נח, רש״י מוסיף שהיד שמגין על ישראל הוא היד שיכניע את האויב 61) זוה״ק 62) מדרש אגדה ע׳ 63) מכילתא שכל טוב,מלבים

In Your great might, You shatter Your opponents.
You send forth Your wrath, it consumes them like straw.[64]

With one mighty swipe, Hashem wiped out the great Egyptian empire, with all its armies and chariots.[65] With one flick, the two magicians Yochni and Mamrai, who had levitated themselves out of the sea, were flung back down to drown.[66]

The verse speaks of the opponents of Hashem. These are the enemies of the Jewish people. Hashem consumes them and will continue to consume them in the future.[67] He needs no weapons to destroy the enemies of the Jewish people. His burning rage alone consumes them.[68] Mortals can only harm their enemies through acts, not emotions. Hashem's divine wrath, however, destroyed the Egyptians.[69] In the sequence of Hashem's war with the Egyptians, He first "crushed" them. Then He "shattered" them, implying greater destruction. Finally, He "consumed" them, implying total annihilation that leaves no residue.[70]

The most wicked of the Egyptians died in the sea like straw. Just as straw sinks very slowly, so too did these evil Egyptians suffer slowly and greatly as they drowned in the sea.[71]

Besides its specific symbolism for the manner of death of the most wicked Egyptians, the burning of straw is also a metaphor for the overall destruction of Egypt. Straw crackles loudly when it burns; the Egyptians cried out in pain as they lay dying on the shore.[72] Straw burns thoroughly, leaving no residue; the Egyptian empire was also thoroughly destroyed.[73] Straw burns quickly; the Egyptians were destroyed with great haste.[74] Moreover, straw is a very lowly substance, and by the time Hashem finished with the Egyptians, they could only be compared to straw. The glory, prestige and power of Egypt were all gone.[75]

---

* Egypt was destroyed by the divine Name of compassionate judgment, Hashem, and therefore, they were granted the kindness of burial. Had they been destroyed by the divine Name of strict judgment, Elokim, they would not have been granted even the slightest consideration. (*Sifsei Kohein*)

---

64) בשלח טו-ז, ברשב"ם מתפרש בענין אחר 65) שכל טוב 66) ילקו"ש רלה 67) רש"י ממכילתא, רוקח 68) אב"ע 69) רש"י, שכל טוב, ראה גם בקול אליהו 70) ע' באר יצחק והעמק דבר על פרש"י 71) מכילתא, במדרש אגדה (מובא גם בהדר זקנים בשלח טו-י) איתא שהרשעים ביותר מתו מיד ואידך מתו כקש וטעמו ונימוקו שיוכלו הרשעים להענש בגיהנים והשאר יקבלו עונשם בעלמא הדין 72) מכילתא 73) שם 74) רלב"ג, שפתי כהן 75) מכילתא, לקח טוב

> *With the breath of Your Nostrils, the waters piled up.*
> *The running waters stood like a wall, the deep waters*
> *congealed in the heart of the sea.[76]*

The metaphor of heat is used to describe how Hashem caused the waters of the sea to congeal. When the waters of the sea returned to form, the metaphor of cool breath describes the melting of the waters and their collapse over the Egyptians. This indicates a miracle within a miracle, for heat usually melts whereas cold congeals.[77]

The manner in which the waters congealed into walls concealed the dangers from the Egyptians.[78] The depths of the sea solidified into a firm floor which allowed the Jewish people to walk straight ahead without descending to the floor of the sea. Only the top third of the sea (symbolized by the heart, which is in the top third of the body) split into a corridor. When the Egyptians saw a corridor going straight ahead they did not realize they were actually entering the sea.[79]

> *The enemy said, "I will pursue, I will overtake,*
> *I will divide the spoils, I will satisfy myself with them.*
> *I will draw my sword, my hand will impoverish them."[80]*

These words were spoken by Pharaoh when he set out in pursuit of the Jewish people.[81] Although the Jewish people were not there at the time, they were aware of Pharaoh's words through *ruach hakodesh*, divine inspiration.[82] Others suggest that Pharaoh spoke these words when he saw that the east wind had congealed the sea. He deluded himself into thinking he would have ample time to overtake the Jewish people and return to shore before the sea melted.[83]

---

79) אונקלוס 78) ע׳ מעם לועז טו-א 77) רש״י, דעת זקנים, ריב״א, וחזקוני בשלח טו-יא, ע׳ מעם לועז טו-יא 76) בשלח טו-ח
81) רש״י 80) בשלח טו-ט, ועי״ש ברש״י וחזקוני מכילתא, ע׳ הדר זקנים, מושב זקנים, מלבים וכן תרגום יונתן
83) מכילתא 82) ע׳ רמב״ן ושפתי כהן

You blew with Your wind, the sea covered them.
The mighty sank deep like lead in the water.[84]

According to another interpretation, they sank deep like lead in the mighty waters.[85] The winds caused the sea to dissolve, covering the Egyptians under it.[86] Miraculously, in the same day and the same place, one wind caused the sea to congeal while another caused it to melt.[87]

The Egyptians that drowned like lead were the least evil. They were covered by the sea and drowned instantly.[88] The symbolism of lead is used here to indicate that the Egyptians were also being punished for placing Yosef's remains in a lead coffin and hiding it in the riverbed of the Nile.[89] It also indicates that the Egyptians were being punished for weighing down the workloads of the Jewish laborers with lead weights to make life more difficult for them.[90]

Who is like You among the mighty, Hashem?
Who is like You, adorned in holiness,
awesome beyond words, performing wonders?[91]

When the nations of the world saw the Egyptians annihilated, their empire destroyed, their idols smashed, they abandoned their idolatrous ways. They joined the Jewish people and angels in Heaven in declaring, "Who is like You among the mighty, Hashem?"[92]

"Good fortune and success is Yours, O Yisrael!" the Divine Spirit responded. "Who is like You?"[93]

In the future, when Mashiach comes, Hashem will again redeem the Jewish people from their exile and annihilate their enemies. At that time, the Jewish people will again acknowledge the awesome power of Hashem by saying, "Who is like You among the mighty, Hashem?"[94]

When Pharaoh saw the miracles at sea and the praise the Jewish people offered to Hashem, he too said, "Who is like You among the mighty, Hashem?" Then he added in the Egyptian language,

---

84) בשלח טו-י, ע' רש"י ומהרש"א מנחות נג.   85) רשב"ם   86) ר' סעדיא גאון   87) מעם לועז   88) ראה לעיל
ציון 71   89) ר' אפרים עה"ת   90) שם   91) בשלח טו-יא   92) מכילתא, רד"ל בפדר"א מב   93) ספרי זאת הברכה,
ע' ברכות ו   94) מכילתא, זוה"ק

"Who is like You, adorned in holiness?"[95]

The verse goes on to say that Hashem is awesome beyond praise. Indeed, it is so beyond the capacity of people to praise Hashem adequately that, in a way, it would be best to remain silent.[96] Nevertheless, we praise Hashem for all the mighty wonders He performed in the past, changing the course of nature and bending it to His will.[97] In the future, the Jewish people will praise Him for even greater miracles He will perform in their behalf.[98]

There are many other implicit praises in the statement of the Jewish people, "Who is like You among the mighty, Hashem?" This praise tells of the great power and compassionate nature He has as Master of the Universe.

Who is like You, Hashem, who restrains Himself from punishing the oppressors of His people and gives them the opportunity to repent?[99]

Who is like You, Hashem, who brings down the arrogant men—such as Pharaoh, Sancheriv and Nevuchadnezzar—who considered themselves gods?[100]

Who is like You, Hashem, who can utter two statements at the same time and hear all the prayers in the world at the same time?[101]

Who is like You, Hashem, who can do wonders and miracles that cannot be duplicated by the most skilled magicians in the world?[102]

Who is like You, Hashem, who surpasses all the praise that can be said of Him?[103]

Who is like You, Hashem, who begins building at the top and continues down to the foundations, creating the sky and then the earth?[104]

Who is like You, Hashem, who can create a man from nothing, give him life and make him able to hear, see and speak?[105]

You stretched forth Your right Hand, the earth swallowed them.[106]

When something fragile is held in one's hand, a simple tilt of the wrist can destroy it. All life is in the palm of Hashem's Hand, so to speak, and when He stretches forth His Hand, it is

---

95) פדר"א מב   96) רש"י, רבנו בחיי, ע' תהלים סה-ב וברש"י בעצם ית' דומיה תהלה ומה ששגור בתפלתנו שבחים ע' מגילה יח. וגם כה   97) ע' מכילתא, ר' אברהם בן הרמב"ם, מנחה בלולה, מלבים 98) מכילתא 99) מכילתא, ע' יומא סט: 100) מכילתא 101) מכילתא 102) שם 103) ר' יהודה החסיד מדרש תהלים קו 104) מכילתא 105) מכילתא 106) בשלח טו-יב

destroyed.[107] The Egyptians were no more to Hashem than a fly to be swatted away.[108]

Furthermore, Hashem swore by His right Hand that He would not hold the sea accountable for burying the Egyptians. When the sea saw Hashem's right Hand, it swallowed the Egyptians, as Hashem instructed.[109] It also spit them out, according to Hashem's instructions, so that the dry land could accept the bodies for burial.[110]

With Your kindness You led this nation You redeemed.
You led them with Your might to Your holy sanctuary.[111]

On their own merits, the Jewish people were not fully deserving of all the great miracles Hashem performed on their behalf. Nonetheless, Hashem did everything out of His abundant kindness.[112] Moreover, He led them in their travels in a most extraordinary way. A mortal king is surrounded by servants and attendants when he travels with his nation. Hashem, on the other hand, attended to His people, leading them with cloud pillars during the day and a pillar of fire at night.[113]

The verse also praises Hashem for the destination of the exodus of Egypt. It was not only a flight from affliction but a triumphant march to Mount Sinai, where they would accept the Torah, and to Eretz Yisrael, where they would live according to its commandments.[114] Ultimately, they would build the Beis Hamikdash, and for that alone, they were worthy of being redeemed from Egypt.[115]

The nations heard, they trembled.
Terror gripped the inhabitants of Philistia.[116]
Then the chiefs of Edom panicked.
Trembling seized the mighty of Moav.
All the inhabitants of Canaan melted away.[117]

When the nations of the world heard about the exodus of the former Jewish slaves from mighty Egypt amidst plagues and

---

miracles, they all trembled with fear.[118]

At first, they were struck dumb with overwhelming awe.[119] Finally, they managed to say, "No slave ever escaped Egypt, yet the Jews left after making the Egyptians suffer plagues and give up all their valuables. Then the sea opened for the Jews and closed over the Egyptians, destroying the great Egyptian empire. If all this could happen to mighty Egypt, how much more likely it is to happen to us!"[120]

All the nations under the domination of the Egyptians who had considered coming to their defense were now determined to avoid any contact with the Jewish people. The prospect was too dangerous and terrifying.[121]* However, this dread and fear of the Jewish people on the part of the nations of the world would only last as long as the Jewish people obeyed the will of Hashem. In the future, when the Jewish people would stray from the righteous path, this fear would be quickly forgotten.[122]

The ring of nations that surrounded Eretz Yisrael were thoroughly demoralized and filled with despair. Edom was in a state of total panic. They had received reports that the Jewish people were not taking the direct route to Eretz Yisrael through the land of the Plishtim. Instead, they were veering east in the direction of Edom. "What will become of us?" they lamented. "The Jewish people are surely coming to settle the accounts of their forefather Yaakov with his brother Eisav, our forefather."[123]

Moav, too, shivered in fear at the prospect of the approach of the Jewish people. "What will become of us?" they lamented. "The Jewish people are surely coming to settle the accounts of their forefather Avraham with his nephew Lot, our forefather."[124] They were probably unaware that Hashem would not permit the Jewish people to make war with Moav.[125]

The distress of Edom and Moav was, of course, not only due to concerns for their own safety. As sworn enemies of the Jewish

---

* Amalek would later be condemned to annihilation. for dispelling this overwhelming dread and fear of the Jewish people. Amalek attacked the Jewish people in the desert at Refidim, and although they lost the battle, they succeeded in promoting the impression that the Jews were ordinary, if powerful, people. (*Zohar, Shemos* 3b, *Beshalach* 65)

---

118) מכילתא 119) פיוט לאחרון של פסח 120) לקח טוב, שפתי כהן מביא שבלעם גופיה אמר כן 121) זוה"ק מט, פסיקתא רבה יב, רבנו בחיי 122) ילקו"ש תתקלח 123) מדרש ויושע, רבנו בחיי, אברבנל, שפתי כהן, חזקוני 124) גור אריה 124) מדרש ויושע, רבנו בחיי, חזקוני, גור אריה 125) מנחה בלולה

people, they found it particularly galling to see so many wondrous and spectacular miracles performed on behalf of the Jews.[126]

The Plishtim had additional cause to fear the Jewish people. They were the closest to Egypt in the easterly direction in which the Jewish people were traveling. Logically, they were the next adversary on the road of conquest to Eretz Yisrael.[127] Furthermore, the Plishtim knew that the Jewish people had not forgotten how they had massacred the people of Shevet Ephraim on the outskirts of Gath, one of the five major cities of the Plishtim. Surely, the Jewish people would want to take revenge.[128]

Most frightened of all these nations, however, were the Canaanim. They knew that the land which they inhabited had been promised to the Jewish people. Nonetheless, they had always felt they could defend themselves and hold on to the land. After hearing about the fate of the Egyptians, however, they realized that resistance was useless. Their hearts melted like wax at the thought of what the future held for them.[129]

The fear of the nations lasted for the entire forty years the Jewish people spent in the desert. When the Jewish people marched into Eretz Yisrael, the nations were still demoralized, as Yehoshua's spies reported.[130]

Not everyone, however, was affected by the reports of Krias Yam Suf in a negative way. When Yisro in Midian heard about all the miracles that occurred at the sea, he converted to Judaism and came to join the Jewish people.[131]

May dread and terror fall upon them, at the greatness of Your Arm may they be still as stone until Your people pass through, Hashem, until these people You have acquired pass through.[132]

From this point on, the Shirah addresses the future. Both in request and prophecy, the Jewish people praise Hashem for His miracles and salvation in the future.[133]

---

126) רש״י ממכילתא, ר' אפרים, פיוט לאחרון ש״פ, ע' שפתי חכמים   127) רש״י ממכילתא, ע' שפתי חכמים
128) רש״י ממכילתא, מדרש ויושע   129) רש״י ממכילתא, מדרש ויושע, פיוט לאחרון ש״פ, רבנו בחיי, אברבנל,
חזקוני   130) ע' יהושע ב-טו וכו', סוטה לד., רש״י ומהרש״א שם, מלבים בלק כב-ה   131) זבחים קטז., רש״י
יתרו יח-א ובשפתי חכמים   132) בשלח טו-טז   133) שכל טוב

"May the fear and awe of the Jews that You have instilled in the nations endure," Moshe prayed to Hashem. "May Plishtim, Edom and Moav never dare go to war against the Jewish people."[134]

For the forty years of the Jewish sojourn in the desert, these nations would bear witness to the cloud pillars and the pillar of fire, and it would frighten them. Moshe prayed that this fear should endure.[135]

Moshe was concerned about these three nations for good reason. Avimelech, king of the Plishtim, had made a peace treaty with Avraham, which the Jewish people would have to honor, putting them at a disadvantage. Conflict with Moav would have to be avoided because they were closely related. Conflict with Edom was dangerous since Eisav, the patriarch of Edom, had been given Yitzchak's blessing of "living by the sword."[136] Therefore, he prayed that they would of their own accord avoid war with the Jewish people.

The verse goes on to pray that the enemies of the Jewish people will fall silent as stone. After the crossing of the sea, Amalek began to organize a confederation of nations intent on destroying the Jewish people. Moshe prayed to Hashem, and they all became mute as a stone, unable to formulate plans of war against the Jewish people.[137]

Moshe and the Jewish people also prayed for salvation in future times of peril. When Moshe sent spies to scout Eretz Yisrael, they were protected by these prayers. Any Canaanite who recognized them as Jewish spies immediately found himself mute as a stone.[138] The prayers at the sea also protected the Jewish people in their battle with Amalek, in their battles against the Amorites near the Arnon River and during the crossing of the Jordan River into Eretz Yisrael.[139]

The verse calls the Jewish people the "people You have acquired." Hashem acquired this nation from Egypt. They were once the slaves of Egypt, and now that He redeemed them, they are in His possession.[140] The entire world is, of course, in Hashem's possession, but Hashem's love for the Jewish people has made them His prized possession, just as a precious object purchased for a large sum of money is held in special esteem by its owner.[141]

---

134) רש"י, רמב"ן, חזקוני, ריב"ש 135) שמו"ר כ-טז שיר רבה ג-ה 136) שפתי כהן 137) מכילתא, רוקח כ' שנשתקקו כאבן הנעבד לעכו"ם 138) מכילתא 139) רש"י ממכילתא, תרגום יונתן, מדרש ויושע, הנס עם אמורי מסופר ברש"י חקת כא-יד 140) אב"ע 141) רש"י ממכילתא

Hashem has four principal possessions, so to speak—the heavens and the earth, the Jewish people, the Torah and the Beis Hamikdash. Hashem wants the nation He possesses to accept the Torah He possesses in the world that exists in their merit. Then He wants them to build the Beis Hamikdash, the fourth of His precious possessions.[142]

You will bring them and implant them on the mountain of Your heritage, a foundation for Your dwelling place
that You, Hashem, have made,
a sanctuary Your Hands established.[143]

In this verse, when Moshe and the Jewish people use the word "them" rather than "us," it is because they are unwittingly saying an important prophecy about themselves. Moshe and the generation of the exodus would not enter Eretz Yisrael. Yehoshua would lead their children into Eretz Yisrael.[144] The use of the word "them" also indicates that this prayer is also directed at the times of Mashiach in the distant future. Moshe prayed for the time when the Jewish people would forever be implanted in Eretz Yisrael.[145]

"The mountain of Your heritage" of the verse refers either to Eretz Yisrael, Yerushalayim or the Beis Hamikdash.[146]

The verse also alludes to an alignment between Hashem's terrestrial temple and His celestial temple. The words "Your heritage" refer to the Beis Hamikdash, while the words "Your dwelling place" refer to the celestial Beis Hamikdash.[147] The knowledge that everything we do in our Beis Hamikdash is paralleled in the Beis Hamikdash in Heaven should impress on us the importance of conducting ourselves and praying there with the proper respect.[148]

In mentioning the sanctuary "Your Hands established," the Jewish people also prophesied that Hashem would bring them the third and everlasting Beis Hamikdash. Unlike the first two that would be destroyed, the Third Beis Hamikdash would be built by Hashem Himself and never destroyed.[149] Furthermore, by building the third Beis Hamikdash with both Hands, so to speak, even though the entire

---

world was created with only one Hand, Hashem showed how precious it is to Him. In the future, when His Name is sanctified, the Shechinah will rest there and reign in all its glory for all eternity.[150]

Hashem shall reign for all eternity.[151]

T he end of the Shirah expresses its unifying theme. "Hashem shall reign for all eternity." The purpose of all the experiences and the miracles was to establish in the minds of the peoples of the world that Hashem is master over the entire world.[152] In the context of this theme, Moshe prayed to Hashem that the Jewish people should live eternally in Eretz Yisrael with the Beis Hamikdash, because only thus would Hashem be recognized as King throughout the world.[153]

On another level, however, Moshe's prayer is on behalf of the Jewish people. Just as Hashem had performed miracles for the Jews and destroyed their enemies at the sea, He should continue to defend the righteous and punish the wicked for all generations to come.[154] Moshe prayed that the Jewish people should never be in the power of malicious kings, only in the power of kings who are kind and benevolent.[155] But the final time of true peace and tranquillity will not come in this world but in the world to come. In the world to come, Hashem will wipe the tears from the faces of man, and we will all rejoice forever in our salvation.[156]

We pray that Hashem shall "reign for all eternity," that Mashiach will come and proclaim Hashem's sovereignty, that the evil Amalek and Eisav will be destroyed along with their worthless idolatry, and that Hashem's mastery over the world will be recognized by all.[157]

In this Shirah, Moshe was the first ever to proclaim Hashem's kingship over the world, and the Jewish people endorsed this proclamation. Therefore, Hashem declared that the one who had crowned Him as King of the World—Moshe—should himself become king of the Jewish people who have also acknowledged His sovereignty.[158]

---

150) רש״י ממכילתא, ראה לקח טוב (151 בשלח טו-יח (152 רבנו בחי (153 אב״ע, רשב״ם (154 רמב״ן, רבנו
בחיי (155 ריב״ש, חזקוני (156 מדרש ויושע (157 מדרש חסרות ויתרות באוצר המדרשים קצט, מדרש החפץ,
הדר זקנים (158 ויקרא רבה ב-ד, ע׳ במכילתא

> *When Pharaoh's horse came with his chariots
> and horsemen into the sea, and Hashem turned back
> upon them the waters of the sea, the Jewish people
> walked on the dry land in the midst of the sea.*[159]

There is question among the commentators regarding this final verse of the Shirah. According to some views, this verse is part of the Shirah, bringing it to a dramatic conclusion by describing one of the great miracles of Krias Yam Suf. It was also sung while the Jewish people were walking through the sea with full faith and confidence that the water inundating the Egyptians would not affect them.[160]

According to other views, this verse is not part of the Shirah but was sung when the Jewish people in the sea saw the Egyptians drowning. Nevertheless, based on the sequence of the Torah, the singing of this verse was so emotional that it inspired the singing of the Shirah by Miriam and the rest of the Jewish women.[161]

159) בשלח טו-יט (160 אב״ע, מעם לועז (161 רמב״ן, רשב״ם, רבנו בחיי

Servants of Hashem

22

On the eighth day after the exodus, the Jewish people were still encamped alongside the Yam Suf. The shores were littered with the *bizas hayam*, the treasures of the Egyptian army that had been disgorged by the sea. The very air still vibrated with the aftershock of the stupendous miracles of the splitting of the sea and glowed with the holiness of the revelation of the Shechinah and the singing of the Shirah. The cloud pillars surrounded the encampment like tall and silent sentries. It was a place of extraordinary spiritual beauty, and every Jew felt it.

Nevertheless, the time had come to move on. Moshe announced the imminent breaking of camp and the continuation of the journey towards Mount Sinai and ultimately Eretz Yisrael. His words were greeted with grumbles of protest.

"Moshe, we can't leave here," one man declared. "Look at all the treasures on the shore. There is so much wealth here. There is more here than what we took out of Egypt. Do you expect us to leave it behind?"

"Of course not," said Moshe. "But you have enough time to pack all of it up and take it with you. Remember, there is a lot of treasure here, but what you see is all of it. There will be no more treasures spewing out of the sea, I assure you. Besides, it's not good to be so attached to wealth. It can only lead to trouble." Moshe's fears would unfortunately be borne out at the incident of the Eigel, the Golden Calf.[1]

"Wait a minute," said another man. "Let's take a logical look at this whole thing. Why did Hashem take us out of Egypt? It seems to me there were five reasons. One, to punish the Egyptians for the crimes they committed against us. Two, to provide us with the escort of these glorious cloud pillars. Three, to perform the miracle of the splitting of the sea so that the entire world will know of the greatness of Hashem. Four, to have the Jewish people sing the Shirah in His honor. What an experience! And five. We can't forget five. Five was, of course, to give us all this fabulous treasure lying on the shore in front of us." He paused dramatically. "Well then, now that all five of these goals have been accomplished, I say . . . we can now go back!"

"Back?" asked Moshe incredulously. "Back where?"

"Why, back to Egypt, of course."

"To Egypt?" said Moshe. "I assured you earlier that this would be the last time you would ever see the Egyptians. Why should you want to go to Egypt? Haven't you had enough of Egypt?"

"Times have changed," said the man. "After all, it's not like we'll really be seeing them. The Egyptians are a shattered people, but Egypt is still prime land. We can just walk in and take over the whole place."

"That's ridiculous," said Moshe. "In your five reasons for Hashem taking us out of Egypt, you left out a few things like going to Mount Sinai and accepting the Torah."[2]

"But wait," said a third man. "I, for one, don't care so much for these Egyptian treasures, and I certainly don't want to go back to Egypt. But I don't see how we can leave this place. We actually saw

---

1) כל"י בשלח טו-כב, ראה רש"י ממכילתא בשלח, ילקו"ש רנד   2) שמו"ר כד-ב, מנחה בלולה, ראה ילקו"ש ושמו"ר, יפ"ת מסביר דסבירא להו לישראל שכדאי להמתין עד שיהיו לעם רב וחזק ואז יכבשו ארץ כנען וע"ז השיב להם משה רבינו שעליהם לשלם חובתם לבוראם תיכף ומיד, עיין במלבים מש"כ עפ"י דרכו

the Shechinah here. We rose to the level of angels and sang the Shirah. Look at this place. It shines with holiness. How can we go away?"[3]

This man's words were greeted with a murmur of approval, and no matter how much Moshe argued with them, he could not convince them to leave the shores of the Yam Suf.

In the end, the cloud pillars and the Shechinah which rested in them moved away from the Jewish encampment deep into the desert. The holiness of the place was visibly diminished, and the Jewish people finally agreed to travel into the desert. They were no longer accompanied by the cloud pillars, and Moshe had to guide and lead them to their next encampment. They were reunited there with the cloud pillars, and Hashem Himself led them for the remainder of their time in the desert.

As the great Jewish multitudes traveled into the barren desert without adequate food to sustain them, they exhibited the highest level of faith in Hashem.[4] Hashem would reward them with another of the spectacular miracles of the exodus. On the sixteenth of Iyar, twenty-four days after the Jewish people left their encampment at the Yam Suf, Hashem sent down *mann* from Heaven to feed the Jewish people. For the forty years they were in the desert, the *mann* would continue to fall daily, except for Shabbos, until the Jewish people were on the doorstep of Eretz Yisrael.

On the sixth of Sivan, over forty days after the great miracle of the splitting of the sea, the Jewish people stood at the foot of Mount Sinai and received the Torah. On that day, the Jewish people repaid Hashem for taking them out of Egypt. From that day forward, they would be identified as the servants of Hashem. They had gone from the lowliest status of Pharaoh's slaves to the highest and most exalted status of Hashem's servants, dedicated to honor Him and His *mitzvos*.

Their two-hundred-and-ten-year exile in Egypt had accomplished its purpose. They had gone down to Egypt somewhat deficient in the level of faith Hashem expected of them. But during the exodus, they reached a level of faith that inspired them to say, "This is my God, and I will beautify Him." They had gone down to Egypt as a proud people unable to understand the concept of subservience.

---

3) זוה"ק ס. 4) מכילתא בשלח טו-כב

They came out of Egypt knowing all too well the meaning of sub-servience to human masters. In their new state of mind, they were more than happy to accept the Torah and the uplifting role of sub-servience to Hashem, the Creator and Master of the Universe.[5]

כִּימֵי צֵאתֵנוּ מֵאֶרֶץ מִצְרַיִם
יִרְאֵנוּ נִפְלָאוֹת בִּמְהֵרָה
בִּמְהֵרָה בְּיָמֵינוּ
בְּקָרוֹב